THE KINGFISHER

WORLD ATLAS

First published 2003 by Kingfisher

This edition published 2008 by Kingfisher
an imprint of Macmillan Children's Books
a division of Macmillan Publishers Limited
The Macmillan Building, 4 Crinan Street, London N1 9XW
Basingstoke and Oxford
Associated companies throughout the world
www.panmacmillan.com

Project Management: Picthall & Gunzi Ltd

ISBN 978-0-7534-1742-3

1 3 5 7 9 8 6 4 2
1TR/0508/TWP/CLSN(CLSN)/130ENSOMA/F

A CIP catalogue record is available from the British Library.

Printed in Singapore

The publisher would like to thank the following for permission to reproduce their material. Every care has been taken
to trace copyright holders. However, if there have been unintentional omissions or failure to trace copyright holders,
we apologise and will, if informed, endeavour to make corrections in any future edition.

Key: b = bottom, c = centre, l = left, r = right, t = top

6bl Corbis; 8t Lloyd Cuff/Corbis; 8b Lloyd Cuff/Corbis; 9t James A. Sugar/Corbis; 9b Jeff Vanuga/Corbis; 10bc Imagebank/
Getty Images; 10br Imagebank/Getty Images; 11tr Annie Griffiths Belt/National Geographic Image Collection; 12tr Darrell
Gulin/Corbis; 12b Laurence Fordyce/Eye Ubiquitous/ Corbis; 13tr Gary Braash/Corbis; 13bl Wolfgang Kaehler/Corbis;
13bc Wolfgang Kaehler/Corbis; 13br DiMaggio/Kalish/Corbis; 14-15 Bill Ross/Corbis; 14bl Adrian Arbib/Corbis;
14br Richard Bickel/Corbis; 15tc Robert Essel NYC/Corbis; 15tr Paul Almasy/Corbis

The publisher would also like to thank the following illustrators for their contribution to this book:
Richard Bonson 11b; Chris Forsey 7tr, 9tr; Jeremy Gower 10bl; Maltings Partnership 8bl; Janos Marphy 6–7;
Maps designed and produced by Anderson Geographics Limited, Warfield, Berkshire

THE KINGFISHER

WORLD ATLAS

KINGFISHER

CONTENTS

PLANET EARTH

The home planet 6–7
The changing Earth 8–9
Weather and climate 10–11
The natural world 12–13
The human world 14–15

THE WORLD

The physical world 16–17
The political world 18–19

THE POLES

The Arctic Ocean 20
Antarctica 21

NORTH AMERICA

North America 22–23
Canada 24–25
Western United States 26–27
Midwestern United States 28–29
Southern United States 30–31
Northeastern United States 32–33
Mexico and Central America 34–35
The Caribbean 36–37

SOUTH AMERICA

South America 38–39
Northern South America 40–41
Southern South America 42–43

The Atlantic Ocean 44–45

EUROPE

Europe 46–47
Northwestern Europe 48–49
The British Isles 50–51
The Low Countries 52–53
France 54–55
The Iberian Peninsula 56–57
Germany 58–59
The Alpine states 60–61
Italy and Malta 62–63
Eastern Europe 64–65
Central Europe 66–67
Southeastern Europe 68–69

AFRICA

Africa 70–71
Northwest Africa 72–73
Northeast Africa 74–75
West Africa 76–77
Central and east Africa 78–79
Southern Africa 80–81

The Indian Ocean 82–83

ASIA

Asia 84–85
The Russian Federation 86–87
West Asia 88–89
Central Asia 90–91
South Asia 92–93
Southeast Asia 94–95
East Asia 96–97
Japan and the Koreas 98–99

AUSTRALASIA AND OCEANIA

Australasia and Oceania 100–101
Australia 102–103
New Zealand 104–105

The Pacific Ocean 106–107

Glossary 108
Index 109–128

KEY TO MAPS

Settlements

■ PARIS	Capital city
◉ Halifax	Administrative region capital
○ São Paulo	Major town
○ Galway	Other town

Political and cultural regions

MEXICO	Country
Corsica (to France)	Dependent territory
ARIZONA	Internal administrative region
TUSCANY	Cultural region

Boundaries

	International border
	Disputed border
	Internal administrative boundary

Drainage features

	Congo	River
	Warrego	Seasonal river
	Albert Canal	Canal
	Angel Falls	Waterfall
	Lake Taupo	Lake
	Lake Mackay	Seasonal lake

Topographic features

△ *Mont Blanc 4,810 m*	Spot height of mountain
▽ *–8,605 m*	Spot depth below sea level
Balearic Islands	Island / island group
Thar Desert	Landscape feature / region

Seas and oceans

INDIAN OCEAN	Ocean
North Sea	Sea
Guinea Basin	Sea feature

Ice features

	Limit of summer pack ice
	Limit of winter pack ice

Land height

4,000 m 13,124 ft
2,000 m 6,562 ft
1,000 m 3,281 ft
500 m 1,640 ft
200 m 656 ft
Sea level

THE HOME PLANET

Planet Earth is roughly spherical in shape and measures 40,075 km around the Equator. As far as we know, it is the only planet that can support life. There are two main reasons for this. First, the Earth has an atmosphere that contains oxygen. Second, the planet is just the right distance from the Sun, our nearest star. Planets that are closer to the Sun are too hot for life. Those further away, such as Mars, are too cold.

The Solar System

The Sun's powerful gravity attracts eight major planets (including the Earth), a dwarf planet called Pluto, and countless minor planets known as asteroids. These and other bodies, including moons and comets, circle the Sun and form its family, or Solar System. The planets of the Solar System were probably created about 4.5 billion years ago from a cloud of gas and dust thrown out by the Sun when it was formed. The smaller planets nearer the Sun are made up of minerals and metals. The outer planets were formed at lower temperatures, and consist of swirling clouds of gases.

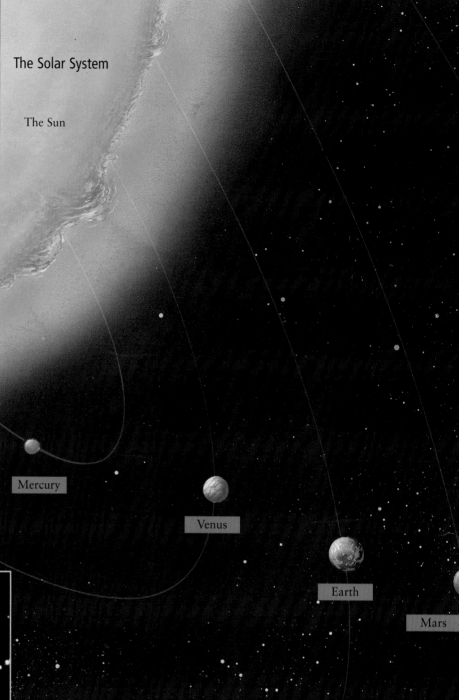

The Solar System

The Sun

Mercury

Venus

Earth

Mars

The Milky Way is an enormous, spiral-shaped galaxy of which our Solar System forms a tiny part. The galaxy contains at least 200 billion stars.

The Earth is the third planet from the Sun (above). It takes 365.25 days for the Earth to complete a full circle of the Sun.

The Sun and Moon

With a diameter of about 1,400,000 km, the Sun is more than 100 times wider than the Earth. Like other stars, the Sun is a great ball of gases. Although it lies about 150 million kilometres from the Earth, the Sun provides the light and warmth needed to make our planet suitable for life. The Moon lies about 384,000 km away from the Earth, and is our planet's closest neighbour in space. Its gravity is weaker than the Earth's, so it cannot hang on to any gases to make an atmosphere. However, the Moon's gravity does pull at our oceans to create tides.

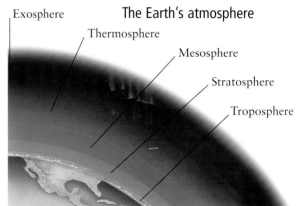

The Earth's atmosphere

Exosphere
Thermosphere
Mesosphere
Stratosphere
Troposphere

The Earth's outer structure

The Earth is surrounded by a layer of air roughly 2,000 km thick, called the atmosphere. It contains the air that we breathe, together with water vapour and tiny pieces of dust. Held by the pull of the Earth's gravity, the atmosphere protects us from the dangerous rays of the Sun, and the cold of outer space. The atmosphere is made up of layers. The layer closest to the Earth is the troposphere. It contains most of the gas in the atmosphere, and is the narrowest layer. Above the troposphere is the stratosphere. It extends from 11 km to 50 km above the Earth. The mesosphere lies between 50 km and 80 km above the Earth. If meteors fall into this layer, they burn up, causing shooting stars. A very thick layer of air called the thermosphere extends from about 80 km to 480 km above the ground. Above this is the exosphere, which has no definite upper limit.

The Earth's inner structure

At the centre of the Earth lies a solid core made of iron and a small amount of nickel. Its temperature is about 4,500°C. Around the core is the outer core, formed of liquid iron and nickel at a temperature of about 3,300°C. Outside the core is the mantle, a layer of rock about 2,900 km thick. The temperature reaches about 3,700°C at the bottom of the mantle, but high pressure there keeps the rock solid. There is less pressure on the top part of the mantle, which is partly molten and can move. We live on the Earth's rocky outer layer, called the crust.

Pluto

Neptune

Uranus

Saturn

Jupiter

Inside the Earth

Rocky crust

Outer mantle

Inner mantle. It is richer in iron than the outer mantle.

Outer core of molten iron and nickel

Inner core of solid iron and nickel

THE CHANGING EARTH

The Earth's crust, which covers the planet's surface, is made up of several sections, called tectonic plates. These plates interlock with each other, like the pieces of an enormous jigsaw puzzle. They are not fixed in position, however, but are moving slowly. As a result, the world's continents have shifted position over millions of years. More than 200 million years ago, the continents made up one single landmass, which gradually split up and moved apart to produce the continent shapes that we see today. The boundaries of the plates are places of huge stress. Sometimes, if plates are drifting apart, new crust is created as hot liquid rock from the mantle below fills the gap. If the plates are pushing towards each other, the land on one side can be pushed upwards, creating mountain ranges.

Earthquakes

Earthquakes occur when two tectonic plates slide past each other and friction is created along the line that lies between them. The friction causes violent vibrations, called tremors, that spread across the ground from the source. Sometimes the crust of the Earth cracks, or is faulted, and the land on one side of the fault line is raised, while on the other side it is lowered.

Sliding plates

The San Andreas Fault extends for over 1,000 km across California. This area is the site of frequent minor earthquakes.

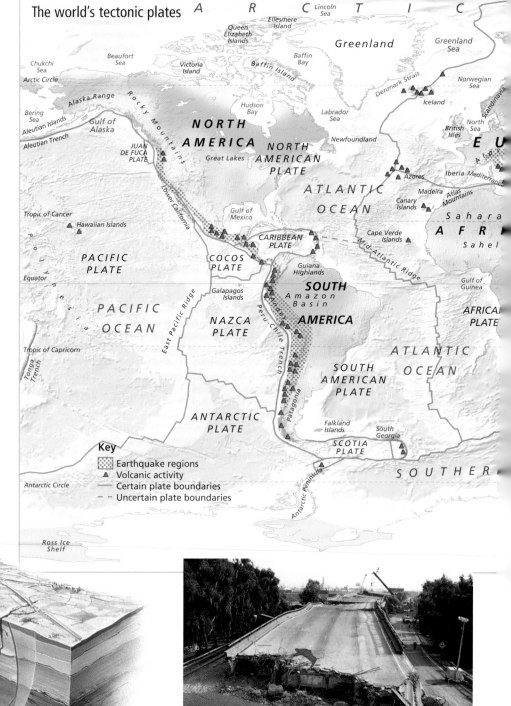

The world's tectonic plates

Key
- ▦ Earthquake regions
- ▲ Volcanic activity
- — Certain plate boundaries
- – – Uncertain plate boundaries

Fault line

Area of friction

Vibrations spreading away from the source

The enormous power of an earthquake can pull down buildings and rip apart roads, sometimes causing death and injury in the process.

Lava flowing from volcanoes can reach temperatures of more than 1,000°C, and move at speeds of up to 60 km/h.

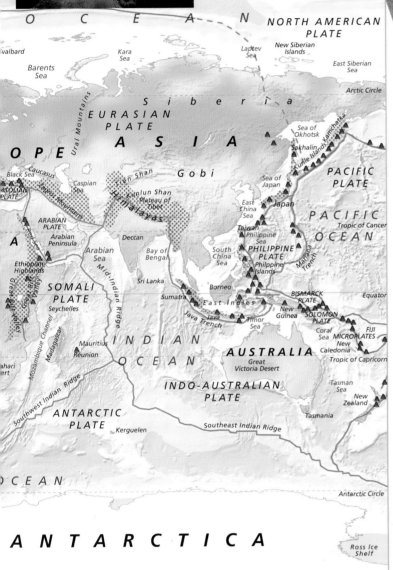

(Map labels)

OCEAN — NORTH AMERICAN PLATE
Svalbard
Barents Sea
Kara Sea
Laptev Sea
New Siberian Islands
East Siberian Sea
Arctic Circle
Siberia
EURASIAN PLATE
Ural Mountains
ASIA
Gobi
OPE
Caucasus
Black Sea
Caspian Sea
Tien Shan
Kunlun Shan
Plateau of Tibet
Himalayas
Sea of Okhotsk
Sakhalin
Kurile Islands
Kamchatka
PACIFIC PLATE
ANATOLIAN PLATE
ARABIAN PLATE
Arabian Peninsula
Arabian Sea
Deccan
Bay of Bengal
Sea of Japan
East China Sea
Japan
PACIFIC OCEAN
Tropic of Cancer
Taiwan
Philippine Sea
PHILIPPINE PLATE
Philippine Islands
Mariana Trench
Ethiopian Highlands
SOMALI PLATE
Seychelles
Mid-Indian Ridge
Sri Lanka
South China Sea
Borneo
East Indies
Sumatra
Java Trench
Timor Sea
New Guinea
BISMARCK PLATE
SOLOMON PLATE
Equator
Great Rift Valley
Mozambique Channel
Madagascar
Mauritius
Réunion
INDIAN OCEAN
Coral Sea
FIJI
MICROPLATES
New Caledonia
Tropic of Capricorn
AUSTRALIA
Great Victoria Desert
INDO-AUSTRALIAN PLATE
Tasman Sea
New Zealand
Kalahari Desert
Southwest Indian Ridge
ANTARCTIC PLATE
Kerguelen
Southeast Indian Ridge
Tasmania
OCEAN
ANTARCTICA
Antarctic Circle
Ross Ice Shelf

An erupting volcano

Smoke, ash and rock
Volcanic cone
Geyser
Layers of cooled lava
Side vent
Magma chamber
Lava flow
Central vent

Volcanoes

When hot liquid rock, or magma, from the Earth's mantle escapes to the surface of the Earth, a volcano is created. Sometimes the magma collects in a huge underground chamber, before it rises through a channel called the central vent, or smaller side vents. Once the magma breaks the surface it is called lava. The lava gradually cools to form the shape of the volcano. Some volcanoes are cone-shaped, while others, called shield volcanoes, are more rounded. During a volcanic eruption, gases, ash and rock are often thrown high into the air.

Geysers

Geysers are found in the volcanic regions of New Zealand, Iceland, Chile, eastern Russian Federation and western USA. Pools of water, in underground caverns made of watertight volcanic rock such as rhyolite, are heated by scorching hot magma. The water boils, and some of it turns to steam. Eventually, the pressure in the cavern builds up, and the water and steam is forced upwards through a crevice to the Earth's surface. Here, the water and steam burst out of the ground, and spurt up into the air.

There are less than 1,000 geysers in the world. A number of them erupt very often and extremely regularly. Some geysers are known to reach heights of more than 100 metres.

CLIMATE AND WEATHER

Climate is the average sunshine, wind, rainfall and humidity that an area receives over a long period of time. The major influence on a region's climate is its latitude (the distance it lies north or south of the equator). The equator receives the most direct rays from the Sun, so the climates there are warm. Places near the poles receive less heat from the Sun, so they have colder climates. Other influences on an area's climate include its distance from an ocean, its height above sea level, ocean currents and wind patterns.

The Earth's climate zones

The Earth's climate varies from place to place. Polar and mountainous zones are freezing and dry all year round. Continental regions are cold in winter and warmer in summer. Steppe areas have cold winters and very hot summers, while temperate regions enjoy a milder climate without extremes of temperature. The tropics are mainly hot and wet all year round. Some subtropical zones have hot, dry summers and warm, wet winters. Arid areas are hot with very little rain at all. Savanna regions are hot throughout the year, but they have a rainy season that lasts about three months.

The greenhouse effect

Certain gases in the atmosphere, such as carbon dioxide, are called greenhouse gases because they act like the glass panes in a greenhouse. These gases let the Sun's rays pass through to the Earth, but they restrict the amount of energy that can pass back into space. The heat becomes trapped in the atmosphere, causing the Earth to warm up.

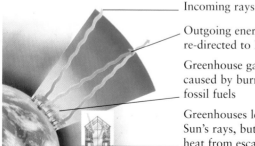

Incoming rays

Outgoing energy re-directed to Earth

Greenhouse gases caused by burning fossil fuels

Greenhouses let in Sun's rays, but keep heat from escaping

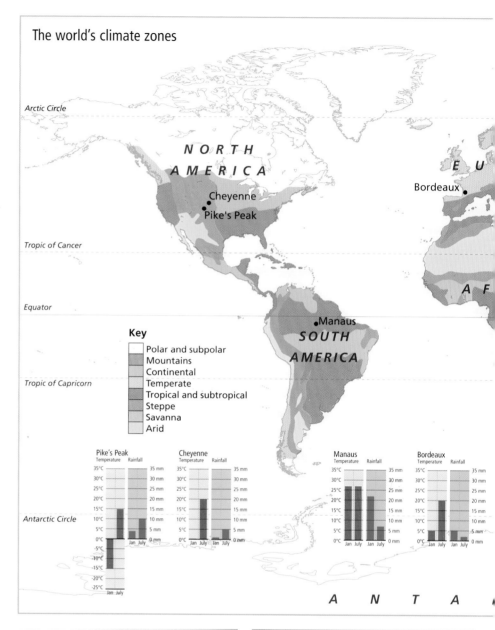

The world's climate zones

Key
- Polar and subpolar
- Mountains
- Continental
- Temperate
- Tropical and subtropical
- Steppe
- Savanna
- Arid

Many deserts are so dry that virtually no plants can grow. The Namib Desert, in southern Africa, receives an average rainfall of only 25 mm per year.

Temperatures on Antarctica reach as low as −88.8°C. A few animals, such as penguins, have adapted to the freezing conditions and howling winds.

Tropical areas, such as the coast of Texas, USA, are wet and hot all year round. During storms, the rain falls in torrents and fierce winds lash trees and houses.

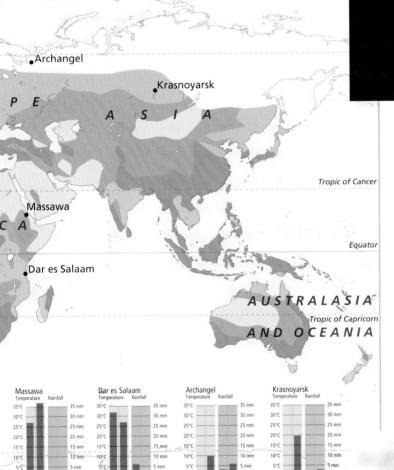

Archangel
Krasnoyarsk
P E
A S I A
Tropic of Cancer
Massawa
C A
Equator
Dar es Salaam
AUSTRALASIA
Tropic of Capricorn
AND OCEANIA

C T I C A

Massawa
Temperature   Rainfall
35°C   35 mm
30°C   30 mm
25°C   25 mm
20°C   20 mm
15°C   15 mm
10°C   10 mm
5°C   5 mm
0°C Jan July Jan July 0 mm

Dar es Salaam
Temperature   Rainfall
35°C   35 mm
30°C   30 mm
25°C   25 mm
20°C   20 mm
15°C   15 mm
10°C   10 mm
5°C   5 mm
0°C Jan July Jan July 0 mm

Archangel
Temperature   Rainfall
35°C   35 mm
30°C   30 mm
25°C   25 mm
20°C   20 mm
15°C   15 mm
10°C   10 mm
5°C   5 mm
0°C   0 mm
-5°C
-10°C   Jan July
-15°C
-20°C
-25°C
     Jan July

Krasnoyarsk
Temperature   Rainfall
35°C   35 mm
30°C   30 mm
25°C   25 mm
20°C   20 mm
15°C   15 mm
10°C   10 mm
5°C   5 mm
0°C   0 mm
-5°C
-10°C   Jan July
-15°C
-20°C
-25°C
     Jan July

Weather

Short-term events in the atmosphere, from showers to hurricanes, make up the world's daily weather. Changes in weather are mainly caused by the movements of large air masses. The temperature and moisture content of these air masses change as they pass over land and water. They also swirl around to produce depressions – bringing cooler, wetter weather – and anticyclones – tending to bring warmer, drier conditions.

The water vapour forms clouds that produce rain or snow

Rivers carry water to the sea

Water runs below the surface of the land to the sea

Moist air is blown towards the land

The Sun heats a body of water, and moisture from its surface evaporates

Water falls back to the land and sea

How the water cycle works

The water cycle

The continuous movement of water across the Earth and through its atmosphere is called the water cycle. Water in the oceans and the ground evaporates as the Sun heats the Earth. The water vapour rises into the sky where it begins to cool down, forming drops of water within clouds. Eventually, the drops of water become heavy enough to fall back to the Earth as rain or snow. The water soaks into the ground and feeds lakes and rivers. Then the cycle starts all over again.

THE NATURAL WORLD

All living things are connected with one another, and rely on each other for food, protection, or even shelter. It is possible to divide the world up into a number of broad zones, in which certain species of plants and animals live together within particular climate conditions. These ecological areas are called biomes.

The harshest habitats

The toughest of the world's biomes are those which have low rainfall, or experience bitterly cold or scorching hot temperatures. Polar regions are permanently covered in ice, so no plants can live in them. Animals, such as the walrus, have developed insulating fat and stocky limbs to survive in the freezing conditions here. With very little soil and large areas of frozen ground, tundra regions are treeless. A few plants, such as lichens and mosses, grow during the summer months. Needleleaf trees, including spruces and pines, are the only type of vegetation that can survive the long, snowy winters in the northern parts of Scandinavia, the Russian Federation and Canada. In mountainous regions, the lower slopes may be forested, but only ground-hugging shrubs can grow above the tree line. Deserts have very little rain. Certain plants and animals are adapted to the extreme temperatures and the lack of water in these regions.

For 50 to 60 days each year, the tundra regions, which are usually frozen, become carpeted with colourful, low-lying plants.

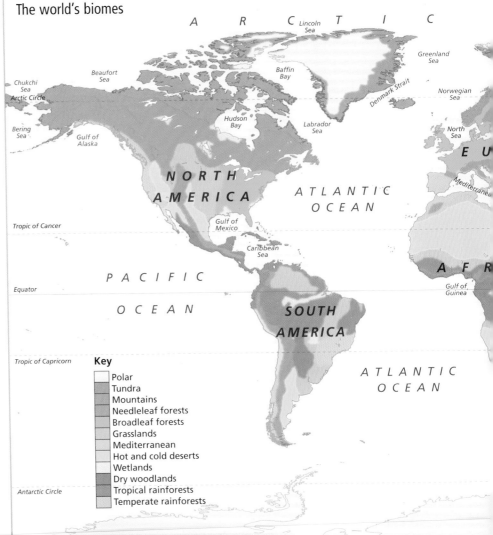

The world's biomes

Key
- Polar
- Tundra
- Mountains
- Needleleaf forests
- Broadleaf forests
- Grasslands
- Mediterranean
- Hot and cold deserts
- Wetlands
- Dry woodlands
- Tropical rainforests
- Temperate rainforests

Mountain peaks are hostile environments. The rocky terrain and thin air at high altitudes make it very difficult for plants and animals to survive.

A wealth of species of trees, ferns and creeping plants are found in tropical rainforests. These regions are also home to various animals, which range from snakes and monkeys to sloths, parrots and countless insects.

Temperate and tropical zones

Much of the northern hemisphere was once covered in broadleaf, deciduous trees, but most of them have now been cleared for settlements. Trees and evergreen shrubs, adapted to dry summers, grow in Mediterranean regions and dry woodlands. The world's major grasslands are found in the centre of the larger continents. These regions are grazed by herbivores, such as bison and zebras. Wetlands are rich feeding grounds for fish and breeding grounds for birds. With plenty of rain and sunshine, the rainforests have the greatest variety of species on Earth.

Biodiversity

The number of plant and animal species, and the variety within each species, make up the Earth's biodiversity. Some plants and animals, such as the kangaroos in Australia, are endemic (found only in one region). Man-made environments, including cities and farms, ruin natural habitats and threaten plant and animal biodiversity. Increasing efforts are now being made to conserve the Earth's wild places.

The grasslands of Africa, with trees dotted here and there, are broad, open habitats where herds of grazing animals range free, while looking out for carnivores such as leopards and lions.

Isolated places have the greatest range of endemic species. Lemurs (above) are only found in Madagascar and Comoros.

The planet's oceans have a huge variety of different species, from enormous whales to the tiniest plankton.

THE HUMAN WORLD

There have been people on planet Earth for over 130,000 years. Humans first evolved in Africa, and they gradually spread across the world. They probably travelled in search of food, either following herds of animals, or looking for fruit. By about 10,000 years ago, people had reached most parts of the globe, and some had started to settle down. Today, there are about six billion people in the world, but they are not distributed evenly. Some areas, including China, India and Europe, are densely populated, while others are not.

Feeding the world

Humans have developed skills to help them survive, and these have had an impact on the Earth. One of the earliest skills was farming. In different parts of the world, people worked out how to raise animals. They also learned how to cultivate crops that grew well in the local environment – from rice in eastern Asia to wheat in North America. Today, almost two-fifths of the planet's land is farmed. Through fishing, we have also changed the oceans. A modern fishing ship can catch entire shoals of fish in one go and some species, such as cod, have suffered badly as a result. Agreements have now been made to reduce the numbers of fish caught, to allow stocks to recover.

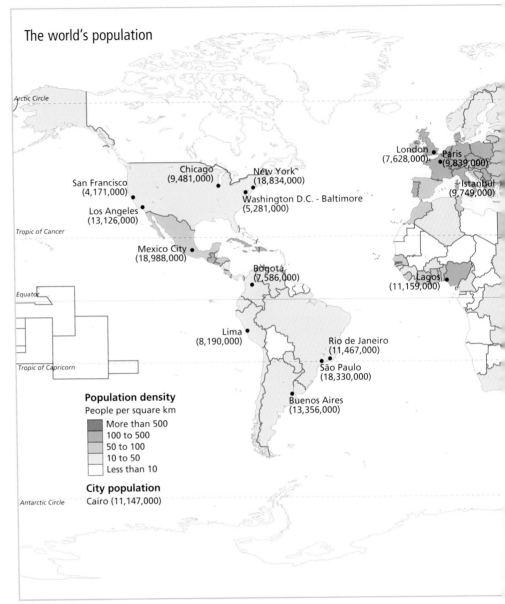

The world's population

San Francisco (4,171,000)
Los Angeles (13,126,000)
Chicago (9,481,000)
New York (18,834,000)
Washington D.C. - Baltimore (5,281,000)
Mexico City (18,988,000)
Bogotá (7,586,000)
Lima (8,190,000)
Rio de Janeiro (11,467,000)
São Paulo (18,330,000)
Buenos Aires (13,356,000)
London (7,628,000)
Paris (9,839,000)
Istanbul (9,749,000)
Lagos (11,159,000)

Arctic Circle
Tropic of Cancer
Equator
Tropic of Capricorn
Antarctic Circle

Population density
People per square km
More than 500
100 to 500
50 to 100
10 to 50
Less than 10

City population
Cairo (11,147,000)

The staple diet of half the world's people, rice has been cultivated for more than 5,000 years. Asia grows 91 per cent of the world's rice.

Traditional fishing methods, shown left, catch enough fish for the local market. But in some places, modern trawlers bring in vast quantities of fish. The catch is usually sold to factories, where it is processed for export.

In 1500, the world's population was about 425 million

In 1600, the world's population was about 545 million

In 1700, the world's population was about 610 million

1500   1600   1700

Cities, such as Tokyo (right), have many amenities, but some are also home to shanty towns (far right) where the very poor live with little or no services.

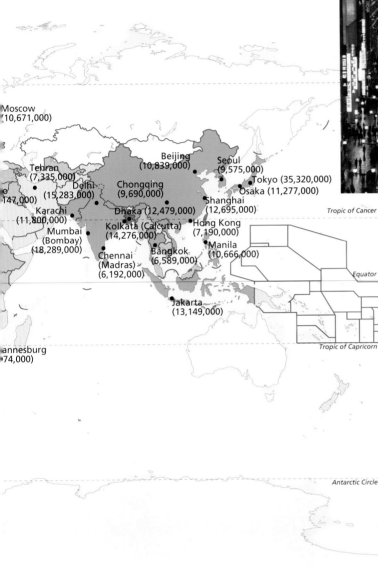

Moscow
(10,671,000)

Beijing
(10,839,000)

Seoul
(9,575,000)

Tehran
(7,335,000)

Tokyo (35,320,000)

Delhi
(15,283,000)

Chongqing
(9,690,000)

Osaka (11,277,000)

147,000)

Shanghai
(12,695,000)

Karachi
(11,800,000)

Dhaka (12,479,000)

Tropic of Cancer

Mumbai
(Bombay)
(18,289,000)

Kolkata (Calcutta)
(14,276,000)

Hong Kong
(7,190,000)

Chennai
(Madras)
(6,192,000)

Bangkok
(6,589,000)

Manila
(10,666,000)

Equator

Jakarta
(13,149,000)

Tropic of Capricorn

annesburg
74,000)

Antarctic Circle

Rushing to the cities

In 2007, around half of the world's population was living in urban environments. This figure is expected to rise to 60 per cent of the total population by 2030. In many developing countries, cities are growing two or three times faster than the overall population. The world's cities are centres of government, education, industry and trade, but they also have problems, including crime, poverty and pollution.

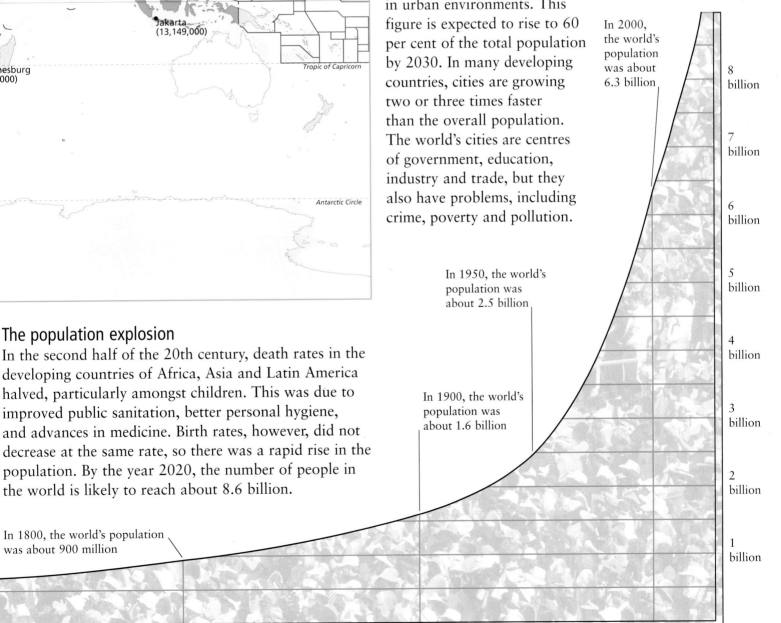

World population growth

In 2000, the world's population was about 6.3 billion

8 billion

7 billion

6 billion

5 billion

In 1950, the world's population was about 2.5 billion

4 billion

3 billion

In 1900, the world's population was about 1.6 billion

2 billion

The population explosion

In the second half of the 20th century, death rates in the developing countries of Africa, Asia and Latin America halved, particularly amongst children. This was due to improved public sanitation, better personal hygiene, and advances in medicine. Birth rates, however, did not decrease at the same rate, so there was a rapid rise in the population. By the year 2020, the number of people in the world is likely to reach about 8.6 billion.

1 billion

In 1800, the world's population was about 900 million

1800

1900

2000

THE PHYSICAL WORLD

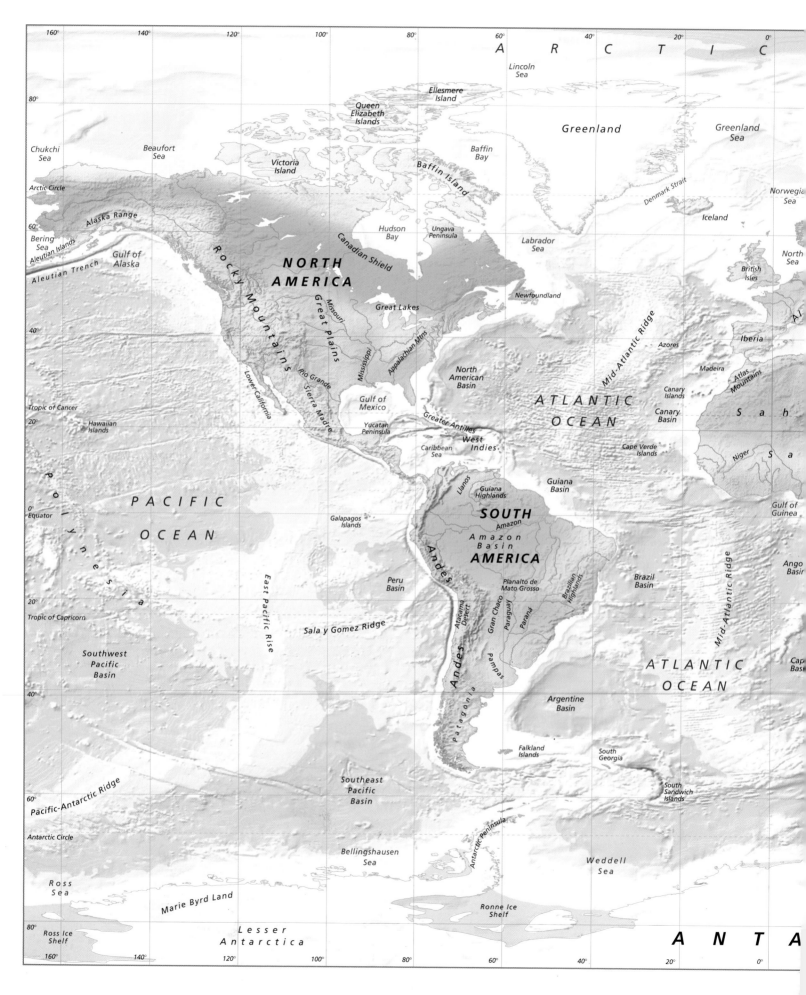

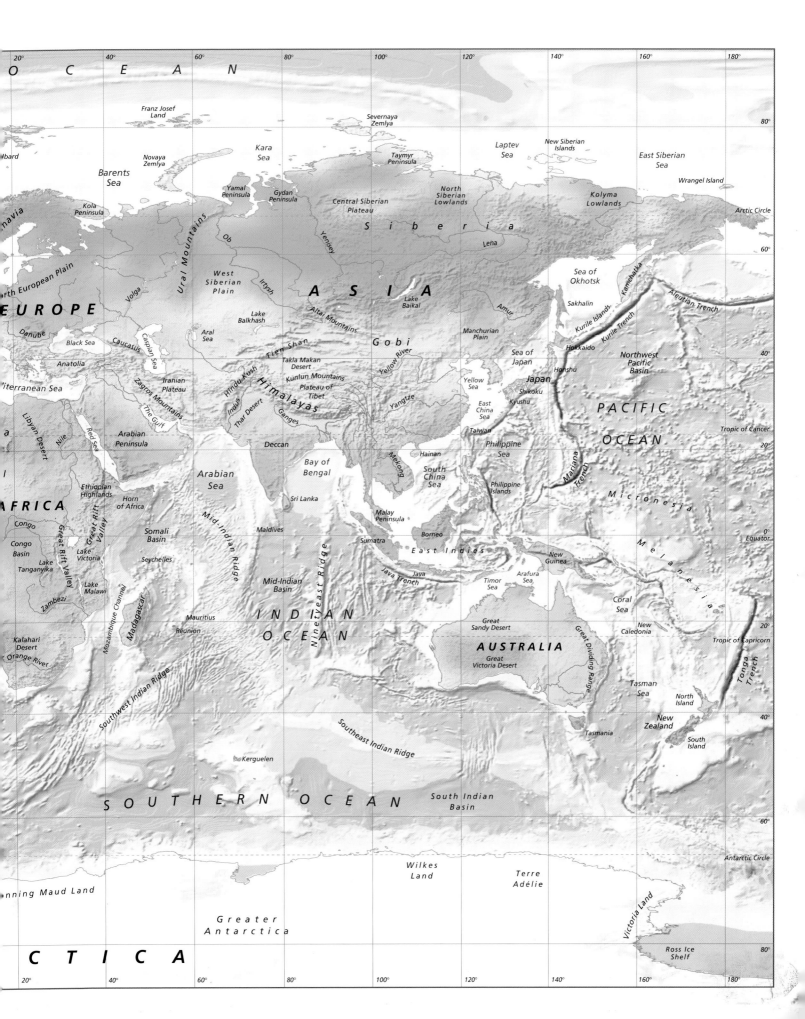

O C E A N

20° 40° 60° 80° 100° 120° 140° 160° 180°

80°

Franz Josef
Land

Severnaya
Zemlya

Laptev
Sea

New Siberian
Islands

East Siberian
Sea

lbard

Novaya
Zemlya

Kara
Sea

Taymyr
Peninsula

Wrangel Island

Barents
Sea

Yamal
Peninsula

Gydan
Peninsula

Central Siberian
Plateau

North
Siberian
Lowlands

Kolyma
Lowlands

Arctic Circle

navia

Kola
Peninsula

S i b e r i a

60°

Ob

Yenisey

Lena

Sea of
Okhotsk

Kamchatka

Aleutian Trench

North European Plain

Ural Mountains

West
Siberian
Plain

A S I A

Sakhalin

EUROPE

Volga

Irtysh

Lake
Baikal

Amur

Kurile Islands

Kurile Trench

Danube

Lake
Balkhash

Altai Mountains

Manchurian
Plain

Hokkaido

Northwest
Pacific
Basin

40°

Black Sea

Caucasus

Caspian Sea

Aral
Sea

Tien Shan

Gobi

Sea of
Japan

Honshu

Anatolia

Iranian
Plateau

Takla Makan
Desert

Yellow
River

Japan

Shikoku

PACIFIC

iterranean Sea

Zagros Mountains

Hindu Kush

Kunlun Mountains

Kyushu

The Gulf

Himalayas

Plateau of
Tibet

Yangtze

Yellow
Sea

East
China
Sea

OCEAN

a

Indus

Thar Desert

Ganges

Taiwan

Tropic of Cancer

Libyan Desert

Nile

Red Sea

Arabian
Peninsula

Deccan

Mekong

Hainan

Philippine
Sea

Mariana Trench

20°

Arabian
Sea

Bay of
Bengal

South
China
Sea

I

Ethiopian
Highlands

Sri Lanka

Philippine
Islands

M i c r o n e s i a

AFRICA

Great Rift Valley

Horn
of Africa

Somali
Basin

Mid-Indian Ridge

Maldives

Malay
Peninsula

Borneo

0°

Congo

Lake
Victoria

Sumatra

East Indies

New
Guinea

Equator

Congo
Basin

Lake
Tanganyika

Seychelles

Mid-Indian
Basin

Java Trench

Java

Ninetyeast Ridge

M e l a n e s i a

Lake
Malawi

Timor
Sea

Arafura
Sea

Zambezi

Mauritius

INDIAN

Coral
Sea

New
Caledonia

20°

Kalahari
Desert

Reunion

OCEAN

Great
Sandy Desert

Tropic of Capricorn

Orange River

Madagascar

Mozambique Channel

AUSTRALIA

Great Dividing Range

Great
Victoria Desert

Tonga Trench

Southwest Indian Ridge

Tasman
Sea

40°

Kerguelen

Southeast Indian Ridge

Tasmania

North
Island

New
Zealand

South
Island

S O U T H E R N   O C E A N

South Indian
Basin

60°

Antarctic Circle

nning Maud Land

Wilkes
Land

Terre
Adélie

Victoria Land

G r e a t e r
A n t a r c t i c a

Ross Ice
Shelf

80°

C T I C A

20° 40° 60° 80° 100° 120° 140° 160° 180°

THE POLITICAL WORLD

Abbreviations
B&H	-	BOSNIA & HERZEGOVINA
CRO.	-	CROATIA
KOS.	-	KOSOVO
LIE.	-	LIECHTENSTEIN
LUX.	-	LUXEMBOURG
MAC.	-	MACEDONIA
MONT.	-	MONTENEGRO
RUSS. FED.	-	RUSSIAN FEDERATION
SAN.	-	SAN MARINO
SWITZ.	-	SWITZERLAND

A R C T I C

Greenland
(to Denmark)

Jan Mayen
(to Norway)

Arctic Circle

UNITED STATES
OF AMERICA
(ALASKA)

ICELAND

Faeroe Islands
(to Denmark)

C A N A D A

A T L A N T I C

UNITED
KINGDOM   DENM

REPUBLIC OF
IRELAND   NETHERLAN

Isle
of Man
(to UK)   BELGIUM

O C E A N

Channel Islands
(to UK)   S
FRANC

St Pierre &
Miquelon
(to France)   MON

ANDORRA

PORTUGAL   SPAIN

UNITED STATES
OF AMERICA

Azores
(to Portugal)   Gibraltar
(to UK)

Bermuda
(to UK)   Madeira
(to Portugal)   MOROCCO

ALGERI

Canary Islands
(to Spain)

Tropic of Cancer

MEXICO   BAHAMAS   WESTERN
SAHARA
(occupied by Morocco)

CUBA   Turks &
Caicos Is. (to UK)   British
Virgin Is. (to UK)

MAURITANIA   MALI

Hawaiian Islands
(to US)   Navassa
Island
(to US)   Virgin Is.
(to US)   Anguilla (to UK)   CAPE VERDE

Cayman Is.
(to UK)   DOMINICAN
REPUBLIC   Montserrat (to UK)
ANTIGUA & BARBUDA   GAMBIA

Johnston Atoll
(to US)   HAITI   Puerto Rico
(to US)   Guadeloupe (to France)   SENEGAL

BELIZE   JAMAICA   DOMINICA   GUINEA-BISSAU   GUINEA

GUATEMALA   HONDURAS   ST KITTS
& NEVIS   Martinique (to France)   SIERRA LEONE   IVORY
COAST

EL SALVADOR   NICARAGUA   ST LUCIA
BARBADOS   LIBERIA   GHAN

Aruba
(to Neth.)   Netherlands
Antilles (to Neth.)   ST VINCENT & THE GRENADINES
GRENADA   TOG

COSTA
RICA   PANAMA   TRINIDAD & TOBAGO   EQUATORIAL GUIN

Clipperton Island
(to France)   VENEZUELA   French
Guiana
(to France)   SÃO TO
& PRINC

P A C I F I C

Kingman Reef (to US)
Palmyra Atoll (to US)   COLOMBIA   GUYANA

SURINAM

Equator   Galapagos Islands
(to Ecuador)   ECUADOR

Jarvis Island
(to US)   Ascension
Island
(to St Helena)

KIRIBATI   O C E A N   PERU   B R A Z I L

American
Samoa
(to US)   Cook
Islands
(to NZ)   BOLIVIA   St Helena
(to UK)

Niue
(to NZ)   French Polynesia
(to France)   PARAGUAY

Tropic of Capricorn   Pitcairn Islands
(to UK)   A T L A N T I C

Easter Island
(to Chile)   URUGUAY   O C E A N

Juan
Fernández Islands
(to Chile)   Tristan da Cunha
(to St Helena)

Gough Island
(to Tristan da Cunha)

Falkland Islands
(to UK)   Bouvet Island
(to Norway)

South Georgia
(to UK)

South Sandwich Islands
(to UK)

Antarctic Circle   S   O   U   T   H

Peter I
Island
(to Norway)

A N T A R C T I C A

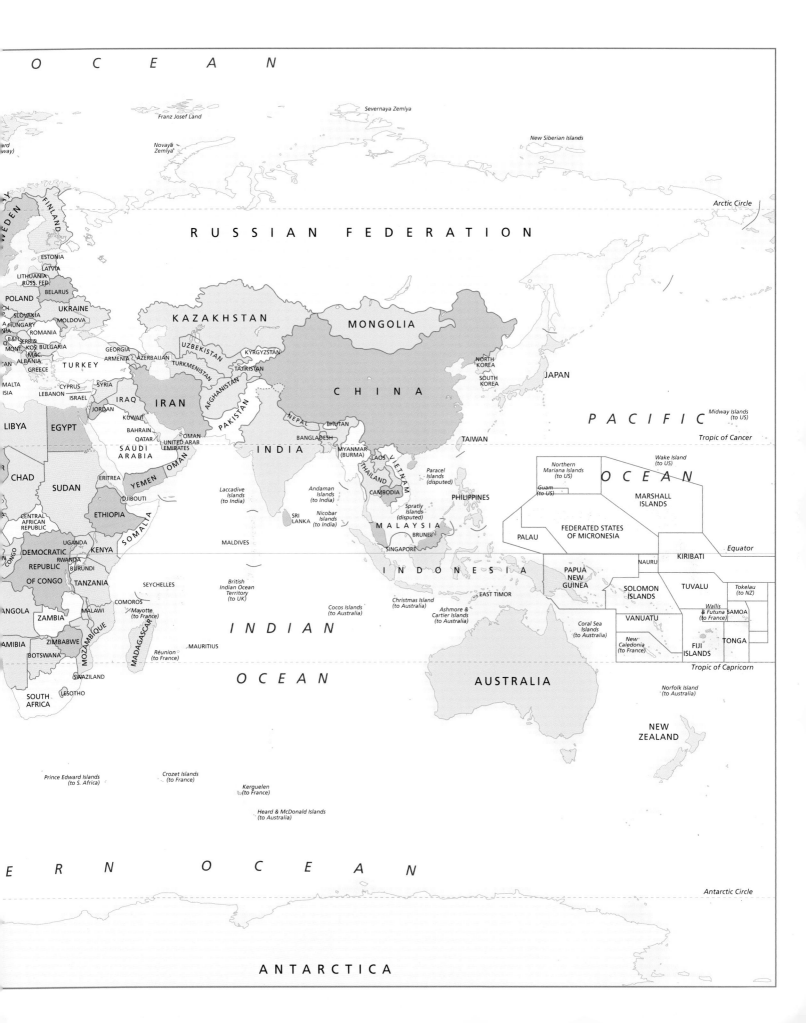

O C E A N

Franz Josef Land

Severnaya Zemlya

New Siberian Islands

Novaya Zemlya

Arctic Circle

SWEDEN

FINLAND

R U S S I A N   F E D E R A T I O N

ESTONIA

LATVIA

LITHUANIA

RUSS. FED.

BELARUS

POLAND

UKRAINE

SLOVAKIA

HUNGARY

MOLDOVA

ROMANIA

B&H

SERBIA

MONT.

KOS.

BULGARIA

MAC.

ALBANIA

GREECE

GEORGIA

ARMENIA

AZERBAIJAN

KAZAKHSTAN

MONGOLIA

UZBEKISTAN

KYRGYZSTAN

TURKMENISTAN

TAJIKISTAN

NORTH KOREA

SOUTH KOREA

JAPAN

TURKEY

MALTA

ISIA

CYPRUS

SYRIA

LEBANON

ISRAEL

IRAQ

JORDAN

IRAN

AFGHANISTAN

CHINA

KUWAIT

BAHRAIN

QATAR

UNITED ARAB EMIRATES

OMAN

PAKISTAN

NEPAL

BHUTAN

P A C I F I C

Midway Islands (to US)

Tropic of Cancer

LIBYA

EGYPT

SAUDI ARABIA

OMAN

BANGLADESH

I N D I A

MYANMAR (BURMA)

LAOS

TAIWAN

Wake Island (to US)

O C E A N

Northern Mariana Islands (to US)

CHAD

SUDAN

ERITREA

YEMEN

DJIBOUTI

Laccadive Islands (to India)

Andaman Islands (to India)

THAILAND

VIETNAM

CAMBODIA

Paracel Islands (disputed)

PHILIPPINES

Guam (to US)

MARSHALL ISLANDS

CENTRAL AFRICAN REPUBLIC

ETHIOPIA

SRI LANKA

Nicobar Islands (to India)

Spratly Islands (disputed)

FEDERATED STATES OF MICRONESIA

SOMALIA

UGANDA

KENYA

MALDIVES

MALAYSIA

BRUNEI

PALAU

CONGO

DEMOCRATIC REPUBLIC OF CONGO

RWANDA

BURUNDI

TANZANIA

SINGAPORE

Equator

SEYCHELLES

British Indian Ocean Territory (to UK)

I N D O N E S I A

NAURU

KIRIBATI

PAPUA NEW GUINEA

TUVALU

Tokelau (to NZ)

ANGOLA

MALAWI

COMOROS

Mayotte (to France)

Christmas Island (to Australia)

Cocos Islands (to Australia)

EAST TIMOR

Ashmore & Cartier Islands (to Australia)

SOLOMON ISLANDS

Wallis & Futuna (to France)

SAMOA

ZAMBIA

MADAGASCAR

Réunion (to France)

MAURITIUS

I N D I A N

Coral Sea Islands (to Australia)

VANUATU

MIBIA

ZIMBABWE

MOZAMBIQUE

New Caledonia (to France)

FIJI ISLANDS

TONGA

Tropic of Capricorn

BOTSWANA

SWAZILAND

O C E A N

AUSTRALIA

Norfolk Island (to Australia)

SOUTH AFRICA

LESOTHO

NEW ZEALAND

Prince Edward Islands (to S. Africa)

Crozet Islands (to France)

Kerguelen (to France)

Heard & McDonald Islands (to Australia)

E R N   O C E A N

Antarctic Circle

A N T A R C T I C A

THE ARCTIC OCEAN

The Poles, at the Earth's northern and southern tips, are the planet's coldest places, where temperatures can fall as low as –80°C in winter. At the North Pole is the Arctic Ocean. With an area of 15,100,000 sq km, it is the smallest ocean on the planet. The Arctic is made up of two large basins divided by three underwater ridges, the greatest of which is the Lomonosov Ridge. Its waters are mainly covered with pack ice. When this ice breaks up, it forms enormous blocks of floating ice, called icebergs. The Arctic is fringed by the northernmost parts of North America, the Russian Federation and Europe.

Despite the region's harsh climate, it has been inhabited for thousands of years by people such as the European Lapps, the Russian Nenet and North American Inuit.

These peoples make their living from herding, hunting and fishing. There are stocks of cod, plaice and haddock in the unfrozen Arctic waters, but numbers have fallen over the years. Now there are restrictions on the amount of fish that people can take from the ocean. The peoples of the Arctic region must import foods, such as grains and vegetables, from elsewhere.

The Arctic is rich in oil, gas and coal, but because of the bitterly cold climate and severe landscape, extracting these resources is difficult and expensive. There are mines and wells in the coastal regions, but these cause pollution and threaten the area's unique wildlife. These industries have also damaged the traditional lifestyles of many of the Arctic region's native peoples.

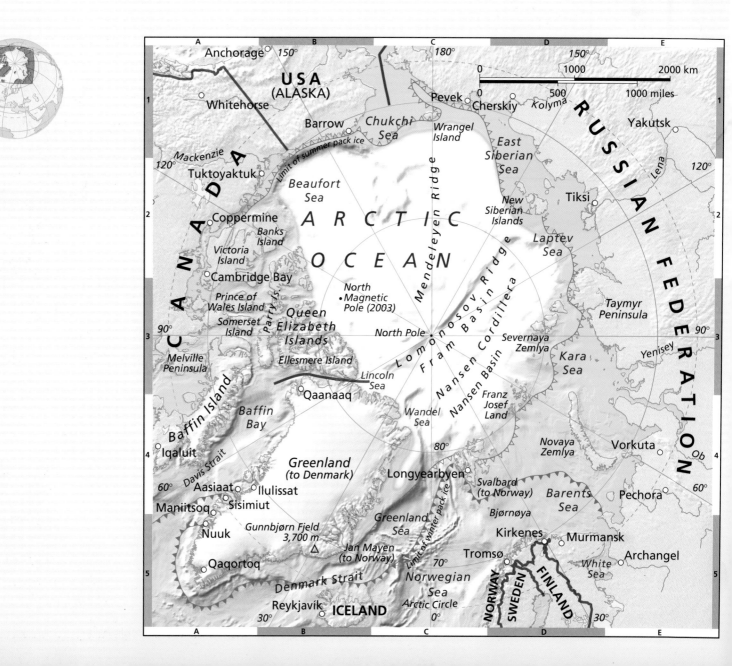

ANTARCTICA

Antarctica, at the Earth's southern tip, is the planet's coldest and smallest continent. It is a frozen world where the land lies beneath a thick layer of ice. Nearly half of the Antarctic coastline is surrounded by ice shelves, which float on the sea. There are two distinct parts to Antarctica. Lesser Antarctica is a series of ice-covered, mountainous islands, which are joined together by ice. Greater Antarctica is a high plateau.

No people live permanently in Antarctica, but teams of scientists visit this region of environmental importance, and stay in research stations for months at a time. These scientists observe the region's wildlife and even study the ice itself. By analyzing chemicals in the ice they can find out how the Earth's atmosphere has changed over the years. Antarctica is governed by Argentina, Brazil, Chile, the United Kingdom, Norway, France, Australia and New Zealand. All these countries have agreed that the continent should only be used for peaceful work.

Colonies of penguins breed along the continent's coastal regions, and there are whales, seals and many fish species living in the surrounding waters. Antarctica has rich mineral reserves, such as gold, iron and coal, and there is natural gas in the seas. The harsh conditions in the region mean that the mining of these resources is too costly and difficult. Each year, between 2,000 and 3,000 tourists visit the Antarctic region. They come to view the unique wildlife and dramatic landscape from the decks of cruise liners.

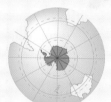

NORTH AMERICA

The continent of North America is shaped like a triangle, stretching from the frozen Arctic in the north to the tropics in the south. In the north, there are two huge countries, Canada and the USA. Smaller countries lie in the south and in the Caribbean Sea. The northern part of the continent has many different types of landscapes. The towering Rocky Mountains to the west give way to the fertile Great Plains, where fertile soils help farmers to grow millions of hectares of crops. To the east are the vast Great Lakes, major rivers such as the Mississippi, and the lower mountains of

the Appalachians. Further south, the Rocky Mountains continue into Mexico and southern North America, where they are called the Sierra Madre. This region also contains high plateaux and low-lying tropical forests, lagoons and mangrove swamps.

North America has a variety of climates, from the frozen wastes and pine forests of northern Canada to the baking deserts of Arizona and Mexico. Areas like these can support few people, but the northeast and west coasts are more densely populated, and North America

is home to some of the world's biggest cities – New York, Los Angeles, Chicago and Mexico City.

Politically, there is a marked difference between northern and southern North America. The USA and Canada have stable administrations in which the central government shares power with the individual states and provinces. The nations of southern North America have been less peaceful, and dictators ruled some countries, such as Nicaragua and Haiti, for many years.

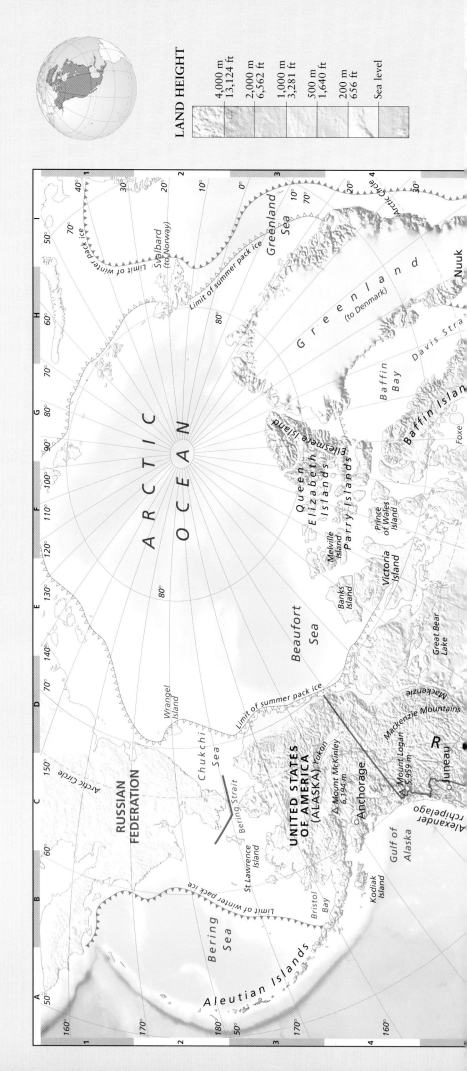

LAND HEIGHT

4,000 m	13,124 ft
2,000 m	6,562 ft
1,000 m	3,281 ft
500 m	1,640 ft
200 m	656 ft
	Sea level

Cape Farewell

*Labrador
Sea*

Limit of winter pack ice

Cape Chidley

Hudson Strait

Ungava Peninsula

Labrador

Cape Breton Island

St Pierre & Miquelon (to France)

Newfoundland

Gulf of St Lawrence

Laurentian Highlands

Smallwood Reservoir

Halifax

C A N A D A

Belcher Islands

James Bay

Hudson Bay

Laurentian Highlands

St Lawrence

Québec

Montréal

OTTAWA

Toronto

Boston

Cape Cod

New York

Long Island

Philadelphia

Baltimore

WASHINGTON D.C.

ATLANTIC

OCEAN

Bermuda (to UK)

Reindeer Lake

Lake Winnipeg

Lake Nipigon

Lake Superior

Lake Huron

Lake Michigan

Lake Ontario

Lake Erie

Great Lakes

Detroit

Cleveland

Columbus

Charlotte

Columbia

Cape Hatteras

Lake Athabasca

Edmonton

Calgary

Saskatoon

Saskatchewan

Winnipeg

Great Plains

Minneapolis

Saint Paul

Milwaukee

Chicago

Indianapolis

Saint Louis

Nashville

Memphis

Atlanta

Jacksonville

Appalachian Mountains

Missouri

Kansas City

UNITED STATES

OF AMERICA

Oklahoma City

Arkansas

Jackson

Baton Rouge

New Orleans

Tampa

Miami

The Everglades

NASSAU

BAHAMAS

Turks & Caicos Islands (to UK)

West Indies

Puerto Rico (to US)

SANTO DOMINGO

S O U T H

A M E R I C A

TRINIDAD & TOBAGO

Peace

Rocky Mountains

Columbia

Mount Rainier 4392 m

Portland

Seattle

Vancouver

Vancouver Island

Coast Mountains

Charlotte Islands

M o u n t a i n s

Great Salt Lake

Great Basin

Mount Whitney 4418 m

Death Valley -86 m

Las Vegas

Grand Canyon Plateau

Colorado

Denver

Phoenix

El Paso

Ciudad Juárez

Hermosillo

Sierra Madre Occidental

Dallas

Fort Worth

Austin

San Antonio

Houston

Mississippi Delta

Gulf of Mexico

Yucatan Peninsula

BELIZE

BELMOPAN

GUATEMALA CITY

GUATEMALA

SAN SALVADOR

EL SALVADOR

HONDURAS

TEGUCIGALPA

MANAGUA

NICARAGUA

Lake Nicaragua

SAN JOSE

COSTA RICA

PANAMA CITY

PANAMA

Caribbean

Sea

Aruba (to Netherlands)

Netherlands Antilles (to Netherlands)

Lesser Antilles

Greater Antilles

Cayman Islands (to UK)

HAVANA

CUBA

Straits of Florida

PORT-AU-PRINCE

HAITI

KINGSTON

JAMAICA

DOMINICAN REPUBLIC

San Francisco

San Jose

Los Angeles

San Diego

Coast Ranges

Lower California

Gulf of California

MEXICO CITY

Popocatépetl 5,452 m

Pico de Orizaba 5,700 m

Sierra Madre del Sur

Acapulco

Guadalajara

Leon

M E X I C O

Sierra Madre Oriental

Monterrey

Rio Grande

PACIFIC

OCEAN

Tropic of Cancer

Equator

2000 km

1000 miles

1000

500

1000

1. ST KITTS & NEVIS
2. ANTIGUA & BARBUDA
3. DOMINICA
4. ST LUCIA
5. BARBADOS
6. ST VINCENT & THE GRENADINES
7. GRENADA

Rio Grande

CANADA

The second-largest country in the world, Canada covers a vast area just north of the USA. This nation has quite a small population of just over 32 million, most of whom live in the south. Some of the people are Native Americans, members of tribes such as the Inuit, Algonquin and Cree. Others are descendants of the Europeans who settled here from the 16th century onwards, especially the French and British.

The landscape of Canada varies greatly. There are mountains in the west and east, and between these two regions is the Canadian Shield. This is a vast area of ancient rocks, low hills, thousands of lakes and huge tracts of forest. In the north, the Arctic regions are cold all year round, and the areas of tundra experience only a slight rise in temperature during summer. Further south, where most of the cities lie, the climate is a little warmer, although winter in many places is long, cold and snowy.

Canadians work in all sorts of businesses, from mining and farming to high-tech industries. The country is rich in minerals such as zinc and iron ore, and it has huge reserves of oil, coal and natural gas. There are good fishing waters off the east and west coasts, and large areas of forest make Canada the world's biggest exporter of timber products. Wheat, which grows well on fertile plains just west of the Canadian Shield, is exported to many countries.

LAND HEIGHT

	4,000 m / 13,124 ft
	2,000 m / 6,562 ft
	1,000 m / 3,281 ft
	500 m / 1,640 ft
	200 m / 656 ft
	Sea level

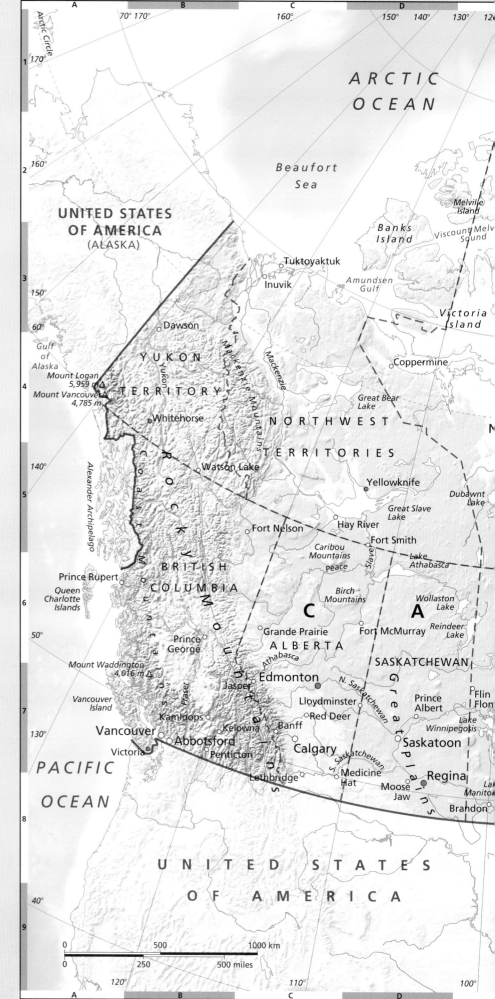

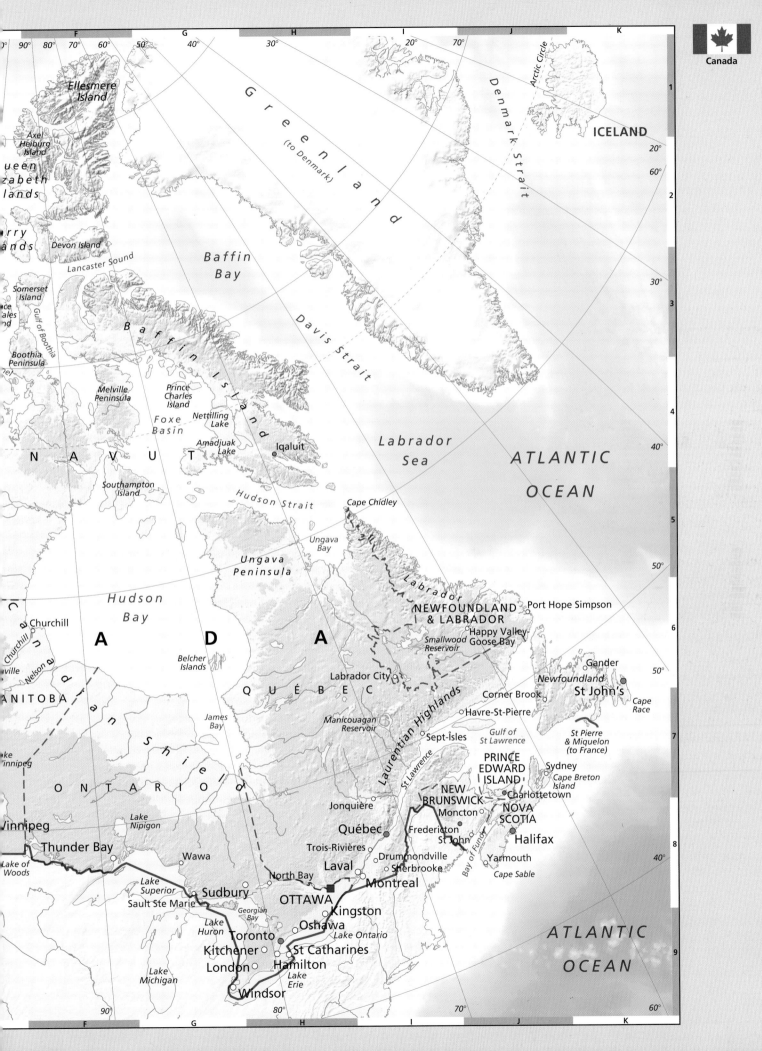

Canada

F 90° 80° 70° 60° G 50° 40° H 30° 20° I 70° J Arctic Circle K

ICELAND

Ellesmere
Island

Axel
Heiberg
Island

Queen
Elizabeth
Islands

Parry
Islands

G r e e n l a n d

(to Denmark)

Denmark Strait

Somerset
Island

ince
ales
nd

Gulf of Boothia

Boothia
Peninsula

Baffin
Bay

Baffin Island

Lancaster Sound

Devon Island

Davis Strait

N U N A V U T

Melville
Peninsula

Prince
Charles
Island

Foxe
Basin

Nettilling
Lake

Amadjuak
Lake

Iqaluit

Southampton
Island

Hudson Strait

Cape Chidley

Ungava
Bay

**Labrador
Sea**

*ATLANTIC
OCEAN*

Churchill

Churchill

Nelson

ville

ANITOBA

ke
nnipeg

Hudson
Bay

Belcher
Islands

C a n a d i a n   S h i e l d

James
Bay

Ungava
Peninsula

C A N A D A

Labrador

**NEWFOUNDLAND
& LABRADOR**

Port Hope Simpson

Smallwood
Reservoir

Happy Valley-
Goose Bay

Gander

Newfoundland

St John's

Cape
Race

Q U É B E C

Labrador City

Manicouagan
Reservoir

Laurentian Highlands

Corner Brook

Havre-St-Pierre

St Lawrence

Sept-Îles

Gulf of
St Lawrence

St Pierre
& Miquelon
(to France)

O N T A R I O

Winnipeg

Thunder Bay

Lake of
Woods

Lake
Nipigon

Wawa

Lake
Superior

Sault Ste Marie

Sudbury

North Bay

Georgian
Bay

Lake
Huron

Toronto

Kitchener

London

Lake
Michigan

Jonquière

Québec

Trois-Rivières

Laval

Drummondville

Sherbrooke

**NEW
BRUNSWICK**

Fredericton

St John

Moncton

**PRINCE
EDWARD
ISLAND**

Charlottetown

Sydney

Cape Breton
Island

**NOVA
SCOTIA**

Halifax

Yarmouth

Bay of Fundy

Cape Sable

OTTAWA

Montreal

Kingston

Oshawa

St Catharines

Hamilton

Lake Ontario

Lake
Erie

Windsor

*ATLANTIC

OCEAN*

90° 80° F 70° G 80° H I 70° J 60° K

1 20° 60° 2 30° 3 4 40° 5 50° 6 50° 7 8 40° 9 60°

WESTERN UNITED STATES

The western states have some of the most dramatic scenery in the USA. All of these states are partly mountainous, and much of the region is arid. In the west, the Central Valley separates the Sierra Nevada mountains from California's Coast Ranges. The area east of the Sierra Nevada contains mountain ranges, river basins, deserts and salt lakes. Off the southwest coast is a chain of volcanoes that emerge from the Pacific Ocean as the Hawaiian islands.

A break in the Earth's crust, known as the San Andreas Fault, runs through California. It is the site of frequent earthquakes. Most of the west has dry, hot summers and to the south of the region, the Sonoran Desert and California's Death Valley are two of the hottest places on Earth. In winter, while the Pacific coast is wet and warm, the temperature inland, in states such as Utah and Idaho, drops dramatically.

With large areas of forest, Oregon and Washington are the USA's major timber-producing states. Alaska is rich in oil and natural gas. In other areas farming is important. There are cattle ranches in Nevada, and the heavily irrigated land of California produces half of the USA's fruit and vegetables.

Manufacturing industries, from aircraft building to clothing, employ many people in this region. The western states' best-known products are the computers and other electronic goods that are made in the famous 'Silicon Valley', just south of San Francisco, California. Tourism is another major industry. Some people come to visit the spectacular physical features, such as the Grand Canyon, while others are lured by the sunny beaches of Hawaii and California.

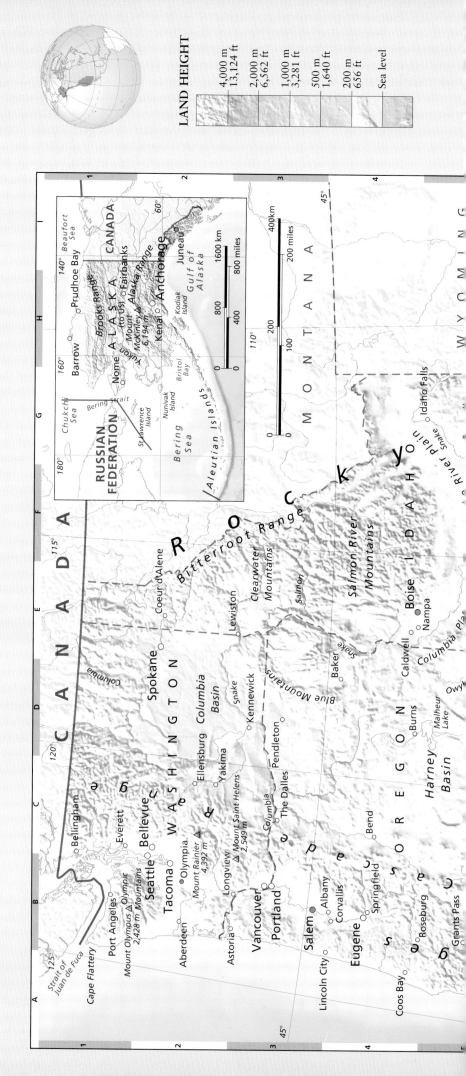

LAND HEIGHT

4,000 m	13,124 ft
2,000 m	6,562 ft
1,000 m	3,281 ft
500 m	1,640 ft
200 m	656 ft
Sea level	

United States
of America

MIDWESTERN UNITED STATES

In the heart of the USA is a large area of land known as the Midwest. To the west, it is bordered by the Rocky Mountains, a huge chain of peaks running all the way from Alaska to New Mexico. Few people live in this rugged landscape, but many of those who do are involved in the mining industry, because the Rockies are rich in coal, natural gas and many metals.

To the east of the Rocky Mountains, much of the Midwest is covered by the Great Plains. These plains were once natural grasslands, where native peoples such as the Crow and Cheyenne hunted buffalo. Today, the plains contain many large cattle ranches and cereal farms. Food processing is a major industry in the cities. Far inland, the plains have quite low rainfall and are hot in summer, so the USA's second-longest river, the Missouri, is a vital source of water for farming. This river is also used to generate electricity and for transporting heavy goods.

Not all of the plains are covered with rich grasslands. In the north are the Badlands. The land here is dry, and few plants and animals can survive in the arid conditions. Storms have washed away the soil to reveal a harsh, stony landscape covered with multi-coloured rocks, such as shales and limestones. This striking terrain makes parts of the Badlands popular with tourists.

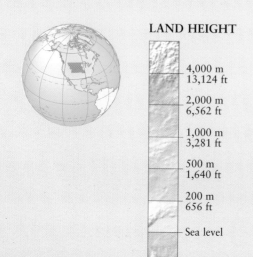

LAND HEIGHT

4,000 m 13,124 ft
2,000 m 6,562 ft
1,000 m 3,281 ft
500 m 1,640 ft
200 m 656 ft
Sea level

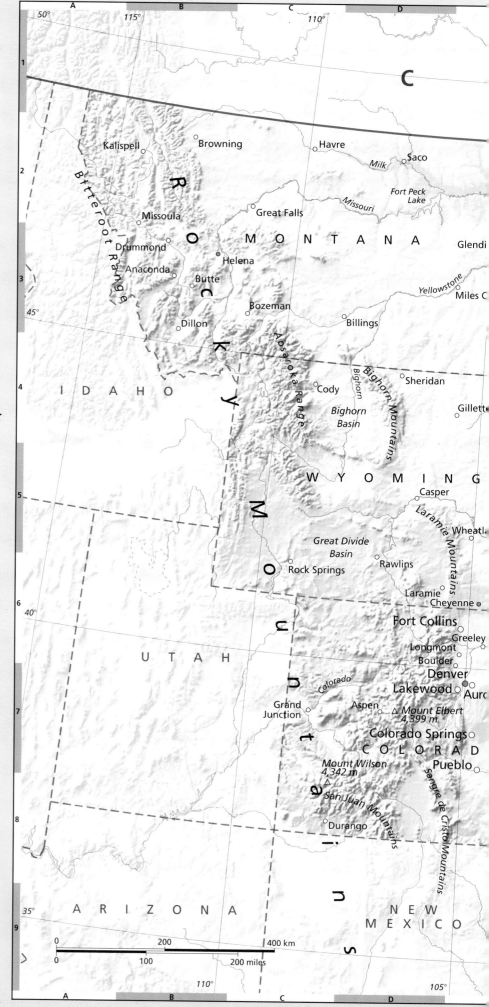

United States
of America

SOUTHERN UNITED STATES

This region of the USA is home to many Native American peoples, such as the Cherokee, Creek and Choctaw. To the south of the area is the large Gulf Coastal Plain. It is drained by many rivers, including the Mississippi, which flows south to a huge swampy delta on the coast of Louisiana. Elsewhere, the landscape ranges from the deserts and mountains of New Mexico to the Everglades, which are southern Florida's swamplands. Further north are uplands, including the Appalachian and Ouachita Mountains. The southern states have a warm climate with mild winters. Summer is generally hot, and the southeastern part of the region can be very humid.

Crops such as peanuts and citrus fruit grow well in the south, while the west contains large cattle ranches and wheat farms. Another typical crop is cotton, which was grown on plantations worked mainly by slaves until the mid-19th century. Many of this region's cities are industrialized, and the states of Texas and Oklahoma are major sources of oil and natural gas. As well as manufacturing and engineering, this area has high-tech computer and aerospace industries. Florida's unique scenery and warm climate make it a favourite tourist destination. People from all over the world come to visit its attractions, including the Everglades National Park.

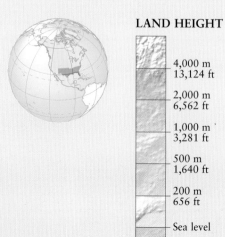

LAND HEIGHT

	4,000 m 13,124 ft
	2,000 m 6,562 ft
	1,000 m 3,281 ft
	500 m 1,640 ft
	200 m 656 ft
	Sea level

United States
of America

WISCONSIN

MICHIGAN

CANADA

PENNSYLVANIA

IOWA

NEW
JERSEY

ILLINOIS

OHIO

DELAWARE

MARYLAND

INDIANA

WEST
VIRGINIA

VIRGINIA

MISSOURI

KENTUCKY

Clarksville   Morristown   Greensboro   Durham NORTH
                                                    CAROLINA
Fayetteville   Oak Ridge   Winston-
        Pocohontas   Salem   Raleigh   Wilson   Cape
ogee   Nashville   Knoxville   Asheville   Hatteras
arkansas   ARKANSAS   Murfreesboro   Gastonia   Jacksonville
Fort Smith   TENNESSEE   Appalachian Mountains   Charlotte Fayeteville
        Memphis   Chattanooga   Blue Ridge   Greenville SOUTH   Wilmington
North Little Rock   Florence   Tennessee   Anderson CAROLINA   Cape Fear
hita Mountains Little   Decatur Huntsville   Columbia
Hot Springs Rock   Athens   Orangeburg
Pine Bluff   Chattahoochee Atlanta   Augusta North Charleston
Greenville   Birmingham   Anniston   Macon   Charleston
                Columbus Tuscaloosa   ATLANTIC
OF   Greenville MISSISSIPPI ALABAMA   Columbus   Savannah
      Monroe   Meridian Selma Montgomery GEORGIA   Savannah
MERICA Shreveport   Jackson   OCEAN
ne   Alexandria   Tombigbee   Albany   Brunswick
      Coastal   Hattiesburg Dothan Valdosta Jacksonville
Charles LOUISIANA Baton Biloxi Mobile   Plain   Tallahassee Gainesville   Daytona Beach
      Rouge Gulfport   Pensacola Panama City   Deltona
Beaumont Metairie   Cape   Orlando Cape Canaveral
Port Arthur New Orleans   San Blas   FLORIDA Melbourne
asadena   Clearwater   Lakeland
Galveston   Mississippi   Saint Petersburg Tampa
port   Delta   Bradenton
                                              Sarasota   Lake   West Palm Beach
                                                      Okeechobee
                              Cape Coral   Hialeah   Fort Lauderdale
                              Naples   The   Hollywood
Gulf   Everglades Miami
                                          Key Largo
of   Cape Sable   BAHAMAS
                                    Florida Keys Straits of Florida
Mexico

MEXICO

CUBA

NORTHEASTERN UNITED STATES

Along the eastern coast of this area are rocky headlands and sandy beaches, with flooded river valleys that make ideal harbours. Inland, beyond the coastal plain, are the Appalachians, an ancient chain of mountains covered in woods. Still further to the west is part of the huge Mississippi basin, with the Great Lakes to the north.

For thousands of years the region was home to native peoples, such as the Iroquois and Delaware. They were expert farmers and fishers. In the 17th century, some of North America's first European settlers arrived here and the native peoples showed the settlers how to grow local crops. In the 19th century, millions of immigrants passed through New York before settling in the region, and today it is still densely populated. The northeast contains major cities such as New York, the country's financial centre, Chicago and Washington D.C., the capital of the USA.

Many farmers in the northeast grow maize or fruit, or raise livestock. Some areas, such as Detroit and the state of Pennsylvania, have for many years been centres of heavy industry, from mining and steel production to manufacturing. Although these are still important, newer, high-tech industries, producing electronic goods, have developed in Massachusetts and New Jersey.

LAND HEIGHT

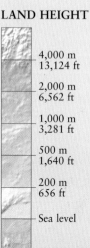

4,000 m
13,124 ft

2,000 m
6,562 ft

1,000 m
3,281 ft

500 m
1,640 ft

200 m
656 ft

Sea level

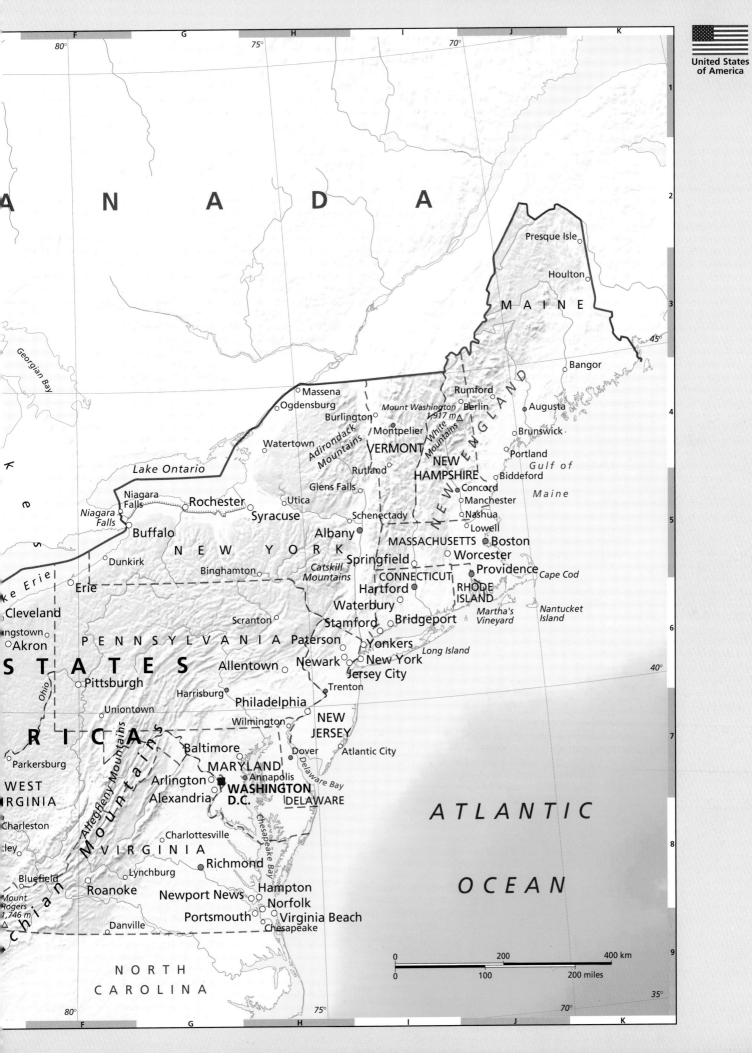

United States
of America

CANADA

Presque Isle

Houlton

MAINE

Bangor

45°

Massena
Ogdensburg
Burlington
Mount Washington
1,917 m
Rumford
Berlin
Augusta
Watertown
Adirondack
Mountains
Montpelier
White
Mountains
VERMONT
NEW
HAMPSHIRE
Brunswick
Portland
Gulf of
Maine
Rutland
Concord
Biddeford
Glens Falls
Manchester
Lake Ontario
Utica
Schenectady
Nashua
Niagara
Falls
Rochester
Lowell
Niagara
Falls
Syracuse
Albany
MASSACHUSETTS
Boston
Buffalo
Springfield
Worcester
Dunkirk
NEW YORK
Catskill
Mountains
CONNECTICUT
Providence
Cape Cod
Erie
Binghamton
Hartford
RHODE
ISLAND
Cleveland
Waterbury
Nantucket
Island
ngstown
Scranton
Stamford
Bridgeport
Martha's
Vineyard
Akron
PENNSYLVANIA
Paterson
Yonkers
Long Island
STATES
Allentown
Newark
New York
40°
Pittsburgh
Harrisburg
Jersey City
Uniontown
Philadelphia
Trenton
Parkersburg
Wilmington
NEW
JERSEY
RICA'S
Baltimore
Dover
Atlantic City
WEST
Arlington
MARYLAND
Annapolis
VIRGINIA
Alexandria
WASHINGTON
D.C.
DELAWARE
Charleston
Charlottesville
ATLANTIC
Bluefield
VIRGINIA
Richmond
Mount
Rogers
1,746 m
Lynchburg
OCEAN
ley
Roanoke
Hampton
Newport News
Norfolk
Danville
Portsmouth
Virginia Beach
Chesapeake

Lake Erie
Ohio
Allegheny Mountains
Georgian Bay
New England
Delaware Bay
Chesapeake Bay
achian
Maine

NORTH
CAROLINA

0		200		400 km
0	100		200 miles	

35°

MEXICO AND CENTRAL AMERICA

A chain of mountains, broken by fertile river valleys, forms the backbone of Mexico and Central America. Lowlands run along the east coast, widening to form Mexico's Yucatan Peninsula and Nicaragua's Mosquito Coast. In the south, Costa Rica and Panama form a narrow neck of land that measures less than 100 km across in some places. The Panama Canal, which was completed in 1914, provides a shipping link between the Atlantic and Pacific Oceans.

Most of the inhabitants of this area are descended from native peoples – such as the Maya and Aztec – and Europeans, especially the Spanish, who conquered the region in the 15th and 16th centuries. They are mainly farmers, either producing corn and beans for local use, or growing crops such as coffee, cotton and bananas for export. The area's major industries include mining, manufacturing and construction.

The population of Mexico and Central America is rising rapidly. Millions of people, unable to make a living from farming, have moved to the towns. Some cities have grown very quickly, and have poor housing, health and education services. The air quality in these urban areas is often low due to pollution from cars and factories. As the cities grow, large areas of tropical forest are being cut down to clear land for building.

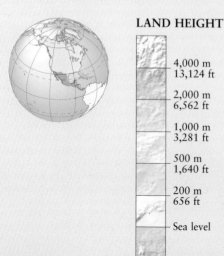

LAND HEIGHT

4,000 m
13,124 ft

2,000 m
6,562 ft

1,000 m
3,281 ft

500 m
1,640 ft

200 m
656 ft

Sea level

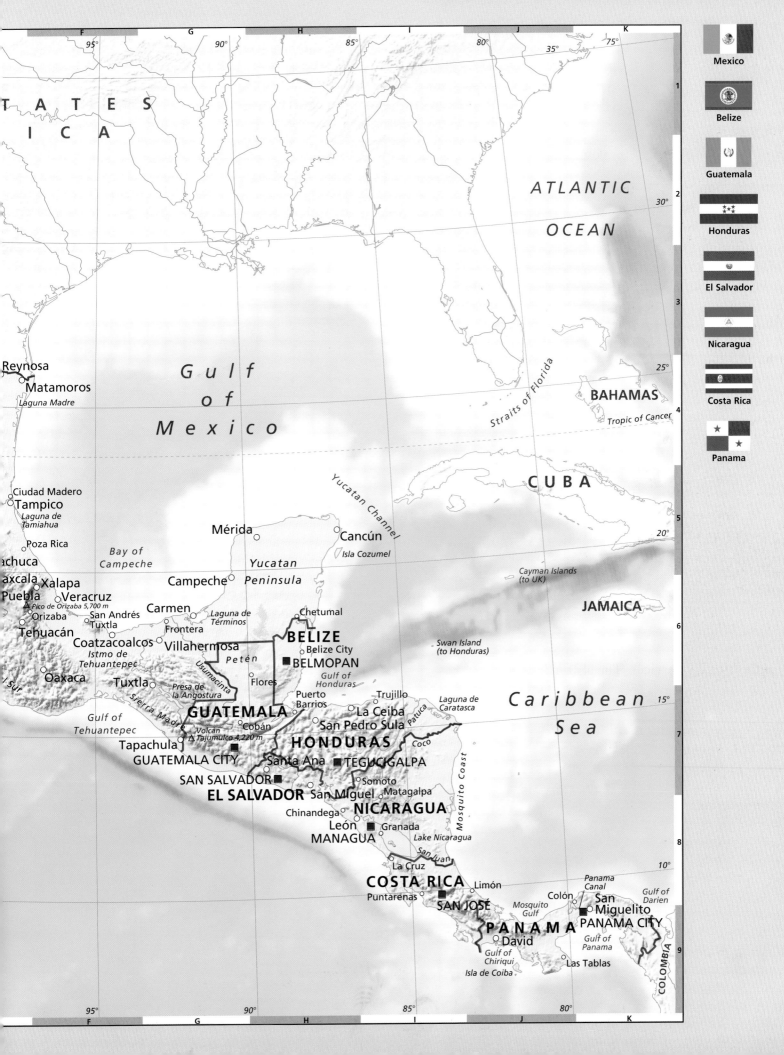

Mexico

Belize

Guatemala

Honduras

El Salvador

Nicaragua

Costa Rica

Panama

STATES
ICA

ATLANTIC

OCEAN

Reynosa
Matamoros
Laguna Madre

Gulf
of
Mexico

Straits of Florida

BAHAMAS

Tropic of Cancer

Ciudad Madero
Tampico
Laguna de
Tamiahua

Poza Rica
achuca

Bay of
Campeche

Mérida

Yucatan Channel

Cancún

Isla Cozumel

CUBA

Cayman Islands
(to UK)

axcala Xalapa
Puebla Veracruz
△*Pico de Orizaba 5,700 m*
Orizaba San Andrés
Tuxtla

Campeche

Yucatan
Peninsula

JAMAICA

Tehuacán
Carmen

Coatzacoalcos
Istmo de
Tehuantepec
Frontera
Villahermosa
Laguna de
Términos

Chetumal

BELIZE
Belize City
BELMOPAN

Swan Island
(to Honduras)

Oaxaca

Tuxtla

Usumacinta
Petén

Presa de
la Angostura

Flores

Gulf of
Honduras

Puerto
Barrios

Trujillo
La Ceiba

Laguna de
Caratasca

Caribbean

Sea

Sierra Madre

GUATEMALA
Cobán
△*Volcán*
Tajumulco 4,220 m

San Pedro Sula

Patuca

Gulf of
Tehuantepec

Tapachula
GUATEMALA CITY

HONDURAS
Santa Ana ■ **TEGUCIGALPA**

Coco

Mosquito Coast

SAN SALVADOR ■
EL SALVADOR San Miguel
Somoto
Matagalpa

Chinandega
NICARAGUA
León
MANAGUA Granada
Lake Nicaragua

San Juan
La Cruz

COSTA RICA Limón
Puntarenas **SAN JOSÉ**

Panama
Canal
Colón San
Miguelito
PANAMA CITY
Gulf of
Darien

Mosquito
Gulf

PANAMA
David
Gulf of
Chiriqui
Isla de Coiba

Gulf of
Panama

Las Tablas

COLOMBIA

THE CARIBBEAN

In the Caribbean Sea there are two mountain ranges, called the Greater and Lesser Antilles, which run from Florida to Trinidad. For part of their length, these mountains are hidden underwater, but where they break the surface they form the islands of the Caribbean. Many of these islands are small and mountainous, but two larger ones, Cuba and Hispaniola (which is divided into Haiti and the Dominican Republic), have a more varied landscape. On Cuba, the mountains are broken up by plains, while on Hispaniola, valleys divide the uplands.

The Caribbean is well known for its warm, sunny climate, but during the hottest months between July and October, violent storms and hurricanes blow in from the Atlantic Ocean and lash the islands. These winds reach up to 250 km/h and they can flatten everything in their path.

The people of the Caribbean are mostly descendants of Africans, Europeans and Asians who settled here over the years, or were brought to the area as slaves. In the past, nearly everyone lived by farming, and these islands still produce large amounts of crops, such as sugar cane and bananas. Today, the Caribbean's warm weather and sandy beaches attract millions of visitors from North America and further afield. Tourism has had a damaging effect on the environment, but it has also brought much-needed money into the region.

LAND HEIGHT

	4,000 m 13,124 ft
	2,000 m 6,562 ft
	1,000 m 3,281 ft
	500 m 1,640 ft
	200 m 656 ft
	Sea level

ATLANTIC

OCEAN

0   250   500 km
0   125   250 miles

25°

West Indies

Acklins
Island

Turks & Caicos Islands
(to UK)

Great
Inagua

20°

Windward Passage

Port-de-Paix
Cap-Haïten
Santiago
Gonaïves   **DOMINICAN**
St Marc   La Vega   **REPUBLIC**
Pico Duarte   San Francisco
3,175 m   de Macorís   Leeward Islands
HAITI Hispaniola   La
Romana   Puerto Rico   British
Cayes   **PORT-AU-PRINCE**   (to US)   Virgin Islands   Anguilla
SANTO   San   Bayamón   (to UK)   (to UK)
Jacmel **DOMINGO** Pedros de   Mayagüez San Juan   St Martin
Macorís   Ponce   Caguas   (to France & Netherlands)
Mona Passage   St Barthélémy (to France)
Netherlands   Barbuda
Virgin Islands   Antilles   St Kitts
(to US)   (to Netherlands)   Nevis   **ANTIGUA & BARBUDA**
BASSETERRE   **ST JOHN'S**
Antilles   **ST KITTS**   Antigua
& NEVIS
Montserrat   Guadeloupe Passage   Grande Terre
(to UK)   Basse Terre   Guadeloupe
(to France)
Basse Terre

DOMINICA ROSEAU

Martinique Passage   15°

Martinique
(to France)
Fort-de-France

ST LUCIA
CASTRIES

St Vincent Passage
BARBADOS
KINGSTOWN St Vincent
Lesser Antilles   **ST VINCENT &**   BRIDGETOWN
THE GRENADINES

Aruba
(to Netherlands)   Netherlands Antilles   ST GEORGE'S
Oranjestad   (to Netherlands)
Bonaire   **GRENADA**
Willemstad Curaçao

Tobago   8

PORT-OF-SPAIN   **TRINIDAD**
& TOBAGO
Arima
Point Fortin   Trinidad   10°

VENEZUELA

70°   65°   60°

SOUTH AMERICA

The continent of South America is shaped like a triangle. It tapers from the warm Caribbean coasts of Colombia and Venezuela to the cold waters of the Southern and Pacific Oceans at the southern tips of Argentina and Chile. Three very different types of landscape dominate the continent. In the west, the Andes stretch for 7,250 km along the entire Pacific coast. These towering mountains reach more than 6,900 m in height. In the hot and humid regions of the northeast, the world's largest rainforest, the Amazon, covers an area of 6.5 million sq km. The mighty Amazon river flows through this region. Further south, there are great open plains of grass and scrub.

Hundreds of years ago, the native peoples of South America built up powerful civilizations, but later, between the 16th and 19th centuries, much of the continent was ruled by the Spanish and Portuguese. As a result, the official language in Brazil is Portuguese, while Spanish is spoken in most of the other countries. The Spanish and Portuguese also developed South America's cities, building on the Atlantic coast for easy access to Europe. Today, most South Americans still live on the coast, in places such as Rio de Janeiro, Montevideo and São Paulo, which is one of the world's largest cities.

South America has rich mineral deposits and fertile farming lands, and most of the countries export goods, including oil and foodstuffs. The wealth is not divided equally. Many people are desperately poor, and large sections of the population cannot read or write. A number of South America's countries have borrowed money from wealthier nations and are struggling to repay their debts.

LAND HEIGHT

4,000 m 13,124 ft	2,000 m 6,562 ft	1,000 m 3,281 ft	500 m 1,640 ft	200 m 656 ft	Sea level

ATLANTIC

OCEAN

PACIFIC

OCEAN

1000 km

500 miles

500

250

South Georgia
(to UK)

Salvador

Sobradinho

Tocar

BRASÍLIA

Brazilian

Goiânia

Highlands

Belo Horizonte

Ribeirão Prêto

Nova
Iguaçu

São Gonçalo

Guarulhos Rio de Janeiro

Uberlândia

Campinas

São Paulo

Curitiba

Rio Grande

Araguaia

Planalto de
Mato Grosso

Campo Grande

Serra Geral

Porto Alegre

Pantanal

Paraná

Lagoa
dos Patos

Juruá

BOLIVIA

Guaporé

Beni

Santa Cruz

Cochabamba

SUCRE

LA PAZ

Lake
Titicaca

Nevado
Sajama
6,542 m

Altiplano

Madre de

PERU

Arequipa

Callao
LIMA

Atacama Desert

Ojos del Salado
6,880 m

Paraguay

Pilcomayo

Gran Chaco

ASUNCIÓN

PARAGUAY

Salado

San Miguel
de Tucumán

Aconcagua
6,960 m

SANTIAGO

*Laguna
Mar Chiquito*

Córdoba

Rosario

Lomas de Zamora

BUENOS AIRES

La

Río de la Plata

MONTEVIDEO

URUGUAY

Mesopotamia

Paraná

Uruguay

Lagoa
Mirim

Plata

ARGENTINA

Pampas

Mar del Plata

Bahía
Blanca

Punta Rasa

Río Negro

Gulf of
San Matias

Patagonia

Gulf of
San Jorge

Bahía
Grande

Strait of Magellan

Tierra
del Fuego

Cape Horn

Isla de
Chiloé

Archipiélago
de los Chonos

Isla
Wellington

Archipiélago
Reina Adelaida

Falkland Islands
(to UK)

Stanley

East
Falkland

West
Falkland

Tropic of Capricorn

Islas de los
Desventurados

Juan Fernández
Islands

ANDES

20°

30°

40°

50°

20°

30°

40°

50°

Tropic of Capricorn

20°

30°

40°

50°

90°

80°

70°

60°

50°

40°

NORTHERN SOUTH AMERICA

The northern part of South America is fringed by uplands – the Guiana Highlands in the north, the Andes in the west and the Brazilian Highlands in the south. This region has many amazing physical features. Lake Titicaca, on the border between Peru and Bolivia, is South America's largest lake. It is also the highest navigable lake in the world. The Angel Falls in Venezuela is the world's highest waterfall. Across the middle of this region is the basin of the Amazon, a river so vast that it carries about one-fifth of the world's fresh water.

Few people live in the interior areas. Most of this region's huge population lives in coastal cities, working in the industries that have grown up around them. These include oil production and metal refining in Venezuela, and chemical and textile industries in Brazil. Mining occurs in most countries. The Amazon region has a thriving timber industry, but loggers are steadily cutting away the rainforest. Large areas of trees have been cleared by farmers for cropland and cattle ranches. Plans to build new oil pipelines and roads across the region will also lead to deforestation. Every year, about eight million hectares of forest disappear from the Amazon, and as about half of the world's known plant and animal species live here, environmentalists are fighting to preserve this important area.

BOLIVIA'S TWO CAPITALS
LA PAZ – legislative and administrative capital
SUCRE – legal captial

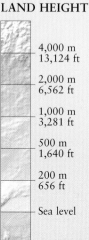

LAND HEIGHT

4,000 m
13,124 ft

2,000 m
6,562 ft

1,000 m
3,281 ft

500 m
1,640 ft

200 m
656 ft

Sea level

ATLANTIC
OCEAN

GRENADA

Isla de
Margarita

TRINIDAD
& TOBAGO

Maturín

Ciudad Guayana

Ciudad Bolívar

*Embalse
de Guri*

GEORGETOWN

GUYANA

PARAMARIBO

*Angel
Falls*

H i g h l a n d s

SURINAME **French
Guiana
(to France)**

Cayenne

Boa Vista

Esequibo

Branco

Negro

Amazon

Macapá

*Mouths of
the Amazon*

Baía de Marajó

*Represa de
Balbina*

*Isla de
Marajó*

Baía de São Marcos

Equator

Manaus

Amazon

Santarém

Belém

Tapajós

Iriri

São Luís

Parnaíba

Sobral

Fortaleza

Amazon

*Represa
Tucuruí*

Imperatriz

Teresina

*Cabo de
São Roque*

Mossoró

Natal

Pôrto Velho

Madeira

B R A Z I L

São Manuel

Xingu

Parnaíba

Juazeiro do Norte

Campina
Grande

João Pessoa

Jaboatão

Olinda

Caruaru

Recife

Juàzeiro

Arapiraca

Maceió

Guaporé

Juruena

Rio das Mortes

Araguaia

Tocantins

*Represa de
Sobradinho*

Taguatinga

Feira de Santana

Aracaju

V I A

Pantanal

*Planalto de
Mato Grosso*

Cuiabá

São Francisco

Alagoinhas

Salvador

Santa Cruz

Jequié

Ilhéus

Corumbá

BRASÍLIA

Goiânia

Anápolis

Vitória da
Conquista

Montes Claros

Brazilian

Teófilo Otoni

Campo
Grande

Paranaíba

Uberlândia

Highlands

Uberaba

Divinópolis

Linhares

Paraná

Dourados

Franca

Rio Grande

Belo Horizonte

Vitória

Ribeirão Prêto

Juiz de Fora

PARAGUAY

Marília

Campinas

Guarulhos

Campos

São Gonçalo

Maringá

Londrina

Nova
Iguaçu

Rio de Janeiro

São Paulo

Santos

Cascavel

Ponta Grossa

Tropic of Capricorn

ATLANTIC
OCEAN

Curitiba

Serra Geral

Joinville

Uruguay

Lages

Florianópolis

E N T I N A

Passo Fundo

Santa Maria

Porto Alegre

Bagé

*Lagoa
dos Patos*

Rio Grande

URUGUAY

Lagoa Mirim

Colombia

Venezuela

Guyana

Suriname

Brazil

Ecuador

Peru

Bolivia

0   500   1000 km

0   250   500 miles

SOUTHERN SOUTH AMERICA

The southern part of South America is made up of Paraguay, Uruguay, Argentina and Chile. The Andes Mountains run from the north to the south, forming the backbone of the region. The Atacama Desert, the driest place on Earth, lies in the northwest. To the east are the forests and grasslands of Gran Chaco, the grasslands of the Pampas, and Patagonia, a high, cold plateau in southern Argentina. The southwest has a dramatic landscape of icy fjords, jagged mountain peaks, U-shaped valleys and frozen glaciers. Further south are the windy islands of Tierra del Fuego.

Most of the people in southern South America live in cities, particularly in the capitals. Buenos Aires, for example, is home to over one-third of Argentina's population. The majority of those who live in this region speak Spanish, the language of the people who ruled the area until the 19th century. In some places, small groups of people still speak the native languages.

The big cities of Chile, Argentina and Uruguay are centres for heavy industries, and some of these have polluted the larger rivers, such as the Paraná and its tributaries. Argentina is famous

for raising cattle on its rich grasslands, and beef from its ranches is exported worldwide. Some of this meat is processed into products such as corned beef in factories in Córdoba and Buenos Aires. Paraguay grows wheat and other crops for its own use, while cotton, coffee, tobacco and oilseeds such as soya, are the country's major export crops. Uruguay's main export is wool. The Chilean Andes, with their deposits of copper, are mined heavily. A wide range of fruits and more specialized crops such as walnuts, and grapes for wine, are grown in Chile's fertile Central Valley.

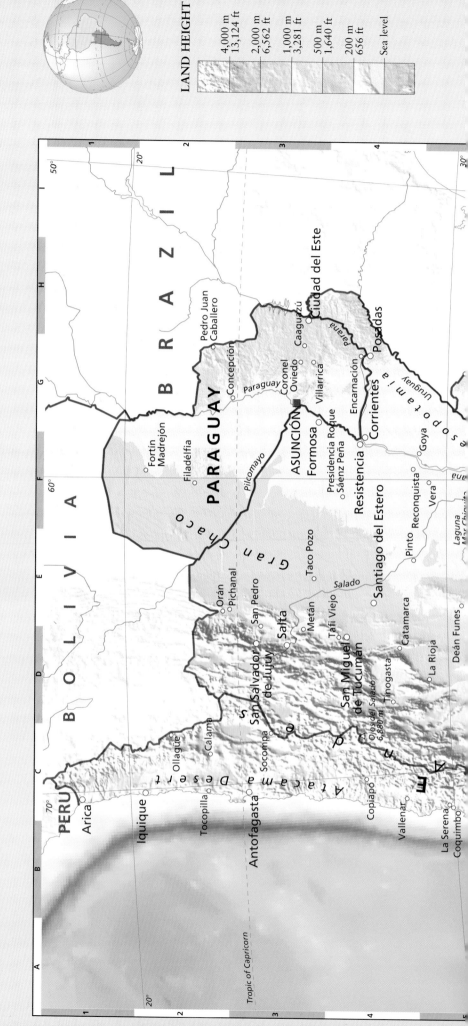

LAND HEIGHT

4,000 m	13,124 ft
2,000 m	6,562 ft
1,000 m	3,281 ft
500 m	1,640 ft
200 m	656 ft
Sea level	

Chile
Paraguay
Argentina
Uruguay

URUGUAY

Lagoa Mirim

Melo
Mercedes
Fray Bentos
Durazno
Florida
San José de Mayo
Minas
San Nicolás de los Arroyos
Gualeguaychú
MONTEVIDEO
Las Piedras
Rosario
San Nicolás de Los Arroyos
Río de la Plata
Punta Norte
BUENOS AIRES
La Plata
Mar del Plata
Lomas de Zamora
Pergamino
Junín
Necochea
Villa María
Río Cuarto
Venado Tuerto
Azul
Punta Rasa
Rufino
Olavarría
San Luis
Tres Arroyos
Bahía Blanca
Mendoza
Godoy Cruz
Mercedes
Coronel Pringles
Punta Alta
Bahía Blanca
Punta Rasa
SANTIAGO
San Bernardo
San Rafael
Bahía Blanca
Viña del Mar
Aconcagua 6,960 m
Andes
Malargüe
Río Colorado
Viedma
Peninsula Valdés
Valparaíso
Rancagua
Salado
Río Negro
Gulf of San Matías
Pichilemu
Talca
Chos Malal
General Roca
San Antonio Oeste
Rawson
Constitución
Colorado
Neuquén
Chillán
Los Ángeles
Zapala
Chubut
Talcahuano
Concepción
Lebu
San Carlos de Bariloche
Esquel
Chico
Temuco
Valdivia
Osorno
Puerto Montt
Nueva Lubecka
Sarmiento
Comodoro Rivadavia
Gulf of San Jorge
Fitz Roy
Cabo Tres Puntas
Puerto Deseado
Isla de Chiloé
Gulf of Corcovado
Puerto Aisén
Coihaique
Deseado
Gobernador Gregores
Puerto San Julián
Archipiélago de los Chonos
Chico
Puerto Santa Cruz
Taitao Peninsula
Isla Wellington
Santa Cruz
El Calafate
Puerto Natales
Gulf of Penas
Archipiélago Reina Adelaida
Río Gallegos
Punta Arenas
Bahía Grande
Strait of Magellan
San Sebastián
Río Grande
Tierra del Fuego
Ushuaia
Isla de los Estados
Cape Horn

ARGENTINA
CHILE
PACIFIC OCEAN
ATLANTIC OCEAN

Falkland Islands (to UK)
West Falkland
East Falkland
Stanley

600 km
300 miles
300
150
0
0

Central Valley

THE ATLANTIC OCEAN

Covering about one-fifth of the planet's surface, the Atlantic is the world's second-largest ocean. To the west are the Americas, and Europe and Africa lie to the east. The Earth's longest mountain chain, the Mid-Atlantic Ridge, dominates the ocean's underwater landscape. In places, the ridge rises above the water as volcanic islands, such as Iceland and the Azores. The deepest part of the Atlantic, the Puerto Rico Trench, plunges to -8,605 m.

Since Portuguese and Spanish explorers began to cross the ocean from Europe to America in the 15th century, the Atlantic has been one of the world's major transport routes. Today, ships carry bulk goods, such as oil, grain and iron, between the ocean's many international ports.

The Atlantic is rich in natural resources. The shallow areas along the coasts have deposits of oil and gas, and in recent years, offshore oil and gas reserves have been exploited in the Gulf of Mexico, the Niger Delta and the North Sea. Sand, gravel and shell deposits are mined by the USA and the United Kingdom for use in the construction industry. The ocean is also a vital source of food. Most of the Atlantic's coastal countries fish in its waters, but in the north Atlantic, stocks of cod, herring and haddock have been reduced by overfishing. The ocean's environment is also threatened by pollution. Oil is discharged into the water by ships and drilling rigs. Industrial waste, fertilizers and sewage enter the Atlantic at the coasts, particularly in the Mediterranean, Baltic and North Sea regions, and off the USA, southern Brazil and eastern Argentina. A number of countries are trying to reach agreements to tackle some forms of pollution.

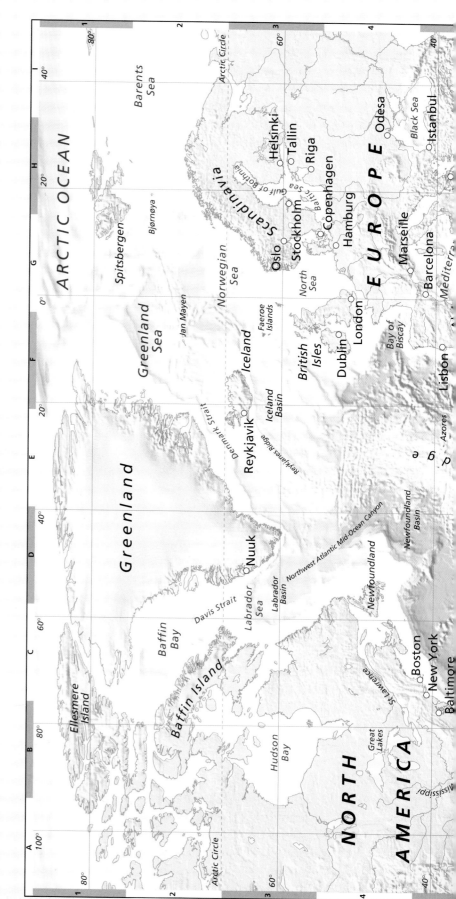

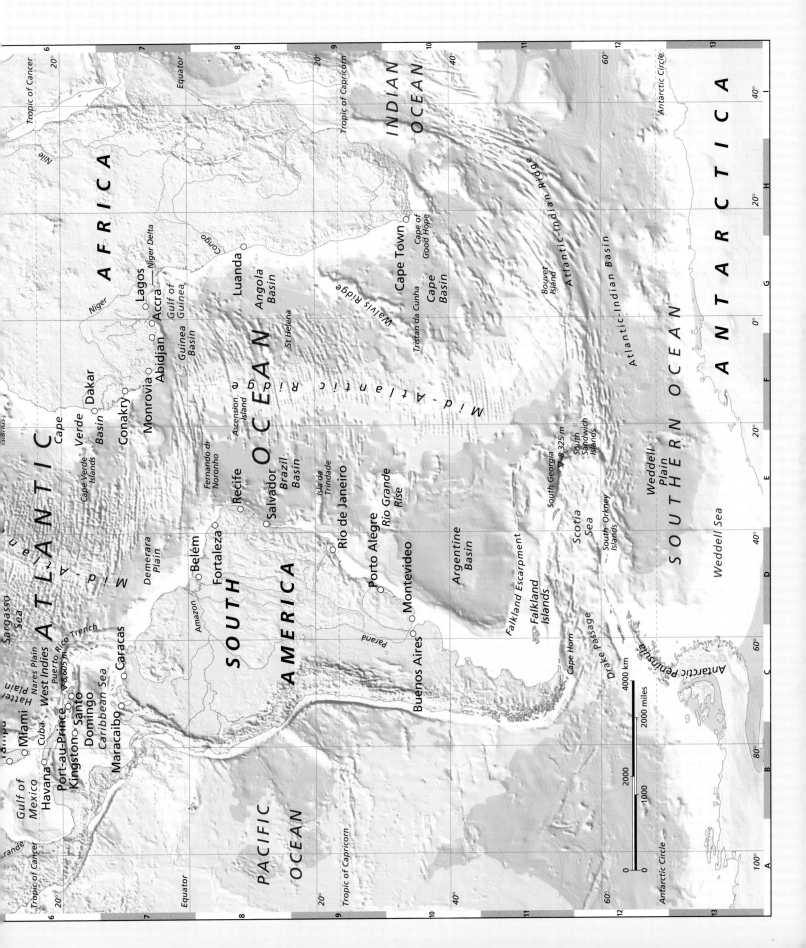

THE ATLANTIC OCEAN

AFRICA

A F R I C A

Tropic of Cancer

Equator

Nile

Niger Delta

Congo

Lagos

Accra

Abidjan

Monrovia

Conakry

Dakar

Cape Verde

Basin

Cape Verde Islands

Cape

Niger

Gulf of Guinea

Guinea Basin

Luanda

Angola Basin

St Helena

Ascension Island

Fernando di Noronho

Tropic of Capricorn

INDIAN OCEAN

Cape Town

Cape of Good Hope

Cape Basin

Tristan da Cunha

Walvis Ridge

Bouvet Island

Atlantic-Indian Ridge

Atlantic-Indian Basin

Antarctic Circle

A N T A R C T I C A

S O U T H E R N   O C E A N

M i d - A t l a n t i c   R i d g e

A T L A N T I C

Sargasso Sea

Hatteras Plain

Nares Plain

West Indies

Puerto Rico Trench

▽8,605 m

Mid-A...n...plain

Demerara Plain

Caracas

Maracaibo

Santo Domingo

Kingston

Port-au-Prince

Havana

Miami

Cuba

Gulf of Mexico

Grande

Tropic of Cancer

Equator

20°

PACIFIC OCEAN

S O U T H

A M E R I C A

Amazon

Belém

Fortaleza

Recife

Salvador

Brazil. Basin

Isla da Trindade

Rio de Janeiro

Porto Alegre

Montevideo

Buenos Aires

Paraná

Rio Grande Rise

Argentine Basin

Cape Horn

Drake Passage

Falkland Escarpment

Falkland Islands

Scotia Sea

South Orkney Islands

South Georgia

South Sandwich Islands

▽8,325 m

Weddell Plain

Weddell Sea

Antarctic Peninsula

Tropic of Capricorn

Antarctic Circle

4000 km

2000 miles

2000

1000

0

Equator

OCEAN

EUROPE

The continent of Europe extends from the Ural Mountains in the east to the Atlantic Ocean in the west, north to the Arctic Ocean and south to the Mediterranean Sea. There are a number of mountain ranges, including the Alps, which rise to more than 4,800 m, and lesser ranges, such as the Carpathians, Pyrenees and Apennines. Most of the continent's population lives between these uplands on the North European Plain. The plain's rich, fertile soil and temperate climate help farmers to grow a variety of crops, such as wheat, fruit and vegetables, and raise both dairy and beef cattle.

During the Industrial Revolution of the 18th and 19th centuries, Europe developed heavy industries, such as iron and steel-making. Today, in western Europe, these businesses are being replaced by high-tech industries and financial services. In the east, however, many old-fashioned factories remain. These cause terrible environmental pollution in some places.

Many of Europe's countries have existed for hundreds of years and some, such as the United Kingdom and France, had large empires. Although these empires no longer exist, the countries that ran them still play a major role in world affairs. In the 20th century, many of western Europe's countries came together to form the European Union. The union is working towards bringing its members closer politically and economically.

LAND HEIGHT

	4,000 m 13,124 ft
	2,000 m 6,562 ft
	1,000 m 3,281 ft
	500 m 1,640 ft
	200 m 656 ft
	Sea level

Barents Sea

North Cape

Novaya Zemlya

Arctic Circle

Ural Mountains

ASIA

Pechora

SWEDEN

Österålen

ten

Murmansk

Kola Peninsula

White Sea

Oulu

FINLAND

Northern Dvina

Archangel

RUSSIAN

FEDERATION

Perm

Tampere

Lake Onega

Kirov

Izhevsk

Turku (Abo)

HELSINKI

Lake Ladoga

Ufa

STOCKHOLM

Gulf of Bothnia

St Petersburg

Yaroslavl

Kazan

Kama

Naberezhnyye Chelny

TALLINN

Gulf of Finland

Ivanovo

ESTONIA

Tver

Nizhniy Novgorod

Gotland

LATVIA

Volga

MOSCOW

Oka

Simbirsk

Tolyatti

Orenburg

Öland

RIGA

Western Dvina

Ryazan

Samara

Ural

Baltic Sea

LITHUANIA

European Plain

Vitsyebsk

Tula

Penza

Volga

Gdansk

RUSS. FED.

VILNIUS

Smolensk

Saratov

Volga

Kaliningrad

MINSK

Bryansk

Lipetsk

North

BELARUS

Kursk

Voronezh

Vistula

Poznan

WARSAW

Homyel

Don

Volgograd

Lodz

KIEV

Kharkiv

Astrakhan

Oder

Wroclaw

Rivne

Caspian Depression

POLAND

UKRAINE

Dnipropetrovsk

Krakow

Lviv

Dniester

Donetsk

Rostov-na-Donu

Caspian Sea

SLOVAKIA

Carpathian Mountains

Krivyy Rih

BRATISLAVA

Tisza

Cluj-Napoca

Iasi

MOLDOVA

Stavropol

BUDAPEST

CHISINAU

Dnieper

Sea of Azov

Krasnodar

Groznyy

HUNGARY

Timisoara

Odesa

Crimean Peninsula

ROMANIA

CROATIA

BELGRADE

BUCHAREST

Sevastopol

Elbrus
△5,642 m

Caucasus

BOSNIA &
HERZEGOVINA

SARAJEVO

Constanta

Danube

Black Sea

SERBIA

MONTENEGRO

BULGARIA

PODGORICA

PRISTINA

KOSOVO

SOFIA

Burgas

SKOPJE

MACEDONIA

Plovdiv

Istanbul

TIRANA

ALBANIA

Thessaloniki

GREECE

Aegean Sea

Ionian Sea

Patra

ATHENS

ASIA

Rhodes

Irakleion

Crete

Mediterranean Sea

| | 500 | 1000 km |
| 0 | 250 | 500 miles |

NORTHWESTERN EUROPE

Denmark, Norway and Sweden, in the far northwest of Europe, are together known as Scandinavia. These countries have similar languages and for part of their history shared the same rulers. Out at sea to the west lies Iceland. Finland is in the east. Until 1917, Finland was a province of the Russian Empire, so it has a very different language and culture to Scandinavia. All of these countries are highly industrialized and have a high standard of living.

Iceland has a unique landscape. Icy and rocky, it is dotted with volcanoes and dramatic hot springs, some of which are tapped to heat buildings. Much of the rest of northwestern Europe is rugged, mountainous and wooded. The landscape is harsh, and most of the population live in the flatter southern areas, where lakes were scraped out by glaciers thousands of years ago. The soil in the south is more fertile than in the north, allowing farmers to grow crops and lush grass for dairy farming. The western coasts have been eroded by the sea and ice into deep inlets known as fjords. The climate in this part of the region is wet, but mild, and many of the people who live here

work in fishing and fish-processing. Further east, the climate is much colder and drier. A great number of those who live inland are employed in the timber industry.

The countries of northwestern Europe produce very little pollution. Most of the region's power is generated from clean hydro-electric stations that harness the fast-flowing mountain streams to produce electricity. However, pollution from elsewhere in Europe blows north and falls as acid rain. This rain poisons forests and lakes, killing the plants and animals living in them.

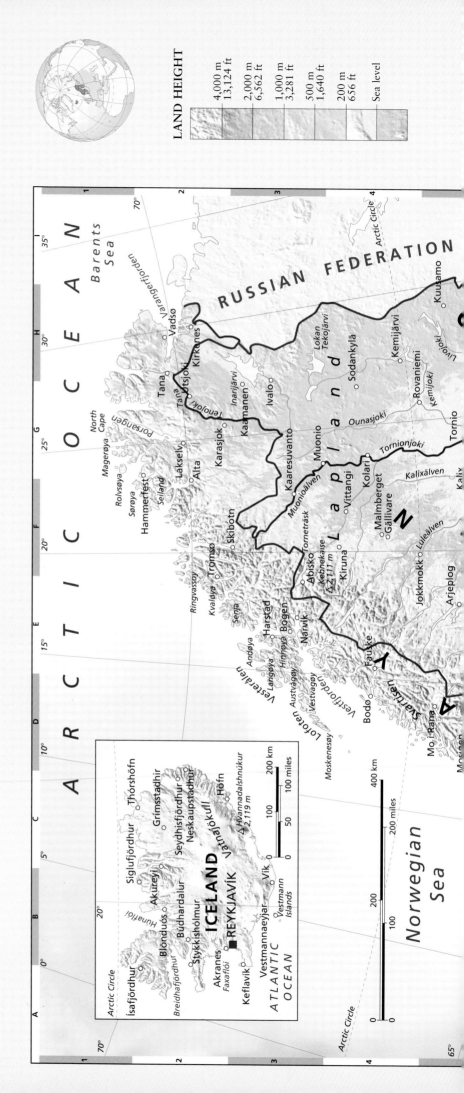

LAND HEIGHT

4,000 m	13,124 ft
2,000 m	6,562 ft
1,000 m	3,281 ft
500 m	1,640 ft
200 m	656 ft
	Sea level

Iceland Norway Sweden Finland Denmark

RUSSIAN FEDERATION

BELARUS

ESTONIA

LATVIA

LITHUANIA

RUSSIAN FEDERATION (KALININGRAD)

POLAND

GERMANY

FINLAND

SWEDEN

NORWAY

DENMARK

Gulf of Finland

Gulf of Riga

Baltic Sea

Gulf of Bothnia

North Sea

Skagerrak

Kattegat

Suomussalmi
Kontiomäki
Kuhmo
Sotkamo
Nurmes
Kajaani
Iisalmi
Pielinen
Joensuu
Orivesi
Parikkala
Imatra
Lappeenranta
Siilinjärvi
Kuopio
Äänekoski
Varkaus
Mikkeli
Saimaa
Kouvola
Kotka
Porvoo
HELSINKI
Kempele
Raahe
Pyhäjoki
Oulujärvi
Keitele
Jyväskylä
Keuruu
Lahti
Riihimäki
Hyvinkää
Vantaa
Espoo
Kokkola (Karleby)
Jakobstad (Pietersaari)
Lapua
Seinäjoki
Alavus
Nokia
Hämeenlinna
Tampere
Salo
Turku (Åbo)
Vaasa (Vasa)
Närpes
Parkano
Kankaanpää
Pori
Rauma
Noormarkku
Kristinestad
Skiftet Kihti
Mariehamn (Maarianhamina)
Åland
Ålands hav

Skellefteälven
Skellefteå
Umeälven
Lycksele
Umeå
Holmsund
Storuman
Vilhelmina
Dorotea
Hoting
Ångermanälven
Örnsköldsvik
Härnösand
Norrtälje
Täby
Uppsala
Tierp
Sollentuna
STOCKHOLM
Sandviken
Söderhamn
Gävle
Hudiksvall
Söderköping
Nyköping
Norrköping
Linköping
Storsjön
Östersund
Strömsund
Kramfors
Timrå
Sundsvall
Ånge
Ljusnan
Ljusdal
Bollnäs
Falun
Borlänge
Dalälven
Sala
Avesta
Västerås
Nora
Askersund
Katrineholm
Mariestad
Vättern
Vetlanda
Gotland
Visby
Borgholm
Färjestaden
Öland
Oskarshamn
Kalmar
Kungsbacka
Varberg
Jönköping
Borås
Ljungby
Växjö
Laholm
Karlskrona
Kristianstad
Helsingborg
Lund
Malmö
Ystad
Trelleborg
Ronne
Bornholm
Halmstad
Ratan
Rättvik
Leksand
Mora
Svenstavik
Idre
Sveg
Malung
Ludvika
Filipstad
Klarälven
Karlstad
Säffle
Örebro
Falköping
Trollhättan
Vänern
Tun
Amål
Mellerud
Uddevalla
Vänersborg
Gothenburg
Mölndal

Glittertind 2,452 m
Galdhøpiggen 2,479 m
Jotunheimen
Dovrefjell
Trondheim
Hell
Hemdal
Storen
Røros
Verdalsøra
Steinkjer
Namsos
Vikna
Smøla
Hitra
Frøya
Kristiansund
Averøya
Molde
Ålesund
Åndalsnes
Dombås
Ringebu
Lillehammer
Gol
Hamar
Mjøsa
Gjøvik
Hønefoss
Drammen
Sandvika
OSLO
Lillestrøm
Moss
Sarpsborg
Halden
Strömstad
Fredrikstad
Skien
Holmestrand
Kongsberg
Haugesund
Haukeligrend
Hardangervidda
Setesdal
Evje
Arendal
Kristiansand
Egersund
Sandnes
Stavanger
Kvinesdal
Leirvik
Boknafjorden
Sognefjorden
Bergen
Voss
Eidfjord
Geilo
Hermansverk
Floro
Trondheimsfjorden
Namsen
Glomma
Lågen
Hardangerjøkulen
Folgefonni

Thisted
Hjørring
Frederikshavn
Ålborg
Hobro
Randers
Viborg
Holstebro
Herning
Århus
Vejle
Billund
Kolding
Odense
Nyborg
Fyn
Ringsted
COPENHAGEN
Zealand
Helsingør
Nykøbing
Falster
Lolland
Rødbyhavn
Store Bælt
Varde
Esbjerg
Jutland
DENMARK

60° 30° 25° 20° 15° 10° 5° 55°

THE BRITISH ISLES

Located in the northwest of Europe, this group of islands contains two countries: the United Kingdom and the Republic of Ireland. The United Kingdom includes the national regions of England, Wales and Scotland, and the province of Northern Ireland. Britain and Ireland are the British Isles' largest islands.

In the north and west of Britain are uplands, fringed by rocky, jagged coasts. To the south and east of the island are lowlands. They range from the flat fens of the east to the rolling hills of the southeast. Ireland has a low-lying plain

in its centre, which is covered by numerous lakes, peat bogs and grassy hills. The plain is surrounded by low coastal mountains.

Sheep and cattle are raised in Britain's uplands, and cereal crops are grown in the east. The flatter areas of the island, such as central England, produce fruit and vegetables. Dairy products and beef are important sources of income for the Republic of Ireland.

early 20th century, the country was a world leader in mining, steel production and textiles. Recently, many of these heavy industries have been replaced by high-tech businesses and financial services. Computer hardware and software companies employ a great number of people in Ireland, Scotland and southern England, while tourism is an important industry throughout the islands. The move away from heavy industry has helped to reduce pollution in the area, but the British Isles is a small, densely populated region with high numbers of cars, so poor air quality is a big problem in large cities.

In the late 18th century, the United Kingdom began to develop heavy industries, and by the

LAND HEIGHT

	4,000 m / 13,124 ft
	2,000 m / 6,562 ft
	1,000 m / 3,281 ft
	500 m / 1,640 ft
	200 m / 656 ft
	Sea level

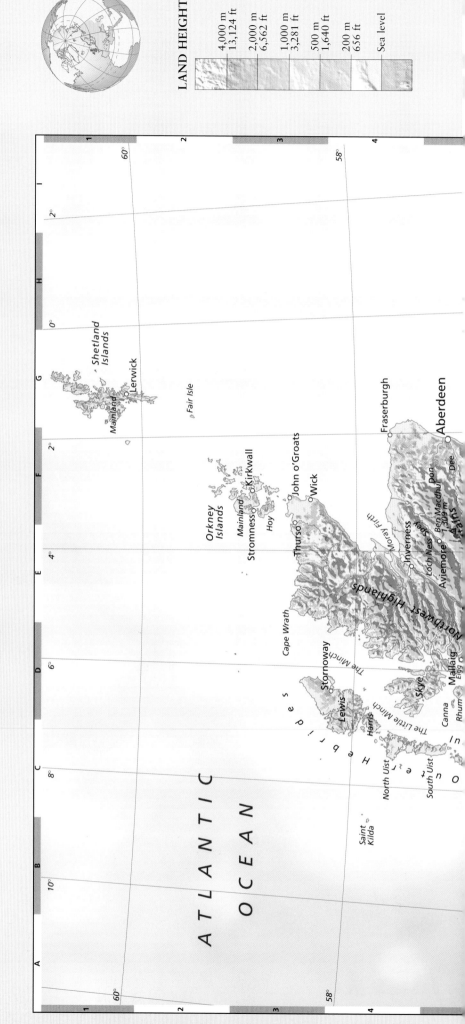

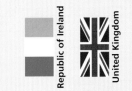

Republic of Ireland

United Kingdom

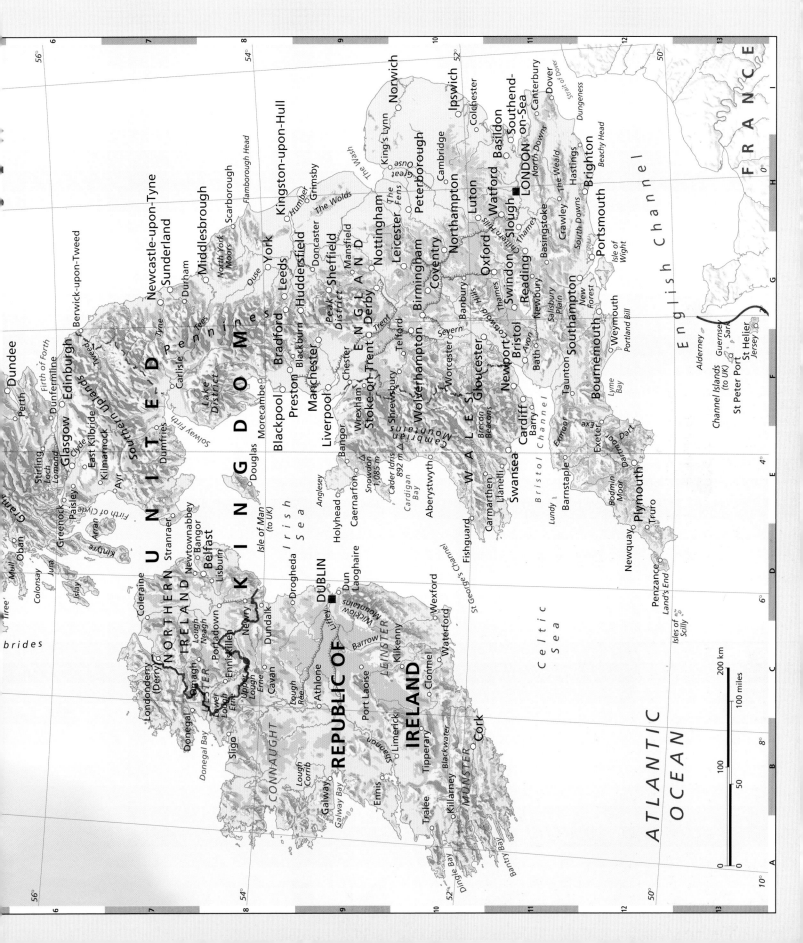

THE BRITISH ISLES

FRANCE

ATLANTIC OCEAN

REPUBLIC OF IRELAND

UNITED KINGDOM

NORTHERN IRELAND

WALES

ENGLAND

CONNAUGHT

LEINSTER

MUNSTER

ULSTER

Scotland and Northern England

Dundee
Perth
Stirling
Loch Lomond
Glasgow
Greenock
Paisley
East Kilbride
Kilmarnock
Ayr
Oban
Mull
Colonsay
Jura
Islay
Tiree
Colonsay
Kintyre
Arran
Firth of Clyde
Dunfermline
Edinburgh
Firth of Forth
Berwick-upon-Tweed
Dumfries
Southern Uplands
Stranraer
Tweed
Newcastle-upon-Tyne
Sunderland
Tyne
Durham
Middlesbrough
Tees
Carlisle
Lake District
Solway Firth
Grampians
Hebrides
Londonderry (Derry)
Coleraine
Omagh
Donegal
Donegal Bay
Sligo
Lower Lough Erne
Upper Lough Erne
Enniskillen
Lough Neagh
Newtownabbey
Bangor
Belfast
Lisburn
Portadown
Newry
Dundalk
Drogheda
Douglas
Isle of Man (to UK)
Irish Sea

Republic of Ireland

Galway
Galway Bay
Lough Corrib
Lough Ree
Athlone
Shannon
Ennis
Limerick
Tralee
Killarney
Dingle Bay
Bantry Bay
Cork
Tipperary
Blackwater
Clonmel
Kilkenny
Barrow
Port Laoise
Cavan
DUBLIN
Dun Laoghaire
Liffey
Wicklow Mountains
Wexford
Waterford
St George's Channel

England and Wales

Cavan
Morecambe
Blackpool
Preston
Blackburn
Bradford
Leeds
Huddersfield
Manchester
Sheffield
Peak District
Liverpool
Chester
Wrexham
Bangor
Anglesey
Holyhead
Caernarfon
Snowdon 1,085 m
Cader Idris 892 m
Cardigan Bay
Aberystwyth
Cambrian Mountains
Stoke-on-Trent
Derby
Nottingham
Mansfield
Trent
Doncaster
York
North York Moors
Scarborough
Flamborough Head
Kingston-upon-Hull
Humber
Grimsby
The Wolds
Ouse
Pennines

Leicester
Birmingham
Coventry
Telford
Shrewsbury
Wolverhampton
Worcester
Severn
Fishguard
Carmarthen
Llanelli
Swansea
Cardiff
Barry
Newport
Gloucester
Brecon Beacons
Bristol
Bath
Avon
Bristol Channel
Lundy
Barnstaple
Exmoor
Exe
Bodmin Moor
Dartmoor
Dart
Exeter
Plymouth
Truro
Newquay
Penzance
Land's End
Isles of Scilly
Celtic Sea

Banbury
Northampton
Cotswold Hills
Swindon
Thames
Oxford
Chilterns
Reading
Newbury
Salisbury Plain
Basingstoke
Luton
Watford
Slough
LONDON
North Downs
Southend-on-Sea
Basildon
Cambridge
Peterborough
King's Lynn
The Fens
Great Ouse
The Wash
Norwich
Ipswich
Colchester
Canterbury
Dover
Strait of Dover
Dungeness
Beachy Head
Hastings
The Weald
Brighton
South Downs
Crawley
Portsmouth
Isle of Wight
Southampton
New Forest
Bournemouth
Poole
Weymouth
Portland Bill
Lyme Bay
English Channel
Channel Islands (to UK)
Alderney
Guernsey
St Peter Port
Sark
Jersey
St Helier

Scale:
200 km
100 miles
100
100
50
0

6° 7° 8° 9° 10° 11° 12° 13°
56° 54° 52° 50°
0°
4°
A B C D E F G H I

THE LOW COUNTRIES

Luxembourg, Belgium and the Netherlands are known as the Low Countries because most of their land is flat and low-lying. Nearly one-third of the Netherlands lies below sea level. The Dutch reclaimed this land from the sea by building dykes to enclose areas of shallow water, which were then drained into canals by pumps. Regions such as these are called polders, and they need constant care to stop them from flooding. Rising to heights of 500 m, the forested hills of the Ardennes, in southern Belgium and Luxembourg, are the Low Countries' only uplands. Two major rivers –

the Meuse and the Rhine – flow through the region on their way to the North Sea.

The reclaimed areas, plus flat plains such as Flanders in northern Belgium, have fertile soils, and provide good conditions for agriculture. Barley, potatoes and flax are the main crops. The Netherlands also produces cut flowers and bulbs, which are exported all over the world. Beef, dairy and pig farming take place in the higher inland parts of this region. Luxembourg is a major centre for banking, and Belgium has a great number of factories. Brussels, which is

the capital of Belgium, is also the administrative capital of the European Union.

Many people work in chemical companies, engineering, the textile industry, and in the new high-tech businesses that are springing up in this region. The majority of people live in towns or cities and the largest urban area is known as *Randstad Holland*. This is a densely-populated, built-up region between Amsterdam and Rotterdam. Most people have a comfortable lifestyle in the cities, but large numbers of cars and factories cause serious air pollution.

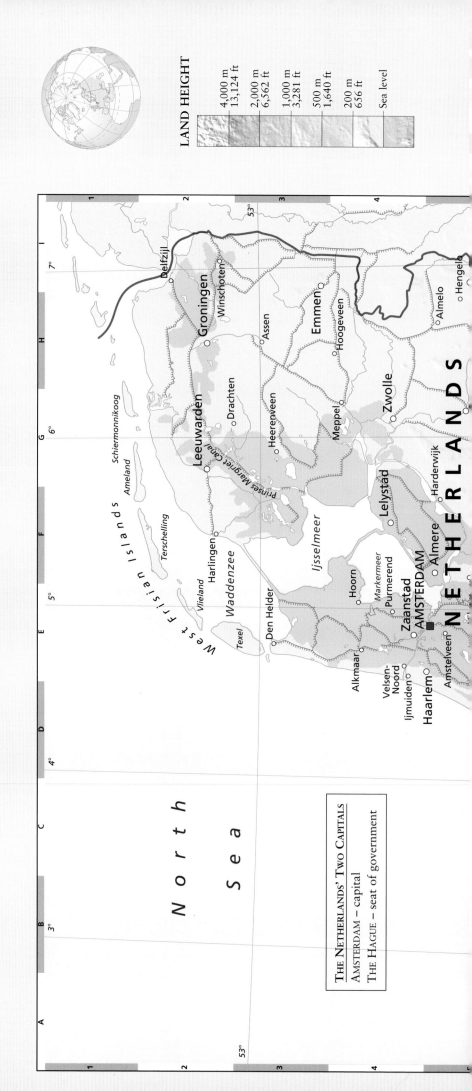

LAND HEIGHT

	4,000 m / 13,124 ft
	2,000 m / 6,562 ft
	1,000 m / 3,281 ft
	500 m / 1,640 ft
	200 m / 656 ft
	Sea level

THE NETHERLANDS' TWO CAPITALS
AMSTERDAM – capital
THE HAGUE – seat of government

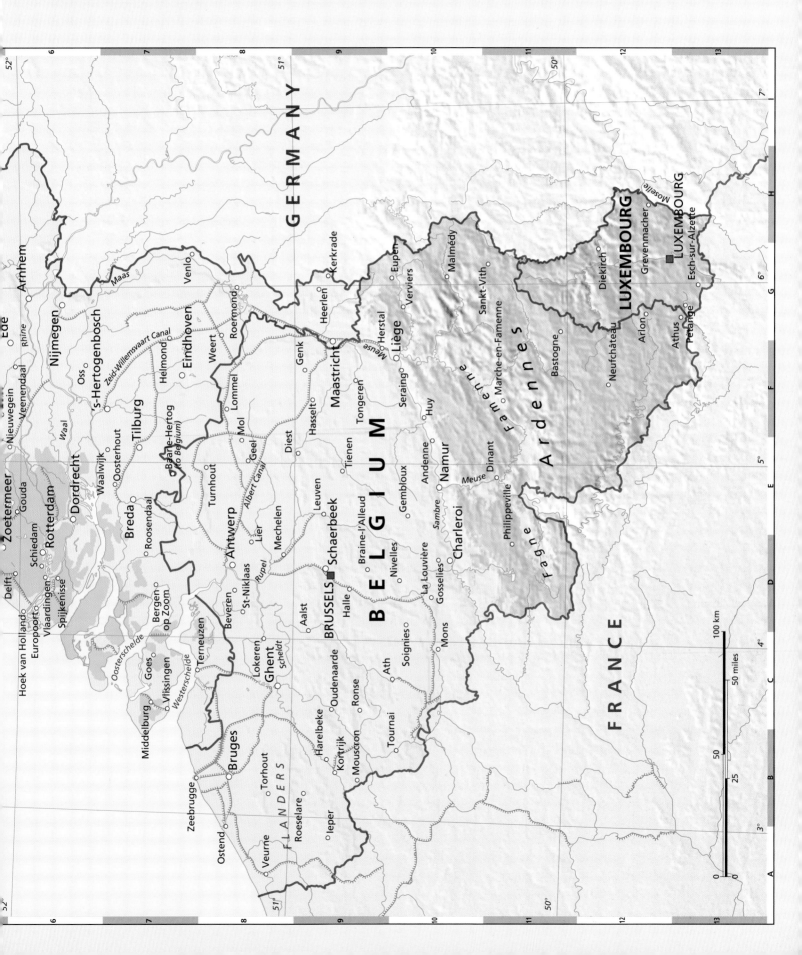

Netherlands
Belgium
Luxembourg

GERMANY

LUXEMBOURG

BELGIUM

FRANCE

FLANDERS

Ardennes

Famenne

Fagne

Arnhem
Ede
Nijmegen
Nieuwegein
Veenendaal
Rhine
Waal
's-Hertogenbosch
Oss
Zoetermeer
Gouda
Delft
Schiedam
Rotterdam
Vlaardingen
Europoort
Spijkenisse
Hoek van Holland
Dordrecht
Breda
Roosendaal
Bergen op Zoom
Middelburg
Goes
Vlissingen
Oosterschelde
Westerschelde
Terneuzen
Zeebrugge
Ostend
Bruges
Torhout
Roeselare
Veurne
Ieper
Harelbeke
Kortrijk
Mouscron
Ronse
Oudenaarde
Aalst
Ghent
Lokeren
scheldt
Beveren
St-Niklaas
Antwerp
Lier
Mechelen
Rupel
Turnhout
Geel
Mol
Lommel
Diest
Oosterhout
Waalwijk
Tilburg
Baarle-Hertog
(to Belgium)
Eindhoven
Weert
Helmond
Venlo
Maas
Roermond
Zeid-Willemsvaart Canal
Genk
Hasselt
Albert Canal
Tienen
Leuven
Schaerbeek
BRUSSELS
Halle
Braine-l'Alleud
Nivelles
Soignies
Ath
Tournai
Mons
La Louvière
Gosselies
Charleroi
Philippeville
Dinant
Gembloux
Andenne
Namur
Meuse
Sambre
Huy
Seraing
Liège
Herstal
Maastricht
Tongeren
Meuse
Heerlen
Kerkrade
Heerlen
Eupen
Verviers
Malmédy
Sankt-Vith
Marche-en-Famenne
Bastogne
Neufchâteau
Arlon
Athus
Pétange
Esch-sur-Alzette
LUXEMBOURG
Grevenmacher
Diekirch
Moselle

100 km
50 miles
50
25
0
0

50°
51°
52°
3°
4°
5°
6°
7°

FRANCE

One of the largest countries in western Europe, France has a variety of landscape types, which fall into two main areas. In the north and west are flat plains and low hills. The plains are drained by three great rivers, the Seine, the Loire and the Garonne. These rivers form basins with rich soils. To the south and east are the uplands – the high plateau of the Massif Central and two mountain ranges, the Pyrenees and the Alps. The Pyrenees form a natural border with Spain. The Alps are crossed by high passes that lead into Italy and Switzerland.

Fertile soils and a temperate climate make France a successful food producer. Wheat and vegetables are grown in the north, and corn and fruit are produced in the south. The lowlands make good dairy pasture and grapes for wine are grown in many areas. France is also highly industrialized. It exports a vast range of products, from cars to clothing. Both the northern and southern coasts suffer from industrial pollution, but because France generates about 80 per cent of its electricity in nuclear power stations, the country is less polluted by the use of fossil fuels than other industrialized nations.

From the 18th–20th centuries, France was a colonial power, with an empire in Africa, Asia and North America. Almost all of its colonies are now independent. Today, France plays a leading role in the European Union.

LAND HEIGHT

4,000 m	13,124 ft
2,000 m	6,562 ft
1,000 m	3,281 ft
500 m	1,640 ft
200 m	656 ft
Sea level	

France

Monaco

Strait of Dover
Dunkerque
Calais
Boulogne-sur-Mer
Lille
Tourcoing
Roubaix
Béthune
Lens
Arras
Valenciennes
Abbeville

BELGIUM

LUXEMBOURG

GERMANY

Dieppe
Rouen
Beauvais
Amiens
St-Quentin
Somme
Oise
Laon
Charleville-Mézières
Compiègne
Creil
Reims
Thionville
Metz
Forbach
Haguenau
Évreux
Pontoise
Argenteuil
PARIS
Créteil
Versailles
Châlons-en-Champagne
CHAMPAGNE
Bar-le-Duc
Nancy
Strasbourg
St-Dié
Colmar
Melun
Seine
Yonne
Troyes
Marne
Épinal
Vosges
Chartres
Sens
Chaumont
Rhine
Orléans
Auxerre
Langres
Mulhouse
Olivet
Belfort
Blois
Clamecy
Vesoul
Montbéliard
Dijon
Besançon
LIECHTENSTEIN
AUSTRIA
Cher
Bourges
Morvan
BURGUNDY
SWITZERLAND
Nevers
ANCE
E
Châteauroux
Loire
Chalon-sur-Saône
Creuse
Montceau-les-Mines
Saône
Lake Geneva
Moulins
Mâcon
Jura
Thonon-les-Bains
Montluçon
Bourg-en-Bresse
Vichy
Roanne
Annemasse
Clermont-Ferrand
Lyon
Annecy
Chamonix
Limoges
Villeurbanne
Mont Blanc 4,810 m
Puy de Sancy 1,885 m
St-Étienne
St-Chamond
Chambéry
Alps
igueux
Brive-la-Gaillarde
Massif
Isère
Grenoble
ITALY
Dordogne
Le Puy
Les Ecrins 4,102 m
Central
Valence
Cahors
Lot
Mende
Gap
Montélimar
Cévennes
Rhône
Maritime Alps
Rodez
Alès
Durance
Digne
Montauban
Tarn
Orange
Albi
Avignon
Nîmes
Tarascon
MONACO
MONACO
Toulouse
Castres
Arles
Aix-en-Provence
Nice
Antibes
Montpellier
Camargue
PROVENCE
Cannes
Canal du Midi
Béziers
Sète
St-Tropez
Fréjus
Carcassonne
Marseille
Toulon
Côte d'Azur
Narbonne
Gulf of Lion
La Seyne-sur-Mer
Îles d'Hyères
Cap Corse
Foix
Bastia
Perpignan
ANDORRA
e e s
Mediterranean Sea
Corsica
Aléria
Ajaccio
Sartène
Bonifacio
Strait of Bonifacio

THE IBERIAN PENINSULA

The Iberian Peninsula is separated from the rest of Europe by the Pyrenees mountains. To the west is the Atlantic Ocean, while the Mediterranean Sea lies in the east. Spain and Portugal occupy most of this large landmass, together with the tiny mountainous state of Andorra, and Gibraltar, a small British territory. The centre of the peninsula is dominated by a vast plateau, which is enclosed by the Cordillera Cantábrica to the north, and the Sierra Morena to the south.

Wheat and barley are Iberia's main crops, but in the south, farmers irrigate the dry land to grow citrus fruits, especially oranges and lemons. Both Spain and Portugal make wines and these two countries also produce two-thirds of the world's cork.

Spain's industries, which are concentrated in the north of the country, make cars, machinery, steel and chemicals. Portugal exports textiles, clothing, shoes and processed fish, and tourism is an important source of income for this entire region.

Soil erosion, which is caused when forests are cleared for farmland, has affected much of the peninsula. High-rise hotels along the Mediterranean coast have spoilt the character of this area, and popular beaches here are extremely overcrowded.

LAND HEIGHT

4,000 m
13,124 ft

2,000 m
6,562 ft

1,000 m
3,281 ft

500 m
1,640 ft

200 m
656 ft

Sea level

Spain

Andorra

Portugal

FRANCE

Gulf of Gascony

Gulf of Lion

tander
San Vicente de Barakaldo
Bilbao
Donostia-San Sebastián
Irún
PAIS VASCO
Pamplona
ria-Gasteiz
NAVARRA
Jaca
Aneto 3,404 m △
ANDORRA LA VELLA
ANDORRA
Llívia (to Spain)
Figueres
Roses
urgos
Logroño
Huesca
Segre
Ripoll
LA RIOJA
Girona
Sistema
Central
Ebro
Monzón
CATALONIA
Manresa
Mataró
Costa Brava
anda
Duero
Soria
Duero
Zaragoza
Lleida
Terrassa
Sabadell
Badalona
Barcelona
Calatayud
ARAGÓN
L'Hospitalet de Llobregat
Daroca
Embalse de Mequinenza
Reus
Tarragona
Alcañiz
Guadalajara
Alcobendas
Alcalá de Henares
MADRID
etafe
Teruel
Tortosa
Amposta
Vinaròs
NUEVA
I
N
Aranjuez
Cuenca
Castelló de la Plana
Costa del Azahar
Ciutadella de Menorca
Mahón
Menorca (Minorca)
Alcúdia
Palma de Mallorca
Andratx
Manacor
Mallorca (Majorca)
Santanyí
Balearic Islands
Alcázar de San Juan
Villarrobledo
La Roda
LA MANCHA
Manzanares
Valdepeñas
Utiel
Júcar
Paterna
Torrente
Alzira
Sagunto
Valencia
Gulf of Valencia
Gandía
Denia
Cabo de la Nao
Albacete
Alcoy
Benidorm
San Antonio Abad
Ibiza
Ibiza
Formentera
Hellín
Elda
Elche (Elx)
Alicante
Costa Blanca
Linares
Orihuela
Murcia
Torrevieja
Mediterranean Sea
én
Huéscar
éticos
Lorca
Cabo de Palos
Cartagena
Baza
Aguilas
Granada
Huércal-Overa
Nevada
Mulhacén 3,478 m
Almería
Motril
Adra
Cabo de Gata
el Sol

ALGERIA

Melilla (to Spain)

GERMANY

Germany lies in the very heart of Europe. There are flat plains in the northern part of the country, and in the south are forests and the Alps. Two of Europe's greatest rivers flow through Germany. The Rhine runs from the south, where it forms a natural border with France, to the north. It is an important transport link between many industrial centres. To the south, the Danube rises in the Black Forest and flows east on its course to the Black Sea.

Germany's northern plains make good farmland – cattle and pigs are raised here, and cereal crops are grown. Livestock farms are located in the south, but the uplands here are often more suited to growing vegetables. Grapes for Germany's successful wine industry also grow well in the mountainous regions, and vineyards cover the slopes surrounding the Rhine and its tributaries. The chemicals industry, car manufacturing and engineering employ many people in and around major cities, especially in Berlin, and in the Ruhr, Rhine and Main valleys. Germany also has strong high-tech industries, producing goods such as computers and telecommunications equipment.

In 1945, Germany was defeated in World War II and the country was divided. East Germany became part of communist Europe. Many people worked in old-fashioned heavy industries, and salaries and working conditions were poor for most people. West Germany made a rapid recovery following the war, and became one of Europe's richest and most powerful countries. In 1990, the two states joined again, and since then, the German government has been trying to unite the country economically and politically. Germany is also an important member of the European Union.

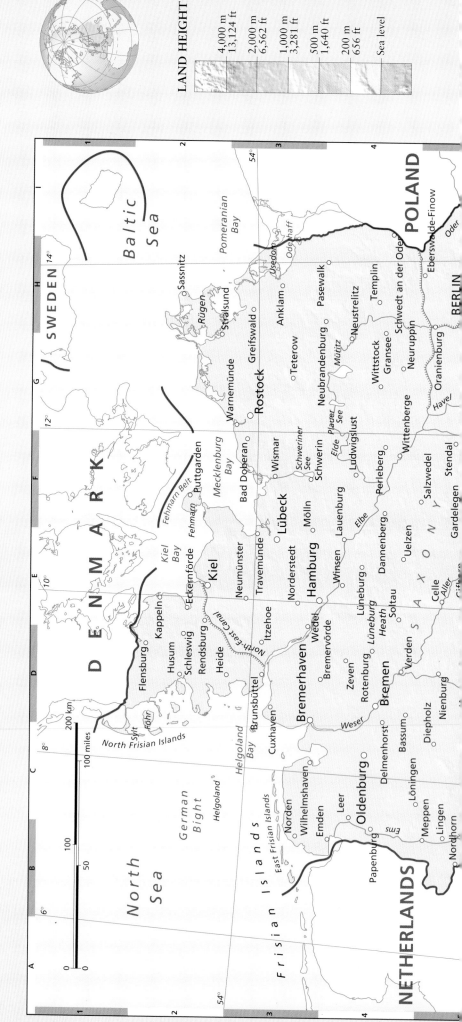

LAND HEIGHT

| 4,000 m 13,124 ft | 2,000 m 6,562 ft | 1,000 m 3,281 ft | 500 m 1,640 ft | 200 m 656 ft | Sea level |

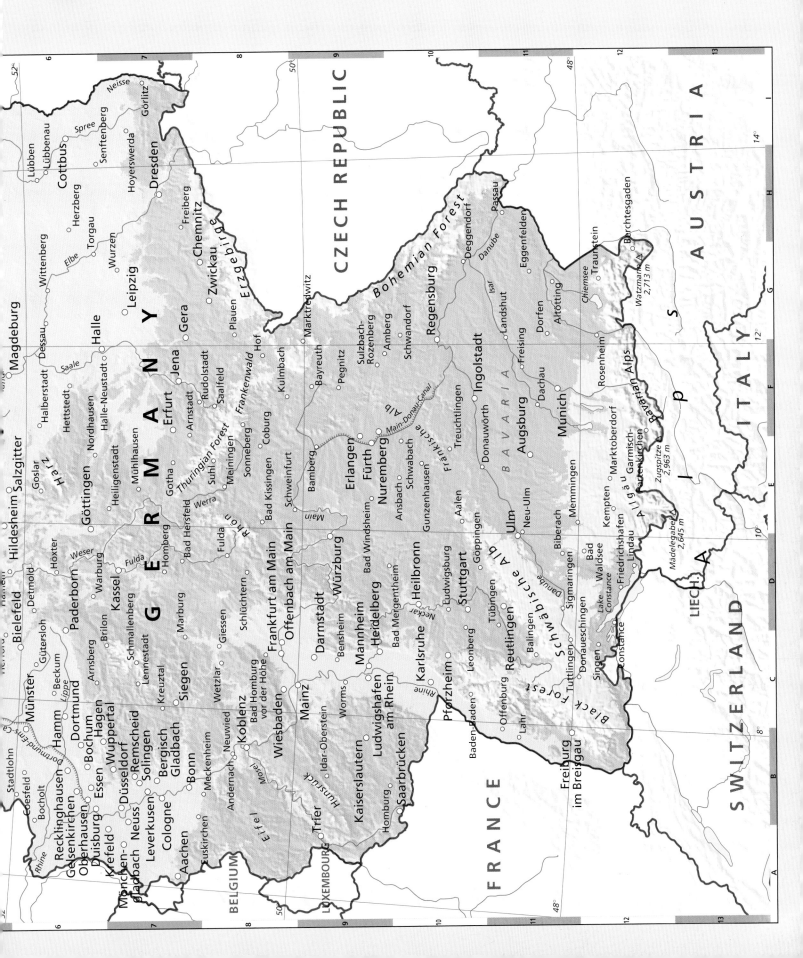

Germany

GERMANY

CZECH REPUBLIC

AUSTRIA

ITALY

SWITZERLAND

FRANCE

BELGIUM

LUXEMBOURG

LIECH.

Magdeburg
Lübben
Lübbenau
Cottbus
Senftenberg
Spree
Neisse
Görlitz
Hoyerswerda
Dresden
Freiberg
Herzberg
Torgau
Wittenberg
Dessau
Halberstadt
Hettstedt
Nordhausen
Halle-Neustadt
Heiligenstadt
Mühlhausen
Göttingen
Halle
Leipzig
Wurzen
Chemnitz
Zwickau
Gera
Jena
Plauen
Hof
Erzgebirge
Erfurt
Gotha
Arnstadt
Rudolstadt
Saalfeld
Suhl
Meiningen
Sonneberg
Coburg
Bad Kissingen
Schweinfurt
Kulmbach
Bayreuth
Pegnitz
Marktredwitz
Bohemian Forest
Deggendorf
Passau
Danube
Regensburg
Amberg
Sulzbach-Rozenberg
Schwandorf
Isar
Landshut
Eggenfelden
Dorfen
Altötting
Chiemsee
Traunstein
Berchtesgaden
Watzmann △ 2,713 m
Erlangen
Fürth
Nuremberg
Ansbach
Schwabach
Gunzenhausen
Treuchtlingen
Ingolstadt
Donauwörth
Freising
Dachau
Munich
Rosenheim
Augsburg
BAVARIA
Fränkische
Main-Donau-Canal
Alb
Bamberg
Würzburg
Bad Windsheim
Bad Mergentheim
Aalen
Göppingen
Ulm
Neu-Ulm
Memmingen
Kempten
Marktoberdorf
Garmisch-Partenkirchen
Zugspitze 2,963 m
Allgäu
Bavarian Alps
Lindau
Friedrichshafen
Bad Waldsee
Biberach
Frankfurt am Main
Offenbach am Main
Darmstadt
Bensheim
Mannheim
Heidelberg
Heilbronn
Neckar
Ludwigsburg
Stuttgart
Leonberg
Reutlingen
Tübingen
Sigmaringen
Balingen
Lake Constance
Constance
Singen
Tuttlingen
Donaueschingen
Schwäbische Alb
Danube
Mädelegabel 2,645 m
Worms
Mainz
Wiesbaden
Bad Homburg vor der Höhe
Giessen
Marburg
Wetzlar
Fulda
Bad Hersfeld
Homberg
Schlüchtern
Rhön
Thuringian Forest
Werra
Fulda
Weser
Kassel
Warburg
Höxter
Paderborn
Brilon
Schmallenberg
Lennestadt
Arnsberg
Beckum
Hamm
Münster
Stadtlohn
Coesfeld
Bocholt
Recklinghausen
Gelsenkirchen
Oberhausen
Duisburg
Krefeld
Mönchen-gladbach
Neuss
Düsseldorf
Leverkusen
Solingen
Remscheid
Wuppertal
Hagen
Bochum
Dortmund
Dortmund-Ems-Canal
Rhine
Lippe
Bielefeld
Gütersloh
Detmold
Hildesheim
Salzgitter
Goslar
Harz
Salzwedel
Wurzburg
Schweinfurt
Karlsruhe
Pforzheim
Baden-Baden
Offenburg
Lahr
Freiburg im Breisgau
Black Forest
Rhine
Ludwigshafen am Rhein
Kaiserslautern
Homburg
Saarbrücken
Idar-Oberstein
Hunsrück
Trier
Mosel
Andernach
Neuwied
Koblenz
Meckenheim
Bonn
Cologne
Bergisch Gladbach
Siegen
Kreuztal
Eifel
Euskirchen
Aachen

THE ALPINE STATES

The Alps, Europe's tallest range of mountains, stretch across the Alpine states – Austria, Liechtenstein, Switzerland and Slovenia. This region in central Europe has a landscape of jagged snow-topped peaks, deep valleys and lakes that were scooped out by glaciers over 20,000 years ago. The mountainous terrain of the Alpine states limits the amount of land that can be cultivated by farmers, although the rich pastures of the lower slopes are used to graze both beef and dairy cattle.

Switzerland and Liechtenstein have few raw materials, so these countries concentrate on producing high-quality goods, including pharmaceuticals and watches. They also act as international centres for banking. Austria is heavily industrialized, and all four countries have strong tourist industries. People from many parts of the world come to the Alpine states to ski and to admire the mountain scenery. The vast numbers of visitors, and the buildings needed to house them, put a strain on the environment. This region lies on the main trading routes across the Alps, so air pollution caused by passing lorries is another environmental problem.

Switzerland takes a neutral position in wars and other conflicts. This policy makes the country an ideal base for a number of important international organizations, including the Red Cross and various agencies of the United Nations.

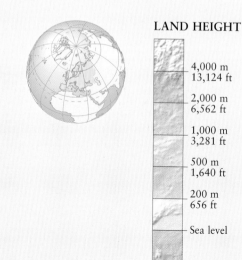

LAND HEIGHT

- 4,000 m / 13,124 ft
- 2,000 m / 6,562 ft
- 1,000 m / 3,281 ft
- 500 m / 1,640 ft
- 200 m / 656 ft
- Sea level

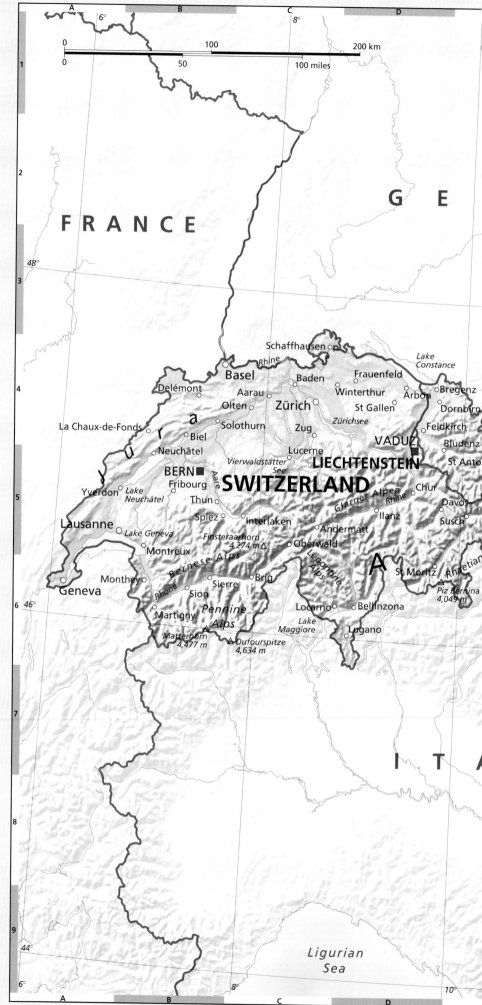

Austria

Switzerland

Liechtenstein

Slovenia

CZECH
REPUBLIC

M A N Y

SLOVAKIA

Gmünd

Mistelbach

Hollabrunn

Krems an
der Donau

Danube

Tulln

VIENNA

Linz

St Pölten

Mödling

Salzach

Wels

Amstetten

48°

Vocklabruck

Steyr

Baden

*Neusiedler
See*

Attersee

Gmunden

Waidhofen
an der Ybbs

Wiener
Neustadt

Eisenstadt

Traunsee

Salzburg

AUSTRIA

Hallein

Bad Ischl

Enns

Neunkirchen

Liezen

Rottenmann

Mürzzuschlag

Kufstein

Wörgl

Bischofshofen

Bruck an der Mur

*Zugspitze
2,963 m*

Bavarian Alps

Kitzbühel

Radstadt

Knittelfeld

Telfs

Schwaz

Niedere Tauern

Judenburg

Graz

I R O L

Mittersill

Mur

Köflach

Raab

andeck

Innsbruck

Hohe Tauern

St Michael
im Langau

Wildon

*Wildspitze
3,774 m*

S

*Grossglockner
3,797 m*

Wolfsberg

HUNGARY

*Ötztaler
Alpen*

p

Lienz

St Veit an
der Glan

Leibnitz

Mur

Spittal-an
der Drau

Drau

Völkermarkt

Murska Sobota

Karnische Alpen

Villach

Klagenfurt

Maribor

Ptuj

Drava

Karawanken

*Triglav
2,864 m*

Jesenice

Celje

*Julian
Alps*

Kranj

Sava

Trbovlje

Tolmin

LJUBLJANA

Krsko

SLOVENIA

Nova
Gorica

Postojna

Novo Mesto

Ribnica

Kocevje

Koper

Kozina

CROATIA

BOSNIA &
HERZEGOVINA

*Adriatic
Sea*

L Y

ITALY AND MALTA

This region stretches from the Alps in the north to the Mediterranean islands of Malta in the south. Much of the Italian peninsula is mountainous, with the Apennines extending along almost the whole length of Italy, and the Dolomites in the northeast. In the south are volcanoes, such as Etna and Vesuvius. This area also experiences earthquakes.

The northern and southern halves of the region are different from each other in several ways. The north, which has a milder climate than the south, is more developed. Big cities, including

Turin, Milan and Genoa, are centres of industry. Here, manufacturing companies make cars, engines and other products. There are also high-tech businesses, and design studios specializing in everything from clothing to furniture. The north is a popular tourist destination, luring many people with its stunning scenery, fine food and historical cities including Venice, Florence and Rome. Lake Garda and Lake Como also attract many visitors. In the north are two tiny countries. The Vatican City, a small area of Rome, is the headquarters of the Catholic

Church. The ancient independent state of San Marino is located near the Adriatic coast.

In the south, the climate is hotter, the towns are generally smaller, and industry is less well developed. The dry soils often have to be irrigated, but some crops, such as olives, citrus fruits, grapes and tomatoes, grow well in the baking sun. Still further south are Sicily and Malta, which have an even hotter climate. Sicily is part of Italy, while the islands of Malta form a separate nation. Tourism and shipping are Malta's major sources of income.

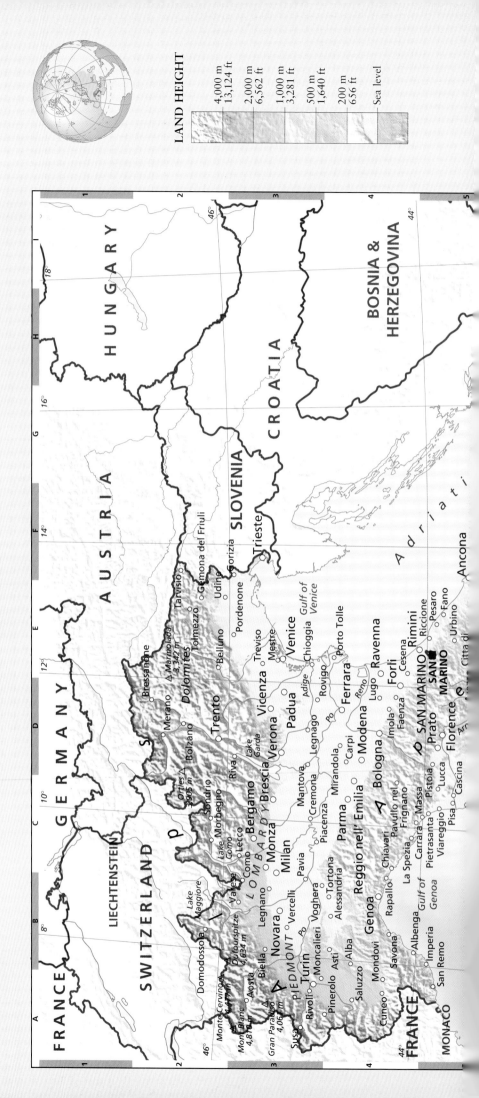

LAND HEIGHT

4,000 m / 13,124 ft
2,000 m / 6,562 ft
1,000 m / 3,281 ft
500 m / 1,640 ft
200 m / 656 ft
Sea level

Italy San Marino Vatican City Malta

EASTERN EUROPE

The countries of eastern Europe have a varied landscape which extends from the cliffs and sandy beaches of the Baltic coast, through the vast Pripet Marshes in southern Belarus, to the great open steppes that cover almost three-quarters of the Ukraine.

Most of the countries in this region have spent long periods of their history under Russian rule. For much of the 20th century, they all formed part of the Soviet Union. The Soviets encouraged the growth of heavy industry and manufacturing, turning these states into industrial nations. When the Soviet Union broke up in 1991, the countries of this area became independent and their old-fashioned factories had to compete with the modern, high-tech businesses of the rest of Europe. For a number of years there were price rises and food shortages. Recently, however, this region has developed new high-tech industries, and the countries have also formed trade links with western Europe.

Farming is the main source of employment for much of the population. The rich black soils of the Ukraine are ideal for growing cereal crops and sugar beet. The smaller countries of the Baltic coast have many cattle and pig farms. The Baltic states have few natural resources, and they have to import goods and services from their larger, richer neighbours.

In 1986, the world's worst nuclear accident took place at the power station at Chernobyl, in the Ukraine near the border with Belarus. Thirty-one people were killed immediately, and radioactive particles spread over a huge area, contaminating farmland and making thousands of people ill.

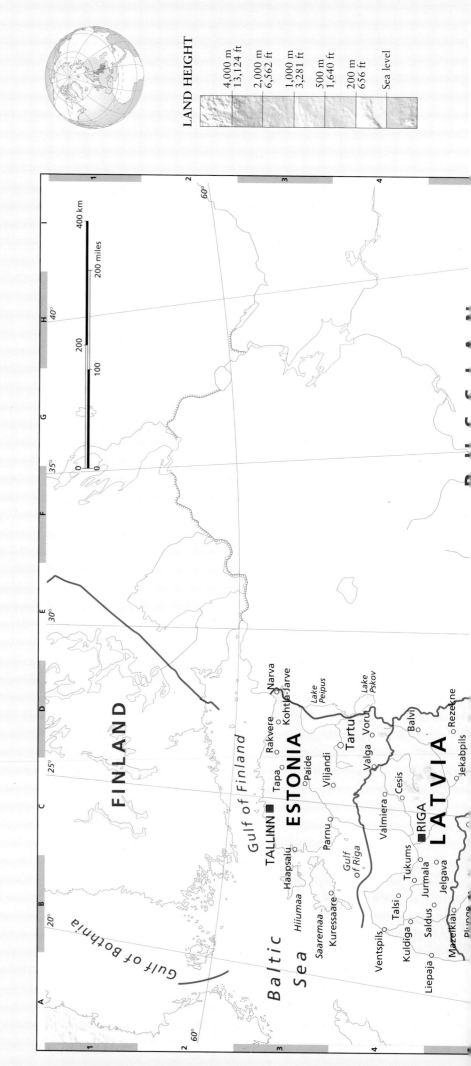

LAND HEIGHT

| 4,000 m / 13,124 ft | 2,000 m / 6,562 ft | 1,000 m / 3,281 ft | 500 m / 1,640 ft | 200 m / 656 ft | Sea level |

Estonia
Latvia
Lithuania
Belarus
Ukraine
Moldova

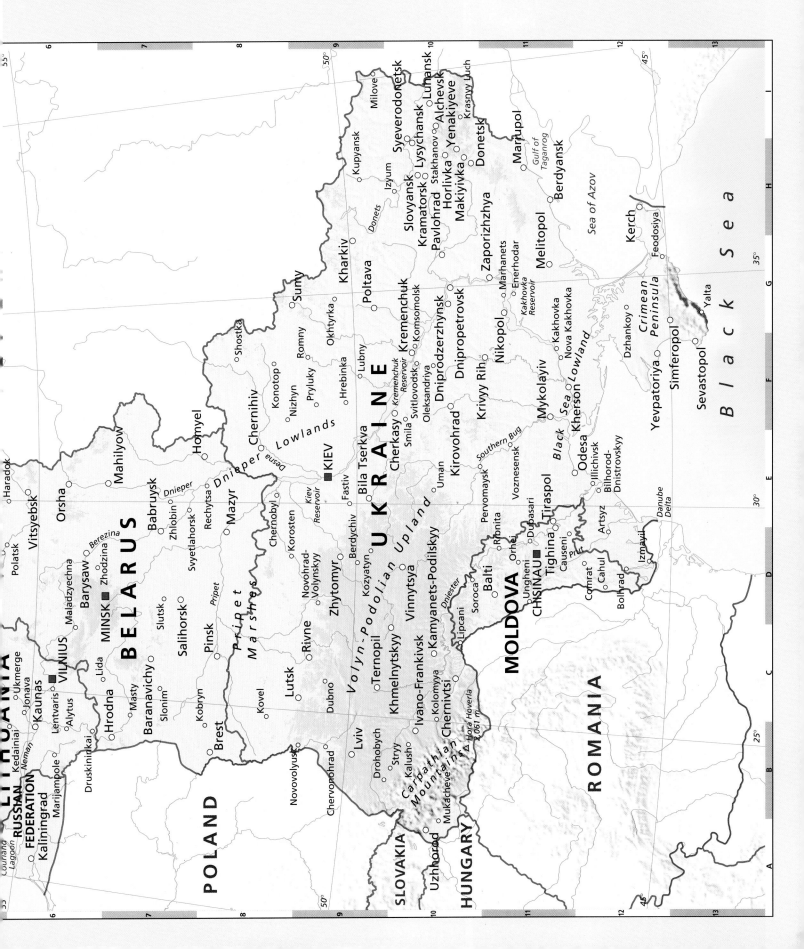

CENTRAL EUROPE

Central Europe is made up of two plains, which are divided by a chain of mountains. To the north, in Poland, is the North European Plain. The Great Hungarian Plain, with its farmlands and grasslands, lies in the south. Much of the land area of the Czech Republic and Slovakia falls in the mountainous region in the centre. For most of the 20th century, these countries were united as Czechoslovakia, but in 1993, they split into two separate nations.

Central Europe's farmers grow cereal crops such as barley, oats, wheat and rye, as well as large quantities of potatoes and sugar beet. They also raise livestock, especially pigs. In Hungary, where the climate is warmer, farmers grow grapes for wine and sweet peppers for paprika, a hot spice that is used in Hungarian cooking. Much of Slovakia is covered with forest and the country has a large timber industry.

Poland has enormous reserves of a brown coal, called lignite, which is exported. A variety of minerals are mined in the mountains of the Czech Republic and Slovakia. Hungary has a wide range of industries, producing vehicles, metals, chemicals, textiles and electrical goods, while the Czech Republic is famous for its breweries and fine glassware.

For much of the 20th century, the countries of central Europe were ruled by communist governments, which were dominated by the powerful, Russian-led Soviet Union. The old-fashioned heavy industries that were developed under communist rule have caused terrible pollution in some places. However, the countries of central Europe are now moving towards more modern, high-tech industries.

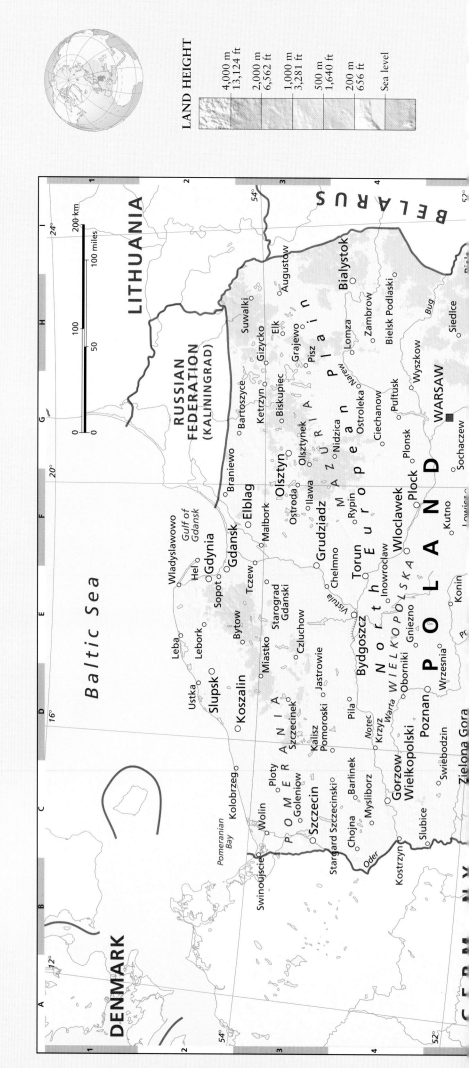

LAND HEIGHT

4,000 m 13,124 ft
2,000 m 6,562 ft
1,000 m 3,281 ft
500 m 1,640 ft
200 m 656 ft
Sea level

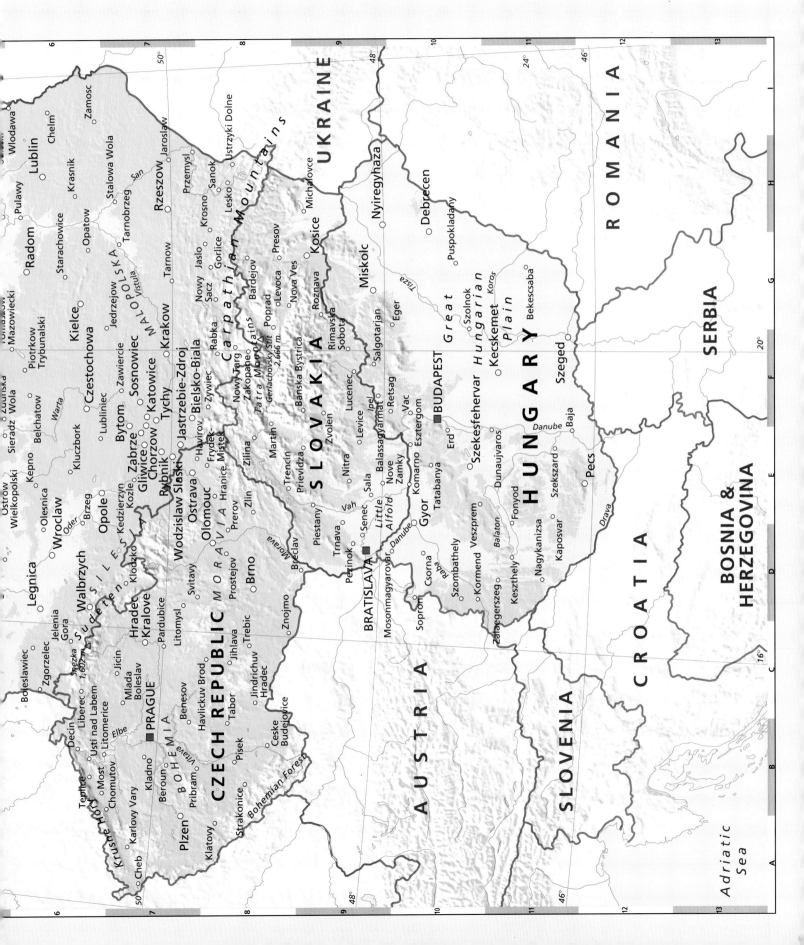

SOUTHEASTERN EUROPE

Southeastern Europe extends east from the Adriatic Sea to the Black Sea, south to the Mediterranean Sea and north to the Carpathian Mountains. The ancient country of Greece, in the south, has been independent since 1829. The rest of this region, including Albania, Bulgaria and Romania, came under communist rule until the 1990s. One communist country, Yugoslavia, broke apart after a civil war in the 1990s. Following Kosovo's declaration of independence from Serbia in 2008, the former Yugoslavia is now made up of seven separate nations.

Southeastern Europe is mainly mountainous, but the northern part of the region has good soils where cereals, vegetables and fruits are grown. The upland areas are used for grazing sheep and goats. Further south, and in the coastal areas, grapes and olives are the main crops. Southeastern Europe has some textile, engineering and manufacturing businesses, and these are concentrated around major cities, such as Zagreb and Bucharest. Fumes from motor vehicles and factories combine to pollute the atmosphere in the urban areas. The Greek government controls the number of vehicles that come into Athens, but despite this, the air quality here is still bad. Mainland Greece and the islands in the Aegean Sea are centres of a thriving tourist trade, while tourism on the Black Sea coast is growing steadily.

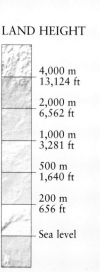

LAND HEIGHT

4,000 m
13,124 ft

2,000 m
6,562 ft

1,000 m
3,281 ft

500 m
1,640 ft

200 m
656 ft

Sea level

Romania

Croatia

Serbia

Bosnia & Herzegovina

Bulgaria

Kosovo

Montenegro

Albania

Macedonia

Greece

AFRICA

Africa, the world's second-largest continent, is separated from Asia by the Red Sea and from Europe by the Mediterranean Sea. A major feature of this huge landmass is the Sahara, the planet's biggest desert. It divides Africa's northern coast from the rest of the continent. South of the Sahara, the landscape consists mainly of broad plateaux, broken by the basins of major rivers, such as the Congo and the Zambezi. The Great Rift Valley cuts through the uplands of east Africa. Some of the rivers have dramatic waterfalls, such as the Victoria Falls, where the Zambezi plunges into a chasm more than 120 m deep. Africa also has high mountains, such as the Atlas range in the northwest and the Drakensberg in the south.

Most experts believe that the human race first evolved in Africa, but the continent's long history has been a troubled one. In the 19th century, European powers such as Britain, France and Belgium took over much of the continent. Most areas won independence from their foreign rulers in the 1960s, to create 53 separate African nations. These contain many different peoples, and have a rich variety of languages. A number of countries, however, have struggled to develop as modern states.

Some African countries rely on income from a single 'cash crop', such as oranges, olives or sugar cane. This means that their economies suffer badly if prices for the crop decrease or the harvests fail. The continent's rapidly rising population is often hit hard by famine, and some countries have suffered war. Africa also has lots of advantages, from its plentiful natural resources to some of the planet's most spectacular scenery and fascinating wildlife.

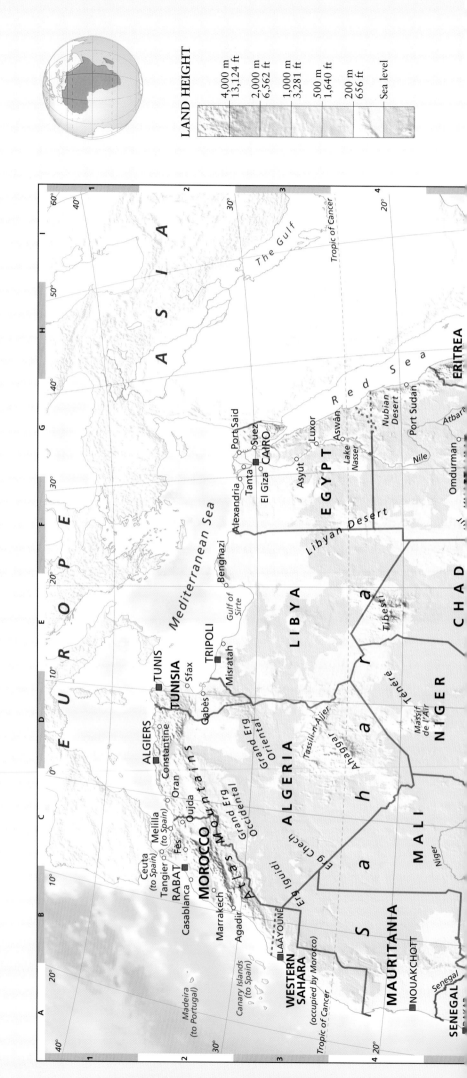

LAND HEIGHT

4,000 m 13,124 ft	2,000 m 6,562 ft	1,000 m 3,281 ft
500 m 1,640 ft	200 m 656 ft	Sea level

NORTHWEST AFRICA

Morocco, Algeria, Tunisia and Libya occupy the coast of northwestern Africa and part of the northern Sahara Desert. The region's uplands, including the Atlas Mountains, stretch from the north of Tunisia to the Atlantic coast of Morocco. Most of the people live in towns and villages on a fertile strip of land along the north coast, although Western Sahara and the southern parts of Algeria and Libya are thinly populated by Tuareg nomads.

On the coast, farmers grow grapes and olives, or raise sheep and goats. The bark of the cork tree is harvested in Morocco and Algeria, and dates are grown at oases in the desert. This region has a thriving textile industry, producing colourful rugs and fabrics, and in the past few decades, oil and natural gas have brought wealth to Libya. Tourism is also a strong industry in the area, with ancient cities and hot weather attracting many overseas visitors.

The main environmental problem in northwest Africa is the northward spread of the Sahara Desert due to droughts and the cutting down of trees and plants for fuel and animal food. As a result, farmers are losing land, and they are forced to overgraze the existing pastures. This puts more stress on the land, and leads to the further expansion of the desert.

LAND HEIGHT

	4,000 m 13,124 ft
	2,000 m 6,562 ft
	1,000 m 3,281 ft
	500 m 1,640 ft
	200 m 656 ft
	Sea level

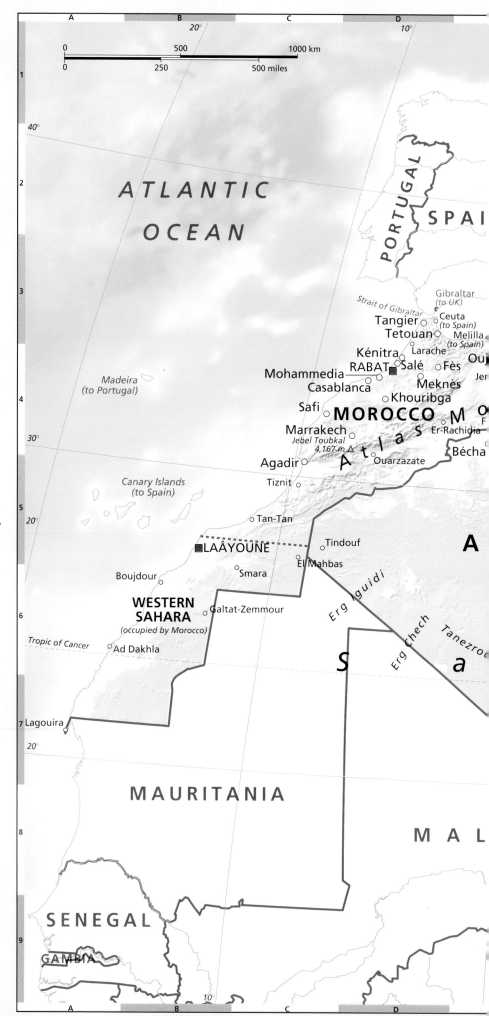

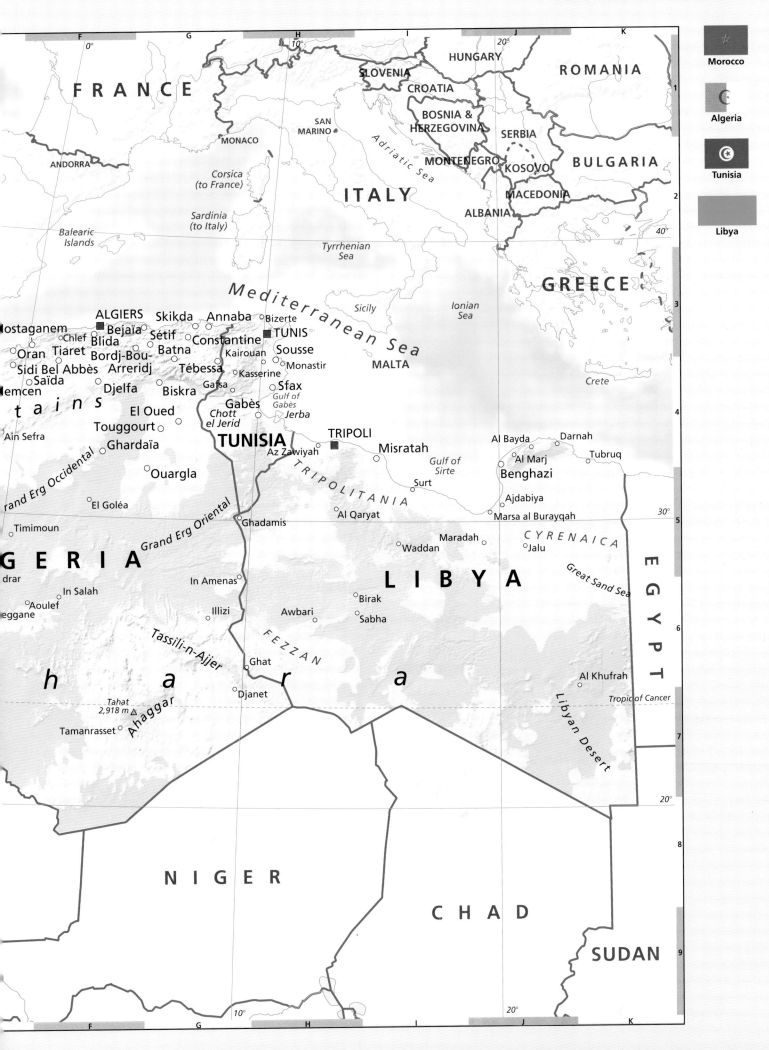

Morocco

Algeria

Tunisia

Libya

FRANCE

ANDORRA

MONACO

SAN MARINO

Corsica
(to France)

Sardinia
(to Italy)

Balearic
Islands

HUNGARY

SLOVENIA

CROATIA

BOSNIA &
HERZEGOVINA

SERBIA

MONTENEGRO

KOSOVO

MACEDONIA

ALBANIA

ROMANIA

BULGARIA

ITALY

Adriatic
Sea

Tyrrhenian
Sea

GREECE

Sicily

Ionian
Sea

Crete

Mediterranean Sea

MALTA

Mostaganem

ALGIERS

Bejaïa

Skikda

Annaba

Bizerte

TUNIS

Chlef

Blida

Sétif

Constantine

Oran

Tiaret

Bordj-Bou-

Batna

Kairouan

Sousse

Sidi Bel Abbès

Arreridj

Tébessa

Monastir

Saïda

Kasserine

Sfax

emcen

Djelfa

Biskra

Gafsa

Gabès

Gulf of
Gabès

El Oued

Chott
el Jerid

Jerba

Touggourt

TUNISIA

Ain Sefra

Ghardaïa

Az Zawiyah

TRIPOLI

Misratah

Al Bayda

Darnah

Ouargla

Surt

Al Marj

Tubruq

Gulf of
Sirte

Benghazi

Grand Erg Occidental

El Goléa

Ajdabiya

Timimoun

Ghadamis

Al Qaryat

Marsa al Burayqah

CYRENAICA

GERIA

Grand Erg Oriental

Maradah

Jalu

Waddan

drar

In Salah

In Amenas

LIBYA

Great Sand Sea

Aoulef

EGYPT

eggane

Illizi

Awbari

Birak

Sabha

Tassili-n-Ajjer

FEZZAN

Al Khufrah

Ghat

Libyan Desert

h

a

r

a

Djanet

Tahat
2,918 m △

Ahaggar

Tropic of Cancer

Tamanrasset

NIGER

CHAD

SUDAN

NORTHEAST AFRICA

The land in the northeastern part of Africa is mainly arid. To the north, Egypt and northern Sudan are desert areas. Only the Nile valley provides a narrow strip of fertile soil, where people can live and farm. Smaller deserts lie in Somalia, Ethiopia and Djibouti. There are some forests on Ethiopia's highlands, but much of the rest of this region is covered by dry scrubland and the occasional tree.

People settled in northeast Africa over 6,000 years ago, and by about 3000 BCE, one of the greatest early civilizations was established in

Egypt. For much of its history, this region was an important international centre of trade, with great cities and monuments. In 1867, the Suez Canal was opened to provide a shipping link between the Red and Mediterranean Seas.

Today, there are few big cities in northeast Africa, and most people live in the countryside and work the land. Farmers have to grow what crops they can in this hot, dry environment, where rainfall is rare and many rivers dry up for much of the year. Cotton and sugar cane are grown along the Nile river, dates grow well in

oases in the desert, and coffee is Ethiopia's main crop. Sheep, goats and cattle are raised on the grasslands, while the region's factories process food. There is also a local textile industry.

In the past few decades, life has been very hard for the people of this region. Rapid population growth has forced farmers to clear land to grow food and to cut down trees for fuel. The removal of trees and plants has allowed the wind to erode the soil, turning large areas into desert. A series of famines and wars have brought death and suffering to millions of people in this area.

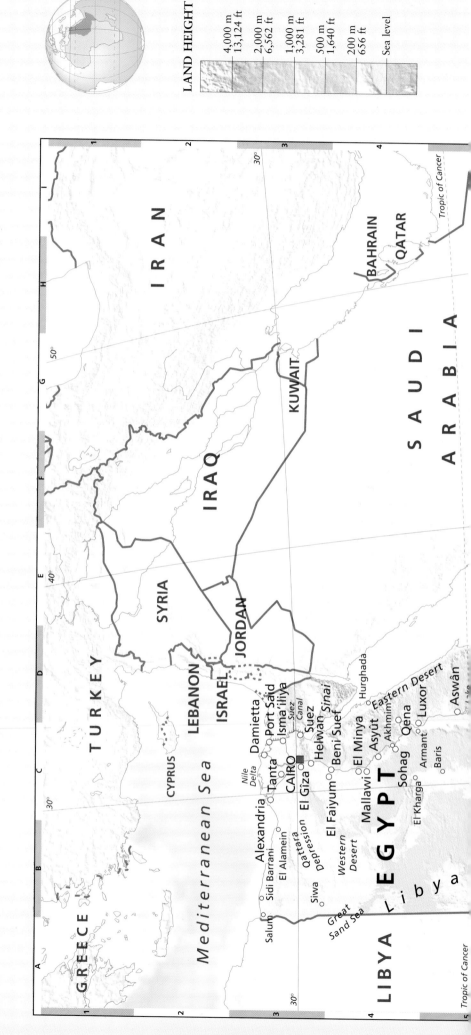

LAND HEIGHT

| 4,000 m / 13,124 ft | 2,000 m / 6,562 ft | 1,000 m / 3,281 ft | 500 m / 1,640 ft | 200 m / 656 ft | Sea level |

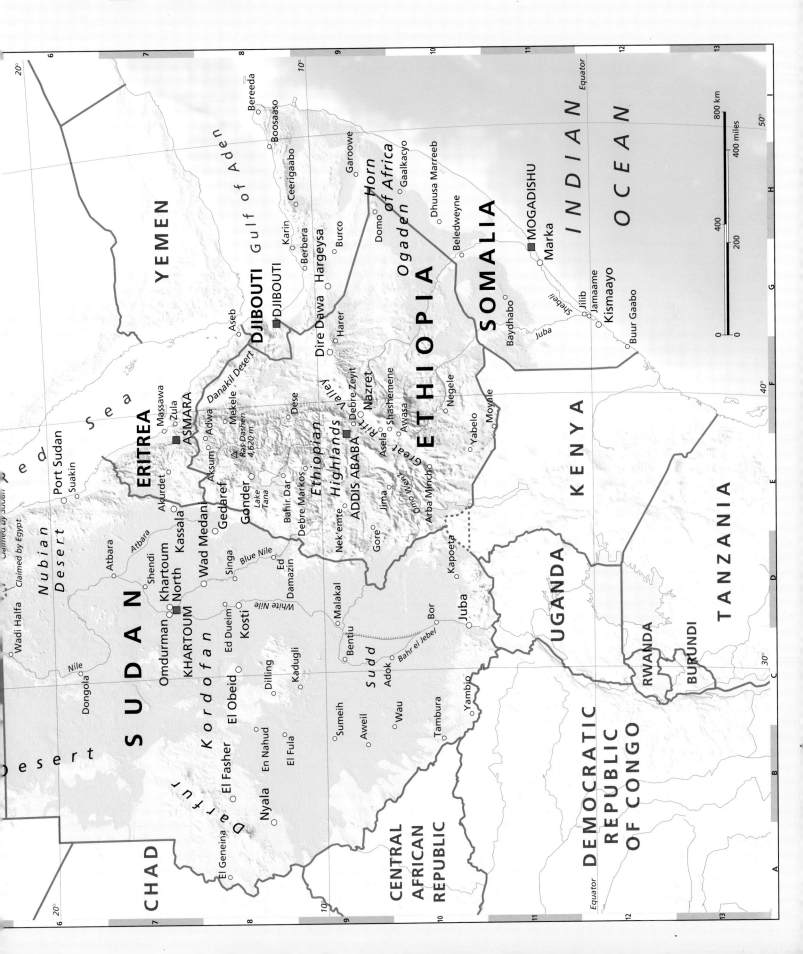

Egypt

Sudan

Eritrea

Ethiopia

Djibouti

Somalia

CHAD

SUDAN

Nubian Desert

Darfur

Kordofan

CENTRAL AFRICAN REPUBLIC

Wadi Halfa

Dongola

Atbara

Shendi

Omdurman

Khartoum North

KHARTOUM

Ed Dueim

Kosti

El Fasher

El Geneina

Nyala

En Nahud

El Fula

Dilling

Kadugli

El Obeid

Singa

Wad Medani

Ed Damazin

Gedaref

Kassala

Akurdet

Port Sudan

Suakin

Red Sea

YEMEN

Gulf of Aden

ERITREA

ASMARA

Massawa

Zula

Aseb

Danakil Desert

Mekele

Adwa

Aksum

Ras Dashen 4,620 m

DJIBOUTI

DJIBOUTI

Dire Dawa

Harer

Karin

Berbera

Hargeysa

Burco

Bereeda

Boosaaso

Ceerigaabo

Garoowe

Horn of Africa

Ogaden

Domo

Dhuusa Marreeb

Beledweyne

SOMALIA

MOGADISHU

Marka

Baydhabo

INDIAN OCEAN

Equator

800 km

400 miles

400

200

50°

ETHIOPIA

Ethiopian Highlands

Great Rift Valley

Dese

Bahir Dar

Debre Markos

Lake Tana

Gonder

Debre Zeyit

Nazret

Asela

Shashemene

Awasa

Jima

Gore

Nek'emte

ADDIS ABABA

Omo Wenz

Arba Minch

Yabelo

Negele

Moyale

KENYA

Shebeli

Juba

Jilib

Jamaame

Kismaayo

Buur Gaabo

UGANDA

Blue Nile

White Nile

Nile

Malakal

Bentiu

Adok

Sudd

Bahr el Jebel

Bor

Juba

Kapoeta

Sumeih

Aweil

Wau

Tambura

Yambio

DEMOCRATIC REPUBLIC OF CONGO

RWANDA

BURUNDI

TANZANIA

Equator

Claimed by Egypt

Claimed by Sudan

Desert

20°

6

7

8

9

10°

10

11

12

13

20°

30°

40°

10°

A

B

C

D

E

F

G

H

I

WEST AFRICA

In the northern part of this region, the edge of the Sahara meets a wide band of semi-desert scrubland called the Sahel, which stretches from Mauritania to Niger. South of the Sahel is a strip of grassland and further south, along the coast, is a region of land where higher rainfall feeds areas of tropical rainforest. Many rivers cross the southern half of this area. The longest of these is the Niger, which forms a vast, swampy delta at the coast.

Cash crops such as cotton, cocoa and peanuts are grown throughout the southern part of this region. Further north, farmers raise sheep and goats, and grow food crops such as yams and cassava. The biggest industries are connected with food – the processing of nuts to extract oil, for example. Many people in Nigeria also work in the chemical industry, or on wells that tap the region's rich supplies of gas and oil.

West Africa is an area with large deposits of minerals, ranging from iron ore to diamonds. In the past, it has been home to successful civilizations, such as the empires of Mali and Asante, which benefited from these resources. In spite of new wealth from oil and tourism, most west Africans remain poor. Their lives are made difficult by frequent droughts and the growth of the desert in the north of the region.

LAND HEIGHT

	4,000 m 13,124 ft
	2,000 m 6,562 ft
	1,000 m 3,281 ft
	500 m 1,640 ft
	200 m 656 ft
	Sea level

MOROCCO

TUNISIA

ALGERIA

LIBYA

Erg Iguidi

Erg Chech

S a h a r a

MALI

Azaouâd

Tessalit

Araouane

Adrar des Ifôghas

Kidal

Séguédine

Assamakka

Arlit

Massif de l'Aïr

Agadez

Talak

Ténéré

Tropic of Cancer

CHAD

Mreyyé

ualâta

ema

Bassikounou

Timbuktu

Gao

Ménaka

Ansongo

NIGER

Ngourti

Nguigmi

Niger Delta

Mopti

Tambao

Tahoua

Diffa

Ségou

Bani

Tillabéri

NIAMEY

Dogondoutchi

Maradi

Zinder

Lake Chad

asso

Koudougou

Ouahigouya

Kaya

Sokoto

Katsina

Kano

Maiduguri

Banfora

Bobo-Dioulasso

Bolgatanga

Dapaong

Natitingou

Kandi

Niger

Gusau

Kaduna

Zaria

Bauchi

Kumo

Korhogo

Ferkessédougou

Tamale

Sokodé

Parakou

Minna

Bida

Jos

Jalingo

IVORY COAST

GHANA

Atakpamé

Ogbomosho

Ilorin

ABUJA

NIGERIA

uaké

YAMOUSSOUKRO

Lake Volta

Oyo

Oshogbo

Akure

Lokoja

Makurdi

Adamawa Highlands

CENTRAL AFRICAN REPUBLIC

aloa

Abengourou

Abeokuta

Ibadan

Enugu

Gagnoa

Kumasi

PORTO-NOVO

Lagos

Onitsha

Abidjan

Asamankese

Tema

LOMÉ

Cotonou

Benin City

Owerri

Aba

Calabar

n-Pédro

Sekondi-Takoradi

ACCRA

Cape Coast

Port Harcourt

Warri

Uyo

CAMEROON

Bight of Benin

Mouths of the Niger

EQUATORIAL GUINEA

CONGO

Gulf of Guinea

SÃO TOMÉ & PRÍNCIPE

GABON

Equator

Niger

Dosso

Black Volta

White Volta

Oti

Niger

Benue

Niger

BURKINA FASO

OUAGADOUGOU

TOGO

BENIN

Shaki

Sahel

Mauritania

Mali

Niger

Cape Verde

Senegal

Gambia

Burkina Faso

Nigeria

Guinea-Bissau

Guinea

Ivory Coast

Ghana

Togo

Benin

Sierra Leone

Liberia

CENTRAL AND EAST AFRICA

This region extends from Africa's Atlantic coast to the Indian Ocean. In the west is the Congo, the continent's second-longest river. Its basin is covered by the Earth's largest tropical rainforest. So far, this area has survived well, but some parts of it are being cut away. In the east is the Great Rift Valley, which runs from the north to the south, and cuts through the uplands and grasslands of Uganda and Tanzania. The Nile river rises in the uplands, and flows north on its way to the Mediterranean Sea.

To the west, among the dense forests of the Democratic Republic of Congo, rubber and oil palm trees are grown in large plantations. The Congo river and its many tributaries provide a source of fish for the local people. Elsewhere, cattle and goats are herded. In the east, farmers grow crops for export, such as vegetables and coffee.

The Democratic Republic of Congo mines its rich supplies of copper, diamonds, silver and cobalt. Other countries, such as Kenya, have developed manufacturing industries. Tourism is growing steadily in Kenya and Tanzania, where each year, thousands of overseas visitors come to visit the countries' amazing wildlife. Although the tourist industry employs a great number of people here, most of the population still makes its living from the land.

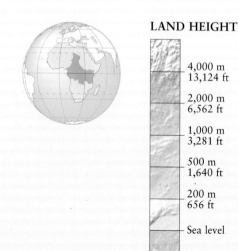

LAND HEIGHT

4,000 m 13,124 ft
2,000 m 6,562 ft
1,000 m 3,281 ft
500 m 1,640 ft
200 m 656 ft
Sea level

A

E G Y P T

SAUDI
ARABIA

S U D A N

ERITREA

YEMEN

DJIBOUTI

E T H I O P I A

Birao

Massif
s Bongo

Bria

Bangassou

Bondo

Uele

Obo

Bumba

Buta

Isiro

Watsa

Gulu

Mungbere

Lira

Lodwar

Moroto

Lake
Turkana

Moyale

Marsabit

SOMALIA

Yangambi

Kisangani

Masindi

UGANDA

KAMPALA

Tororo

Mbale

Eldoret

K E N Y A

Lake Albert

Albert Nile

Aruwimi

Entebbe

Jinja

Kakamega

Meru

EMOCRATIC

Ikoli

Lake Edward

Mbarara

Kisumu

Nakuru

Kirinyaga 5,199 m

Nyeri

Garissa

Equator

huapa

REPUBLIC

Kabale

Goma

Lake
Victoria

Thika

NAIROBI

OF CONGO

Kindu

Lake Kivu

KIGALI

Bukavu

RWANDA

Mwanza

Serengeti
Plain

Machakos

Kilimanjaro
5,895 m

Malindi

Lomani

Lualaba

BUJUMBURA

BURUNDI

Arusha

Moshi

Kongolo

Kigoma

Shinyanga

Masai
Steppe

Tanga

Pemba

I N D I A N

Kananga

Kabinda

Kasongo

Tabora

Singida

Zanzibar

Zanzibar

Mbuji-Mayi

Kabalo

Kalémié

Lake
Tanganyika

DODOMA

Morogoro

Dar es Salaam

O C E A N

Mwene-Ditu

Mpanda

Mafia

Kamina

Lake
Mweru

Sumbawanga

T A N Z A N I A

Iringa

Rufiji

Mohoro

Aldabra Group
(to Seychelles)

Mbeya

Makumbako

Lindi

Dilolo

Kolwezi

Likasi

Lake
Nyasa

Masasi

Mtwara

Songea

Ruvuma

Lubumbashi

MALAWI

COMOROS

Z A M B I A

MOZAMBIQUE

Mayotte
(to France)

Great Rift Valley

Rift Valley

SOUTHERN AFRICA

This region has a huge variety of scenery, from the parched Namib and Kalahari deserts of the west to the eastern grasslands and the Drakensberg mountains in the southeast. Off the eastern coast of southern Africa is Madagascar, a large island that split from the mainland about 1,345 million years ago. Madagascar's wildlife, from lemurs to chameleons, includes many species of plants and animals that cannot be found anywhere else in the world.

Cattle are farmed on the grasslands, while much of the land in the south is used for growing fruit for the export market. With rich deposits of precious minerals and metals, such as diamonds and gold, South Africa is the wealthiest part of this region. The country also has many other industries, including food canning, steel production, manufacturing and textiles. These types of businesses are found in other countries in southern Africa, but on a smaller scale.

In many areas, trees have been cut down for fuel, and the soils have been blown away, leaving barren, infertile deserts. The region also has political problems. For much of the 20th century, the black South Africans were denied basic human rights by the South African government. This system, known as apartheid, was abolished in 1994, when black South Africans were allowed to vote for the first time, and the country became a truly democratic state.

LAND HEIGHT

4,000 m	13,124 ft
2,000 m	6,562 ft
1,000 m	3,281 ft
500 m	1,640 ft
200 m	656 ft
	Sea level

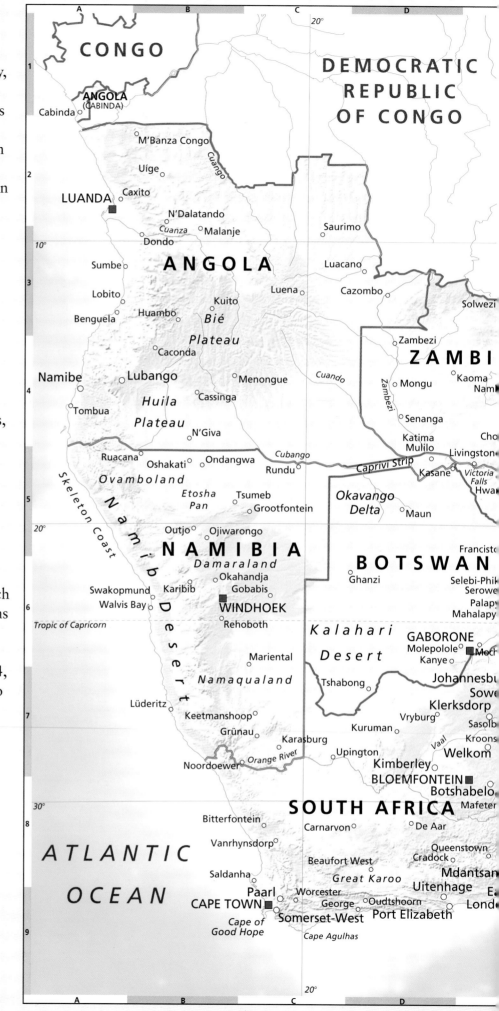

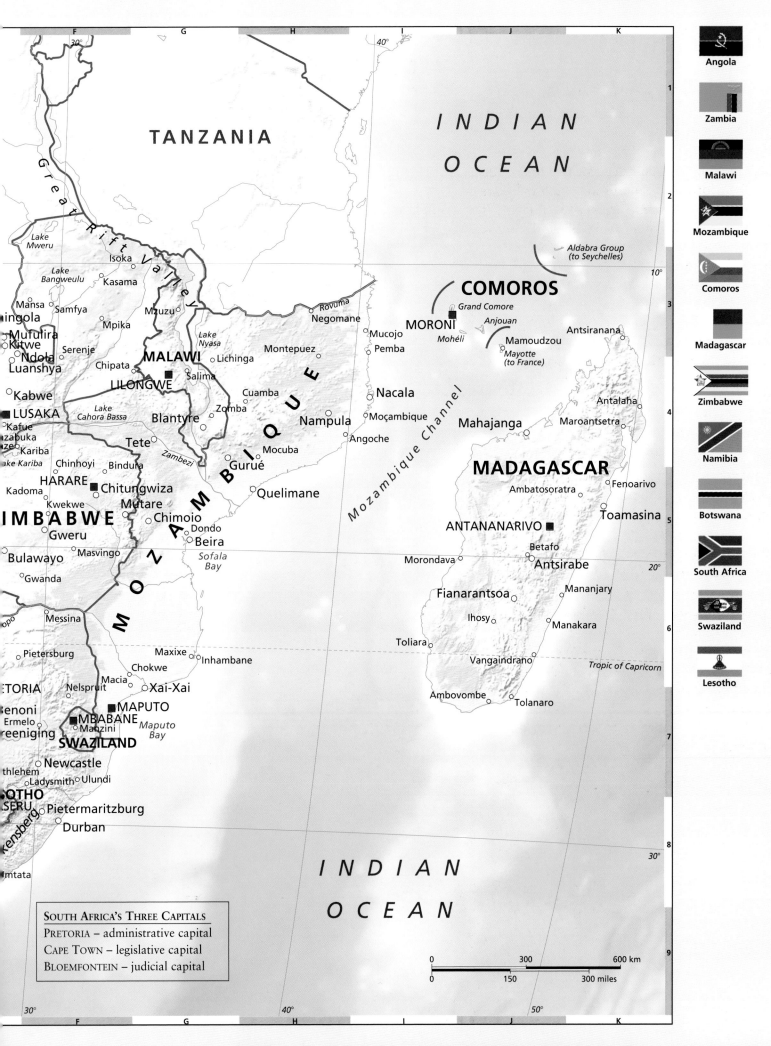

TANZANIA

INDIAN OCEAN

Great Rift Valley

Lake Mweru
Lake Bangweulu
Isoka
Kasama
Mansa   Samfya
Mpika
Mzuzu
ingola
Mufulira
Kitwe
Ndola   Serenje
Luanshya   Chipata
Kabwe
LUSAKA   Lake Cahora Bassa
Kafue   Blantyre
zabuka
ze   Kariba
ake Kariba   Chinhoyi   Bindura
HARARE   Chitungwiza
Kadoma   Kwekwe   Mutare
IMBABWE   Gweru   Chimoio
Bulawayo   Masvingo   Dondo
Gwanda   Beira

Rovuma
Negomane
Lichinga
Montepuez
Cuamba
Zomba
Mocuba
Gurué
Quelimane

MALAWI
LILONGWE
Salima
Lake Nyasa

Mucojo
Pemba
Nacala
Moçambique
Nampula
Angoche

MOZAMBIQUE

Tete
Zambezi

Sofala Bay

COMOROS

Grand Comore
MORONI   Anjouan
Mohéli   Mamoudzou
Mayotte (to France)

Aldabra Group (to Seychelles)

Antsiranana
Antalaha
Mahajanga   Maroantsetra

MADAGASCAR

Ambatosoratra   Fenoarivo
ANTANANARIVO   Toamasina
Betafo
Morondava   Antsirabe
Fianarantsoa   Mananjary
Ihosy   Manakara
Toliara
Vangaindrano
Ambovombe
Tolanaro

Mozambique Channel

Messina
po
Pietersburg
Maxixe   Inhambane
Chokwe
Macia
Nelspruit   Xai-Xai
TORIA
enoni
Ermelo   MAPUTO
reeniging   MBABANE
Manzini   Maputo Bay
SWAZILAND
Newcastle
thlehem
Ladysmith   Ulundi
OTHO
SERU   Pietermaritzburg
kensberg   Durban
mtata

Tropic of Capricorn

INDIAN OCEAN

SOUTH AFRICA'S THREE CAPITALS
PRETORIA – administrative capital
CAPE TOWN – legislative capital
BLOEMFONTEIN – judicial capital

| 0 | 300 | 600 km |
| 0 | 150 | 300 miles |

Angola
Zambia
Malawi
Mozambique
Comoros
Madagascar
Zimbabwe
Namibia
Botswana
South Africa
Swaziland
Lesotho

30°   40°   50°

THE INDIAN OCEAN

From the coast of Africa in the west to Australia and the islands of southeast Asia in the east, the Indian Ocean measures almost 10,000 km across at its widest point. Under the water are three ridges that form an upside-down 'Y' shape. The ridges mark where three continental plates meet. Here, volcanic activity is common.

The climate of the Indian Ocean varies according to latitude. The regions in the north, near India, have a warm climate. In the south, freezing temperatures have created pack ice and icebergs. Monsoon winds bring heavy rainfall to many coastal countries. They also have an effect on the ocean's currents, which reverse direction completely between March and August.

For thousands of years, the Indian Ocean has provided important trade routes between the eastern and western parts of the world. Among the first traders to sail its waters were the ancient Egyptians, who travelled along the east African coast more than 4,000 years ago. In the 15th century, European explorers made pioneering journeys across the Indian Ocean to Asia. They were soon followed by merchants who brought back silks, spices and tea from India and China. Today, huge tankers carry oil from the Persian Gulf to many of the ocean's international ports. A large number of these boats travel along the Red Sea and through the Suez Canal to reach Europe.

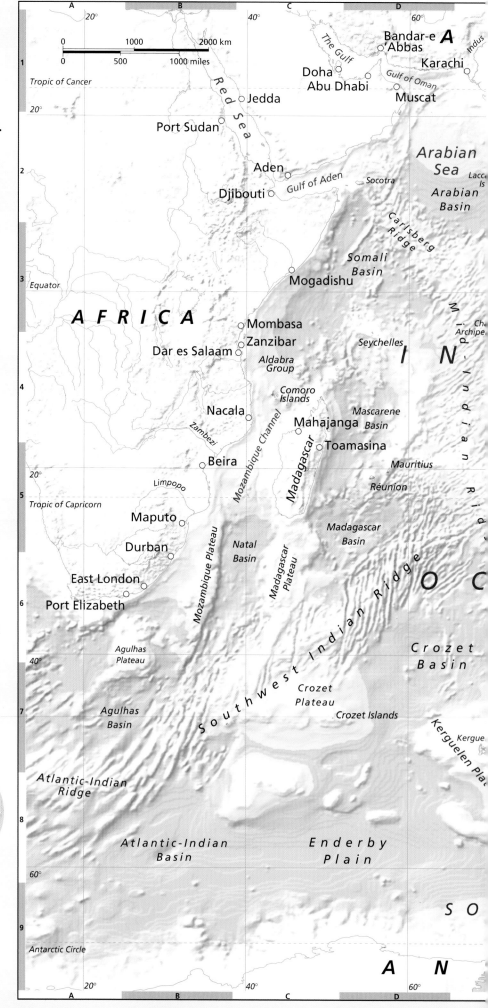

F   G   100°   H   120°   I   J   140°   K

80°

I **A**

Ganges   Brahmaputra

Chittagong   1

Tropic of Cancer

Sittwe   20°

mbai   Godavari   Irrawaddy   Salween

mbay)   Moulmein

ennai   **P A C I F I C**

dras)   Bay of   2

Cochin   Bengal   South   **O C E A N**

Trivandrum   Andaman   China

Islands   Sea

ombo   Sri   Andaman

Lanka   Sea   Strait of Malacca

dives   Nicobar

Islands

Equator   3

Ceylon   Padang   Borneo

Plain   Sumatra

I A N

Mid-Indian   Java Trench   Java

Basin   Investigator Ridge   Christmas   North

Island   Australian   Darwin   4

Cocos   Basin

Islands

Ninetyeast Ridge

20°

Wharton   5

Basin   Tropic of Capricorn

Broken Ridge   **A U S T R A L I A**

A N   Perth

Basin

Amsterdam Island   Perth   Great Australian   Adelaide   6

Bight

aul   South Australian   Melbourne

nd   Basin

40°

Southeast Indian Ridge   Tasmania   Hobart

South Australian   Tasman   7

Plain   Plateau

rd and

onald Islands

8

South Indian

Basin

60°

HERN   O C E A N   9

Antarctic Circle

A R C T I C A

80°   F   100°   G   H   120°   I   J   140°   K

ASIA

Stretching from the Black Sea in the west to Japan in the east, Asia is the world's largest continent. There are many types of landscapes, from the snowy Mount Everest, the world's highest mountain, to the Arabian Desert. Uplands stretch across much of the middle of Asia and there are great rivers, such as China's Yangtze and India's Ganges. The Earth's lowest place, the Dead Sea, is located on the border of Israel and Jordan.

Asia has a variety of peoples with many different beliefs, languages and lifestyles. The huge communist state of China is the most populous country in the world. India, with over 1 billion people, is the world's largest democratic nation. The break-up of the Soviet Union, which stretched from the eastern edge of the Russian Federation to Iran, created four countries in central Asia – Kazakhstan, Kyrgyzstan, Tajikistan and Turkmenistan. These, and the older states to the west, are mainly Muslim nations.

Few people live in the cold and windswept areas of central and northern Asia. Those who inhabit these regions are often poor, and live without many of the luxuries of modern life. Further south are some of the world's major cities, such as Mumbai, Beijing and Tokyo. The cities and countries of western Asia have grown rich from oil, while those of the Pacific coast have modern industries that have brought a high standard of living to many people.

LAND HEIGHT

	4,000 m 13,124 ft
	2,000 m 6,562 ft
	1,000 m 3,281 ft
	500 m 1,640 ft
	200 m 656 ft
	Sea level

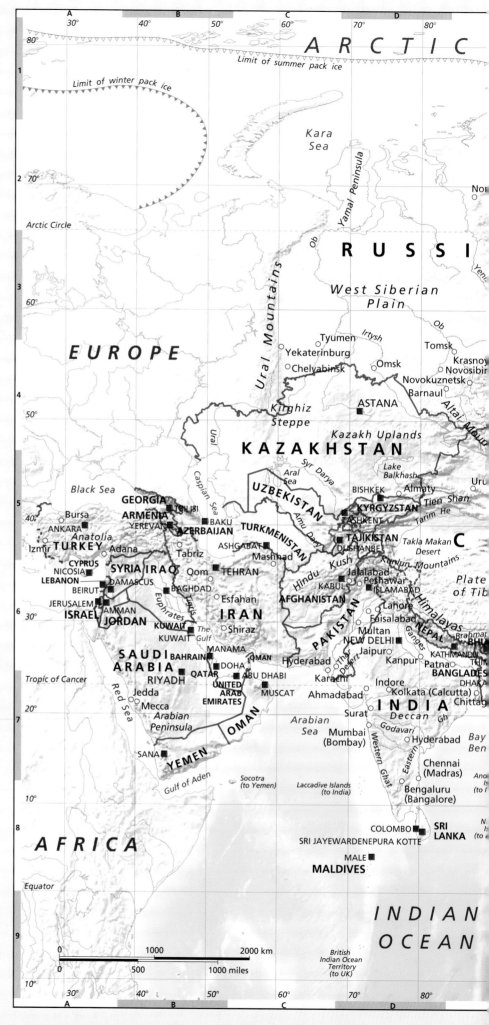

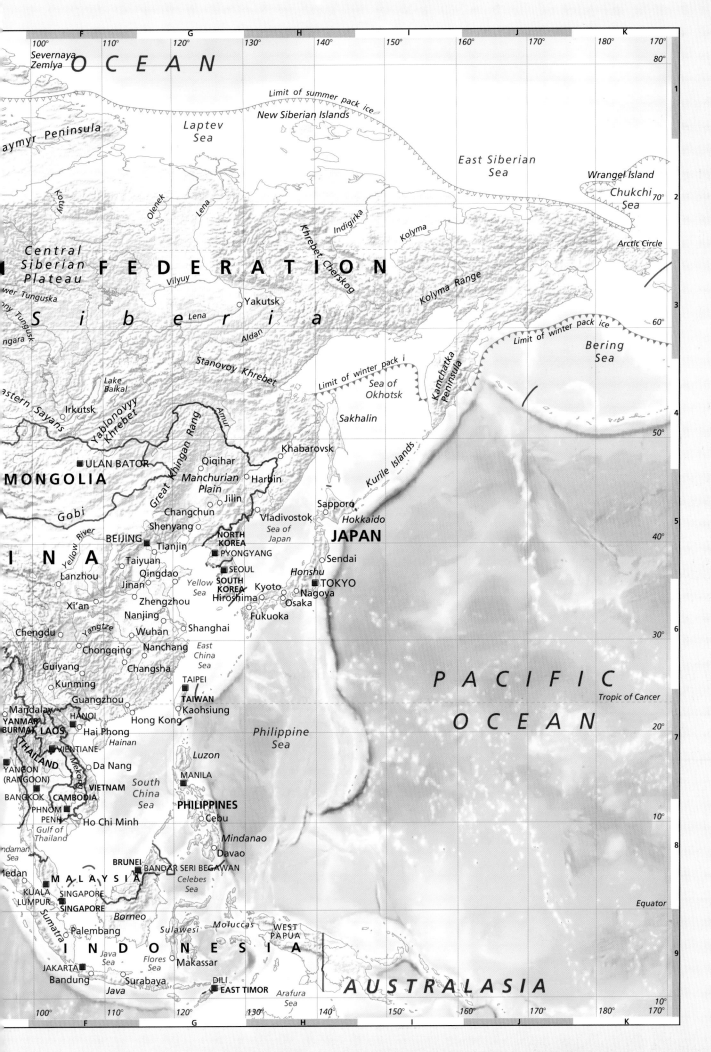

OCEAN

Severnaya Zemlya

100°   110°   120°   130°   140°   150°   160°   170°   180°   170°   80°

Limit of summer pack ice

Laptev Sea

New Siberian Islands

aymyr Peninsula

East Siberian Sea

Wrangel Island

Chukchi Sea 70°

Arctic Circle

Central Siberian Plateau

FEDERATION

Khrebet Cherskog

Indigirka

Kolyma

Kolyma Range

wer Tunguska

ny Tunguska

ngara

S i b e r i a

Olenek

Lena

Vilyuy

○ Yakutsk

Lena

Aldan

60°

Limit of winter pack ice

Bering Sea

Stanovoy Khrebet

Kamchatka Peninsula

Limit of winter pack i

Sea of Okhotsk

Lake Baikal

astern Sayans

○ Irkutsk

Yablonovyy Khrebet

Amur

Sakhalin

50°

Khabarovsk

Great Khingan Rang

■ ULAN BATOR

○ Qiqihar

Manchurian Plain

○ Harbin

Kurile Islands

MONGOLIA

Gobi

○ Jilin

○ Changchun

○ Sapporo

Hokkaido

○ Shenyang

○ Vladivostok

Sea of Japan

JAPAN

40°

Yellow River

■ BEIJING

○ Tianjin

NORTH KOREA

■ PYONGYANG

○ Sendai

INA

○ Taiyuan

○ Qingdao

■ SEOUL

Honshu

○ Lanzhou

○ Jinan

SOUTH KOREA

○ Kyoto

● TOKYO

○ Zhengzhou

Yellow Sea

○ Hiroshima

○ Nagoya

○ Xi'an

○ Nanjing

○ Fukuoka

○ Osaka

○ Chengdu

Yangtze

○ Wuhan

○ Shanghai

30°

○ Chongqing

○ Nanchang

East China Sea

○ Guiyang

○ Changsha

○ Kunming

□ TAIPEI

PACIFIC

○ Guangzhou

TAIWAN

○ Mandalay

■ HANOI

○ Kaohsiung

YANMAR

BURMA **LAOS**

○ Hai Phong

○ Hong Kong

Hainan

OCEAN

Tropic of Cancer

20°

THAILAND

■ VIENTIANE

Philippine Sea

YANGON (RANGOON)

○ Da Nang

Luzon

■ BANGKOK

CAMBODIA

VIETNAM

□ MANILA

South China Sea

■ PHNOM PENH

○ Ho Chi Minh

PHILIPPINES

Gulf of Thailand

○ Cebu

10°

ndaman Sea

Mindanao

□ BRUNEI

○ Davao

M A L A Y S I A

■ BANDAR SERI BEGAWAN

Celebes Sea

○ Medan

□ KUALA LUMPUR

○ SINGAPORE

SINGAPORE

Borneo

Equator

Sumatra

○ Palembang

Sulawesi

Moluccas

WEST PAPUA

Java Sea

I N D O N E S I A

Flores Sea

○ Makassar

9

■ JAKARTA

○ Bandung

○ Surabaya

Java

□ DILI

EAST TIMOR

Arafura Sea

A U S T R A L A S I A

10°

100°   110°   120°   130°   140°   150°   160°   170°   180°   170°

THE RUSSIAN FEDERATION

The western part of the Russian Federation falls in Europe, while the area east of the Ural Mountains is in Asia. Just east of the mountains is a flat region of marshes and streams, called the West Siberian Plain. The plain gradually rises to the Central Siberian Plateau, and then again to highlands in the south and east. Great coniferous forests cover most of this land. Much of European Russia lies on the North European Plain. This region is covered in large forests of birch and pine trees, and is watered by several great rivers, including the Volga. In the far north is frozen tundra.

In the east, a cold climate and harsh living conditions keep the population low. Many of those who do live here herd reindeer or work in forestry. The majority of people live in the west, where farmers grow root crops and wheat. This part of the country is highly industrialized, producing goods such as chemicals, cars and textiles. The region is also one of Europe's main sources of oil.

The Russian Federation was created when the communist Soviet Union broke up in 1991. The communists controlled farming, and they developed heavy industries, many of which caused pollution. Today, the country is modernizing its industries, and tackling the environmental problems caused during the Soviet period.

LAND HEIGHT

	4,000 m / 13,124 ft
	2,000 m / 6,562 ft
	1,000 m / 3,281 ft
	500 m / 1,640 ft
	200 m / 656 ft
	Sea level

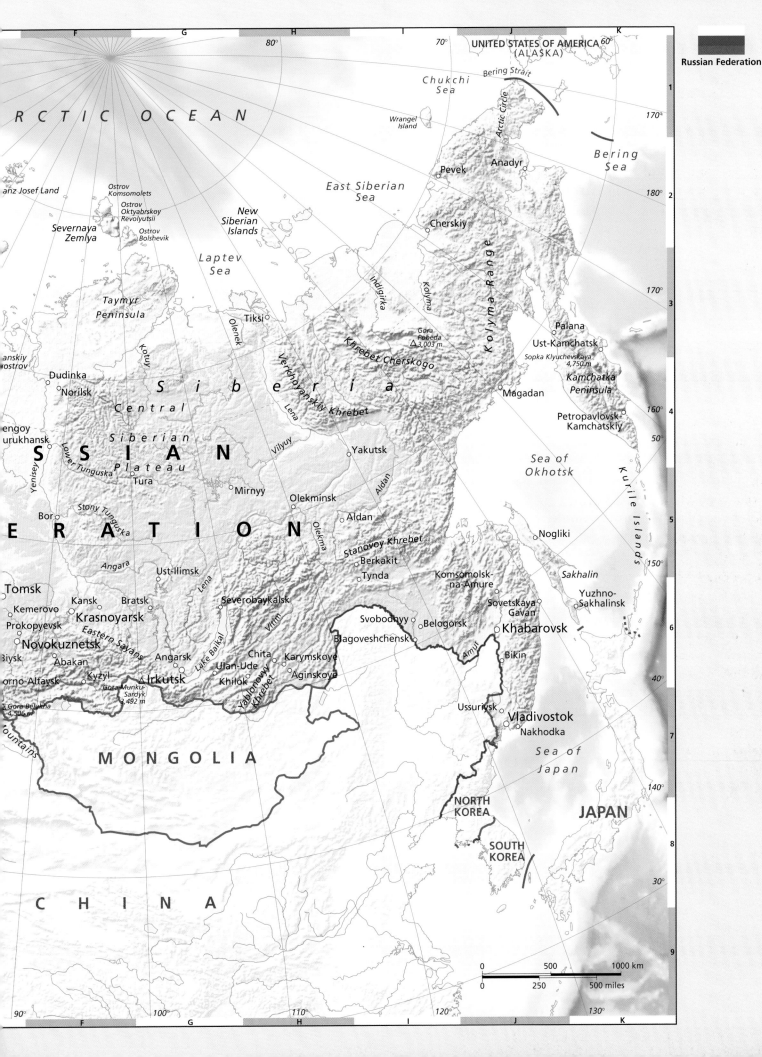

Russian Federation

ARCTIC OCEAN

UNITED STATES OF AMERICA (ALASKA)

Chukchi Sea

Bering Strait

Arctic Circle

Bering Sea

Wrangel Island

anz Josef Land

Ostrov Komsomolets
Ostrov Oktyabrskoy Revolyutsii
Ostrov Bolshevik

Severnaya Zemlya

East Siberian Sea

New Siberian Islands

Pevek

Anadyr

Laptev Sea

Cherskiy

Taymyr Peninsula

anskiy ostrov

Kotuy

Tiksi

Olenek

Indigirka

Kolyma

Khrebet Cherskogo

Gora Pobeda △ 3,003 m

Kolyma Range

Palana

Ust-Kamchatsk

Sopka Klyuchevskaya 4,750 m

Dudinka

Norilsk

S i b e r i a

Verkhoyanskiy Khrebet

Kamchatka Peninsula

Central Siberian Plateau

Lena

Magadan

engoy urukhansk

Vilyuy

Yakutsk

Petropavlovsk-Kamchatskiy

R S S I A N

Yenisey

Lower Tunguska

Tura

Mirnyy

Aldan

Sea of Okhotsk

Bor

Stony Tunguska

Olekminsk

Olekma

Aldan

Kurile Islands

E R A T I O N

Angara

Ust-Ilimsk

Lena

Stanovoy Khrebet

Berkakit

Nogliki

Sakhalin

Tomsk

Kansk

Bratsk

Severobaykalsk

Tynda

Komsomolsk-na-Amure

Yuzhno-Sakhalinsk

Kemerovo

Krasnoyarsk

Vittim

Svobodnyy

Belogorsk

Sovetskaya Gavan

Prokopyevsk

Eastern Sayans

Lake Baikal

Khabarovsk

Novokuznetsk

Angarsk

Chita

Karymskoye

Blagoveshchensk

Amur

Biysk

Abakan

Ulan-Ude

Khilok

Aginskoye

Bikin

orno-Altaysk

Kyzyl

Gora Munku-Sardyk 3,492 m

△ Irkutsk

Yablonovvy Khrebet

X Gora Belukha 4,506 m

ountains

MONGOLIA

Ussuriysk

Vladivostok

Nakhodka

Sea of Japan

NORTH KOREA

JAPAN

SOUTH KOREA

C H I N A

0   500   1000 km
0 250 500 miles

WEST ASIA

In the north of west Asia lie the Taurus Mountains and the plateau of Anatolia. The eastern part of this region is also dominated by uplands, including the Elburz and Zagros Mountains. In the south is the huge Arabian Peninsula, which is separated from the rest of Asia by the valleys of the Tigris and Euphrates rivers. Mountains run along the peninsula's Red Sea coast, and much of the rest of this region is covered in dry, barren deserts.

West Asia has a long history. Some of the world's first great civilizations developed in Iraq about 5,000 years ago, and the Arabian Peninsula was the home of the prophet Muhammad, and the first Muslims. This region is still mainly Muslim, although it also contains the Jewish state of Israel.

Oil and natural gas are important sources of income for many of the countries in west Asia. Other industries produce a range of goods, from industrial machinery in Georgia to carpets in Iran. Cattle and sheep are raised in the north, while goats are herded on the southern tip of the Arabian Peninsula. Hazelnuts are the main crop along the Black Sea coast, root crops are produced in Anatolia, and olives, figs, grapes and peaches are cultivated on Turkey's southern coast. Wheat is harvested in the fertile valleys of the Euphrates and Tigris rivers. Cotton, dates and fruits for the export market are also grown here.

LAND HEIGHT

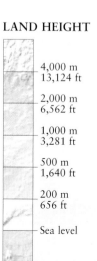

4,000 m
13,124 ft

2,000 m
6,562 ft

1,000 m
3,281 ft

500 m
1,640 ft

200 m
656 ft

Sea level

RUSSIAN FEDERATION

KAZAKHSTAN

UZBEKISTAN

Turkey

Georgia

Armenia

Azerbaijan

Iran

Syria

Iraq

Cyprus

Lebanon

Israel

Jordan

Saudi Arabia

Kuwait

Bahrain

Oman

Qatar

United Arab Emirates

Yemen

CENTRAL ASIA

A wall of mountains cuts through central Asia in a diagonal line from the Tien Shan in the northeast, through the Pamirs in the centre, to the Hindu Kush in the southwest. In the northwest are the sandy deserts of Uzbekistan and Turkmenistan. There are rolling grasslands in Kazakhstan, in the north. Central Asia receives very little rain and the region experiences extremes of temperature – winters are cold and summers are very hot.

With very few large cities, the peoples of central Asia live mainly in rural areas and make their living from the land. Farming is difficult in the desert and mountain regions, so agriculture is concentrated around the river valleys in the east. Here, a variety of cereals and fruits, including peaches, melons and apricots, are grown. Cotton, which is central Asia's main export, is grown on land irrigated by the Amu Darya river. Herds of cattle, sheep and goats are raised in the south and east, and on the grasslands of Kazakhstan in the north.

Fossil fuels, including oil, gas and coal, are extracted and processed throughout the region.

There are a number of traditional industries, which make products such as carpets and leather goods. The main industrial area is located in the east, in the Fergana Valley, where old-fashioned factories cause air pollution.

Once the fourth largest lake in the world, the Aral Sea has shrunk by almost half its size since 1960. This is because the rivers feeding the lake have been diverted to irrigate fields of cotton. The dry climate, combined with poor vegetation cover, means that desertification is another environmental problem in central Asia.

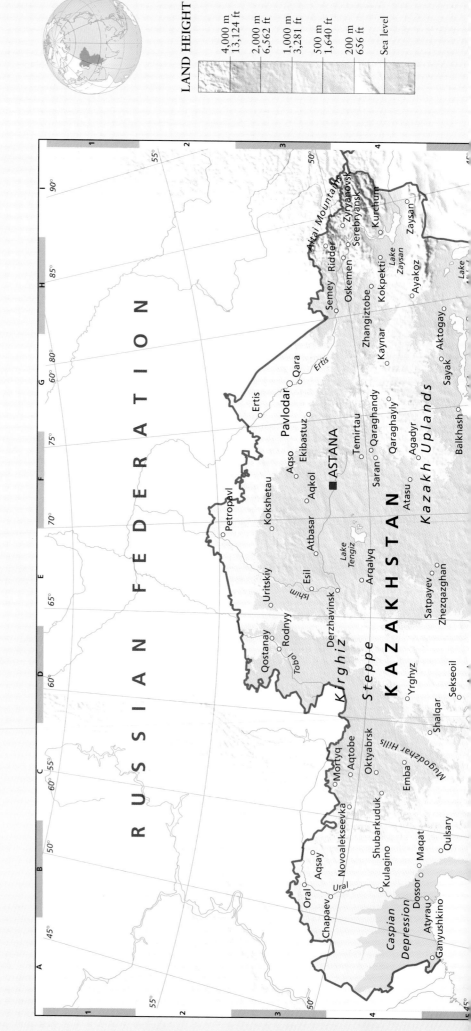

LAND HEIGHT

4,000 m	13,124 ft
2,000 m	6,562 ft
1,000 m	3,281 ft
500 m	1,640 ft
200 m	656 ft
Sea level	

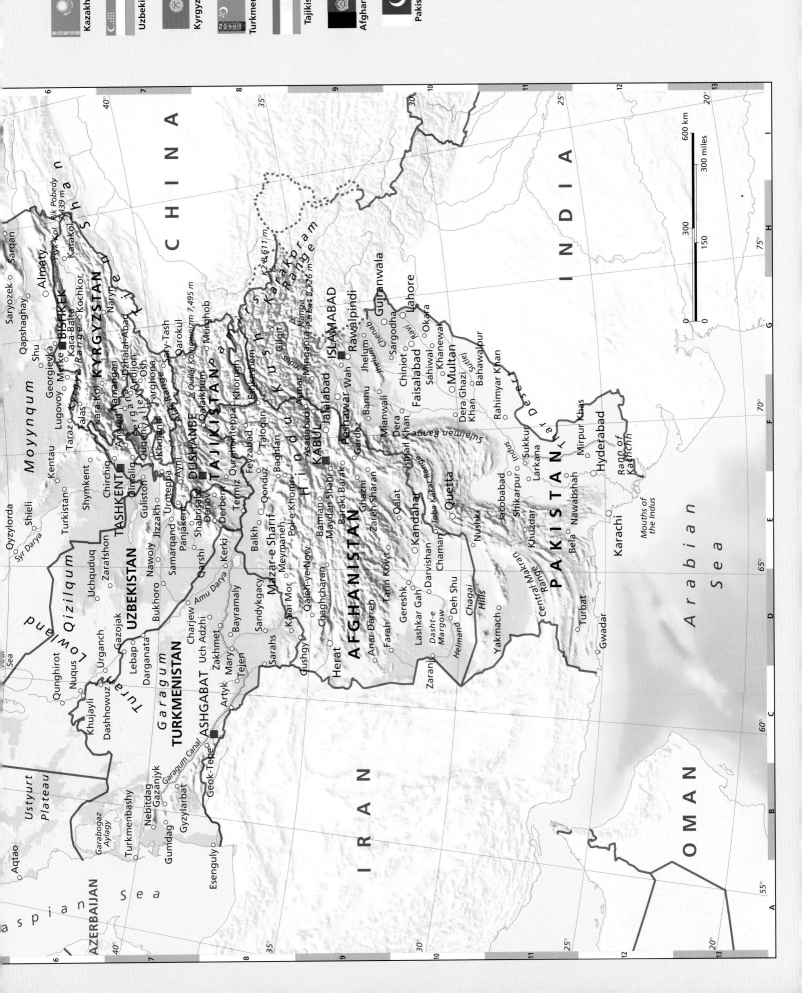

Kazakhstan

Uzbekistan

Kyrgyzstan

Turkmenistan

Tajikistan

Afghanistan

Pakistan

SOUTH ASIA

South Asia is separated from the rest of Asia by the Thar Desert in the northwest and a wall of mountains, including the towering Himalayas, in the north and east. The great floodplains of the Ganges, Brahmaputra and Indus rivers lie at the foothills of the mountains. Further south are rolling plateaux, which are fringed by a line of coastal hills, called the Eastern and Western Ghats. To the southeast are the mountainous islands of Sri Lanka.

More than half of south Asia's population makes its living from agriculture. Farmers grow rice in the wet areas of the east and west, while corn and millet are the main crops on the Deccan plateau. Elsewhere, groundnuts are grown for cooking oil, and tea for the export market is harvested on huge plantations. Livestock are raised throughout the region, and fishing is common along the entire coast.

Large-scale industries, from car manufacturing to chemicals, have expanded in the region's cities in recent years. Service industries are also growing steadily. In the countryside, a number of people work in traditional trades, providing goods to the local people. Products such as clothing, leather and jewellery are among south Asia's leading exports.

This part of Asia's huge population is growing rapidly. The majority of the people live in rural areas, but increasing numbers are moving to the cities in search of work. There is serious overcrowding in both rural and urban regions, and slums have developed in the larger cities. Deforestation is also a major problem, with trees being cut down in the southern and Himalayan regions for fuel.

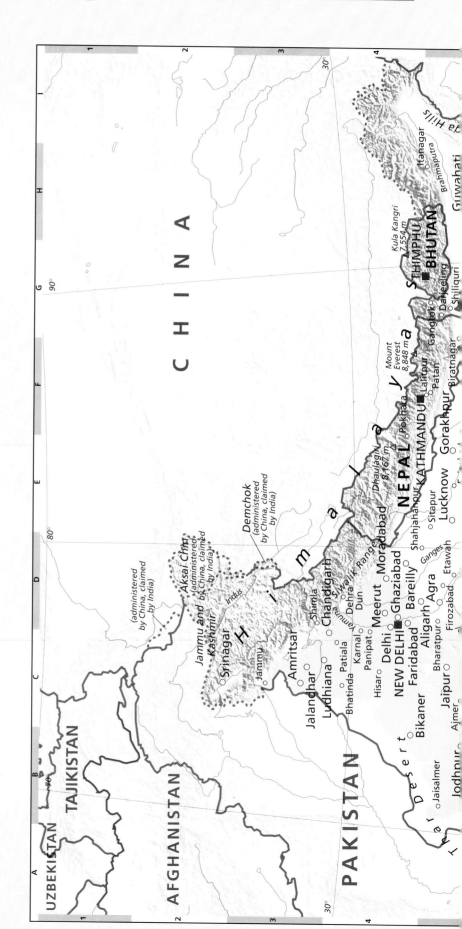

LAND HEIGHT

4,000 m
13,124 ft

2,000 m
6,562 ft

1,000 m
3,281 ft

500 m
1,640 ft

200 m
656 ft

Sea level

SOUTHEAST ASIA

Southeast Asia is made up of many thousands of tropical islands and a mainland area. The landscape of the mainland is dominated by a string of mountain ranges, which are covered in dense forests and crossed by wide river valleys. The many islands to the southeast of the mainland are also forested. Most of these islands were formed by volcanoes, many of which are still active. In the centre of the region is the island of Borneo. The third-largest island in the world, it is divided between the countries of Malaysia, Indonesia and Brunei.

Rice is the main food crop in this region, while bananas, pineapples and sugar cane are grown as cash crops. Large quantities of fish are caught in the surrounding waters. Over the last few decades, the types of industries in southeast Asia have changed dramatically. There are still a number of traditional companies, which process the area's raw materials, including timber and metals, but many parts of the region now have large high-tech industries.

The forests of southeast Asia are home to thousands of unique species of plants and animals. This wildlife is now under threat, however, because vast numbers of trees are being cut away for use in the region's timber industry. In Indonesia, trees are burned to clear land for crops. The smoke from the fires creates terrible smog.

LAND HEIGHT

	4,000 m 13,124 ft
	2,000 m 6,562 ft
	1,000 m 3,281 ft
	500 m 1,640 ft
	200 m 656 ft
	Sea level

115° F 120° G 125° H 130° I 135° J 140° K 145°

Myanmar

Laos

Vietnam

Thailand

Philippines

Cambodia

Malaysia

Brunei

Singapore

Indonesia

East Timor

Tropic of Cancer

25°

20°

TAIWAN

Batan Islands

Luzon Strai

Babuyan Islands

15°

Laoag   Aparri

Luzon   Ilagan

San Fernando   Baguio

Dagupan   Cabanatuan

Angeles   San Fernando

MANILA   Catanduanes

Batangas   Naga

Mindoro   Legaspi

Calbayog   *Samar*

Calamian   Masbate

Group   Roxas City   *Leyte* Tacloban

Iloilo   *Panay* Cadiz   Ormoc

San Carlos   Bacolod City

Cebu Cebu   Surigao

Puerto   Dumaguete   *Bohol*   Butuan

Princesa   *Negros*   Cagayan de Oro

Iligan   *Mindanao*

Zamboanga   Mount Apo   Davao

Basilan   2,954 m

Jolo   General Santos

Tawitawi

Sulu Archipelag

PACIFIC

OCEAN

15°

10°

FEDERATED STATES
OF MICRONESIA

PALAU

South China

Sea

PHILIPPINES

Spratly
Islands

Palawan

Sulu Sea

Balabac Strait

Kudat

Gunung Kinabalu

Kota Kinabalu   △4,094 m   Sandakan

Ranau

GAWAN   SABAH

BRUNEI

Miri

RAWAK   Tarakan

Crocker Range

Tanjungredeb

Kapuas
Mountains

Borneo

Rajang   *Kayan*

Samarinda

Mahakan

ALIMANTAN   Balikpapan

Barito

njarmasin

Martapura

O

Makassar

Madura

urabaya

Jember   *Bali* Lombok Sumbawa

alang   Mataram

Denpasar

Sumba

115°   F   120°   G

Celebes
Sea

Talaud
Islands

Sangir
Islands

Manado

Gorontalo

Gulf of
Tomini

Palu

Poso

Sulawesi

N

Malunda

Parepare

Muna

Buton

Selayar

Flores Sea

Flores

Lesser Sunda Islands

Morotai

Halmahera

Ternate

Molucca
Sea

Halmahera
Sea

Bacan   Sorong

Peleng   Obi

Sula
Islands

Moluccas   Misool

Ceram Sea

Seram

Buru   Ambon

E

Waigeo

Manokwari

Biak

Jazirah
Doberai

Yapen   Jayapura

WEST
PAPUA

Kai
Islands

Aru
Islands

Mamberamo

Puncak Jaya   △ *Pegunungan*
5,030 m   *Maoke*

S   I   A

Yos
Sudarso

PAPUA NEW GUINEA

Wetar

Alor

Banda Sea

Tanimbar
Islands

Arafura

Sea

DILI

EAST TIMOR

Timor

Kupang

Timor
Sea

AUSTRALIA

120°   H   125°   I   130°   J   135°   K   140°

Equator

10°

5°

Equator

5°

10°

1

2

3

4

5

6

7

8

9

EAST ASIA

East Asia's landscape may be divided into four main areas. In the southwest is the Plateau of Tibet. Here, high mountain peaks surround small areas of pasture and arid deserts. There are dry highlands in the northwest, and in the north there are cold deserts. Great plains lie to the east. These plains were formed from soils that were carried to the region by China's rivers.

Although most of China's land is either too poor or too mountainous for cultivation, almost three-quarters of this country's enormous population of about 1.3 billion people make their living from farming. The majority of the people live in the east, where the land is flatter and more fertile. Wheat, corn, soya beans and cotton are grown on the plains, and further south, rice is the main crop. Pigs are raised here in large numbers. In Mongolia, in the north, farmers mainly herd sheep.

China became a communist country in 1949, and since then, it has become a major industrial nation. The country's industries, including iron and steel production, chemicals, engineering and textiles, are concentrated in the cities on the east coast, such as Qingdao and Shanghai. Hong Kong and Beijing are also major financial centres. Taiwan exports electronic goods, shoes and textiles throughout the world, while Mongolia's economy is mainly based on agriculture.

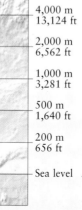

LAND HEIGHT

4,000 m
13,124 ft

2,000 m
6,562 ft

1,000 m
3,281 ft

500 m
1,640 ft

200 m
656 ft

Sea level

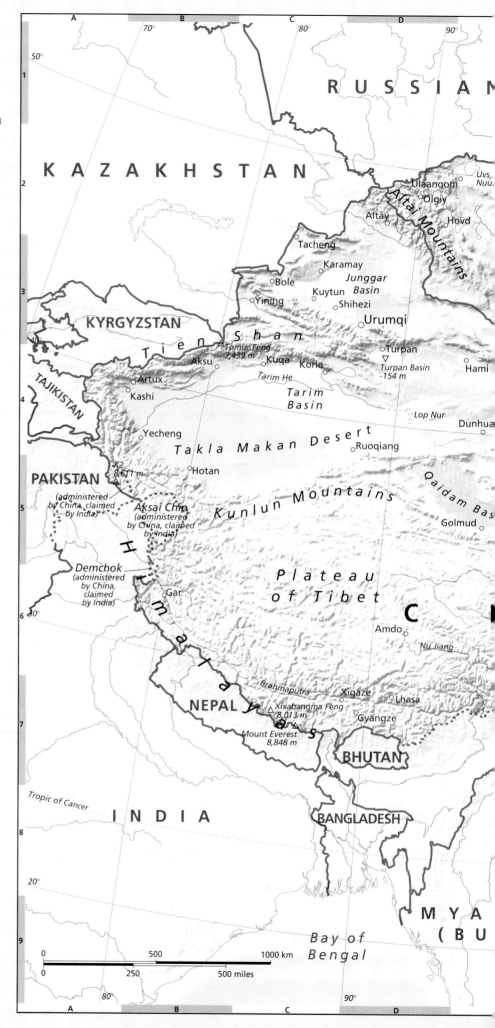

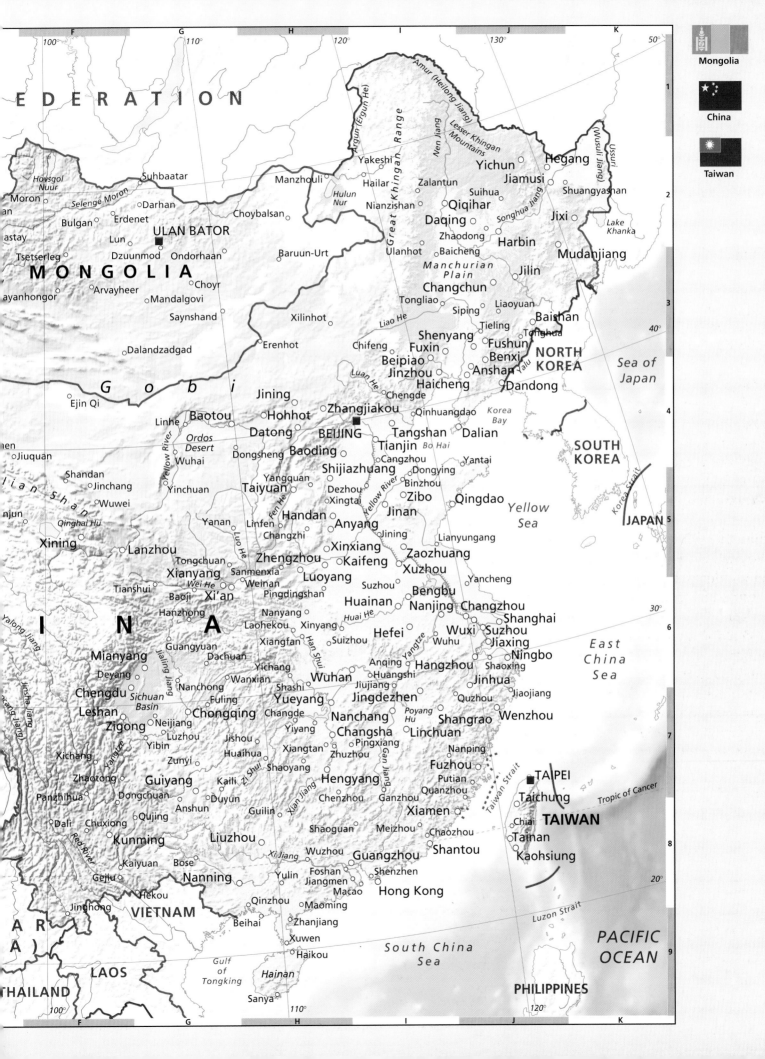

Mongolia

China

Taiwan

E D E R A T I O N

Hovsgol Nuur

Moron
an
astay
Tsetserleg
Bulgan · Erdenet
Lun
Dzuunmod · Ondorhaan
ULAN BATOR
Suhbaatar
Darhan

Selenge Moron

Manzhouli
Hailar
Nianzishan
Choybalsan
Baruun-Urt

M O N G O L I A
ayanhongor · Arvayheer
Mandalgovi
Choyr
Saynshand
Dalandzadgad

Xilinhot
Erenhot

G o b i
Ejin Qi
Linhe · Baotou
Jining
Hohhot
Datong
Dongsheng · Baoding

Yakeshi
Hulun Nur

Great Khingan Range
Argun (Ergun He)
Amur (Heilong Jiang)
Nen Jiang
Lesser Khingan Mountains

Yichun · Hegang
Zalantun · Jiamusi
Suihua · Shuangyashan
Qiqihar
Daqing · Jixi
Zhaodong *Songhua Jiang*
Ulanhot · Baicheng · Harbin · Mudanjiang
Manchurian Plain
Tongliao · Changchun · Jilin
Siping · Liaoyuan
Tieling · Baishan
Chifeng · Shenyang · Tonghua
Fuxin · Fushun **NORTH KOREA**
Beipiao · Benxi
Jinzhou · Anshan
Haicheng *Yalu*
Chengde · Dandong

Luan He
Zhangjiakou · Qinhuangdao
Korea Bay
Tangshan · Dalian
BEIJING
Tianjin *Bo Hai*
Cangzhou · Yantai
Shijiazhuang · Dongying
Dezhou · Binzhou
Xingtai · Zibo
Jinan · Qingdao
Yellow Sea

Ulsuri (Wusuli Jiang)
Lake Khanka

Sea of Japan

SOUTH KOREA
Korea Strait
JAPAN

Jiuquan
Ulian Shan
Shandan · Jinchang
Wuwei
njun
Qinghai Hu
Xining
Lanzhou
Tongchuan
Xianyang · Sanmenxia
Tianshui · Weinan
Baoji · Xi'an
Hanzhong

Wuhai
Yinchuan
Yangquan
Taiyuan
Yanan
Linfen
Fen He
Handan
Changzhi
Zhengzhou
Luoyang
Luo He
Pingdingshan
Wei He

Yellow River
Anyang
Xinxiang
Kaifeng
Jining
Xuzhou
Zaozhuang
Lianyungang
Yancheng

Xiaguan
Yalong Jiang
Jinsha Jiang
eng Jiang

Mianyang
Deyang
Chengdu *Sichuan Basin*
Leshan
Zigong
Neijiang
Xichang
Zhaotong
Yangtze
Guiyang
Panzhihua
Dongchuan
Dali · Chuxiong
Kunming
Kaiyuan
Gejiu
Jinghong

Nanyang
Laohekou · Xinyang
Xiangfan
Guangyuan · Dachuan
Nanchong
Yichang
Wanxian
Jialing Jiang
Shashi
Fuling
Chongqing
Changde
Yiyang
Luzhou
Yibin
Zunyi
Jishou
Huaihua
Zi Shui
Shaoyang
Duyun
Kaili
Anshun
Qujing
Guilin
Liuzhou

Huai He
Suzhou
Huainan
Bengbu
Hefei
Suizhou
Han Shui
Wuhan
Huangshi
Jiujiang
Jingdezhen
Poyang Hu
Nanchang
Pingxiang
Zhuzhou
Xiangtan
Changsha
Xiang Jiang
Hengyang
Chenzhou
Ganzhou
Gan Jiang
Shaoguan
Meizhou
Chaozhou

Nanjing
Changzhou
Anqing *Yangtze*
Wuhu
Hangzhou
Jinhua
Quzhou
Shangrao
Linchuan

Shanghai
Wuxi · Suzhou
Jiaxing
Ningbo
Shaoxing
East China Sea
Jiaojiang
Wenzhou

Nanping
Fuzhou
Putian
Quanzhou
Xiamen
Shantou
TAIPEI
Taichung
Chiai
TAIWAN
Tainan
Kaohsiung
Tropic of Cancer
Taiwan Strait

I N A
Xingyang
Zhanjiang
Red River
Hekou
VIETNAM

Nanning
Bose
Yulin
Xi Jiang
Wuzhou
Foshan
Jiangmen
Macao
Guangzhou
Shenzhen
Hong Kong
Maoming
Qinzhou
Beihai
Zhanjiang
Xuwen
Haikou
Hainan
Sanya

Yueyang
Shashi
Jingdezhen

Gulf of Tongking

South China Sea

Luzon Strait

PACIFIC OCEAN

PHILIPPINES

LAOS
THAILAND
AR
A

JAPAN AND THE KOREAS

South and North Korea lie on a peninsula that juts out from the northeast coast of China. To the east is Japan, a long chain of more than 4,000 islands in the Pacific Ocean. Mountains and hills dominate the landscape of these three countries, so most of this region's cities and towns are located on lower-lying land near the coasts.

Rice is grown throughout this region, and large quantities of fish are caught off the coasts. North Korea's communist government controls its industries and farms, and this country does very little trade with other nations. South Korea and Japan, however, export goods all over the globe. These two countries have few natural resources, so they have specialized in the production of high-value goods. South Korea makes cars, ships and textiles, while Japan is a world leader in the production of high-tech goods, such as cameras, computers and electronics, as well as cars.

Japan's environment suffers from acid rain caused by pollution from the factories of North Korea and the Russian Federation. Nuclear waste is dumped in the Sea of Japan. This country is also located in a major earthquake zone. Although buildings are constructed to withstand tremors, major quakes, such as the one that destroyed Kobe in 1995, are still a big threat in Japan.

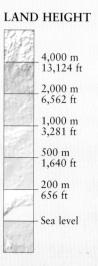

LAND HEIGHT

	4,000 m 13,124 ft
	2,000 m 6,562 ft
	1,000 m 3,281 ft
	500 m 1,640 ft
	200 m 656 ft
	Sea level

Japan

North Korea

South Korea

RUSSIAN FEDERATION

135° 140° 145°

La Perouse Strait
Soya-misaki

Sea of Okhotsk

Kurile Islands
(administered by Russian Federation)

Rebun-to
Rishiri-to
Wakkanai

Nayoro
Shiretoko-misaki
Monbetsu
Abashiri
Rumoi
Kitami
Shibetsu
Takikawa
Asahikawa
△ Asahi-dake
2,290 m
Kussharo-ko
Otaru
Ebetsu
Hokkaido
Nemuro
Iwanai
Sapporo
Chitose
Obihiro
Kushiro
Tomakomai
Uchiura-wan
Muroran

Okushiri-to
Hakodate
Erimo-misaki
Tsugaru-kaikyo
Shimokita-hanto
Mutsu-wan
Aomori
Hirosaki
Hachinohe
Noshiro

Sea of Japan

Oga
Morioka
Akita
Miyako
Yokote
Sakata
Kesennuma
Furukawa
Sado-shima
Ishinomaki
Yamagata
Sendai
Ryotsu
Sendai-wan
Niigata
Fukushima
Nagaoka
Koriyama
JAPAN
Honshu
Noto-hanto
Joetsu
Iwaki
Toyama-wan
Nikko
Kuroiso
Takaoka
Toyama
Kanazawa
Nagano
Utsunomiya
Hitachi
Matto
Ueda
Maebashi
Komatsu
Matsumoto
Takasaki
Mito
Fukui
Chino
Oyama
Tsuchiura
Takayama
Urawa
Funabashi
Wakasa-wan
Tsuruga
Kofu
TOKYO
Choshi
shoto
Ogaki
Gifu
Fujinomiya
Kawasaki
Chiba
ottori
Maizuru
Otsu
Yokkaichi
Nagoya
△ Mount Fuji
3,776 m
Ichihara
go
Biwa-ko
Toyota
Fujieda
Shizuoka
Yokohama
Fuji
Yaizu
ayama
Himeji
Kyoto
Nara
Okazaki
Toyohashi
Nojima-zaki
Kurashiki
Otsu
Osaka
Tsu
Hamamatsu
Kobe
Sakai
Ise
Ise-wan
Takamatsu
Wakayama
chi
Tokushima
Izu-shoto
Kii-suido
Tanabe
Sagami-nada
Muroto-zaki
Shiono-misaki

PACIFIC OCEAN

PACIFIC OCEAN

0 — 200 — 400 km
0 — 100 — 200 miles

0 — 200 — 400 km
0 — 100 — 200 miles

East China Sea

Amami-o-shima
Naze

Tokuno-shima

Ryukyu Islands
Okinawa
Kume-jima
Okinawa
Naha

Miyako-jima
Philippine Sea

Iriomote-jima
Ishigaki-jima

135° 140° 145° 30°

AUSTRALASIA AND OCEANIA

Australasia and Oceania is made up of 14 countries. They include the vast landmass of Australia, the islands of New Zealand and Papua New Guinea, and the many thousands of coral atolls and islands that extend into the Pacific Ocean.

Before European explorers started to visit this part of the globe during the 16th century, the region was occupied by native peoples who lived by traditional means, such as hunting and gathering. Eventually, the Europeans began to settle and take over these lands. Some of the islands became overseas territories of the United Kingdom, France and the USA. In the past 20 years, a number of these dependencies, such as Palau, have become independent nations.

Natural resources are of major economic importance throughout Australasia and Oceania. Australia exports raw materials, such as coal, iron ore and bauxite. Sheep are raised for their wool and meat in New Zealand and Australia, and fishing is important throughout the Pacific islands. Manufacturing companies are found only in the large coastal cities of Australia and New Zealand. Until recently, both of these countries relied on Europe for trade. However, they have now begun to form trade links with the neighbouring countries of east and southeast Asia.

LAND HEIGHT

4,000 m	13,124 ft
2,000 m	6,562 ft
1,000 m	3,281 ft
500 m	1,640 ft
200 m	656 ft
Sea level	

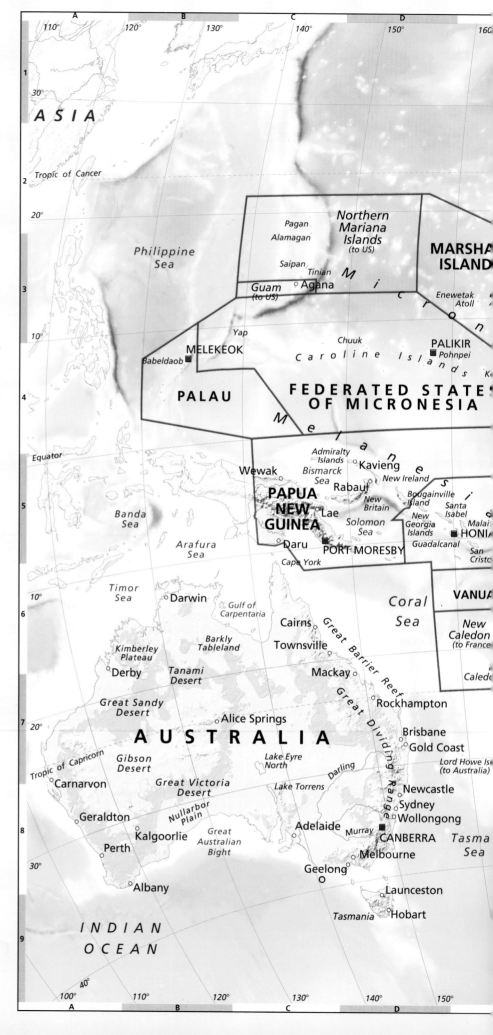

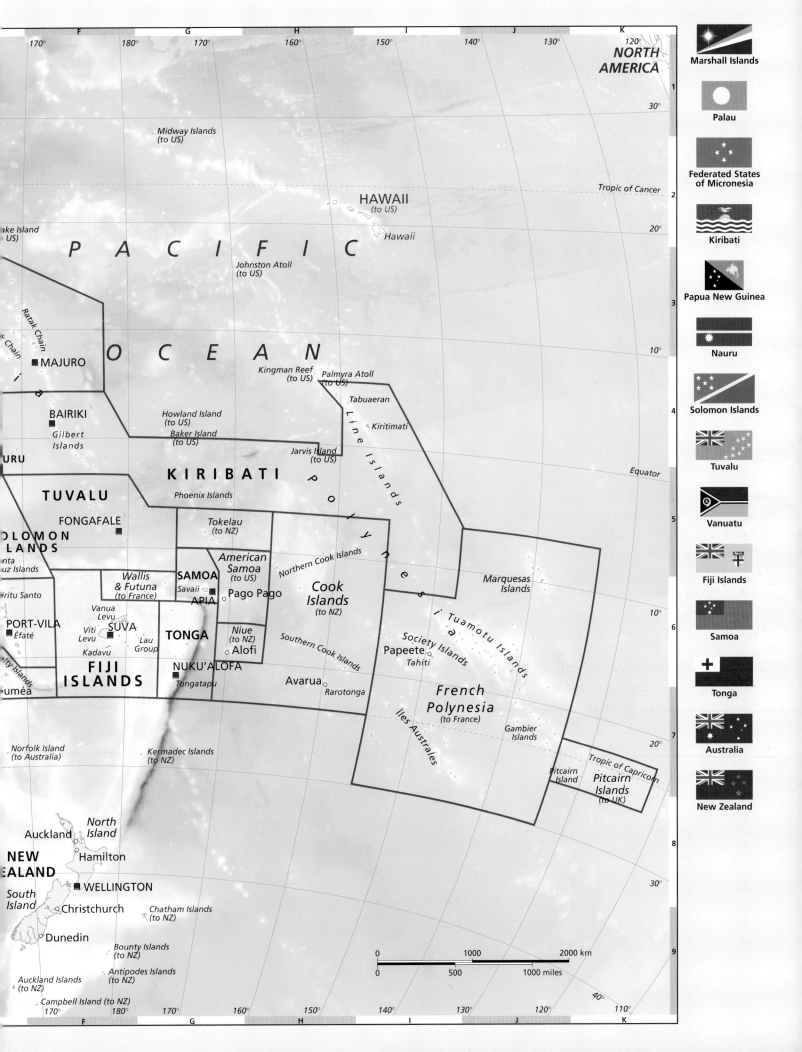

NORTH
AMERICA

170° *180°* *170°* *160°* *150°* *140°* *130°* *120°*

30°

Tropic of Cancer

20°

Midway Islands
(to US)

HAWAII
(to US)

Hawaii

ake Island
US)

P   A   C   I   F   I   C

Johnston Atoll
(to US)

O   C   E   A   N

10°

Ratak Chain

■ MAJURO

Chain

i

Kingman Reef
(to US)

Palmyra Atoll
(to US)

Tabuaeran

Equator

BAIRIKI
Gilbert
Islands

Howland Island
(to US)

Baker Island
(to US)

Jarvis Island
(to US)

Kiritimati

Line Islands

URU

K   I   R   I   B   A   T   I

P

TUVALU

Phoenix Islands

o

10°

FONGAFALE

Tokelau
(to NZ)

l

OLOMON
LANDS

American
Samoa
(to US)

Northern Cook Islands

y

Marquesas
Islands

5°

nta
uz Islands

SAMOA
Savaii

SUVA
Kadavu

Wallis
& Futuna
(to France)

APIA

Pago Pago

Cook
Islands
(to NZ)

n

e

Tuamotu Islands

iritu Santo

PORT-VILA
Éfaté

Vanua
Levu

Viti
Levu

TONGA

Niue
(to NZ)
○ Alofi

Southern Cook Islands

Society Islands

PAPEETE

s

i

10°

Lau
Group

Tahiti

uméa

FIJI
ISLANDS

NUKU'ALOFA
Tongatapu

Avarua○
Rarotonga

French
Polynesia
(to France)

a

Norfolk Island
(to Australia)

Kermadec Islands
(to NZ)

Îles Australes

Gambier
Islands

Tropic of Capricorn

20°

Pitcairn
Island

Pitcairn
Islands
(to UK)

North
Island

Auckland

NEW
EALAND

Hamilton

■ WELLINGTON

8°

South
Island

○ Christchurch

Chatham Islands
(to NZ)

○ Dunedin

Bounty Islands
(to NZ)

30°

Auckland Islands
(to NZ)

Antipodes Islands
(to NZ)

0   1000   2000 km

0   500   1000 miles

40°

Campbell Island (to NZ)

170° *180°* *170°* *160°* *150°* *140°* *130°* *120°* *110°*

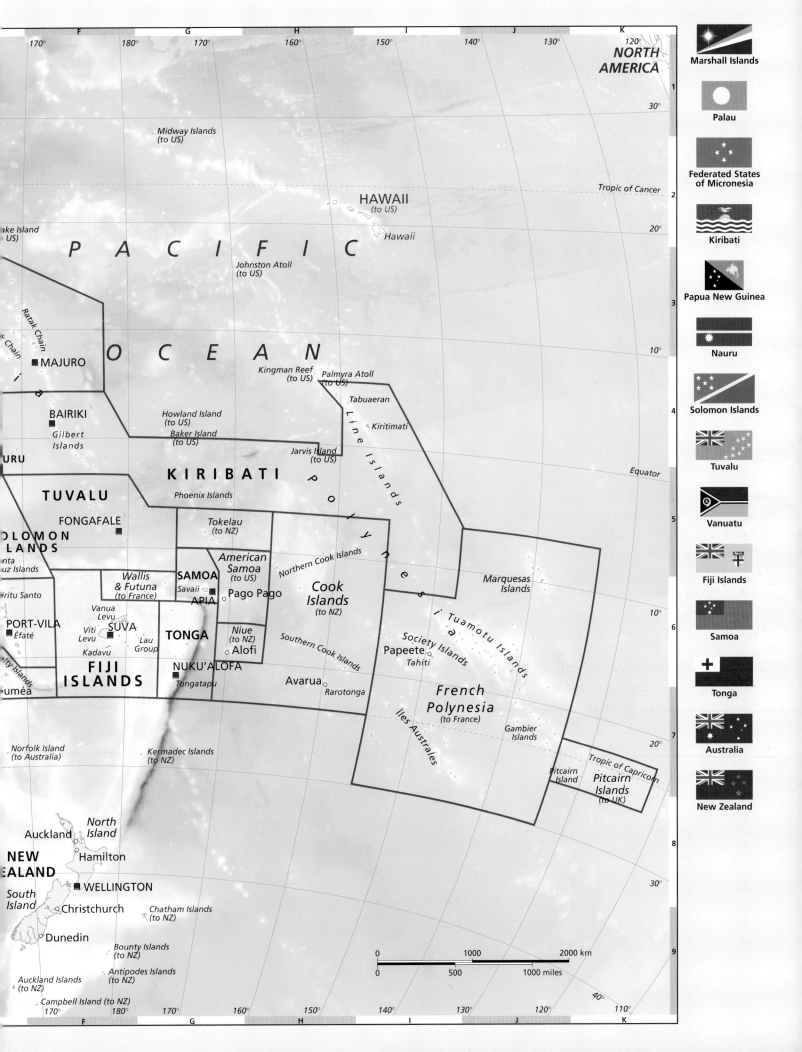
Marshall Islands

Palau

Federated States
of Micronesia

Kiribati

Papua New Guinea

Nauru

Solomon Islands

Tuvalu

Vanuatu

Fiji Islands

Samoa

Tonga

Australia

New Zealand

AUSTRALIA

One of the world's largest countries, Australia is located in the southern Pacific Ocean. Despite its huge size, this nation has a relatively small population of about 20 million people, because much of the land is dry. In the west are semi-arid plains of scrub and grassland, while in the east the land rises to the peaks of the Great Dividing Range. In the north, there are tropical rainforests and mangrove swamps.

Sugar cane is harvested near the east coast. In the south and west, grapes for Australia's successful wine industry are produced, along with wheat. Large numbers of sheep and cattle are raised in the southwest and on the Great Artesian Basin in the east. These provide meat and wool for export.

The first inhabitants of Australia were the Aboriginal peoples. Today, they are a tiny minority, and the majority of Australians are of European origin. Most people work and live in cities in the south and east, and around Perth in the west. In these urban areas are engineering and manufacturing businesses, and thriving service industries.

Australia has one of the world's biggest mining industries, which exploits the rich resources of gold, copper, coal and iron ore. Tourism is another important source of income, especially along the northeast coast, where people come to visit the sunny beaches and the Great Barrier Reef.

LAND HEIGHT

	4,000 m 13,124 ft
	2,000 m 6,562 ft
	1,000 m 3,281 ft
	500 m 1,640 ft
	200 m 656 ft
	Sea level

Australia

PAPUA NEW GUINEA

Arafura Sea

Torres Strait

Wessel Islands
Prince of Wales Island Cape York

Van Diemen Gulf

Darwin

Cape Arnhem

Cape York Peninsula *Princess Charlotte Bay*

Katherine

Arnhem Land

Gulf of Carpentaria

Mataranka

Groote Eylandt

Sir Edward Pellew Group

Coral Sea

Victoria River Roadhouse

Daly Waters

Wellesley Islands

Cooktown

Lake Woods

Barkly Tableland

Normanton

Cairns

Tanami Desert

Croydon

Georgetown

Forsayth

Great Barrier Reef

Tennant Creek

Camooweal

Mitchell

Townsville

NORTHERN

Flinders

Charters Towers

TERRITORY

Mount Isa

Cloncurry

Richmond

Torrens Creek

Proserpine

Duchess

Hughenden

Mackay

Georgina

Winton

Macdonnell Ranges

Boulia

QUEENSLAND

Cape Townshend

RALIA

Alice Springs

Clermont

Longreach

Jericho

Emerald

Rockhampton

Lake Amadeus

Δ Uluru (Ayers Rock) 867 m

Simpson Desert

Great Artesian

Blackall

Gladstone

Tropic of Capricorn

Birdsville

Diamantina

Thomson

Basin

Buckland Tableland

Theodore

Bundaberg

Hervey Bay

Fraser Island

Charleville

Injune

Maryborough

Oodnadatta

Lake Eyre North

Sturt Desert

Quilpie

Durham Downs

Mitchell

Roma

Miles

Gympie

Maroochydore-Mooloolaba

Cooper Creek

Warrego

Toowoomba

Caloundra

SOUTH AUSTRALIA

Coober Pedy

Lake Blanche

Cunnamulla

Saint George

Ipswich

Brisbane

Lake Eyre South

Marree

Dirranbandi

Warwick

Gold Coast

Talwood

Goondiwindi

Ballina

Tarcoola

Lake Torrens

Bourke

Moree

Lismore

Lake Frome

Grafton

Penong

Lake Everard

Flinders Ranges

Darling

Walgett

Coffs Harbour

Ceduna

Lake Gairdner

Broken Hill

Wilcannia

Coonamble

Armidale

Streaky Bay

Port Augusta

NEW SOUTH WALES

Tamworth

Port Macquarie

Elliston

Kyancutta

Port Pirie

Ivanhoe

Dubbo

Forster-Tuncurry

Great Australian Bight

Whyalla

Orange

Newcastle

Port Lincoln

Waikerie

Lachlan

Bathurst

Gosford

York Peninsula

Gawler

Mildura

Sydney

Spencer Gulf

Adelaide

Balranald

Hay

Wagga Wagga

Wollongong

Gulf St Vincent

Murray Bridge

Murray

Goulburn

Keith

VICTORIA

Albury

CANBERRA

Kangaroo Island

Horsham

Wodonga

AUSTRALIAN CAPITAL TERRITORY

Naracoorte

Bendigo

Cooma

Δ Mount Kosciuszko 2,230 m

Ballarat

Mount Gambier

Hamilton

Melbourne

Portland

Geelong

Sale

Cape Howe

Cape Otway

South East Point

Bass Strait

Tasman Sea

King Island

Flinders Island

Furneaux Group

Stanley

Burnie

Devonport

Launceston

Δ Mount Ossa 1,617 m

TASMANIA

Hobart

NEW ZEALAND

New Zealand lies in the southern Pacific Ocean, 1,600 km southeast of Australia. This country consists of two large islands – North Island and South Island – and many smaller ones. In the far north of North Island are coastal inlets, which are fringed by mangrove swamps. Further south are geysers, boiling mud pools and fertile plains that rise to volcanic peaks, such as Mount Egmont and Mount Ruapehu. There are also volcanoes in South Island, where the landscape is dominated by the Southern Alps. This towering mountain range stretches more than 480 km along the western side of the island. Many rivers flow down from these uplands to the east coast.

The first inhabitants of New Zealand were the Maori, a Polynesian people. In the 19th century, Europeans began to settle here, and they now make up more than 90 per cent of the whole population. The people are mainly concentrated in the country's coastal towns and cities, especially in Auckland, on North Island.

New Zealand has rich and fertile land that provides good pasture for millions of sheep and cattle. Fruits, such as apples, peaches, oranges and kiwi fruit, are grown and exported to many countries throughout the world.

New Zealand has a strong timber industry, and in the cities, high-tech businesses that produce electronic goods and computers are expanding. Agricultural products, however, such as lamb, wool and milk, remain the country's major exports. Tourism is also an important source of income. New Zealand's environment is generally unpolluted due to its low population and lack of heavy industries.

LAND HEIGHT

4,000 m	13,124 ft
2,000 m	6,562 ft
1,000 m	3,281 ft
500 m	1,640 ft
200 m	656 ft
Sea level	

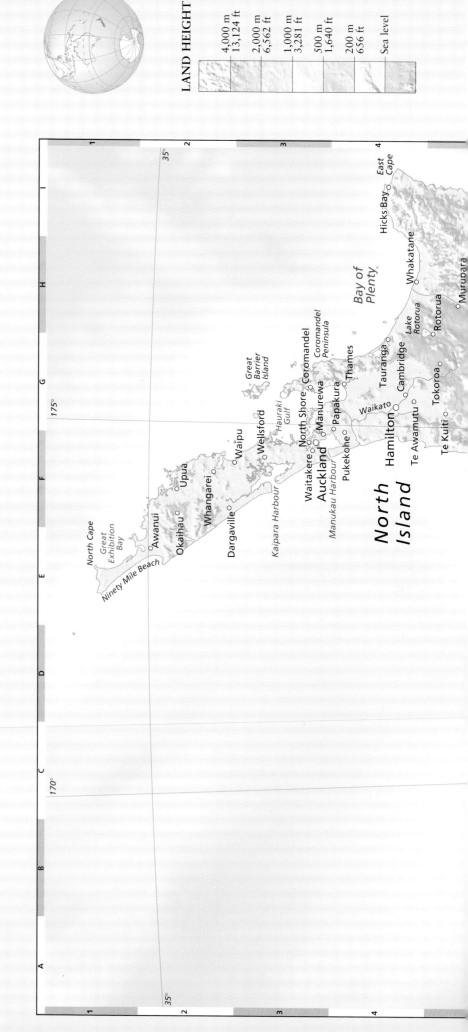

New Zealand

PACIFIC

OCEAN

200 km

100 miles

100

50

Tasman

Sea

NEW

ZEALAND

South
Island

Cook Strait

Cape Egmont
(Taranaki)
△ 2,518 m

Opunake
Hawera
Stratford
Wanganui

△Mount Ngauruhoe 2,291 m
△Mount Ruapehu 2,797 m

Waiouru
Mangaweka
Feilding
Palmerston North
Levin
Poirirua
Lower Hutt
WELLINGTON

Napier
Hastings
Waipukurau
Herbertville
Masterton

Wairoa
Hawke
Bay
Mahia
Peninsula

Cape Palliser

South Taranaki
Bight

Cape Farewell
Golden
Bay
Collingwood

D'Urville
Island
Tasman
Bay
Motueka
Nelson
Owen River

Picton
Blenheim

Cloudy
Bay
Clarence
Kaikoura

Parnassus

Rotherham
Waipara

Pegasus
Bay
Christchurch
Banks
Peninsula
Lake
Ellesmere

Karamea
Bight
Waimangaroa
Westport
Reefton

Rangiora
Sheffield
Dunsandel
Ashburton
Canterbury Plains
Lake Tekapo

Canterbury
Bight

Cape Foulwind
Greymouth
Hokitika

Southern Alps
△Mount Cook
3,754 m

Timaru

Oamaru

Palmerston
Dunedin
Otago
Peninsula
Milton
Balclutha

Fox Glacier

Omarama
Lake Hawea
Wanaka

Kurow

Cromwell
Alexandra
Roxburgh
Beaumont
Clutha

Haast

Mount Aspiring △
3,030 m
Lake
Wanaka
Lake
Wakatipu
Queenstown
Kingston

Lumsden
Gore
Mataura

Cascade
Point

Milford Sound
Lake
Te Anau
Te Anau
Mossburn
Ohai
Waiau

Tuatapere
Invercargill

Fiordland

Resolution
Island
West
Cape
South West
Cape

Foveaux Strait
Halfmoon Bay

Stewart Island

40°
45°
175°
170°
40°
45°

THE PACIFIC OCEAN

Stretching over about one-third of the Earth's surface, the Pacific is the planet's largest ocean. It extends east from Japan to the Americas, and south from the Arctic Ocean to Antarctica. The ocean's floor is generally deeper in the west than in the east, and at its deepest point, the Mariana Trench, the Pacific plunges to –11,034 m.

The many thousands of islands scattered across the Pacific Ocean were created by volcanic eruptions. Some of these islands became fringed with coral, and the islands eventually dropped back into the sea, leaving circles of coral, or atolls. A string of active volcanoes, known as the 'Ring of Fire', surrounds the ocean. The Pacific region is plagued by tropical storms, called typhoons. The area is also prone to tidal waves, which are caused by volcanic eruptions or underwater earthquakes.

The peoples of the Pacific mainly grow food for their own consumption, although a few islands grow crops, such as coconuts and oil palms, for export. Many of the small islands rely heavily on fishing for much-needed foreign income. These fish industries tend to be small and are forced to compete with the large fishing fleets of Japan and the Russian Federation. With palm-fringed beaches, spectacular coral reefs and a warm, sunny climate, the islands of the Pacific Ocean have become popular tourist destinations.

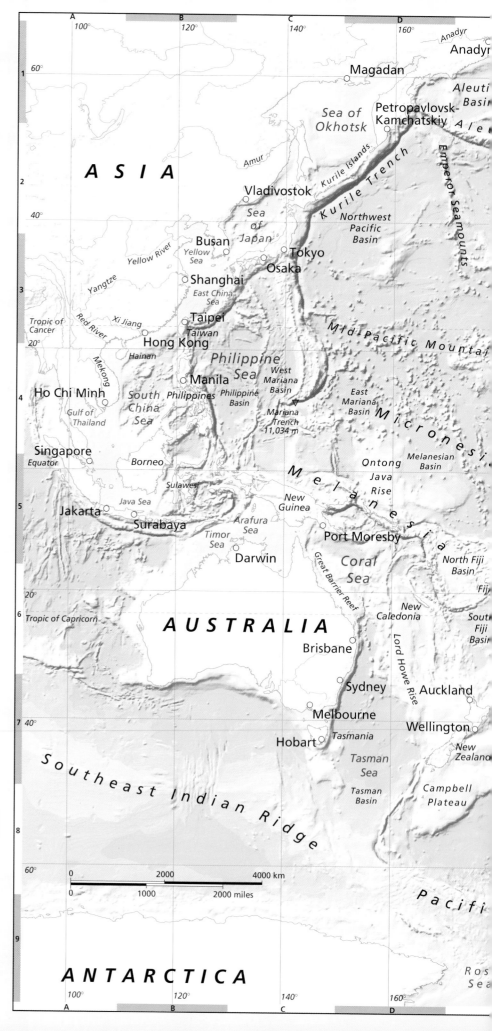

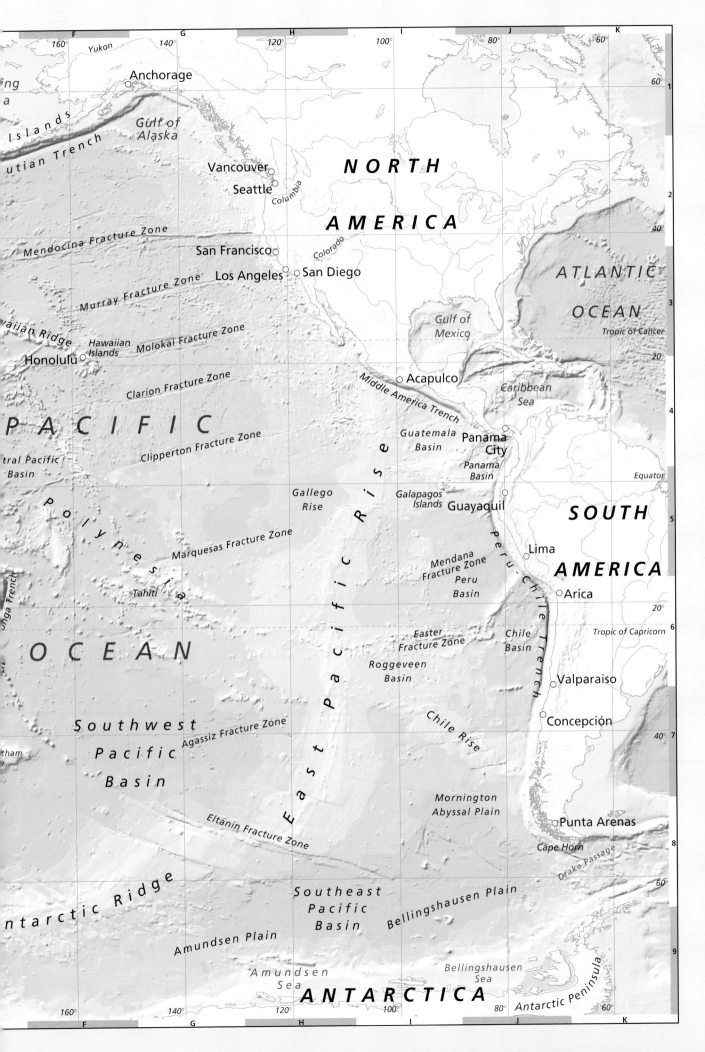

F   160°   Yukon   140°   G   120°   H   100°   I   80°   J   60°   K

ng
a

Anchorage   60°   1

Islands   Gulf of
utian Trench   Alaska

NORTH

Vancouver   2
Seattle
Columbia   AMERICA   40°

Mendocina Fracture Zone

San Francisco   *Colorado*   ATLANTIC
Los Angeles ○ San Diego   OCEAN   3
Murray Fracture Zone
aiian Ridge   Gulf of   Tropic of Cancer
Hawaiian   Molokai Fracture Zone   Mexico   20°
Honolulu ○ Islands

Clarion Fracture Zone   Acapulco   Caribbean   4
Middle America Trench   Sea

P A C I F I C   Clipperton Fracture Zone   Guatemala   Panama
tral Pacific   Basin   City
Basin   Panama   Equator
Basin

Gallego   Galapagos
Rise   Islands   Guayaquil   SOUTH   5

Polynesia   Marquesas Fracture Zone   Lima   AMERICA
Mendana
Fracture Zone
Tahiti   Peru
Basin   Arica   20°

onga Trench   O C E A N   Easter   6
Fracture Zone   Chile   Tropic of Capricorn
Roggeveen   Basin
Basin   Valparaiso

S o u t h w e s t   Agassiz Fracture Zone
tham   P a c i f i c   Chile Rise   Concepción   40°   7
e   B a s i n

Mornington
Abyssal Plain
Eltanin Fracture Zone   Punta Arenas   8
Cape Horn   *Drake Passage*
60°
ntarctic Ridge   S o u t h e a s t
P a c i f i c   Bellingshausen Plain
Basin
Amundsen Plain   9
Bellingshausen
Amundsen   *Sea*
Sea   A N T A R C T I C A   Antarctic Peninsula
160°   140°   120°   100°   80°   60°
F   G   H   I   J   K

GLOSSARY

The following glossary explains certain geographical and technical terms used in this atlas.

Acid rain
Rain and snow that has absorbed gases released by power stations and vehicle exhausts. Acid rain can cause severe environmental damage.

Arctic Circle
An imaginary line (latitude) that runs east-west around the Earth. The Arctic Circle lies at a latitude of 66° 32'N.

Biodiversity
The quantity of different plant or animal species in a given area.

Cash crops
Crops grown for sale, often for the export market, rather than for consumption in the area in which they are grown.

Climate
The average weather conditions in a given region.

Deforestation
The cutting down of large areas of forest for timber, farmland or urban development. It can lead to soil erosion, flooding and landslides.

Delta
A low-lying, fan-shaped area at a river mouth. It is formed when the river drops layers of sediment as it slows down when entering the sea.

Desertification
The gradual spread of desert conditions in arid or semi-arid regions. Desertification may be caused by changes in the climate or by human activities, such as overgrazing and deforestation.

Equator
The imaginary line (latitude) which circles the middle of the Earth. Lying at 0°, it is equidistant from the North and South Poles.

European Union (EU)
A group of European countries that have joined together to promote trade, industry and agriculture. The EU was formed in 1965, and was formerly known as the European Economic Community (EEC), then the European Community (EC).

Flood plain
The broad, flat part of a river valley, bordering the river. Flood plains are formed by sediment deposited during flooding.

Heavy industry
A type of industry that uses vast amounts of energy and raw materials to make heavy goods such as machinery and ships.

High-tech industry
A type of industry that produces high-value, technologically advanced goods, such as computers and other electronic equipment.

Ice shelf
Floating ice attached to the edge of a coast. The edge facing the sea is usually a steep cliff up to 30 m high.

Irrigation
The artificial supply of water to land. It usually involves the construction of canals and the diversion of natural watercourses.

Manufacturing
A type of industry that makes vast quantities of finished goods, from clothes to cars, which are sold to large numbers of people.

Natural resources
Fuel and raw materials, such as oil, ores and timber, which occur naturally and are found in large quantities in a given area.

Peninsula
A thin strip of land that juts out into the sea, and is surrounded by water on three of its sides. Large examples include Florida and the Koreas.

Plain
A flat, level region of land. It is often relatively low-lying.

Service industry
A type of industry that does not produce goods, but provides services such as banking and tourism.

Shanty town
An area in or around a city where people live in makeshift shacks, usually without basic facilities such as running water.

Tropics
The area between the **Tropic of Cancer** and the **Tropic of Capricorn** where the **climate** is hot.

Tropic of Cancer
An imaginary circle around the Earth, north of the Equator. It lies at a latitude of 23° 28'N.

Tropic of Capricorn
An imaginary circle around the Earth, south of the Equator. It lies at a latitude of 23° 28'S.

United Nations (UN)
An association of countries that was established in 1945. It seeks to maintain international peace and security, and promote co-operation over economic, social, cultural and humanitarian problems.

INDEX

The following index lists all the placenames and features on the regional and continental maps in this atlas. The entry names are settlements unless otherwise indicated by the use of italicized definitions. Each name is located within a region, country, sea or ocean. Physical feature names that are made up of a proper name and a description, such as Mount Etna, are positioned alphabetically by the proper name. The description appears after the proper name. For example, Mount Etna appears as 'Etna, Mount' in the index.

The first number at the end of each entry is the page number of the map on which the feature or place may be found. The letter and figure after the page number give the grid square in which the name is located.

A

Aachen Germany 59 A7
Aalen Germany 59 E10
Aalst Belgium 53 D9
Äänekoski Finland 49 H7
Aarau Switzerland 60 C4
Aare *river* Switzerland 60 B5
Aasiaat Greenland 20 A4
Aba Nigeria 71 D7, 77 I8
Abadan Iran 89 G4
Abakan Russian Federation 87 F6
Abashiri Japan 99 J2
Abbeville France 55 F1
Abbotsford British Columbia, Canada 24 B7
'Abd Al Kuri *island* Yemen 89 H9
Abéché Chad 78 E3
Abengourou Ivory Coast 77 F7
Abeokuta Nigeria 77 H7
Aberdeen Scotland, United Kingdom 50 F5
Aberdeen South Dakota, USA 29 G4
Aberdeen Washington, USA 26 B2
Aberystwyth Wales, United Kingdom 51 E10
Abha Saudi Arabia 89 F8
Abidjan Ivory Coast 71 B7, 77 F8
Abilene Texas, USA 30 D5
Abisko Sweden 48 E3
Åbo *see* Turku
Abrantes Portugal 56 B5
Absaroka Range *mountain range* Montana/Wyoming, USA 28 C3
Abu Dhabi *country capital* United Arab Emirates 84 C7, 89 I6
Abuja *country capital* Nigeria 71 D6, 77 I7
Abu Kamal Syria 89 E3
Acapulco Mexico 23 D11, 34 E6
Acarigua Venezuela 40 D1
Accra *country capital* Ghana 71 C6, 77 G8
Acklins Island *island* Bahamas 36 E3
Aconcagua *mountain* Argentina 39 C9, 43 C6

Adamawa Highlands *plateau* Cameroon/Nigeria 71 D6, 77 J7, 78 C5
Adana Turkey 84 A5, 88 D2
Adapazari Turkey 88 C1
Adare, Cape *headland* Antarctica 21 C5
Ad Dahna *desert* Saudi Arabia 89 G5
Ad Dakhla Western Sahara 72 A6
Ad Dammam Saudi Arabia 89 G5
Addis Ababa *country capital* Ethiopia 71 H6, 75 H8
Adelaide *state capital* South Australia, Australia 100 C8, 103 G7
Adelaide Island *island* Antarctica 21 A2
Adélie Land *physical region* Antarctica 21 D4
Aden Yemen 89 F9
Aden, Gulf of *gulf* SW Arabian Sea 71 I5, 75 H8, 82 C2, 84 B8
Adige *river* Italy 62 D3
Adirondack Mountains *mountain range* New York, USA 33 H4
Admiralty Islands *island group* Papua New Guinea 100 C4
Adok Sudan 75 G8
Adour *river* France 54 D7
Adra Spain 57 F8
Adrano Italy 63 G11
Adrar Algeria 73 E5
Adriatic Sea *sea* N Mediterranean Sea 46 E7, 62 F5, 68 C4
Adwa Ethiopia 75 F8
Aegean Sea *sea* NE Mediterranean Sea 47 F8, 69 G6
Aeolian Islands *island group* Italy 63 G10
Afghanistan *country* C Asia 84 C6, 91 D9
Africa *continent* 70–81
Africa, Horn of *physical region* Ethiopia/Somalia 71 I6, 75 H9
Agadez Niger 77 I5
Agadir Morocco 70 B2, 72 C4

Agadyr Kazakhstan 90 F4
Agana *island group* Guam 100 C3
Agartala India 93 H6
Agassiz Fracture Zone *undersea feature* S Pacific Ocean 107 G7
Agen France 55 E7
Aginskoye Russian Federation 87 H6
Agios Nikolaos Greece 69 H9
Agra India 92 D5
Agrigento Italy 63 E11
Agropoli Italy 63 G8
A Guardia Spain 56 B3
Aguascalientes Mexico 34 D5
Aguilas Spain 57 G7
Agulhas Basin *undersea feature* W Indian Ocean 82 A7
Agulhas, Cape *headland* South Africa 71 E13, 80 C9
Agulhas Plateau *undersea feature* W Indian Ocean 82 B6
Ahaggar *plateau* Algeria 70 D4, 73 G7
Ahmadabad India 84 D7, 93 B6
Ahmadnagar India 93 C7
Ahvaz Iran 89 G4
Ain Sefra Algeria 73 E4
Aïr, Massif de l' *mountain range* Niger 70 D4, 77 I4
Aix-en-Provence France 55 H7
Aizawl India 93 H6
Ajaccio Corsica, France 55 K9
Ajdabiya Libya 73 J5
Ajman United Arab Emirates 89 I6
Ajmer India 92 C5
Akhmim Egypt 74 C4
Akita Japan 99 H4
Akjoujt Mauritania 76 C4
Akola India 93 C7
Akranes Iceland 48 B2
Akron Ohio, USA 33 E6
Aksai Chin *disputed region* China/India 92 D2, 96 B5
Aksu China 96 B4
Aksum Ethiopia 75 E8
Aktogay Kazakhstan 90 H5
Akurdet Eritrea 75 E7
Akure Nigeria 77 H7
Akureyi Iceland 48 C2
Alabama *river* Alabama/Georgia, USA 31 H5
Alabama *state* USA 31 G5
Alagoinhas Brazil 41 J5
Al Ahmadi Kuwait 89 G5
Alai Range *mountain range* Kazakhstan/Kyrgyzstan 91 F7
Alakol, Lake *lake* Kazakhstan 90 H5
Alamagan *island* North Mariana Islands 100 C2
Al 'Amarah Iraq 89 G4
Alamogordo New Mexico, USA 30 B5
Åland *island* Finland 49 F9
Ålands hav *strait* Baltic Sea/Gulf of Bothnia 49 E9
Alaska *state* USA 26 H1
Alaska, Gulf of *gulf* Canada/USA 22 B4, 26 H2
Alaska Range *mountain range* Alaska, USA 226 H1
Alavus Finland 49 G7
Al 'Ayn United Arab Emirates 89 I6
Alba Italy 62 B4
Albacete Spain 57 G6
Al Bahah Saudi Arabia 89 E7
Alba Iulia Romania 69 F2
Albania *country* SE Europe 47 E8, 68 E5
Albany Western Australia, Australia 100 B8, 102 C7
Albany Georgia, USA 31 I5
Albany *state capital* New York, USA 33 I5
Albany Oregon, USA 26 B4
Al Bayda Libya 73 J4
Albenga Italy 62 B4
Albergaria-a-Velha Portugal 56 B4
Alberta *province* Canada 24 C6
Albert Canal *canal* Belgium 53 E8
Albert, Lake *lake* Democratic Republic of Congo/Uganda 79 G6
Albert Lea Minnesota, USA 29 I5
Albert Nile *river* Uganda 79 H6
Albi France 55 F7

Ålborg Denmark 49 B11
Albuquerque New Mexico, USA 30 B4
Albury New South Wales, Australia 103 I7
Alcácer do Sal Portugal 56 B6
Alcalá de Henares Spain 57 E4
Alcañiz Spain 57 H4
Alcántara, Embalse de *reservoir* Spain 56 C5
Alcázar de San Juan Spain 57 E5
Alchevsk Ukraine 65 I10
Alcobendas Spain 57 E4
Alcoy Spain 57 H6
Alcúdia Balearic Islands, Spain 57 J5
Aldabra Group *island group* Seychelles 71 I9, 79 K9, 81 J2, 82 C4
Aldan *river* Russian Federation 85 H3, 87 I5
Aldan Russian Federation 87 H5
Alderney *island* Channel Islands, United Kingdom 51 F13
Aleg Mauritania 76 D5
Aleksinac Serbia 69 F4
Alençon France 54 E3
Alentejo *physical region* Portugal 56 B7
Aleppo Syria 88 D3
Aléria Corsica, France 55 K9
Alès France 55 G7
Alessandria Italy 62 B4
Ålesund Norway 49 B7
Aleutian Islands *island group* Alaska, USA 22 A2, 26 F2, 106 E2
Aleutian Trench *undersea feature* N Pacific Ocean 107 E2
Alexander Archipelago *island group* Alaska, USA 22 C5
Alexandra New Zealand 105 C11
Alexandria Egypt 70 G3, 74 C3
Alexandria Romania 69 G3
Alexandria Louisiana, USA 31 F5
Alexandria Virginia, USA 33 G7
Alexandroupoli Greece 69 H5
Algarve *cultural region* Portugal 56 B7
Algeciras Spain 56 D9
Algeria *country* N Africa 70 C3, 73 E5
Alghero Italy 63 B8
Algiers *country capital* Algeria 70 D2, 73 F3
Al Hasakah Syria 89 E3
Al Hillah Iraq 89 F4
Al Hufuf Saudi Arabia 89 G6
Alicante Spain 46 B8, 57 H6
Alice Springs Northern Territory, Australia 100 B7, 103 F4
Aligarh India 92 D5
Al Jawf Saudi Arabia 88 E4
Al Jazirah *physical region* Iraq/Syria 89 E3
Al Kharj Saudi Arabia 89 G6
Al Khasab Oman 89 I5
Al Khufrah Libya 73 K6
Alkmaar Netherlands 52 E4
Al Kut Iraq 89 F4
Al Ladhiqiyah Syria 88 D3
Allahabad India 89 F4
Allegheny Mountains *mountain range* NE USA 33 F8
Allentown Pennsylvania, USA 33 H6
Alleppey India 93 C11
Aller *river* Germany 58 E5
Allgäu *mountain range* Germany 59 E12
Al Mahrah *mountain range* Yemen 89 H8
Al Majma'ah Saudi Arabia 89 F6
Al Marj Libya 73 J4
Almaty Kazakhstan 84 D5, 91 G6
Almelo Netherlands 52 H4
Almendra, Embalse de *reservoir* Spain 56 C4
Almere Netherlands 52 F5
Almeria Spain 57 F8
Al Mukalla Yemen 89 G9
Alofi Niue 101 G6
Alor Indonesia 95 H9
Alor Setar Malaysia 94 B6
Alphen aan de Rijn Netherlands 53 E5
Alps *mountain range* C Europe 46 D6, 55 I6, 60 D6, 62 B3
Al Qamishli Syria 89 E2

Al Qaryat Libya 73 H5
Alqueva Reservoir Portugal 56 B6
Al Qunfidhah Saudi Arabia 89 E7
Al Qurayyat Saudi Arabia 88 D4
Al Qurnah Iraq 89 G4
Alta Norway 48 G2
Altai Mountains *mountain range* Asia/Europe 84 E4, 87 E7, 90 H3, 96 D2
Altamura Italy 63 H8
Altar Desert *desert* Mexico/USA 34 A1
Altay China 96 D2
Altay Mongolia 97 E3
Altiplano *physical region* W South America 39 C6, 40 D6
Altötting Germany 59 G11
Alturas California, USA 27 C6
Altun Shan *mountain range* China 96 C4
Al Wajh Saudi Arabia 88 D5
Al Wari'ah Saudi Arabia 89 G5
Alzira Spain 57 H6
Alytus Lithuania 65 B6
Amadeus, Lake *seasonal lake* Northern Territory, Australia 103 E4
Amadjuak Lake *lake* Nunavut, Canada 25 G4
Amami-o-shima *island* Japan 99 J8
Amarapura Myanmar 94 B2
Amarillo Texas, USA 30 C4
Amazon *river* N South America 38 F4, 40 D4
Amazon Basin *physical region* N South America 38 C3, 40 D3
Amazon, Mouths of the *delta* Brazil 38 G3, 41 H3
Ambato Ecuador 40 B3
Ambatosoratra Madagascar 81 K5
Amberg Germany 59 F9
Ambon Indonesia 95 I8
Ambovombe Madagascar 81 J7
Amdo China 96 D6
Ameland *island* Netherlands 52 F1
American Samoa *US dependent territory* C Pacific Ocean 101 G5
Amersfoort Netherlands 53 F5
Amery Ice Shelf *ice shelf* Antarctica 21 E2
Ames Iowa, USA 29 I5
Amiens France 55 F2
Amman *country capital* Jordan 84 A6, 88 D4
Amol Iran 89 H3
Amorgos *island* Greece 69 H8
Amposta Spain 57 H4
Amravati India 93 D7
Amritsar India 92 C3
Amstelveen Netherlands 52 E5
Amsterdam *country capital* Netherlands 46 D5, 52 E5
Amsterdam Island *island* C Indian Ocean 83 E6
Amstetten Austria 61 I3
Am Timan Chad 78 E4
Amu Darya *river* C Asia 84 C5, 91 D7
Amundsen Gulf *gulf* SE Beaufort Sea 24 D3
Amundsen Plain *undersea feature* S Pacific Ocean 107 G9
Amur *river* China/Russian Federation 85 G4, 87 J6, 97 I1
Anaconda Montana, USA 28 B3
Anadyr Russian Federation 87 J2
Anaheim California, USA 27 D11
Anantapur India 93 C9
Anápolis Brazil 41 H6
Anar Darreh Afghanistan 91 D9
Anatolia *plateau* Turkey 84 A5, 88 C2
Anchorage Alaska, USA 22 C4, 26 H2
Anchuma, Nevado de *mountain* Bolivia 40 D6
Ancona Italy 62 F5
Åndalsnes Norway 49 B7
Andalucia *cultural region* Spain 56 D7
Andaman Islands *island group* India 83 G2, 84 E7, 93 H9
Andaman Sea *sea* NE Indian Ocean 83 G2, 95 E8, 94 A5
Andenne Belgium 53 E10
Andermatt Switzerland 60 C5

Andernach Germany 59 B8
Anderson Indiana, USA 32 C7
Anderson South Carolina, USA 31 I4
Andes *mountain range* W South America 39 C10, 40 C5, 42 C5
Andijon Uzbekistan 91 F7
Andong South Korea 98 C6
Andorra *country* SW Europe 46 C7, 55 F8, 57 I2
Andorra la Vella *country capital* Andorra 46 B7, 57 I2
Andøya *island* Norway 48 E3
Andratx Balearic Islands, Spain 57 J5
Andria Italy 63 H7
Andros Greece 69 G7
Andros Island *island* Bahamas 36 C2
Aneto *mountain* Spain 57 H2
Angara *river* Russian Federation 85 E3, 87 F5
Angarsk Russian Federation 87 G6
Ånge Sweden 49 D7
Ángel de la Guarda, Isla *island* Mexico 34 A2
Angeles Philippines 95 G4
Angel Falls *waterfall* Venezuela 41 E2
Ångermanälven *river* Sweden 49 E6
Angers France 54 D4
Anglesey *island* Wales, United Kingdom 51 E9
Angoche Mozambique 81 H7
Angola *country* SW Africa 71 E9, 80 B3
Angola Basin *undersea feature* E Atlantic Ocean 45 G8
Angostura, Presa de la *reservoir* Mexico 35 H6
Angoulême France 54 E6
Angren Uzbekistan 91 F7
Anguilla *UK dependent territory* E West Indies 37 J5
Anjouan *island* Comoros 81 J3
Anju North Korea 98 B4
Ankara *country capital* Turkey 84 A5, 88 D2
Anklam Germany 58 H3
Annaba Algeria 73 G3
Annamitique, Chaine *mountain range* Laos/Vietnam 94 D3
Annapolis *state capital* Maryland, USA 33 H7
Ann Arbor Michigan, USA 32 D5
An Nasiriyah Iraq 89 F4
Annecy France 55 I5
Annemasse France 55 I5
Anniston Alabama, USA 31 H4
Anqing China 97 I6
Ansbach Germany 59 E10
Anshan China 97 J4
Anshun China 97 G7
Ansongo Mali 77 G5
Antalaha Madagascar 81 K4
Antalya Turkey 88 C2
Antananarivo *country capital* Madagascar 71 I10, 81 J5
Antarctica *continent* 21 C3
Antarctic Peninsula *peninsula* Antarctica 21 A2, 45 C13
Antibes France 55 I7
Antigua *island* Antigua & Barbuda 37 J5
Antigua & Barbuda *country* E West Indies 23 I12, 37 J5
Antipodes Islands *island group* New Zealand 101 F9
Antofagasta Chile 42 C3
Antsirabe Madagascar 81 J5
Antsiranana Madagascar 81 K3
Antwerp Belgium 53 D8
Anuradhapura Sri Lanka 93 D11
Anyang China 97 H5
Anyang South Korea 98 B5
Anzio Italy 63 E7
Aomori Japan 99 H4
Aosta Italy 62 A3
Aoulef Algeria 73 E6
Aparri Philippines 95 G3
Apeldoorn Netherlands 52 G5
Apennines *mountain range* Italy 46 D7, 62 C4

Apia *country capital* Samoa 101 G6

Apo, Mount *volcano* Philippines 95 H5

Appalachian Mountains *mountain range* E USA 23 F9, 31 H4, 32 E9

Appennino Lucano *mountain range* Italy 63 G8

Appleton Wisconsin, USA 32 C4

Apure *river* Venezuela 38 C2, 40 D2

Aqaba Jordan 88 D5

Aqköl Kazakhstan 90 F3

Aqsay Kazakhstan 90 B3

Aqso Kazakhstan 90 F3

Aqtao Kazakhstan 91 A6

Aqtobe Kazakhstan 90 C4

Aquitaine *cultural region* France 54 D7

Arabian Basin *undersea feature* N Indian Ocean 82 D2

Arabian Peninsula *peninsula* SW Asia 84 B7, 89 E5

Arabian Sea *sea* NW Indian Ocean 82 D2, 84 C7, 91 D13, 93 A8

Aracaju Brazil 41 J5

Arad Romania 69 F2

Arafura Sea *sea* W Pacific Ocean 85 H9, 95 I9, 100 B5, 103 F1

Aragón *cultural region* Spain 57 F3

Araguaia *river* Brazil 39 F6, 41 H5

Arak Iran 89 G3

Arakan Yoma *mountain range* Myanmar 94 A2

Aral Kazakhstan 90 D5

Aral Sea *inland sea* Kazakhstan/Uzbekistan 84 C5, 91 D5

Aranda de Duero Spain 57 E3

Aranjuez Spain 57 E5

Arao Japan 98 D3

Araouane Mali 77 F4

Arapiraca Brazil 41 J5

'Ar'ar Saudi Arabia 89 E4

Aravali Range *mountain range* India 93 B6

Arba Minch Ethiopia 75 E10

Arbil Iran 89 F3

Arbon Switzerland 60 D4

Arcachon France 54 D6

Archangel Russian Federation 47 H2, 86 C3

Arctic Ocean *ocean* 20 B2

Ardabil Iran 89 G2

Ardennes *physical region* Belgium/France 53 E11

Arendal Norway 49 B10

Arequipa Peru 39 C6, 40 D6

Arezzo Italy 62 D5

Argenteuil France 55 F3

Argentina *country* S South America 39 C10, 43 D7

Argentine Basin *undersea feature* C Atlantic Ocean 45 D10

Argostoli Greece 69 E7

Argun *river* China/Russian Federation 97 I2

Argyle, Lake *salt lake* Western Australia, Australia 102 E2

Århus Denmark 49 B12

Arica Chile 42 C1

Arima Trinidad & Tobago 37 J8

Arizona *state* USA 27 G10

Arjeplog Sweden 48 E5

Arkansas *river* C USA 23 E9, 29 G3, 31 F4

Arkansas *state* USA 31 E4

Arkansas City Kansas, USA 29 H8

Arles France 55 H7

Arlington Texas, USA 30 E5

Arlington Virginia, USA 33 G7

Arlit Niger 77 I4

Arlon Belgium 53 G12

Armant Egypt 74 C4

Armenia *country* SW Asia 84 B5, 89 F2

Armenia Colombia 40 C2

Armidale New South Wales, Australia 103 J6

Arnhem Netherlands 53 G6

Arnhem, Cape *headland* Northern Territory, Australia 103 G1

Arnhem Land *physical region* Northern Territory, Australia 103 F2

Arno *river* Italy 62 D5

Arnsberg Germany 59 C6

Arnstadt Germany 59 F7

Arqalyq Kazakhstan 90 E4

Ar Ramadi Iraq 89 F3

Arran *island* Scotland, United Kingdom 51 D6

Ar Raqqah Syria 88 E3

Arras France 55 F1

Ar Rub' al Khali *desert* SW Asia 89 G7

Ar Rustaq Oman 89 I6

Arta Greece 69 E7

Artesia New Mexico, USA 30 B5

Artigas Uruguay 42 G5

Artsyz Ukraine 65 D12

Artux China 96 B4

Artyk Turkmenistan 91 C8

Aru Islands *island* Indonesia 95 J8

Arusha Tanzania 71 H8, 79 I7

Aruwimi *river* Democratic Republic of Congo 79 F6

Arvayheer Mongolia 97 F3

Arvidsjaur Sweden 49 F5

Asadabad Afghanistan 91 F9

Asahi-dake *mountain* Japan 99 I2

Asahikawa Japan 99 I2

Asamankese Ghana 77 G8

Asansol India 93 F6

Ascension Island *island* C Atlantic Ocean 45 F8, 71 A9

Ascoli Piceno Italy 63 F6

Aseb Eritrea 75 G8

Asela Ethiopia 75 F9

Ashburton *river* Western Australia, Australia 102 B4

Ashburton New Zealand 105 D10

Asheville North Carolina, USA 31 I3

Ashgabat *country capital* Turkmenistan 84 C5, 91 C8

Ashland Oregon, USA 27 B5

Asia *continent* 84–99

Asir *mountain range* Saudi Arabia 89 F7

Askersund Sweden 49 D10

Asmar Afghanistan 91 F9

Asmara *country capital* Eritrea 70 H5, 75 E7

Aspen Colorado, USA 28 D7

Aspiring, Mount *mountain* New Zealand 105 B10

Assamakka Niger 77 I4

Assen Netherlands 52 H3

Assisi Italy 63 E6

As Sulaymaniyah Iraq 89 F3

As Sulayyil Saudi Arabia 89 F7

Astana *country capital* Kazakhstan 84 D4, 90 F4

Asti Italy 62 B4

Astoria Oregon, USA 26 B3

Astrakhan Russian Federation 47 J6, 86 B4

Asunción *country capital* Paraguay 39 E8, 42 G3

Aswân Egypt 70 G4, 74 D5

Asyût Egypt 70 G3, 74 C4

Atacama Desert *desert* Chile 39 C7, 42 C4

Atakpamé Togo 77 G7

Atar Mauritania 76 D4

Atasu Kazakhstan 90 F5

Atbara *river* NE Africa 70 G5, 75 D7

Atbara Sudan 75 D7

Atbasar Kazakhstan 90 E3

Athabasca *river* Alberta, Canada 24 C6

Athabasca, Lake *lake* Alberta/Saskatchewan, Canada 23 E6, 24 D6

Athens *country capital* Greece 47 F8, 69 G7

Athens Georgia, USA 31 I4

Athlone Republic of Ireland 51 C9

Athus Belgium 53 G13

Atlanta Georgia, USA 23 F9, 31 I4

Atlantic City New Jersey, USA 33 H7

Atlantic-Indian Basin *undersea feature* Atlantic Ocean/Indian Ocean 45 G11, 82 B8

Atlantic-Indian Ridge *undersea feature* Atlantic Ocean/Indian Ocean 45 F12, 82 A8

Atlantic Ocean *ocean* 31 J5, 44–45, 50 A2

Atlas Mountains *mountain range* NW Africa 70 C2, 72 C5

At Ta'if Saudi Arabia 88 E7

Attersee Austria 61 H3

Atyrau Kazakhstan 90 B5

Auch France 54 E7

Auckland New Zealand 101 F8, 104 F3

Auckland Islands *island group* New Zealand 101 E9

Augsburg Germany 59 E11

Augusta Western Australia, Australia 102 B7

Augusta Georgia, USA 31 I4

Augusta *state capital* Maine, USA 33 J4

Augustow Poland 66 H3

Aurangabad India 93 C7

Aurora Colorado, USA 28 E7

Austin *state capital* Texas, USA 23 E10, 30 D6

Austin Minnesota, USA 29 I4

Australasia *continent* 100–105

Australes, Îles *island group* French Polynesia 101 I7

Australia *country* SW Pacific Ocean 100 B7, 102–103

Australian Capital Territory *state* Australia 103 I7

Austria *country* C Europe 46 E6, 61 H4

Austvågøy *island* Norway 48 D3

Auxerre France 55 G4

Avarua Cook Islands 101 H6

Aveiro Portugal 56 B4

Avellino Italy 63 F8

Averoya *island* Norway 48 B7

Avesta Sweden 49 E9

Avezzano Italy 63 E7

Aviemore Scotland, United Kingdom 50 E4

Avignon France 55 H7

Ávila Spain 56 D4

Avilés Spain 56 D1

Avola Italy 63 G12

Avon *river* England, United Kingdom 51 F11

Avranches France 54 D3

Awanui New Zealand 104 E2

Awasa Ethiopia 75 F10

Awbari Libya 73 H6

Aweil Sudan 75 B9

Axel Heiburg Island *island* Nunavut, Canada 25 F1

Axios *river* Greece/Macedonia 69 F5

Ayacucho Peru 40 C6

Ayakoz Kazakhstan 90 H4

Aydin Turkey 88 C2

Ayers Rock *see* Uluru

Aynĭ Tajikistan 91 E7

'Ayoûn El 'Atroûs Mauritania 76 E5

Ayr Scotland, United Kingdom 51 E7

Azahar, Costa del *coastal region* Spain 57 H5

Azaouâd *desert* Mali 77 G4

Azerbaijan *country* SE Asia 84 B5, 89 G2

Azores *island group* SW Europe 44 E5

Azov, Sea of *sea* NE Black Sea 47 H6, 65 H12

Azuaga Spain 56 D7

Azul Argentina 43 F7

Azur, Côte d' *coastal region* France 55 I8

Az Zarqa Jordan 88 D4

Az Zawiyah Libya 73 H4

B

Baarle-Hertog Belgium 53 E7

Babeldaob *island* Palau 100 B4

Bab el Mandeb *strait* Gulf of Aden/Red Sea 89 F9

Babol Iran 89 H3

Babruysk Belarus 65 E7

Babuyan Islands *island group* Philippines 95 G3

Bacan *island* Indonesia 95 H7

Bacau Romania 69 H2

Bacolod City Philippines 95 G5

Badajoz Spain 56 C6

Badalona Spain 57 I3

Bad Doberan Germany 58 F3

Baden Austria 61 J3

Baden Switzerland 60 C4

Baden-Baden Germany 59 C10

Bad Hersfeld Germany 59 D7

Bad Homburg vor der Höhe Germany 59 C8

Bad Ischl Austria 61 H4

Bad Kissingen Germany 59 E8

Badlands *physical region* North Dakota, USA 29 E3

Bad Mergentheim Germany 59 D9

Bad Waldsee Germany 59 D12

Bad Windsheim Germany 59 E9

Bafatá Guinea-Bissau 76 C6

Baffin Bay *bay* Canada/Greenland 20 A4, 22 G4, 25 G3, 44 C2

Baffin Island *island* Nunavut, Canada 22 G4, 25 F3

Bafia Cameroon 78 B5

Bafoussam Cameroon 78 B5

Bagé Brazil 41 G9

Baghdad *country capital* Iraq 84 B6, 89 F4

Bagheria Italy 63 E11

Baghlan Afghanistan 91 E8

Baguio Philippines 95 G3

Bahamas *country* N West Indies 23 G11, 36 D2

Bahawalpur Pakistan 91 F10

Bahir Dar Ethiopia 75 E8

Bahrain *country* SW Asia 84 B6, 89 H5

Bahr el Jebel *river* Sudan 75 C10

Baia Mare Romania 69 F1

Baicheng China 97 I3

Baikal, Lake *lake* Russian Federation 85 F4, 87 G6

Bairiki *country capital* Kiribati 101 F4

Baishan China 97 J3

Baja Hungary 67 E11

Baker Oregon, USA 26 D4

Baker Island *US dependent territory* C Pacific Ocean 101 G4

Bakersfield California, USA 27 C10

Bakhtaran Iran 89 G3

Baku *country capital* Azerbaijan 84 B5, 89 G2

Balabac Strait *strait* Malaysia/Philippines 95 F5

Balassagyarmat Hungary 67 F9

Balaton *lake* Hungary 67 D11

Balbina, Represa de *reservoir* Brazil 41 F3

Balclutha New Zealand 105 C12

Balearic Islands *island group* Spain 46 B8, 57 I5

Baleshwar India 93 G7

Bali *island* Indonesia 94 D8

Balikesir Turkey 88 C1

Balikpapan Indonesia 95 F7

Balingen Germany 59 C11

Balkan Mountains *mountain range* Bulgaria/Serbia & Montenegro 69 F4

Balkh Afghanistan 91 E8

Balkhash Kazakhstan 90 G5

Balkhash, Lake *lake* Kazakhstan 84 D5, 90 G5

Ballarat Victoria, Australia 103 H8

Ballary (Bellary) India 93 C9

Ballina New South Wales, Australia 103 J6

Balranald New South Wales, Australia 103 H7

Balsas *river* Mexico 34 D6

Balti Moldova 65 D11

Baltic Sea *sea* NE Atlantic Ocean 47 E4, 58 H2, 64 A3, 66 D1

Baltimore Maryland, USA 23 G9, 33 G7

Balvi Latvia 64 D3

Bam Iran 89 I4

Bamako *country capital* Mali 71 B5, 76 E6

Bambari Central African Republic 78 E5

Bamberg Germany 59 E9

Bamenda Cameroon 78 B5

Bamian Afghanistan 91 E9

Banbury England, United Kingdom 51 G10

Bandaaceh Indonesia 94 A6

Bandar-e 'Abbas Iran 89 I5

Bandar-e Bushehr Iran 89 H5

Bandar-e Lengeh Iran 89 I5

Bandar Seri Begawan *country capital* Brunei 85 F8, 94 D6

Banda Sea *sea* Indonesia 95 H8

Bandundu Democratic Republic of Congo 78 D7

Bandung Indonesia 85 F9, 94 D9

Banff Alberta, Canada 24 C7

Banfora Burkina 77 F6

Bangassou Central African Republic 79 E5

Bangka *island* Indonesia 94 D7

Bangkok *country capital* Thailand 85 F7, 94 C4

Bangladesh *country* S Asia 84 E6, 93 G6

Bangor Maine, USA 33 J4

Bangor Northern Ireland, United Kingdom 51 D7

Bangor Wales, United Kingdom 51 E9

Bangui *country capital* Central African Republic 71 E7, 78 D5

Bangweulu, Lake Zambia 81 F3

Bani *river* Ivory Coast/Mali 77 F6

Banja Luka Bosnia & Herzegovina 68 D3

Banjarmasin Indonesia 95 F8

Banjul *country capital* Gambia 70 A5, 76 C5

Banks Island *island* Northwest Territories, Canada 22 E4, 24 B3

Banks Peninsula *peninsula* New Zealand 105 E10

Bannu Pakistan 91 F9

Banska Bystrica Slovakia 67 F9

Bantry Bay *bay* Republic of Ireland 51 A11

Baoding China 97 H4

Baoji China 97 G6

Baoro Central African Republic 78 D5

Baotou China 97 G4

Ba'qubah Iraq 89 F3

Baraki Barak Afghanistan 91 F9

Baranavichy Belarus 65 C7

Barbados *country* SE West Indies 23 I12, 37 K7

Barbuda *island* Antigua & Barbuda 37 J5

Barcelona Spain 46 C7, 57 I3

Barcelona Venezuela 40 E1

Bardejov Slovakia 67 G8

Bareilly India 92 D4

Barents Sea *sea* Arctic Ocean 20 D4, 44 I2

Bari Italy 46 E8, 63 H7

Barinas Venezuela 40 D2

Baris Egypt 74 C5

Barisal Bangladesh 93 G6

Barito *river* Indonesia 95 F8

Barkly Tableland *plateau* Northern Territory/Queensland, Australia 100 B6, 103 F2

Barlad Romania 69 H2

Barlavento, Ilhas de *island group* Cape Verde 76 A4

Bar-le-Duc France 55 H3

Barlee, Lake *seasonal lake* Western Australia, Australia 102 C6

Barletta Italy 63 H7

Barlinek Poland 66 C4

Barnaul Russian Federation 84 D4, 87 E6

Barnstaple England, United Kingdom 51 E11

Barquisimeto Venezuela 39 C2, 40 D1

Barra *island* Scotland, United Kingdom 50 C5

Barranquilla Colombia 38 B1, 40 C1

Barreiro Portugal 56 A6

Barrow *river* Republic of Ireland 51 C9

Barrow Alaska, USA 26 H1

Barry Wales, United Kingdom 51 F11

Bartoszyce Poland 66 G3

Baruun-Urt Mongolia 97 H3

Barysaw Belarus 65 D6

Basel Switzerland 60 B4

Basento *river* Italy 63 H8

Basilan *island* Philippines 95 G6

Basildon England, United Kingdom 51 H11

Basingstoke England, United Kingdom 51 G11

Basra Iraq 89 G4

Bassein Myanmar 94 A3

Basse Terre *island* Antigua & Barbuda 37 J6

Basse Terre Antigua & Barbuda 37 J6

Basseterre St Kitts & Nevis 37 J6

Bassikounou Mauritania 77 E5

Bass Strait *strait* Tasmania/Victoria, Australia 103 H8

Bassum Germany 58 D4

Bastia Corsica, France 55 K8

Bastogne Belgium 53 G11

Bata Equatorial Guinea 78 B6

Batangas Philippines 95 G4

Batan Islands *island group* Philippines 95 G2

Bath England, United Kingdom 51 F11

Bathurst New South Wales, Australia 103 I7

Bathurst Island *island* Northern Territory, Australia 103 E1

Batman Turkey 89 E2

Batna Algeria 73 G3

Baton Rouge *state capital* Louisiana, USA 23 E10, 31 F6

Battambang Cambodia 94 C4

Batticaloa Sri Lanka 93 E11

Battipaglia Italy 63 G8

Batumi Georgia 89 F1

Bauchi Nigeria 77 J6

Bavaria *cultural region* Germany 59 E11

Bavarian Alps *mountain range* Austria/Germany 60 B6, 61 F4

Bayamo Cuba 36 D4

Bayamón Puerto Rico 37 H5

Bayanhongor Mongolia 97 F3

Bay City Michigan, USA 32 D5

Baydhabo Sudan 75 G11

Bayonne France 54 D8

Bayramaly Turkmenistan 91 D8

Bayreuth Germany 59 F9

Baza Spain 57 F7

Beachy Head *headland* England, United Kingdom 51 H12

Bear *river* C USA 26 G5

Beaufort Sea *sea* Arctic Ocean 20 B2, 24 C2

Beaufort West South Africa 80 D8

Beaumont New Zealand 105 C12

Beaumont Texas, USA 31 F6

Beauvais France 55 F2

Beawar India 92 C5

Béchar Algeria 72 E4

Beckley West Virginia, USA 33 E8

Beckum Germany 59 C6

Bedford Indiana, USA 32 C7

Be'ér Sheva Israel 88 D4

Beihai China 97 H9

Beijing *country capital* China 85 G5, 97 I4

Beipiao China 97 I3

Beira Mozambique 71 G10, 81 G5

Beirut *country capital* Lebanon 84 A6, 88 D3

Beja Portugal 56 B7

Bejaïa Algeria 73 G3

Bekescsaba Hungary 67 G11

Bela Pakistan 91 E11

Belarus *country* E Europe 47 F5, 65 D7

Belchatow Poland 67 F6

Belcher Islands *island group* Québec, Canada 23 F6, 25 G6

Beledweyne Sudan 75 G10

Belém Brazil 38 G4, 41 H3

Belfast Northern Ireland, United Kingdom 46 B4, 51 D8

Belfort France 55 I4

Belgaum India 93 C8

Belgium *country* NW Europe 46 B5, 53 D9

Belgorod Russian Federation 86 A4

Belgrade *country capital* Serbia 47 F7, 69 E3

Belitung *island* Indonesia 94 D8

Belize *country* Central America 23 E12, 35 H6

Belize City Belize 35 H6

Belle Île *island* France 54 C4
Bellevue Washington, USA 26 C2
Bellingham Washington, USA 26 C1
Bellingshausen Plain *undersea feature* SE Pacific Ocean 107 I9
Bellingshausen Sea *sea* N Atlantic Ocean 21 A3
Bellinzona Switzerland 60 D6
Belluno Italy 62 E2
Belmopan *country capital* Belize 23 E12, 35 H6
Belogorsk Russian Federation 87 I6
Belo Horizonte Brazil 39 H7, 41 I7
Belukha, Gora *mountain* Russian Federation 87 E7
Bemidji Minnesota, USA 29 H2
Benavente Spain 56 D3
Bend Oregon, USA 26 C4
Bendigo Victoria, Australia 103 H8
Benesov Czech Republic 67 B7
Benevento Italy 63 F8
Bengal, Bay of *bay* N Indian Ocean 83 F2, 84 E7, 93 G8, 96 C9
Bengaluru (Bangalore) India 84 D7, 93 D9
Bengbu China 97 I6
Benghazi Libya 70 E2, 73 J4
Bengkulu Indonesia 94 C8
Benguela Angola 71 E9, 80 A3
Beni *river* Bolivia 39 C6, 40 D6
Benidorm Spain 57 H6
Benin *country* W Africa 71 C6, 77 G7
Benin, Bight of *bay* E Atlantic Ocean 76 H8
Benin City Nigeria 71 D6, 77 H8
Beni Suef Egypt 74 C4
Ben Macdhui *mountain* Scotland, United Kingdom 50 E5
Ben Nevis *mountain* Scotland, United Kingdom 50 E5
Benoni South Africa 81 E7
Bensheim Germany 59 C9
Bentiu Sudan 75 C9
Benue *river* Cameroon/Nigeria 71 D6, 77 J7
Benxi China 97 J4
Beppu Japan 98 D8
Berat Albania 68 E6
Berbera Somalia 75 G9
Berbérati Central African Republic 78 D5
Berchtesgaden *mountain* Germany 59 G12
Berdyansk Ukraine 65 H11
Berdychiv Ukraine 65 D9
Bereeda Somalia 75 I8
Berezina *river* Belarus 65 D6
Berezniki Russian Federation 86 C4
Bergamo Italy 62 C3
Bergen Norway 46 D3, 49 A8
Bergen op Zoom Netherlands 53 D7
Bergerac France 54 E6
Bergisch Gladbach Germany 59 B7
Bering Sea *sea* N Pacific Ocean 85 F3
Bering Strait *strait* Bering Sea/Chukchi Sea 22 C3, 26 G1
Berkakit Russian Federation 87 I5
Berkeley California, USA 27 B8
Berkner Island *island* Antarctica 21 B2
Berlin *country capital* Germany 46 E5, 58 H5
Berlin New Hampshire, USA 33 I4
Bermuda *island* NW Atlantic Ocean 45 C5
Bermuda *UK dependent territory* NW Atlantic Ocean 23 H10
Bern *country capital* Switzerland 46 D6, 60 B5
Bernese Alps *mountain range* Switzerland 60 B6
Bernina, Piz *mountain* Italy/Switzerland 60 D6
Beroun Czech Republic 67 B7
Bertoua Cameroon 78 C5
Berwick-upon-Tweed England, United Kingdom 51 F6
Besançon France 55 H4

Betafo Madagascar 81 J5
Betanzos Spain 56 B2
Bethlehem South Africa 81 E7
Béthune France 55 F1
Béticos, Sistemas *mountain range* Spain 56 D8
Beveren Belgium 53 D8
Beyneu Kazakhstan 91 B5
Béziers France 55 G8
Bhadravati India 93 C9
Bhagalpur India 93 F5
Bhamo Myanmar 94 B2
Bharatpur India 92 D5
Bharuch India 93 B6
Bhatinda India 92 C4
Bhatpara India 93 G6
Bhavnagar India 93 B6
Bhilai India 93 E7
Bhilwara India 93 C5
Bhima *river* India 93 C7
Bhiwandi India 93 B7
Bhopal India 93 D6
Bhubaneshwar India 93 F7
Bhusawal India 93 C7
Bhutan *country* S Asia 84 E6, 92 G4
Biak *island* Indonesia 95 J7
Biala Podlaska Poland 66 I5
Bialystok Poland 66 H4
Biarritz France 54 D8
Biberach Germany 59 D11
Bida Nigeria 77 H7
Biddeford Maine, USA 33 J5
Biel Switzerland 60 B4
Bielefeld Germany 59 C6
Biella Italy 62 B3
Bielsko-Biala Poland 67 F7
Bielsk Podlaski Poland 66 I4
Bien Hoa Vietnam 94 D5
Bié Plateau *plateau* Angola 71 E9, 80 B3
Bighorn *river* Montana/Wyoming, USA 28 B5
Bighorn Basin *physical region* Wyoming, USA 28 C4
Bighorn Mountains *mountain range* Wyoming, USA 28 D4
Big Spring Texas, USA 30 C5
Big Springs Nebraska, USA 29 F6
Bihac Bosnia & Herzegovina 68 C3
Bikaner India 92 B4
Bikin Russian Federation 87 J6
Bikini Atoll *island* Marshall Islands 100 E3
Bilaspur India 93 E6
Bila Tserkva Ukraine 65 E9
Bilbao Spain 46 B6, 57 F2
Bilhorod-Dnistrovskyy Ukraine 65 E11
Billings Montana, USA 28 D3
Billund Denmark 49 B12
Biloxi Mississippi, USA 31 G6
Biltine Chad 78 E3
Bindura Zimbabwe 81 F4
Binghamton New York, USA 33 H5
Binzhou China 97 I5
Bioko *island* Equatorial Guinea 78 B5
Birak Libya 73 H6
Birao Central African Republic 79 E4
Biratnagar Nepal 92 G5
Birch Mountains *mountain range* Alberta, Canada 24 C6
Birdsville Queensland, Australia 103 G5
Birjand Iran 89 I3
Birmingham England, United Kingdom 46 C5, 51 G4
Birmingham Alabama, USA 31 H4
Bir Mogreïn Mauritania 76 D2
Birzai Lithuania 64 C5
Bischofshofen Austria 61 H4
Bishkek *country capital* Kyrgyzstan 84 D3, 91 G6
Biskra Algeria 73 G4
Biskupiec Poland 66 G3
Bismarck *state capital* North Dakota, USA 29 F3
Bismarck Sea *sea* W Pacific Ocean 100 C5
Bissau *country capital* Guinea Bissau 71 A5, 76 C6
Bistrita Romania 69 G1
Bitlis Turkey 89 F2
Bitola Macedonia 69 F5
Bitonto Italy 63 H8

Bitterfontein South Africa 80 C8
Bitterroot Range *mountain range* Idaho/Montana, USA 26 E2, 28 A2
Biwa-ko *lake* Japan 99 F7
Biysk Russian Federation 87 E6
Bizerte Tunisia 73 H3
Bjørnøya *island* NW Europe 20 D4, 44 H2
Blackall Queensland, Australia 103 I5
Blackburn England, United Kingdom 51 F8
Black Forest *forest* Germany 59 C12
Blackpool England, United Kingdom 51 F8
Black River *river* China/Vietnam 94 C2
Black Sea *sea* Asia/Europe 47 H7, 65 F13, 69 J4, 84 A5
Black Sea Lowland *physical region* Ukraine 65 F11
Black Volta *river* W Africa 77 F7
Blackwater *river* Republic of Ireland 51 B10
Blagoevgrad Bulgaria 69 F5
Blagoveshchensk Russian Federation 87 I6
Blanca, Bahía *bay* Argentina 39 E10, 43 F8
Blanca, Costa *coastal region* Spain 57 H7
Blanche, Lake *seasonal lake* South Australia, Australia 103 G6
Blanc, Mont *mountain* France/Italy 46 C6, 55 I5, 62 A3
Blantyre Malawi 71 G10, 81 G4
Blenheim New Zealand 105 F8
Blida Algeria 73 F3
Blois France 55 F4
Blönduós Iceland 48 B2
Bloemfontein *judicial capital* South Africa 71 F12, 80 E7
Bloomington Illinois, USA 32 B6
Bloomington Indiana, USA 32 C7
Bloomington Minnesota, USA 29 I4
Bludenz Switzerland 60 D5
Bluefield West Virginia, USA 33 E8
Blue Mountains *mountain range* Oregon/Washington, USA 26 D3
Blue Nile *river* Ethiopia/Sudan 71 G5, 75 D8
Blue Ridge *mountain range* E USA 31 I3
Bo Sierra Leone 76 D7
Boa Vista Brazil 41 F3
Boa Vista *island* Cape Verde 76 A4
Bobo-Dioulasso Burkina 77 F6
Bocholt Germany 59 B6
Bochum Germany 59 B6
Boden Sweden 48 F5
Bodmin Moor *moorland* England, United Kingdom 51 E12
Bodø Norway 48 D4
Bodrum Turkey 88 B2
Bogen Norway 48 E3
Bogor Java, Indonesia 94 D8
Bogotá *country capital* Colombia 38 B3, 40 C2
Bogra Bangladesh 93 G5
Bo Hai *bay* China 97 I4
Bohang South Korea 98 C6
Bohemia *cultural region* Czech Republic 67 B7
Bohemian Forest *forest* C Europe 59 G10, 67 B8
Bohol *island* Philippines 95 H5
Boise *state capital* Idaho, USA 26 E4
Boise City Oklahoma, USA 30 C3
Bojnurd Iran 89 I2
Bokaro India 93 F6
Boknafjorden *fjord* Norway 49 A9
Bole China 96 C3
Bolesławiec Poland 67 C6
Bolgatanga Ghana 77 G6
Bolhrad Ukraine 65 D11
Bolivia *country* W South America 39 D6, 40 D6
Bollnäs Sweden 49 E8
Bologna Italy 46 D7, 62 D4
Bolovens Plateau *plateau* Laos 94 D4

Bolsena, Lake *lake* Italy 63 D6
Bolshevik, Ostrov *island* Russian Federation 87 G2
Bolzano Italy 62 D2
Boma Democratic Republic of Congo 78 C8
Bombay *see* Mumbai
Bonaire *island* Netherlands Antilles 37 H8
Bonaparte, Archipelago *island group* Western Australia, Australia 102 D2
Bondo Democratic Republic of Congo 79 F5
Bongo, Massif des *plateau* Central African Republic 79 E4
Bongor Chad 78 D4
Bonifacio Corsica, France 55 K9
Bonifacio, Strait of *strait* C Mediterranean Sea 55 K9, 63 B7
Bonn Germany 59 B7
Boosaaso Somalia 75 I8
Boothia, Gulf of *gulf* Nunavut, Canada 25 E3, 47 F3, 49 F7
Boothia Peninsula *peninsula* Nunavut, Canada 25 E3
Bor Russian Federation 87 F5
Bor Sudan 75 D10
Borås Sweden 49 C11
Bordeaux France 54 D6
Bordj-Bou-Arreridj Algeria 73 F3
Børgefjellet *mountain range* Norway 49 D5
Borger Texas, USA 30 C4
Borgholm Sweden 49 E11
Borlänge Sweden 49 D9
Borneo *island* Brunei/Indonesia/Malaysia 83 H3, 85 F9, 94 E7
Bornholm *island* Denmark 49 D12
Borujerd Iran 89 G3
Bose China 97 G8
Bosna *river* Bosnia & Herzegovina 68 D3
Bosnia & Herzegovina *country* SE Europe 47 E7, 68 D3
Bossangoa Central African Republic 78 D5
Boston Massachusetts, USA 23 H8, 33 J5
Botosani Romania 69 H1
Botshabelo South Africa 80 E7
Botswana *country* S Africa 71 F11, 80 D6
Bouaké Ivory Coast 77 F7
Bouar Central African Republic 78 D5
Bougainville Island *island* Papua New Guinea 100 D5
Boujdour Western Sahara 72 B6
Boulder Western Australia, Australia 102 C6
Boulder Colorado, USA 28 E6
Boulia Queensland, Australia 103 G4
Boulogne-sur-Mer France 55 F1
Bountiful Utah, USA 27 G6
Bounty Islands *island group* New Zealand 101 F9
Bourg-en-Bresse France 55 H5
Bourges France 55 F4
Bourke New South Wales, Australia 103 I6
Bournemouth England, United Kingdom 51 G12
Bouvet Island *island* SE Atlantic Ocean 45 G11
Bowling Green *state capital* Kentucky, USA 32 C8
Bozeman Montana, USA 28 C3
Brac *island* Croatia 68 C4
Bradenton Florida, USA 31 I7
Bradford England, United Kingdom 51 G8
Braga Portugal 56 B3
Bragança Portugal 56 C3
Brahmapur India 93 F7
Brahmaputra *river* S Asia 84 E6, 92 H5, 96 C7
Braila Romania 69 H3
Braine-L'alleud Belgium 53 D9
Brainerd Minnesota, USA 29 I3
Branco *river* Brazil 38 D3, 41 F3
Brandenburg Germany 58 G5
Brandon Manitoba, Canada 24 E8
Braniewo Poland 66 F2

Brasília *country capital* Brazil 39 G6, 41 H6
Brasov Romania 69 G2
Bratislava *country capital* Slovakia 47 E6, 67 D9
Bratsk Russian Federation 87 G6
Braunschweig Germany 59 E5
Brava, Costa *coastal region* Spain 57 J3
Bravo del Norte, Río *river* Mexico/USA 34 C2 *see also* Grande, Rio
Brawley California, USA 27 E12
Brazil *country* South America 38 D5, 40 E4
Brazil Basin *undersea feature* W Atlantic Ocean 45 E 8
Brazilian Highlands *physical region* Brazil 39 G6, 41 H6
Brazos *river* Texas, USA 30 D4
Brazzaville *country capital* Congo 71 E8, 78 D7
Brcko Bosnia & Herzegovina 68 D3
Breclav Czech Republic 67 D9
Brecon Beacons *mountain range* Wales, United Kingdom 51 E10
Breda Netherlands 53 E7
Bregenz Switzerland 60 D4
Breidhafjördhur *bay* Iceland 48 A2
Bremen Germany 46 D5, 58 D4
Bremerhaven Germany 58 D3
Bremervörde Germany 58 D3
Brescia Italy 62 C3
Bressanone Italy 62 D2
Brest Belarus 65 D8
Brest France 54 B3
Bria Central African Republic 79 E5
Bridgeport Connecticut, USA 33 I6
Bridgetown *country capital* Barbados 37 K7
Brig Switzerland 60 C6
Brigham City Utah, USA 27 G6
Brighton England, United Kingdom 51 H12
Brilon Germany 59 C7
Brindisi Italy 63 I8
Brisbane *state capital* Queensland, Australia 100 D7, 103 J5
Bristol England, United Kingdom 51 F11
Bristol Bay *bay* Alaska, USA 22 B3, 26 G2
Bristol Channel *channel* England/Wales, United Kingdom 51 E11
British Colombia *province* Canada 24 B6
British Indian Ocean Territory *UK dependent territory* United Kingdom 84 D9
British Isles *island group* NW Europe 44 F3
British Virgin Islands *UK dependent territory* E West Indies 37 I5
Brittany *cultural region* France 54 C3
Brive-la-Gaillarde France 55 F6
Brno Czech Republic 67 D8
Broken Arrow Oklahoma, USA 30 E4
Broken Hill New South Wales, Australia 103 H6
Broken Ridge *undersea feature* C Indian Ocean 83 F6
Brooks Range *mountain range* Alaska, USA 26 H1
Broome Western Australia, Australia 102 C3
Browning Montana, USA 28 B2
Bruck an der Mur Austria 61 I4
Bruges Belgium 53 B8
Brunei *country* SE Asia 85 F8, 95 F6
Brunsbüttel Germany 58 D3
Brunswick Georgia, USA 31 J5
Brunswick Maine, USA 33 J4
Brussels *country capital* Belgium 46 D5, 53 D9
Bryansk Russian Federation 47 G5, 86 B4
Brzeg Poland 67 E6
Bucaramanga Colombia 38 B2, 40 C2

Buchanan Liberia 76 D8
Bucharest *country capital* Romania 47 G7, 69 H3
Buckland Tableland *plateau* Queensland, Australia 103 I5
Budapest *country capital* Hungary 47 E6, 67 F10
Búdhardalur Iceland 48 B2
Buea Cameroon 78 B5
Buenaventura Colombia 40 C2
Buenos Aires *country capital* Argentina 39 E10, 43 F6
Buffalo New York, USA 33 F5
Bug *river* N Europe 66 H5
Bujumbura *country capital* Burundi 71 G8, 79 G7
Bukan Iran 89 F3
Bukavu Democratic Republic of Congo 79 G7
Bukhoro Uzbekistan 91 D7
Bulawayo Zimbabwe 71 F11, 81 E5
Bulgan Mongolia 97 F2
Bulgaria *country* SE Europe 47 F7, 69 G5
Bumba Democratic Republic of Congo 79 E6
Bunbury Western Australia, Australia 102 B7
Bundaberg Queensland, Australia 103 J5
Bungo-suido *strait* Japan 98 E8
Buraydah Saudi Arabia 89 F5
Burco Somalia 75 G9
Burgas Bulgaria 47 G7, 69 H4
Burgos Spain 57 E3
Burgundy *cultural region* France 55 G4
Burkina *country* W Africa 71 C5, 77 G6
Burlington Colorado, USA 29 F7
Burlington Iowa, USA 29 J6
Burlington Vermont, USA 33 I4
Burma *see* Myanmar
Burnie Tasmania, Australia 103 H9
Burns Oregon, USA 26 D4
Bursa Turkey 84 A5, 88 C1
Buru *island* Indonesia 95 H8
Burundi *country* C Africa 71 G8, 79 G7
Burylbaytal Kazakhstan 91 G5
Busan South Korea 98 C7
Busselton Western Australia, Australia 102 B7
Buta Democratic Republic of Congo 79 F6
Buton *island* Indonesia 95 G8
Butte Montana, USA 28 B3
Butuan Philippines 95 H5
Buur Gaabo Somalia 75 F12
Buzau Russia 69 H3
Bydgoszcz Poland 66 E4
Bytom Poland 67 F7
Bytow Poland 66 E3

C

Caaguazú Paraguay 42 G3
Cabinda *province* Angola 71 D8, 80 A1
Cacak Serbia 69 E4
Cáceres Spain 56 C5
Caconda Angola 80 B4
Cader Idris *mountain* Wales, United Kingdom 51 E10
Cadiz Philippines 95 G5
Cádiz Spain 56 C8
Cádiz, Gulf of *gulf* Portugal/Spain 56 B8
Caen France 54 E3
Caernarfon Wales, United Kingdom 51 E9
Cagayan de Oro Philippines 95 H5
Cagliari Italy 46 D8, 63 B9
Caguas US 37 H5
Cahora Bassa, Lake Mozambique 81 F4
Cahors France 55 F7
Cahul Moldova 65 D12
Cairns Queensland, Australia 100 C6, 103 I3
Cairo *country capital* Egypt 70 G3, 74 C3
Cajamarca Peru 40 C5
Cakovec Croatia 68 C2

Calabar Nigeria 77 I8
Calabria cultural region Italy 63 H10
Calafat Romania 69 F4
Calais France 55 F1
Calama Chile 42 C2
Calamian Group island group Philippines 95 F4
Calarasi Romania 69 H3
Calatayud Spain 57 G4
Calbayog Philippines 95 H4
Calcutta see Kolkata
Caldas de Rainha Portugal 56 A5
Caldwell Idaho, USA 26 F6
Calgary Alberta, Canada 23 D6, 24 C7
Cali Colombia 38 B3, 40 C3
Calicut India 93 C10
California state USA 27 B9
California, Gulf of gulf Mexico 23 C10, 34 A2
Callao Peru 39 B6, 40 C5
Caloundra Queensland, Australia 103 J5
Caltanissetta Italy 63 F11
Camagüey Cuba 36 D4
Camargue physical region France 55 G7
Cambodia country SE Asia 85 F7, 94 C4
Cambrian, Mountains mountain range Wales, United Kingdom 51 E10
Cambridge New Zealand 104 G4
Cambridge England, United Kingdom 51 H10
Cameroon country W Africa 71 D7, 78 C5
Camooweal Queensland, Australia 103 G3
Campbell Island island New Zealand 101 F9
Campeche Mexico 35 G5
Campeche, Bay of bay S Gulf of Mexico 35 F5
Cam Pha Vietnam 94 D2
Campina Grande Brazil 41 F7
Campinas Brazil 39 G8, 41 H7
Campobasso Italy 63 G7
Campo Grande Brazil 39 F7, 41 G7
Campos Brazil 41 I7
Cam Ranh Vietnam 94 D4
Canada country N North America 23 D6, 24 C6
Canadian river SW USA 30 C3
Canadian Shield physical region C Canada 24 E6
Canary Islands island group NW Africa 45 F6, 70 A3, 72 B5
Canaveral, Cape headland Florida, USA 31 J6
Canberra country capital Australian Capital Territory, Australia 100 D8, 103 I7
Cancún Mexico 35 H5
Cangzhou China 97 I4
Canicattì Italy 63 F11
Cannanore India 93 C10
Cannes France 55 I7
Cantábrica, Cordillera mountain range Spain 56 C2
Canterbury England, United Kingdom 51 I11
Canterbury Bight bay New Zealand 105 D10
Canterbury Plains physical region New Zealand 105 D10
Can Tho Vietnam 94 D5
Cape Basin undersea feature SE Atlantic Ocean 45 G10
Cape Breton Island island Nova Scotia, Canada 23 I8, 25 J7
Cape Coast Ghana 77 G8
Cape Coral Florida, USA 31 J7
Cape Town legislative capital South Africa 71 E13, 80 C9
Cape Verde country W Africa 76 A4
Cape Verde Basin undersea feature E Atlantic Ocean 45 E6
Cape Verde Islands island group W Africa 45 E6
Cape York Peninsula peninsula Queensland, Australia 103 H1
Cap-Haïten Dominican Republic 37 F4
Capri island Italy 63 F8
Caprivi Strip cultural region Namibia 80 D5

Caquetá river Brazil/Colombia 38 C3, 40 C3 see also Japurá
Caracas country capital Venezuela 38 C1, 40 D1
Caransebes Romania 69 F3
Caratasca, Laguna de lagoon Honduras 35 I7
Carbonara, Capo headland Italy 63 B10
Carbondale Illinois, USA 32 B8
Carbonia Italy 63 A11
Carcassonne France 55 F8
Cardiff Wales, United Kingdom 46 C5, 51 F11
Cardigan Bay bay SE Irish Sea 51 E10
Carey, Lake seasonal lake Western Australia, Australia 102 D6
Caribbean Sea sea W Atlantic Ocean 35 J7, 36 C6, 45 C7
Caribou Mountains mountain range Alberta, Canada 24 C5
Carlisle England, United Kingdom 51 F7
Carlsberg Ridge undersea feature N Indian Ocean 82 D2
Carmarthen Wales, United Kingdom 51 E11
Carmen Mexico 35 G6
Carmona Spain 56 D7
Carnarvon Western Australia, Australia 100 A7, 102 B5
Carnarvon South Africa 80 D8
Carnegie, Lake seasonal lake Western Australia, Australia 102 D5
Carney Island island Antarctica 21 A4
Car Nicobar island Nicobar Islands, India 93 I10
Carnot Central African Republic 78 D5
Caroline Islands island group Micronesia 100 C4
Carpathian Mountains mountain range C Europe 47 F6, 65 B10, 67 G8, 69 G1
Carpentaria, Gulf of gulf Northern Territory, Australia 100 B6, 103 G2
Carpi Italy 62 D4
Carrara Italy 62 C4
Carson City state capital Nevada, USA 27 C7
Cartagena Colombia 38 B2, 40 C1
Cartagena Spain 57 G7
Caruarú Brazil 41 J5
Casablanca Morocco 70 B2, 72 D4
Casa Grande Arizona, USA 27 G12
Cascade Point headland New Zealand 105 B10
Cascade Range mountain range Oregon/Washington, USA 26 B5
Cascavel Brazil 41 G8
Cascina Italy 62 C5
Caserta Italy 63 F8
Casper Wyoming, USA 28 D5
Caspian Depression physical region Kazakhstan/Russian Federation 47 I6, 90 A4
Caspian Sea inland sea Asia/Europe 47 J6, 84 B5, 86 A7, 89 G1, 91 A5
Cassinga Angola 80 B4
Cassino Italy 63 F7
Castelló de la Plana Spain 57 H5
Castelo Branco Portugal 56 B5
Castelvetrano Italy 63 E11
Castilla-Nueva cultural region Spain 56 D5
Castilla-Vieja physical region Spain 56 E4
Castres France 55 F7
Castries country capital St Lucia 37 K7
Castrovillari Italy 63 H9
Catalonia cultural region Spain 57 H3
Catamarca Argentina 42 D4
Catanduanes island Philippines 95 H4
Catania Italy 63 G11
Catanzaro Italy 63 H10
Cat Island island Bahamas 36 E2
Catskill Mountains mountain range New York, USA 33 H5

Cauca river Colombia 40 C2
Caucasus mountain range Georgia/Russian Federation 47 I7, 89 F11
Causeni Moldova 65 D11
Cavan Republic of Ireland 51 C8
Caxito Angola 80 A2
Cayenne French Guiana 38 F2, 41 G2
Cayes Haiti 37 E5
Cayman Islands island group United Kingdom 36 B4
Cayman Islands UK dependent territory W West Indies 23 F11
Cazombo Angola 80 D3
Cebu island Philippines 95 G5
Cebu Philippines 85 G8, 95 H5
Cecina Italy 63 C5
Cedar river Iowa/Minnesota, USA 29 J5
Cedar City Utah, USA 27 G8
Cedar Falls Iowa, USA 29 J5
Cedar Rapids Iowa, USA 29 J5
Cedros, Isla island Mexico 34 A3
Ceduna South Australia, Australia 103 F6
Ceerigaabo Somalia 75 H9
Cefalù Italy 63 F11
Celebes Sea sea Indonesia/Philippines 85 G8, 94 G6
Celje Slovenia 61 I6
Celle Germany 58 E5
Celtic Sea sea NE Atlantic Ocean 46 B5, 51 C11
Central African Republic country C Africa 71 E6, 78 D5
Central Makran Range mountain range Pakistan 91 D11
Central Pacific Basin undersea feature C Pacific Ocean 107 E4
Central Siberian Plateau plateau Russian Federation 85 F3, 87 F4
Central, Sistema mountain range Spain 56 D4
Central Valley valley Chile 43 C7
Central Valley valley California, USA 27 B7
Ceram Sea sea Indonesia 95 H7
Cerignola Italy 63 G7
Cervino, Monte mountain Italy/Switzerland 62 A2
Cesena Italy 62 E4
Cesis Latvia 64 C4
Ceske Budejovice Czech Republic 67 B8
Cetraro Italy 63 G9
Ceuta Spanish dependent territory N Africa 56 D9, 70 C2, 72 D3
Cévennes mountain range France 55 G7
Ceylon Plain undersea feature N Indian Ocean 83 F3
Chabahar Iran 89 J5
Chad country C Africa 70 E5, 78 D3
Chad, Lake lake C Africa 71 E5, 77 K6, 78 C3
Chagai Hills hill range Afghanistan/Pakistan 91 D10
Chaghcharan Afghanistan 91 E9
Chagos Archipelago island group N Indian Ocean 82 E4
Chagos-Laccadive Plateau undersea feature N Indian Ocean 82 E4
Chalkida Greece 69 G7
Chalkidiki peninsula Greece 69 G6
Challans France 54 D4
Châlons-en-Champagne France 55 G3
Chalon-sur-Saône France 55 H5
Chaman Pakistan 91 E10
Chambal river India 92 C5
Chambéry France 55 H6
Chamonix France 55 I5
Champagne cultural region France 55 G3
Chandigarh India 92 C4
Chandler Arizona, USA 27 G11
Chandrapur India 93 D7
Changchun China 85 G5, 97 J3
Changde China 97 H7
Changsha China 85 F6, 97 H7
Changzhi China 97 H5
Changzhou China 97 J6
Chania Greece 69 G9
Channel Islands island group United Kingdom 46 C5, 51 F13

Channel Islands island group California, USA 27 C11
Chanthaburi Thailand 94 C4
Chaozhou China 97 I8
Chapaev Kazakhstan 90 B4
Chapala, Lago de lake Mexico 34 D5
Charente river France 54 D6
Chari river Central African Republic/Chad 78 D4
Charjew Turkmenistan 91 D7
Charleroi Belgium 53 D10
Charleston state capital West Virginia, USA 33 E8
Charleston South Carolina, USA 31 J4
Charleville Queensland, Australia 103 H6, 25 H5
Charleville-Mézières France 55 H2
Charlotte North Carolina, USA 23 G9, 31 J3
Charlottesville Virginia, USA 33 G8
Charlottetown Prince Edward Island, Canada 25 J7
Charters Towers Queensland, Australia 103 I3
Chartres France 55 F3
Chasong North Korea 98 B3
Châteauroux France 55 F5
Châtellerault France 55 E5
Chatham Islands island group New Zealand 101 G9
Chatham Rise undersea feature SW Pacific Ocean 107 E7
Chattahoochee river SE USA 31 H4
Chattanooga Tennessee, USA 31 H4
Chaumont France 55 H3
Chaves Portugal 56 B3
Cheb Czech Republic 67 A7
Cheboksary Russian Federation 86 C4
Chech'on South Korea 98 C5
Chelm Poland 67 I6
Chelmno Poland 66 E3
Chelyabinsk Russian Federation 84 C4, 86 C5
Chemnitz Germany 59 G8
Chenab river India/Pakistan 91 G9
Chengde China 97 I4
Chengdu China 85 F6, 97 F6
Chennai India 84 D7, 93 D9
Chenzhou China 97 H7
Cher river France 55 F4
Cherbourg France 54 D2
Cherepovets Russian Federation 86 B3
Cherkasy Ukraine 65 F10
Cherkessk Russian Federation 86 A5
Chernihiv Ukraine 65 E8
Chernivtsi Ukraine 65 C10
Chernobyl Ukraine 65 E8
Cherskiy Russian Federation 87 I2
Cherskogo, Khrebet mountain range Russian Federation 87 H3
Chervonohrad Ukraine 65 B9
Chesapeake Virginia, USA 33 H9
Chesapeake Bay inlet NE USA 33 H8
Chester England, United Kingdom 51 F9
Chetumal Mexico 35 H6
Cheyenne state capital Wyoming, USA 28 E6
Cheyenne river South Dakota/Wyoming, USA 29 F4
Cheyenne Wells Colorado, USA 29 F7
Chiai Taiwan 97 J8
Chiang Mai Thailand 94 B3
Chiang Rai Thailand 94 B3
Chiavari Italy 62 C4
Chiba Japan 99 H6
Chicago Illinois, USA 23 F8, 32 C5
Chiclana de la Frontera Spain 56 C8
Chiclayo Peru 40 B4
Chico river Argentina 43 D11, 43 D10
Chico California, USA 27 B7

Chidley, Cape headland Newfoundland & Labrador/Québec, Canada 23 H6, 25 H5
Chiemsee lake Germany 59 G12
Chieti Italy 63 F6
Chifeng China 97 I3
Chihuahua Mexico 34 C3
Chile country SW South America 39 C12, 43 C8
Chile Basin undersea feature E Pacific Ocean 107 J6
Chile Rise undersea feature E Pacific Ocean 107 I7
Chillán Chile 43 C7
Chiloé, Isla de island Chile 39 C11, 43 B9
Chilpancingo Mexico 34 E6
Chiltern Hills hill range England, United Kingdom 51 G11
Chimborazo mountain Ecuador 38 A4, 40 B3
Chimbote Peru 40 C5
Chimoio Mozambique 81 G5
China country E Asia 85 E5, 96 D6
Chinandega Nicaragua 35 H8
Chindwin river Myanmar 94 B2
Chingola Zambia 81 E3
Chinguetti Mauritania 76 D4
Chinhoyi Zimbabwe 81 F4
Chiniot Pakistan 91 G10
Chino Japan 99 G6
Chioggia Italy 62 E3
Chios Greece 69 H7
Chios island Greece 69 H7
Chipata Zambia 81 G4
Chiquita, Laguna Mar lake Argentina 42 E5
Chirchiq Uzbekistan 91 F7
Chiriqui, Gulf of gulf Panama 35 J9
Chisinau country capital Moldova 47 G6, 65 D11
Chita Russian Federation 87 H6
Chitose Japan 99 I2
Chittagong Bangladesh 84 E7, 93 H6
Chitungwiza Zimbabwe 81 F5
Chlef Algeria 73 F3
Chojna Poland 66 C4
Chokwe Mozambique 81 F6
Cholet France 54 D4
Choma Zambia 80 E4
Chomutov Czech Republic 67 B7
Ch'onan South Korea 98 C5
Chon Buri Thailand 94 C4
Ch'ongjin North Korea 98 D3
Chongju North Korea 98 B4
Ch'ongju South Korea 98 C5
Chongqing China 85 F6, 97 G7
Chongup South Korea 98 B6
Chonos, Archipiélago de los island group Chile 39 C11, 43 B10
Chorzow Poland 67 E7
Ch'osan North Korea 98 B3
Choshi Japan 99 H6
Chos Malal Argentina 43 C7
Choybalsan Mongolia 97 H2
Choyr Mongolia 97 G3
Christchurch New Zealand 101 F8, 105 E9
Christmas Island island E Indian Ocean 83 H4
Chubut river Argentina 43 D9
Chukchi Sea sea Arctic Ocean 20 B1, 85 K2
Chula Vista California, USA 27 D12
Chumphon Thailand 94 B5
Ch'ungju South Korea 98 C6
Chur Switzerland 60 D5
Churchill Manitoba, Canada 25 F6
Churchill river Manitoba, Canada 25 E6
Chuuk island group Micronesia 100 C3
Chuxiong China 97 F8
Ciechanow Poland 66 G4
Ciego de Ávila Cuba 36 C3
Cienfuegos Cuba 36 C3
Cijara, Embalse de reservoir Spain 56 D5
Cilacap Indonesia 94 D9
Cincinnati Ohio, USA 32 D7
Cirebon Indonesia 94 D8
Ciro Marina Italy 63 H9
Citta di Castello Italy 62 E5
Ciudad Bolívar Venezuela 41 E2

Ciudad del Este Paraguay 42 H3
Ciudad Guayana Venezuela 41 E2
Ciudad Juárez Mexico 23 D9, 34 C2
Ciudad Madero Mexico 35 E5
Ciudad Obregón Mexico 34 B3
Ciudad Real Spain 56 E6
Ciudad-Rodrigo Spain 56 C4
Ciudad Victoria Mexico 34 E4
Ciutadella de Menorca Balearic Islands, Spain 57 K5
Civitanova Marche Italy 62 F5
Civitavecchia Italy 63 D7
Clamecy France 55 G4
Clarence New Zealand 105 F8
Clarion Fracture Zone undersea feature E Pacific Ocean 107 G4
Clarksville Tennessee, USA 31 H3
Clearwater Florida, USA 31 I6
Clearwater Mountains mountain range Idaho, USA 26 E3
Clermont Queensland, Australia 103 I4
Clermont-Ferrand France 55 G5
Cleveland Ohio, USA 23 G8, 33 E6
Clipperton Fracture Zone undersea feature C Pacific Ocean 107 G4
Cloncurry Queensland, Australia 103 H4
Clonmel Republic of Ireland 51 C10
Cloudy Bay bay New Zealand 105 F8
Clovis New Mexico, USA 30 C4
Cluj-Napoca Romania 47 F6, 69 F2
Clutha river New Zealand 105 C12
Clyde river Scotland, United Kingdom 51 E6
Clyde, Firth of inlet Scotland, United Kingdom 51 E7
Coast Mountains mountain range Canada/USA 23 C5, 24 B5
Coast Ranges mountain range W USA 23 B7, 27 B7
Coats Land physical region Antarctica 21 B2
Coatzacoalcos Mexico 35 F6
Cobán Guatemala 35 G7
Coburg Germany 59 F8
Cochabamba Bolivia 39 D6, 40 E6
Cochin India 93 C10
Coco river Honduras/Nicaragua 35 I7
Cocos Islands island group E Indian Ocean 83 G4
Cod, Cape headland Massachusetts, USA 23 H8, 33 J5
Cody Wyoming, USA 28 C4
Coesfeld Germany 59 B6
Coeur d'Alene Idaho, USA 26 E2
Coffs Harbour New South Wales, Australia 103 J6
Cognac France 54 E6
Coiba, Isla de island Panama 35 J9
Coihaique Chile 43 C10
Coimbatore India 93 C10
Coimbra Portugal 56 B5
Colby Kansas, USA 29 F7
Colchester England, United Kingdom 51 I10
Coleraine Northern Ireland, United Kingdom 51 D7
Colima Mexico 34 D6
Coll island Scotland, United Kingdom 51 C5
Collingwood New Zealand 105 E7
Colmar France 55 I3
Cologne Germany 46 D5, 59 B7
Colombia country NW South America 38 B3, 40 C3
Colombo country capital Sri Lanka 84 D8, 93 D11
Colón Panama 35 J8
Colonna, Capo headland Italy 63 H10
Colonsay island Scotland, United Kingdom 51 C5
Colorado river Argentina 43 D7
Colorado river Mexico/USA 23 C9, 27 G9, 28 C7, 30 D5
Colorado state USA 28 D7

COLORADO PLATEAU–DUNHUANG . 113

Colorado Plateau *plateau* W USA 23 C8, 27 G8
Colorado Springs Colorado, USA 28 E7
Columbia *river* Canada/USA 23 C7, 26 D1
Columbia Missouri, USA 29 J7
Columbia *state capital* South Carolina, USA 23 G9, 31 J4
Columbia Basin *physical region* Washington, USA 26 D2
Columbia Plateau *plateau* Idaho/Oregon, USA 26 E5
Columbus Georgia, USA 31 H5
Columbus Mississippi, USA 31 G4
Columbus Nebraska, USA 29 H6
Columbus *state capital* Ohio, USA 23 F9, 32 E7
Comilla Bangladesh 93 H6
Como Italy 62 B3
Comodoro Rivadavia Argentina 43 D10
Como, Lake *lake* Italy 62 C2
Comoro Islands *island group* Comoros 82 C4
Comoros *country* W Indian Ocean 71 H9, 81 J3
Compiègne France 55 F2
Comrat Moldova 65 D11
Conakry *country capital* Guinea 71 A6, 76 C7
Concepción Chile 43 B7
Concepción Paraguay 42 G2
Conception, Point *headland* California, USA 27 B10
Conchos *river* Mexico 34 C3
Concord California, USA 27 B8
Concord *state capital* New Hampshire, USA 33 I5
Concordia Argentina 43 G5
Congo *country* C Africa 71 E8, 78 D6
Congo *river* Congo/Democratic Republic of Congo 71 E8, 78 D7
Congo Basin *physical region* C Africa 71 E7, 78 E6
Congo, Democratic Republic of *country* C Africa 71 F8, 79 F6
Connaught *cultural region* Republic of Ireland 51 B8
Connecticut *state* USA 33 I5
Constance Germany 59 D12
Constance, Lake *lake* Germany/Switzerland 59 D12, 60 D4
Constanta Romania 47 G7, 69 I3
Constantine Algeria 70 D2, 73 G3
Constitución Chile 43 B7
Coober Pedy South Australia, Australia 103 F6
Cook Islands *NZ dependent territory* C Pacific Ocean 101 H6
Cook, Mount *mountain* New Zealand 105 C10
Cook Strait *strait* New Zealand 105 F7
Cooktown Queensland, Australia 103 I2
Coolgardie Western Australia, Australia 102 C6
Cooma New South Wales, Australia 103 I8
Coonamble New South Wales, Australia 103 I6
Cooper Creek *seasonal river* Queensland/South Australia, 103 G5
Coorow Western Australia, Australia 102 B6
Coos Bay Oregon, USA 26 A4
Copenhagen *country capital* Denmark 46 E4, 49 C12
Copiapó Chile 42 C4
Coppermine Nunavut, Canada 24 D4
Coquimbo Chile 42 C5
Coral Sea *sea* SW Pacific Ocean 100 D6, 103 J2, 106 D5
Corcovado, Gulf of *gulf* Chile 43 C9
Córdoba Argentina 39 D9, 43 E5
Córdoba Spain 46 A7, 56 D7
Corfu *island* Greece 68 E6
Corigliano Calabro Italy 63 H9
Corinth Greece 69 F7
Corinth, Gulf of *gulf* Aegean Sea/Ionian Sea 69 F7
Cork Republic of Ireland 51 B10
Corner Brook Newfoundland & Labrador, Canada 25 J7
Corno Grande *mountain* Italy 63 F6
Coro Venezuela 40 D1
Coromandel New Zealand 104 G3
Coromandel Coast *coastal region* India 93 D10
Coromandel Peninsula *peninsula* New Zealand 104 G3
Coronel Oviedo Paraguay 42 G3
Coronel Pringles Argentina 43 F7
Coropuna, Nevado *mountain* Peru 40 D6
Corpus Christi Texas, USA 30 D7
Corrib, Lough *lake* Republic of Ireland 51 B9
Corrientes Argentina 42 F4
Corrientes, Cabo *headland* Mexico 34 C5
Corse, Cap *headland* Corsica, France 55 K8
Corsica *island* France 46 D7, 55 K9
Cortona Italy 63 D5
Coruche Portugal 56 B6
Corum Turkey 88 D1
Corumba Brazil 41 F7
Corvallis Oregon, USA 26 B4
Cosenza Italy 63 H9
Costa Rica *country* Central America 23 F13, 35 I8
Cotonou Benin 77 H7
Cotopaxi *volcano* Ecuador 40 B3
Cotswold Hills *hill range* England, United Kingdom 51 G11
Cottbus Germany 59 I6
Council Bluffs Iowa, USA 29 H6
Courland Lagoon *lagoon* Lithuania/Russian Federation 65 A6
Coventry England, United Kingdom 51 G10
Covilha Portugal 56 B5
Cowan, Lake *seasonal lake* Western Australia, Australia 102 D6
Cozumel, Isla *island* Mexico 35 H5
Cradock South Africa 80 D8
Craiova Romania 69 G3
Crawley England, United Kingdom 51 H11
Creil France 55 F2
Cremona Italy 62 C3
Cres *island* Croatia 68 B3
Crescent City California, USA 27 A5
Crete *island* Greece 47 F9, 69 G9
Créteil France 55 F3
Crete, Sea of *sea* NE Mediterranean Sea 69 H9
Creuse *river* France 55 E5
Crimean Peninsula *peninsula* Ukraine 47 H6, 65 G12
Croatia *country* SE Europe 47 E7, 68 C2
Cromwell New Zealand 105 C11
Crotone Italy 63 H10
Croydon Queensland, Australia 103 H3
Crozet Basin *undersea feature* S Indian Ocean 82 D6
Crozet Islands *island group* SW Indian Ocean 82 C7
Crozet Plateau *undersea feature* SW Indian Ocean 82 C7
Csorna Hungary 67 D10
Cuamba Mozambique 81 H4
Cuando *river* S Africa 71 E10, 80 C4
Cuango *river* Angola/Democratic Republic of Congo 71 E9, 80 B2
Cuanza *river* Angola 80 B3
Cuautla Mexico 34 E6
Cuba *country* W West Indies 23 F11, 36 C3
Cubango *river* S Africa 71 E10, 80 C5
Cúcuta Colombia 38 B2, 40 C2
Cuddapah India 93 D9
Cuenca Ecuador 40 B4
Cuenca Spain 57 F5
Cuernavaca Mexico 34 E6
Cuiabá Brazil 41 G6
Culiacán Mexico 34 C4
Cumaná Venezuela 40 E1
Cuneo Italy 62 A4
Cunnamulla Queensland, Australia 103 H5
Curaçao *island* Netherlands Antilles 37 G8
Curitiba Brazil 39 G8, 41 H8
Cusco Peru 40 D6
Cuttack India 93 F7
Cuxhaven Germany 58 D3
Cyclades *island group* Greece 69 G8
Cyprus *country* W Asia 84 A6, 88 C3
Cyrenaica *cultural region* Libya 73 I5
Czech Republic *country* C Europe 46 E6, 67 B8
Czestochowa Poland 67 F6
Czluchow Poland 66 E3

D

Dachau Germany 59 D11
Dachuan China 97 G6
Daegu South Korea 98 C6
Daejon South Korea 98 B6
Dagupan Philippines 95 G3
Dakar *country capital* Senegal 70 A5, 76 C5
Dalälven *river* Norway/Sweden 49 D9
Dalandzadgad Mongolia 97 F3
Da Lat Vietnam 94 D4
Dali China 97 F8
Dalian China 97 J4
Dallas Texas, USA 23 E9, 30 E5
Dalmatia *cultural region* Croatia 68 D4
Daloa Ivory Coast 77 E7
Daly *river* Northern Territory, Australia 103 E2
Daly Waters Northern Territory, Australia 103 F2
Daman India 93 B7
Damaraland *physical region* Namibia 80 B6
Damascus *country capital* Syria 84 A6, 88 D3
Damavand, Qolleh ye *mountain* Iran 89 H3
Damietta Egypt 74 C3
Danakil Desert *desert* Ethiopia 75 F8
Da Nang Vietnam 85 F7, 94 D4
Dandong China 97 J4
Dannenberg Germany 59 G11
Danube *river* C Europe 47 F7, 59 C9, 61 J3, 67 E11, 69 F3
Danube Delta *delta* Romania/Ukraine 65 E12, 69 I3
Danville Virginia, USA 33 F9
Dapaong Togo 77 G6
Daqing China 97 J2
Darabani Romania 69 H1
Darbhanga India 92 F5
Dar es Salaam Tanzania 71 H8, 79 J8
Darfur *cultural region* Ethiopia/Sudan 70 F5, 75 C8
Darganata Turkmenistan 91 D7
Dargaville New Zealand 104 F2
Darhan China 97 G2
Darien, Gulf of *gulf* S Caribbean Sea 35 K8, 40 C2
Darjeeling Bhutan 92 G5
Darling *river* SW Australia 100 C7, 103 H6
Darmstadt Germany 59 C9
Darnah Libya 73 J4
Darnley, Cape *headland* Antarctica 21 E2
Daroca Spain 57 G4
Dart *river* England, United Kingdom 51 E12
Dartmoor *moorland* England, United Kingdom 51 E12
Daru Papua New Guinea 100 C5
Darvishan Afghanistan 91 D10
Darwin *state capital* Northern Territory, Australia 100 B6, 103 E1
Dashhowuz Turkmenistan 91 C6
Datong Mongolia 97 H4
Daugavpils Latvia 64 D5
Davangere India 93 C9
Davao Philippines 85 G8, 95 H5
Davenport Iowa, USA 29 J6
David Panama 35 J9
Davis Strait *strait* Baffin Bay/Labrador Sea 22 H4, 25 H3, 44 C2
Davos Switzerland 60 D5
Dawson Yukon Territory, Canada 24 B3
Dax France 54 D7
Dayr az Zawr Syria 89 E3
Dayton Ohio, USA 32 D7
Daytona Beach Florida, USA 31 J6
De Aar South Africa 80 D8
Deán Funes Argentina 42 E5
Death Valley *valley* California, USA 23 C8, 27 D9
Debrecen Hungary 67 H10
Debre Markos Ethiopia 75 E9
Debre Zeyit Ethiopia 75 F9
Decatur Alabama, USA 31 H4
Decatur Illinois, USA 32 B7
Deccan *plateau* India 84 D7, 93 C7
Decin Czech Republic 67 B6
Dee *river* Scotland, United Kingdom 50 F5
Deggendorf Germany 59 G10
Dehra Dun India 92 D4
Deh Shu Afghanistan 91 D10
Delano California, USA 27 C9
Delaware *state* USA 33 H7
Delaware Bay *inlet* NE USA 33 H7
Delémont Switzerland 60 B4
Delft Netherlands 53 D6
Delfzijl Netherlands 52 I2
Delhi India 92 D4
Delicias Mexico 34 C3
Delmenhorst Germany 58 D4
Del Rio Texas, USA 30 C6
Deltona Florida, USA 31 J6
Demchok *disputed region* China/India 92 D3, 97 B6
Demerara Plain *undersea feature* W Atlantic Ocean 45 D7
Den Helder Netherlands 52 E3
Denia Spain 57 H6
Denizli Turkey 88 C2
Denmark *country* N Europe 46 D4, 49 B12
Denmark Strait *strait* Greenland/Iceland 20 B5, 25 J1, 44 E2
Denov Uzbekistan 91 E8
Denpasar Indonesia 95 F9
Denver *state capital* Colorado, USA 23 D8, 28 E7
Dera Ghazi Khan Pakistan 91 F10
Dera Ismail Khan Pakistan 91 F10
Derbent Uzbekistan 91 E8
Derby England, United Kingdom 51 G9
Derby Western Australia, Australia 100 A6, 102 D3
Derry *see* Londonderry
Derzhavinsk Kazakhstan 90 E4
Dese Somalia 75 F8
Deseado *river* Argentina 43 D10
Des Moines *river* C USA 29 I5
Des Moines *state capital* Iowa, USA 29 I6
Desna *river* Russian Federation/Ukraine 65 E8
Dessau Germany 59 G6
Desventurados, Islas de los *island group* Chile 39 A8
Detmold Germany 59 D6
Detroit Michigan, USA 23 F8, 32 F5
Deva Romania 69 F2
Deventer Netherlands 52 G5
Devon Island *island* Nunavut, Canada 25 F2
Devonport Tasmania, Australia 103 H9
Deyang China 97 G6
Dezful Iran 89 G4
Dezhou China 97 I5
Dhahran Saudi Arabia 89 G6
Dhaka *country capital* Bangladesh 84 E7, 93 H6
Dhamar Yemen 89 F9
Dhanbad India 93 F6
Dhaulagiri *mountain* Nepal 92 E4
Dhole India 93 C7
Dhuusa Marreeb Somalia 75 H10
Diamantina *seasonal river* Queensland/South Australia, Australia 103 G5
Dickinson North Dakota, USA 29 F3
Diekirch Luxembourg 53 G12
Diepholz Germany 58 C5
Dieppe France 55 E2
Diest Belgium 53 E9
Diffa Niger 77 J6
Digne France 55 I7
Dijon France 55 H4
Dili *country capital* East Timor 85 G9, 95 H9
Dilling Sudan 75 C8
Dillon Montana, USA 29 B3
Dilolo Democratic Republic of Congo 79 E9
Dinajpur Bangladesh 92 G5
Dinant Belgium 53 E11
Dinaric Alps *mountain range* Bosnia & Herzegovina 68 D4
Dingle Bay *bay* Republic of Ireland 51 A10
Diourbel Senegal 76 C5
Dire Dawa Ethiopia 71 H6, 75 F9
Dirk Hartog Island *island* Western Australia, Australia 102 A5
Dirranbandi Queensland, Australia 103 I6
Disappointment, Lake *seasonal lake* Western Australia, Australia 102 C4
Divinópolis Brazil 41 H7
Diyarbakir Turkey 89 E2
Djambala Congo 78 C7
Djanet Algeria 73 G6
Djelfa Algeria 73 F4
Djibouti *country* E Africa 71 H5, 75 G8
Djibouti *country capital* Djibouti 71 H6, 75 G8
Dnieper *river* E Europe 47 G6, 65 E7
Dnieper Lowlands *physical region* Ukraine Belarus 65 E8
Dniester *river* Moldova/Ukraine 47 F6, 65 D10
Dniprodzerzhynsk Ukraine 65 G10
Dnipropetrovsk Ukraine 47 H6, 65 G10
Doberai, Jazirah *peninsula* Indonesia 95 I7
Doboj Bosnia & Herzegovina 68 D3
Dobrich Bulgaria 69 I4
Dodecanese *island group* Greece 69 H8
Dodge City Kansas, USA 29 G8
Dodoma *country capital* Tanzania 71 G8, 79 I8
Dogo *island* Japan 98 E6
Dogondoutchi Niger 77 H6
Doha *country capital* Qatar 84 B6, 89 H6
Dolisie Congo 78 C7
Dolomites *mountain range* Italy 62 D2
Dombås Norway 49 B7
Dominica *country* E West Indies 23 I12, 37 J6
Dominican Republic *country* C West Indies 23 H11, 37 G4
Domo Ethiopia 75 H9
Domodossola Italy 62 B2
Don *river* Russian Federation 47 H5, 86 A5
Don *river* Scotland, United Kingdom 50 F5
Donaueschingen Germany 59 C12
Donauwörth Germany 59 D10
Don Benito Spain 56 D6
Doncaster England, United Kingdom 51 G9
Dondo Angola 80 B3
Dondo Mozambique 81 G5
Donegal Republic of Ireland 51 C7
Donegal Bay *bay* NE Atlantic Ocean 51 B8
Donets *river* Russian Federation/Ukraine 65 H9
Donetsk Ukraine 47 H6, 65 H10
Dongara Western Australia, Australia 102 B6
Dongchuan China 97 F8
Donghae South Korea 98 C5
Dong Hoi Vietnam 94 D3
Dongola Sudan 75 C6
Dongsheng China 97 G4
Dongying China 97 I5
Donostia-San Sebastián Spain 57 F2
Dordogne *river* France 55 F6
Dordrecht Netherlands 53 E6
Dorfen Germany 59 G11
Dornbirn Switzerland 60 D4
Dorotea Sweden 49 E6
Dortmund Germany 59 B6
Dortmund-Ems-Canal *canal* Germany 59 B6
Dos Hermanas Spain 56 D8
Dosso Niger 77 H6
Dossor Kazakhstan 90 B4
Dostyk Kazakhstan 90 I5
Dothan Alabama, USA 31 H5
Douala Cameroon 71 D7, 78 B5
Douglas Isle of Man 51 E8
Dourados Brazil 41 G7
Douro *river* Portugal/Spain 46 A7, 56 B4 *see also* Duero
Dover England, United Kingdom 51 I11
Dover *state capital* Delaware, USA 33 H7
Dover, Strait of *strait* France/United Kingdom 51 I11, 55 E1
Dovrefjell *plateau* Norway 49 B7
Dozen *island* Japan 98 E6
Drachten Netherlands 52 G2
Drakensberg *mountain range* Lesotho/South Africa 71 F12, 81 E8
Drake Passage *strait* E Atlantic Ocean 45 C12
Drama Greece 69 G5
Drammen Norway 49 C9
Drau *river* Austria 61 H5
Drava *river* C Europe 61 J6, 67 E12, 68 D2
Dresden Germany 59 H7
Drina *river* Bosnia & Herzegovina/Serbia 68 E3
Drobeta-Turnu Severin Romania 69 F3
Drogheda Republic of Ireland 51 D8
Drohobych Ukraine 65 B9
Dronning Maud Land *physical region* Antarctica 21 C1
Drummond Montana, USA 28 B3
Drummondville Québec, Canada 25 I8
Druskininkai Lithuania 65 B6
Duba Saudi Arabia 88 D5
Dubai United Arab Emirates 89 I6
Dubasari Moldova 65 D11
Dubawnt Lake *lake* Nunavut, Canada 24 E5
Dubbo New South Wales, Australia 103 I7
Dublin *country capital* Republic of Ireland 46 B4, 51 D9
Dubno Ukraine 65 C9
Dubrovnik Croatia 68 D4
Dubuque Iowa, USA 29 J5
Duchess Queensland, Australia 103 G4
Dudinka Russian Federation 87 F4
Duero *river* Portugal/Spain 57 F3 *see also* Douro
Dufourspitze *mountain* Italy/Switzerland 60 C6, 62 B3
Duisburg Germany 59 B6
Duluth Minnesota, USA 29 I3
Dumaguete Philippines 95 G5
Dumfries Scotland, United Kingdom 51 E7
Dumont d'Urville Sea *sea* S Pacific Ocean 21 D5
Dunaujvaros Hungary 67 E11
Dundalk Republic of Ireland 51 D8
Dundee Scotland, United Kingdom 51 F5
Dunedin New Zealand 101 F9, 105 D12
Dunfermline Scotland, United Kingdom 51 F6
Dungeness *headland* England, United Kingdom 51 I12
Dungun Malaysia 94 C6
Dunhuang China 96 E4

Dunkerque France 55 F1
Dunkirk New York, USA 33 F5
Dun Laoghaire Republic of Ireland 51 D9
Dunsandel New Zealand 105 E10
Durance river France 55 H7
Durango Mexico 34 D4
Durango Colorado, USA 28 C8
Durazno Uruguay 43 G6
Durban South Africa 71 G12, 81 F8
Durg India 93 E7
Durgapur India 93 G6
Durham England, United Kingdom 51 G7
Durham North Carolina, USA 31 J3
Durham Downs Queensland, Australia 103 J5
Durres Albania 68 E5
D'Urville Island island New Zealand 105 F7
Dushanbe country capital Tajikistan 84 D5, 91 F8
Düsseldorf Germany 59 D7
Duyun China 97 H7
Dzhalal-Abad Kyrgyzstan 91 G7
Dzhankoy Ukraine 65 G12
Dzuunmod Mongolia 97 G2

E

East Cape headland New Zealand 104 I4
East China Sea sea W Pacific Ocean 85 G6, 97 K6, 98 B8
Easter Fracture Zone undersea feature E Pacific Ocean 107 I6
Eastern Desert desert Egypt 74 D4
Eastern Ghats mountain range India 84 D7, 93 D10
Eastern Sayans mountain range Mongolia/Russian Federation 85 E4, 87 F6
East Falkland island Falkland Islands 39 E13, 43 F12
East Frisian Islands island group Germany 58 B3
East Kilbride Scotland, United Kingdom 51 E6
East London South Africa 71 F12, 80 E8
East Mariana Basin undersea feature W Pacific Ocean 106 D4
East Pacific Rise undersea feature SE Pacific Ocean 107 H8
East Siberian Sea sea Arctic Ocean 20 D1, 85 J2
East Timor country SE Asia 85 G9, 95 H9
Eau Claire Wisconsin, USA 32 A4
Eberswalde-Finow Germany 58 H5
Ebetsu Japan 99 I2
Eboli Italy 63 G8
Ebolowa Cameroon 78 C6
Ebro river Spain 57 G3
Écija Spain 56 D7
Eckernförde Germany 58 E2
Ecuador country N South America 38 A3, 40 B3
Ed Damazin Sudan 75 D8
Ed Dueim Sudan 75 D8
Ede Netherlands 52 F6
Edessa Greece 69 F6
Edinburgh Scotland, United Kingdom 46 C4, 51 F6
Edirne Turkey 88 B1
Edmonton Alberta, Canada 23 D6, 24 C7
Edward, Lake lake Democratic Republic of Congo/Uganda 79 G6
Edwards Plateau plateau Texas, USA 30 C5
Éfaté island Vanuatu 101 E6
Eger Hungary 67 G10
Egersund Norway 49 A10
Eggenfelden Germany 59 G11
Egmont, Cape headland New Zealand 105 E6
Egmont, Mount mountain New Zealand 105 F6
Egypt country NE Africa 70 F3, 74 D4
Eidfjord Norway 49 B8

Eifel mountain range Germany 59 A8
Eigg island Scotland, United Kingdom 50 D5
Eight Degree Channel channel India/Maldives 93 B11
Eighty Mile Beach coastal region Western Australia, Australia 102 C3
Eindhoven Netherlands 53 F7
Eisenstadt Austria 61 K3
Ejin Qi China 97 F4
Ekibastuz Kazakhstan 90 G3
El Alamein Egypt 74 C3
Elat Israel 88 D4
Elazig Turkey 88 E2
Elba island Italy 63 C6
Elbasan Albania 69 E5
Elbe river Czech Republic/Germany 46 D5, 58 F4, 67 B7
Elbert, Mount mountain Colorado, USA 28 D7
Elblag Poland 66 F3
Elbrus mountain Russian Federation 47 I7, 86 A6
Elburz Mountains mountain range Iran 89 G3
El Calafate Argentina 43 C12
Elche Spain 57 G6
Elda Spain 57 G6
Elde river Germany 58 F4
Eldoret Kenya 79 H6
Eleuthera Island island Bahamas 36 D2
El Faiyum Egypt 74 C4
El Fasher Sudan 75 B8
El Fula Sudan 75 B8
El Geneina Sudan 75 A8
El Gîza Egypt 70 G3, 74 C3
El Goléa Algeria 73 F5
Elk Poland 66 H3
El Kharga Egypt 74 C4
Elko Nevada, USA 27 E6
Ellensburg Washington, USA 26 C2
Ellesmere Island island Nunavut, Canada 22 G4, 25 F1
Ellesmere, Lake lake New Zealand 105 E10
Elliston South Australia, Australia 103 F7
Ellsworth Land physical region Antarctica 21 A3
El Mahbas Morocco 73 C5
El Minya Egypt 74 C4
El Mreyyé desert Mauritania 77 E4
El Obeid Sudan 71 G5, 75 C8
El Oued Algeria 73 G4
El Paso Texas, USA 23 D9, 30 B5
El Puerto de Santa María Spain 56 C8
El Salvador country Central America 23 E12, 35 G7
Eltanin Fracture Zone undersea feature SE Pacific Ocean 107 G8
Elvas Portugal 56 B6
Elx see Elche
Elvas Portugal 56 B6
Emamshahr Iran 89 H3
Emba Kazakhstan 90 C4
Emden Germany 58 B4
Emerald Queensland, Australia 103 I4
Emmen Netherlands 52 I3
Emperor Seamounts undersea feature N Pacific Ocean 106 D2
Emporia Kansas, USA 29 H7
Empty Quarter see Ar Rub' al Khali
Ems river Germany 58 B4
Encarnación Paraguay 42 G4
Enderby Land physical region Antarctica 21 C8
Enderby Plain undersea feature S Indian Ocean 82 C8
Enerhodar Ukraine 65 G11
Enewetak Atoll island Marshall Islands 100 E3
Enggano island Indonesia 94 C8
England national region United Kingdom 51 F9
English Channel channel NE Atlantic Ocean 46 B5, 51 G12
Enid Oklahoma, USA 30 D3
Enna Italy 63 F11
En Nahud Sudan 75 C8
Ennis Republic of Ireland 51 B9

Enniskillen Northern Ireland, United Kingdom 51 C8
Enns river Austria 61 I4
Enschede Netherlands 52 I5
Ensenada Mexico 34 A1
Entebbe Uganda 79 H6
Enugu Nigeria 77 I7
Equatorial Guinea country C Africa 71 D7, 78 B6
Erd Hungary 67 E10
Erdenet Mongolia 97 F2
Erenhot China 97 H3
Erfurt Germany 59 F7
Erg Chech desert Algeria/Mali 70 C3, 72 D6, 77 F3
Erg Iguidi desert Algeria/Mauritania 70 B3, 72 D6, 77 F2
Ergun He see Argun
Erie Pennsylvania, USA 33 F6
Erie, Lake lake Canada/USA 23 G8, 25 H9, 33 E6
Erimo-misaki headland Japan 99 I3
Eritrea country E Africa 70 H5, 75 E7
Erlangen Germany 59 E9
Ermelo South Africa 81 F7
Ermoupoli Greece 69 G8
Ernakulam India 93 C10
Erode India 93 D10
Er-Rachidia Morocco 73 D4
Ertis river NW Asia 90 G3 see also Irtysh
Erzgebirge mountain range Germany 59 G8
Erzurum Turkey 89 F2
Esbjerg Denmark 49 A12
Escanaba Michigan, USA 32 C3
Esch-Sur-Alzette Luxembourg 52 G13
Escondido California, USA 27 D11
Esenguly Turkmenistan 91 B8
Esfahan Iran 84 B6, 89 H4
Eshkashem Afghanistan 91 F8
Esil Kazakhstan 90 E3
Eskisehir Turkey 88 C2
Española, Isla island Galapagos Islands 40 B9
Esperance Western Australia, Australia 102 D7
Espichel, Cabo headland Portugal 56 A6
Espiritu Santo island Vanuatu 101 E6
Espoo Finland 49 G9
Esquel Argentina 43 C9
Essen Germany 46 D5, 59 B6
Essequibo river Guyana 41 F2
Estados, Isla de los island Argentina 43 E13
Estepona Spain 56 D8
Estonia country NE Europe 47 F4, 64 C4
Estoril Portugal 56 A6
Estrela, Serra da mountain range Portugal 56 B5
Estremoz Portugal 56 B6
Esztergom Hungary 67 E10
Etawah India 92 D5
Ethiopia country E Africa 71 H6, 75 F10
Ethiopian Highlands mountain range Ethiopia 71 H6, 75 E9
Etna, Mount volcano Italy 46 E8, 63 G11
Etosha Pan salt lake Namibia 80 B5
Euboea island Greece 69 G7
Eugene Oregon, USA 26 B4
Eugenia, Punta headland Mexico 34 A3
Eupen Belgium 53 G10
Euphrates river SW Asia 84 B6, 89 F4
Eureka California, USA 27 A6
Europe continent 46–69
Europoort Netherlands 53 D6
Euskirchen Germany 59 B7
Evansville Indiana, USA 32 C8
Everard, Lake seasonal lake South Australia, Australia 103 F6
Everest, Mount mountain China/Nepal 92 F4
Everett Washington, USA 26 C1
Everglades, The wetland Florida, USA 23 F10, 31 J7
Evje Norway 49 B10

Évora Portugal 56 B6
Évreux France 55 E3
Evros river Bulgaria/Turkey 69 H5
Exe river England, United Kingdom 51 F12
Exeter England, United Kingdom 51 F12
Exmoor moorland England, United Kingdom 51 E11
Exmouth Gulf gulf Western Australia, Australia 102 A4
Eyre, Lake lake Australia 100 C7
Eyre North, Lake seasonal lake South Australia, Australia 103 G5
Eyre South, Lake seasonal lake South Australia, Australia 103 G6

F

Faenza Italy 62 D4
Faeroe Islands Danish dependent territory N Atlantic Ocean 44 F3, 46 C2
Fagaras Romania 69 G2
Fagne hill range Belgium 53 D11
Fairbanks Alaska, USA 26 H1
Fair Isle island Scotland, United Kingdom 50 F3
Fairmont Minnesota, USA 29 I4
Faisalabad Pakistan 84 D6, 91 G10
Faizabad India 92 E5
Falam Myanmar 94 A2
Falkland Escarpment undersea feature SW Atlantic Ocean 45 D11
Falkland Islands island group S South America 45 D11
Falkland Islands UK dependent territory S South America 39 E12, 43 F12
Falkoping Sweden 49 D10
Falster island Denmark 49 C13
Falun Sweden 49 D9
Famenne physical region Belgium 53 F11
Fano Italy 62 E5
Fano, Isla island Galapagos Islands 40 B9
Farah Afghanistan 91 D10
Farewell, Cape headland Greenland 23 I5
Farewell, Cape headland New Zealand 105 D7
Farghona Uzbekistan 91 F7
Fargo North Dakota, USA 29 H3
Faribault Minnesota, USA 29 I4
Faridabad India 92 D4
Färjestaden Sweden 49 E11
Farmington New Mexico, USA 30 A3
Faro Portugal 56 B8
Fastiv Ukraine 65 E9
Fauske Norway 48 E4
Faxaflói bay Iceland 48 A3
Faya Chad 78 D2
Fayetteville North Carolina, USA 31 J3
Fayetteville Arkansas, USA 31 F3
Fdérik Mauritania 76 D3
Fear, Cape headland North Carolina, USA 31 K4
Fehmarn island Germany 58 F2
Fehmarn Belt strait Denmark/Germany 58 F2
Feilding New Zealand 105 G6
Feira de Santana Brazil 41 J5
Feldkirch mountain Switzerland 60 D4
Fen He river China 97 H5
Fenoarivo Mozambique 81 K5
Fens, The marsh England, United Kingdom 51 H10
Feodosiya Ukraine 65 G12
Fergana Valley physical region Tajikistan/Uzbekistan 91 F7
Fergus Falls Minnesota, USA 29 H3
Ferkessédougou Ivory Coast 77 F7
Fermo Italy 63 F5
Fernandina, Isla island Galapagos Islands 40 B9
Fernando di Noronho island group E South America 45 D8
Ferrara Italy 62 D4
Ferret, Cap headland France 54 D7
Ferrol Spain 56 B1

Fès Morocco 70 C2, 72 D4
Feyzabad Afghanistan 91 F8
Fezzan physical region Libya 73 H6
Fianarantsoa Madagascar 71 I11, 81 J6
Fier Albania 68 E6
Figueira da Foz Portugal 56 A5
Figueres Spain 57 J2
Figuig Morocco 72 E4
Fiji country C Pacific Ocean 101 F6
Filadélfia Paraguay 42 F2
Filchner Ice Shelf ice shelf Antarctica 21 B2
Filipstad Sweden 49 D9
Fimbul ice shelf Antarctica 21 C1
Finland country N Europe 47 F3, 48 G7
Finland, Gulf of gulf NE Baltic Sea 47 F4, 49 H9, 64 C3
Finsteraarhorn mountain Switzerland 60 C5
Fiordland physical region New Zealand 105 A11
Firozabad India 92 D5
Fishguard Wales, United Kingdom 51 E10
Fitz Roy Argentina 43 D10
Fitzroy river Western Australia, Australia 102 D3
Fitzroy Crossing Western Australia, Australia 102 D3
Flagstaff Arizona, USA 27 G10
Flamborough Head headland England, United Kingdom 51 H8
Flanders cultural region Belgium 53 A8
Flattery, Cape headland Washington, USA 26 B1
Flensburg Germany 58 D2
Flinders river Queensland, Australia 103 H3
Flinders Island island Tasmania, Australia 103 I8
Flinders Ranges mountain range South Australia, Australia 103 G6
Flin Flon Manitoba, Canada 24 E7
Flint Michigan, USA 32 D5
Florence Italy 46 D7, 62 D5
Florence Alabama, USA 31 G4
Florencia Colombia 40 C3
Flores Guatemala 35 H6
Flores island Indonesia 95 G9
Flores Sea sea Indonesia 85 G9, 95 F9
Florianópolis Brazil 41 H8
Florida state USA 31 J6
Florida Uruguay 43 G6
Florida Keys island group Florida, USA 31 J8
Florida, Straits of strait Atlantic Ocean/Gulf of Mexico 23 F11, 31 J8, 36 C2
Florø Norway 49 A7
Foca Bosnia & Herzegovina 68 D4
Focsani Romania 69 H2
Foggia Italy 63 G7
Föhr island Germany 58 C2
Foix France 55 F8
Follonica Italy 63 D6
Fongafale country capital Tuvalu 101 F5
Fonyod Hungary 67 E11
Forbach France 55 I2
Forli Italy 62 D4
Formentera island Balearic Islands, Spain 57 I6
Formia Italy 63 F7
Formosa Argentina 42 G3
Forsayth Queensland, Australia 103 H3
Forster-Tuncurry New South Wales, Australia 103 J7
Fortaleza Brazil 38 I4, 41 J4
Fort Collins Colorado, USA 28 E6
Fort-de-France Martinique 37 J7
Fort Dodge Iowa, USA 29 I5
Forth, Firth of inlet Scotland, United Kingdom 51 F6
Fort Lauderdale Florida, USA 31 J7
Fort McMurray Alberta, Canada 24 D6
Fort Nelson British Columbia, Canada 24 C5

Fort Peck Lake lake Montana, USA 28 D2
Fort-Shevchenko Kazakhstan 91 A5
Fort Smith Northwest Territories, Canada 24 D5
Fort Smith Arkansas, USA 31 E4
Fort Wayne Indiana, USA 32 D6
Fort William Scotland, United Kingdom 50 D5
Fort Worth Texas, USA 23 E9, 30 E5
Foshan China 97 H8
Foulwind, Cape headland New Zealand 105 D8
Fouman Cameroon 78 B5
Fouta Djallon mountain range Guinea 76 D3
Foveaux Strait strait New Zealand 105 A12
Foxe Basin sea NW Atlantic Ocean 22 G5, 25 G4
Fox Glacier New Zealand 105 C9
Fram Basin undersea feature Arctic Ocean 20 C3
Franca Brazil 41 H7
France country W Europe 46 C6, 54–55
Franceville Gabon 78 C7
Francistown Botswana 71 F11, 80 E5
Frankenwald physical region Germany 59 F8
Frankfort state capital Kentucky, USA 32 D8
Frankfurt am Main Germany 46 D5, 59 C8
Frankfurt an der Oder Germany 59 I5
Fränkische Alb mountain range Germany 59 E10
Franz Josef Land island group Russian Federation 87 E2
Fraser river British Columbia, Canada 24 B7
Fraserburgh Scotland, United Kingdom 50 F4
Fraser Island island Queensland, Australia 103 J5
Frauenfeld Switzerland 60 D4
Fray Bentos Uruguay 43 F6
Fredericton New Brunswick, Canada 25 I8
Frederikshavn Denmark 49 B11
Fredrikstad Norway 49 C9
Freeport Bahamas 36 C1
Freeport Texas, USA 31 E6
Freetown country capital Sierra Leone 71 A6, 76 C7
Freiberg Germany 59 H7
Freiburg im Breisgau Germany 59 B11
Freising Germany 59 F11
Fréjus France 55 I8
Fremantle Western Australia, Australia 102 B7
Fremont California, USA 27 B8
French Guiana French dependent territory N South America 38 F3, 41 G2
French Polynesia French dependent territory C Pacific Ocean 101 I7
Fresno California, USA 27 C9
Fribourg Switzerland 60 B5
Friedrichshafen Germany 59 D12
Frisian Islands island group N Europe 58 F13
Frome, Lake seasonal lake South Australia, Australia 103 G6
Frontera Mexico 35 G4
Frøya island Norway 49 B6
Frydek-Mistek Czech Republic 67 E8
Fuengirola Spain 56 D8
Fuenlabrada Spain 56 E5
Fuerte river Mexico 34 B3
Fujairah United Arab Emirates 89 I6
Fuji Japan 99 G7
Fujieda Japan 99 G7
Fuji, Mount mountain Japan 99 G7
Fujinomiya Japan 99 G7
Fukue-jima island Japan 98 C8
Fukui Japan 99 F6
Fukuoka Japan 85 H6, 98 D7
Fukushima Japan 99 G6
Fukuyama Japan 98 E7
Fulda Germany 59 D8
Fulda river Germany 59 D7

FULING–HALMAHERA . 115

Fuling China 97 G7
Funabashi Japan 99 H6
Fundy, Bay of *bay* New Brunswick/Nova Scotia, Canada 25 J8
Furneaux Group *island group* Tasmania, Australia 103 I8
Fürth Germany 59 E9
Furukawa Japan 99 H5
Fushun China 97 J3
Fuxin China 97 I3
Fuzhou China 97 J7
Fyn *island* Denmark 49 B12

G

Gaalkacyo Somalia 75 H10
Gabès Tunisia 70 D2, 73 H4
Gabès, Gulf of S Mediterranean Sea 73 H4
Gabon *country* C Africa 71 D8, 78 B6
Gaborone *country capital* Botswana 71 F11, 80 E6
Gabrovo Bulgaria 69 G4
Gadag India 93 C8
Gaeta Italy 63 F7
Gaeta, Gulf of *gulf* N Tyrrhenian Sea 63 E8
Gafsa Tunisia 73 G4
Gagnoa Ivory Coast 77 E8
Gainesville Florida, USA 31 I6
Gairdner, Lake *seasonal lake* South Australia, Australia 103 F6
Galapagos Islands *island group* Ecuador 40 A8
Galati Romania 69 I2
Galdhopiggen *mountain* Norway 49 B8
Galicia *cultural region* Spain 56 B2
Galle Sri Lanka 93 D12
Gallego Rise *undersea feature* E Pacific Ocean 107 H5
Gallipoli Italy 63 I8
Gallipoli Turkey 88 B1
Gällivare Sweden 48 F4
Gallup New Mexico, USA 30 A3
Galtat-Zemmour Western Sahara 72 B6
Galveston Texas, USA 31 E6
Galway Republic of Ireland 51 B9
Galway Bay *bay* Republic of Ireland 51 B9
Gambia *country* W Africa 70 A5, 76 C5
Gambia *river* Gambia 76 D6
Gambier Islands *island group* French Polynesia 101 J7
Ganca Azerbaijan 89 G1
Gander Newfoundland & Labrador, Canada 25 K6
Gandhinagar India 93 B6
Gandhi Sagar *lake* India 93 C5
Gandia Spain 57 H6
Ganges *river* Bangladesh/India 84 D6, 92 D5
Ganges, Mouths of the *delta* Bangladesh/India 93 G7
Gangneung South Korea 98 C5
Gangtok Bhutan 92 G5
Gan Jiang *river* China 97 I7
Ganyushkino Kazakhstan 90 A5
Ganzhou China 97 I7
Gao Mali 77 G5
Gap France 55 I7
Gar China 96 B6
Garabogaz Aylagy *bay* Turkmenistan 91 B6
Garagum *desert* Turkmenistan 91 C7
Garagum Canal *canal* Turkmenistan 91 B7
Garda, Lake *lake* Italy 62 D3
Gardelegen Germany 58 F5
Garden City Kansas, USA 29 F8
Gardez Afghanistan 91 F9
Gargano Peninsula *peninsula* Italy 63 G7
Garissa Kenya 79 J6
Garland Texas, USA 30 E5
Garmisch-Partenkirchen Germany 59 F12
Garmsar Iran 89 H3
Garonne *river* France 46 C6, 55 E7
Garoowe Somalia 75 H9
Garoua Cameroon 78 C4
Garut Indonesia 94 D9
Garwolin Poland 66 G5
Gary Indiana, USA 32 C6
Gascony *cultural region* France 54 D7
Gascony, Gulf of *gulf* France/Spain 57 F1, 54 C7
Gastonia North Carolina, USA 31 I3
Gastouni Greece 69 F7
Gata, Cabo de *headland* Spain 57 F8
Gävle Sweden 49 E9
Gawler South Australia, Australia 103 G7
Gaya India 93 F5
Gaza Israel 88 D4
Gazanjyk Turkmenistan 91 B7
Gaziantep Turkey 88 E2
Gazojak Turkmenistan 91 D7
Gdansk Poland 47 E5, 66 E2
Gdansk, Gulf of *gulf* S Baltic Sea 66 F2
Gdynia Poland 66 E2
Gebze Turkey 88 C1
Gedaref Sudan 75 E8
Geel Belgium 53 E8
Geelong Victoria, Australia 100 D8, 103 H8
Geilo Norway 49 B8
Gejiu China 97 F8
Gela Italy 63 F12
Gelsenkirchen Germany 59 B6
Gembloux Belgium 53 E10
Gemena Democratic Republic of Congo 78 E5
Gemona del Friuli Italy 62 E2
General Roca Argentina 43 D8
General Santos Philippines 95 H6
Geneva Switzerland 60 A6
Geneva, Lake *lake* France/Switzerland 55 I5, 60 B5
Genk Belgium 53 F9
Genoa Italy 46 D7, 62 B4
Genoa, Gulf of *gulf* N Ligurian Sea 62 B5
Geok-Tepe Turkmenistan 91 C8
George South Africa 80 D9
Georgetown Queensland, Australia 103 H3
Georgetown *country capital* Guyana 38 F2, 41 F2
George Town Malaysia 94 B6
George V Land *physical region* Antarctica 21 D5
Georgia *country* SW Asia 84 B5, 89 E1
Georgia *state* USA 31 I5
Georgian Bay *lake bay* Ontario, Canada 25 H9, 33 E3
Georgievka Kazakhstan 91 G6
Georgina *seasonal river* C Australia 103 G4
Gera Germany 59 G7
Geraldton Western Australia, Australia 100 A8, 102 B6
Gereshk Afghanistan 91 D10
Gerlachovsky Stit *mountain* Slovakia 67 F8
German Bight *bay* SE North Sea 58 C2
Germany *country* W Europe 46 D5, 58–59
Getafe Spain 57 E5
Ghadamis Libya 73 G5
Ghaghara *river* S Asia 92 E5
Ghana *country* W Africa 71 C6, 77 G7
Ghanzi Botswana 80 D6
Ghardaïa Algeria 73 F4
Ghat Libya 73 G6
Ghazal, Bahr El *river* Sudan 75 C9
Ghaziabad India 92 D4
Ghazni Afghanistan 91 E9
Ghent Belgium 53 C8
Gibraltar *UK dependent territory* SW Europe 46 A8, 56 D9
Gibraltar, Strait of *strait* Atlantic Ocean/ Mediterranean Sea 46 A8, 56 C9, 72 D3
Gibson Desert *desert* Western Australia, Australia 100 A7, 102 D5
Giessen Germany 59 C8
Gifhorn Germany 58 E5
Gifu Japan 99 G7
Gijón Spain 56 D1
Gila *river* Arizona, USA 27 F12
Gilbert Islands *island group* Kiribati 101 F4
Gilgit Pakistan 91 G8
Gillette Wyoming, USA 28 E4
Gioia del Colle Italy 63 H8
Girona Spain 57 J3
Gironde *estuary* France 54 D6
Gisborne New Zealand 104 I5
Giurgiu Romania 69 H3
Gizycko Poland 66 H3
Gjøvik Norway 49 C8
Gladstone Queensland, Australia 103 J5
Glarner Alpen *mountain range* Switzerland 60 D5
Glasgow Scotland, United Kingdom 46 C4, 51 E6
Glen Canyon *canyon* Arizona/Utah, USA 27 G9
Glendale Arizona, USA 27 G11
Glendale California, USA 27 D11
Glendive Montana, USA 28 E3
Glens Falls New York, USA 33 I5
Glittertind *mountain* Norway 49 B8
Gliwice Poland 67 E7
Glogow Poland 67 D5
Glomma *river* Norway 49 C8
Gloucester England, United Kingdom 51 F10
Gmünd Austria 61 I2
Gmunden Austria 61 H3
Gniezno Poland 66 E4
Gobabis Namibia 80 C6
Gobernador Gregores Argentina 43 D11
Gobi *desert* China/Mongolia 85 F5, 97 F4
Godavari *river* India 84 D7, 93 D7
Godoy Cruz Argentina 43 C6
Goes Netherlands 53 C7
Goiânia Brazil 39 G6, 41 H6
Gol Norway 49 B8
Gold Coast Queensland, Australia 100 D7, 103 J6
Golden Bay *bay* New Zealand 105 E7
Goleniow Poland 66 C3
Golmud China 96 E5
Goma Democratic Republic of Congo 79 G6
Gonabad Iran 89 I3
Gonaïves Haiti 37 F4
Gonbad-e Kavus Iran 89 H2
Gonder Ethiopia 75 E8
Gondia India 93 D7
Good Hope, Cape of *headland* South Africa 45 H10, 71 E13, 80 C9
Goondiwindi Queensland, Australia 103 J6
Göppingen Germany 59 D10
Gorakhpur India 92 E5
Gore Ethiopia 75 E9
Gore New Zealand 105 C12
Gorgan Iran 89 H2
Gorizia Italy 62 F3
Gorlice Poland 67 G8
Görlitz Germany 59 I7
Gorno-Altaysk Russian Federation 87 E6
Gorontalo Indonesia 95 G7
Gorzow Wielkopolski Poland 66 C4
Gosford New South Wales, Australia 103 J7
Goslar Germany 59 E6
Gosselies Belgium 53 D10
Gostivar Macedonia 69 E5
Gotha Germany 59 E7
Gothenburg Sweden 46 E4, 49 C11
Gotland *island* Sweden 47 E4, 49 E11
Goto-retto *island group* Japan 98 C8
Göttingen Germany 59 E6
Gouda Netherlands 53 E6
Goulburn New South Wales, Australia 103 I7
Goya Argentina 42 F4
Gozo *island* Malta 63 F13
Grafton New South Wales, Australia 103 J6
Grajewo Poland 66 H3
Grampian Mountains *mountain range* Scotland, United Kingdom 50 E5
Granada Nicaragua 35 I8
Granada Spain 57 E8
Gran Chaco *physical region* C South America 39 D8, 42 E3
Grand Bahama Island *island* Bahamas 36 C1
Grand Canyon *canyon* Arizona, USA 23 C8, 27 F9
Grand Cayman *island* Cayman Islands 36 B4
Grand Comore *island* Comoros 81 J3
Grande, Bahia *bay* Argentina 39 D12, 43 D12
Grande Prairie Alberta, Canada 24 C6
Grand Erg Occidental *desert* Algeria 70 C3, 73 F3
Grande, Rio *river* Brazil 23 D9, 39 F7, 41 H7
Grande, Rio *river* Mexico/USA 30 B5, 34 D2 *see also* Bravo del Norte, Río
Grande Terre *island* Guadeloupe 37 J6
Grand Forks North Dakota, USA 29 H2
Grand Island Nebraska, USA 29 G6
Grand Junction Colorado, USA 28 C7
Grand Rapids Michigan, USA 32 D5
Grand River *river* South Dakota, USA 29 E3
Gran Paradiso *mountain* Italy 62 A3
Gransee Germany 58 H4
Grants Pass Oregon, USA 26 B5
Granville Lake *lake* Manitoba, Canada 25 E6
Graz Austria 61 J5
Great Abaco *island* Bahamas 36 D1
Great Artesian Basin *physical region* Queensland, Australia 103 H5
Great Australian Bight *bay* South Australia, Australia 83 I6, 100 B8, 103 E7
Great Barrier Island *island* New Zealand 104 G3
Great Barrier Reef *reef* Queensland, Australia 100 C6, 103 I1
Great Basin *physical region* W USA 23 C8, 27 E7
Great Bear Lake *lake* Northwest Territories, Canada 22 E5, 24 D4
Great Bend Kansas, USA 29 G7
Great Channel *channel* Andaman Sea/Indian Ocean 93 I12
Great Divide Basin *physical region* Wyoming, USA 28 C5
Great Dividing Range *mountain range* E Australia 100 C7, 103 H3
Greater Antarctica *plateau* Antarctica 21 D3
Greater Antilles *island group* West Indies 23 F11, 36 B4
Great Exhibition Bay *bay* New Zealand 104 E1
Great Falls Montana, USA 28 C2
Great Hungarian Plain *physical region* Hungary 67 F10
Great Inagua *island* Bahamas 37 E4
Great Karoo *plateau* South Africa 80 D8
Great Khingan Range *mountain range* China 85 G5, 97 I2
Great Lakes *lakes* Canada/USA 23 F7, 32 C2
Great Nicobar *island* Nicobar Islands, India 93 I11
Great Ouse *river* England, United Kingdom 51 H10
Great Plains *physical region* Canada/USA 23 E7, 24 D7, 29 E3, 30 C2
Great Rift Valley *valley* E Africa 71 E8, 75 F9, 79 G7, 81 F2
Great Salt Lake *salt lake* Utah, USA 23 D8, 27 G6
Great Salt Lake Desert *physical region* Utah, USA 27 F6
Great Sand Sea *desert* Ethiopia/Libya 73 K5, 74 A4
Great Sandy Desert *desert* Australia 100 A7, 102 C4
Great Slave Lake *lake* Northwest Territories, Canada 23 E5, 24 D5
Great Victoria Desert *desert* South Australia/Western Australia, Australia 100 B7, 102 D6
Greece *country* SE Europe 47 F8, 69 F7
Greeley Colorado, USA 28 E6
Green Bay Wisconsin, USA 32 C4
Greenland *Danish dependent territory* NE North America 20 B4, 22 H3
Greenland *island* NE North America Ocean 44 D1
Greenland Sea *sea* Arctic Ocean 20 C5, 44 F2
Greenock Scotland, United Kingdom 51 E6
Greensboro North Carolina, USA 31 J3
Greenville Liberia 76 D8
Greenville Mississippi, USA 31 F5
Greenville South Carolina, USA 31 I4
Greifswald Germany 58 H3
Grenada *country* SE West Indies 23 I12, 37 J8
Grenadines, The *island group* St Vincent & the Grenadines 37 J7
Grenoble France 55 H6
Grevena Greece 69 F6
Grevenmacher Luxembourg 53 H12
Greymouth New Zealand 105 D9
Grimsby England, United Kingdom 51 H9
Grímsstadhir Iceland 48 C2
Grojec Poland 66 G5
Groningen Netherlands 52 H2
Groote Eylandt *island* Northern Territory, Australia 103 G2
Grootfontein Namibia 80 C5
Grosseto Italy 63 D6
Grossglockner *mountain* Austria 61 G5
Groznyy Russian Federation 47 J7, 86 A6
Grudziadz Poland 66 F3
Grums Sweden 49 D9
Grünau Namibia 80 C7
Guadalajara Mexico 23 D11, 34 D5
Guadalajara Spain 57 F4
Guadalcanal *island* Solomon Islands 100 D5
Guadalquivir *river* Spain 46 A7, 56 D7
Guadeloupe *French dependent territory* E West Indies 37 K6
Guadeloupe Passage *channel* Antigua & Barbuda/Guadeloupe 37 J6
Guadiana *river* Portugal/Spain 56 B7
Gualeguaychu Argentina 43 F6
Guam *US dependent territory* W Pacific Ocean 100 C3
Guangyuan China 97 G6
Guangzhou China 85 F7, 97 I8
Guantánamo Cuba 36 E4
Guaporé *river* Bolivia/Brazil 39 D6, 41 E5
Guarda Portugal 56 C4
Guarulhos Brazil 39 G8, 41 H7
Guatemala *country* Central America 23 E12, 35 G7
Guatemala Basin *undersea feature* E Pacific Ocean 107 I4
Guatemala City *country capital* Guatemala 23 E12, 35 G7
Guaviare *river* Colombia/Venezuela 38 C3, 40 D2
Guayaquil Ecuador 38 A4, 40 B4
Guayaquil, Gulf of *gulf* Ecuador/Peru 40 B4
Guaymas Mexico 34 B3
Gubbio Italy 63 E5
Guernsey *island* Channel Islands 51 F13
Guiana Highlands *physical region* N South America 38 D2, 40 E2
Guilin China 97 H8
Guimarães Portugal 56 B3
Guinea *country* W Africa 71 A6, 76 D6
Guinea Basin *undersea feature* E Atlantic Ocean 45 F9
Guinea-Bissau *country* W Africa 71 A5, 76 C6
Guinea, Gulf of *gulf* E Atlantic Ocean 45 G7, 71 C7, 77 G9, 78 A5
Guiyang China 85 F6, 97 G7
Gujranwala Pakistan 91 G9
Gulf Coastal Plain *physical region* S USA 30 E6
Gulfport Mississippi, USA 31 G6
Gulf, The *gulf* SW Asia 82 C1, 84 B6, 89 G5
Guliston Uzbekistan 91 E7
Gulu Uganda 79 H6
Gumdag Turkmenistan 91 B7
Gunnbjørn Fjeld *mountain* Greenland 20 B5
Gunsan South Korea 98 B6
Guntur India 93 E8
Gunzenhausen Germany 59 E10
Guri, Embalse de *reservoir* Venezuela 41 E2
Gurué Mozambique 81 G4
Gusau Nigeria 77 I6
Gushgy Turkmenistan 91 D9
Guspini Italy 63 B9
Gütersloh Germany 59 C6
Guwahati India 92 H5
Guyana *country* N South America 38 E2, 41 F2
Gwadar Pakistan 91 D12
Gwalior India 92 D5
Gwanda Zimbabwe 81 F5
Gwangju South Korea 98 B6
Gweru Zimbabwe 71 G10, 81 F5
Gyangze China 96 D7
Gydanskiy Poluostrov *peninsula* Russian Federation 87 E3
Gyeongju South Korea 98 C6
Gympie Queensland, Australia 103 J5
Gyor Hungary 67 E10
Gytheio Greece 69 F8
Gyumri Armenia 89 F1
Gyzylarbat Turkmenistan 91 B7

H

Haapsalu Estonia 64 C3
Haarlem Netherlands 52 E5
Haast New Zealand 105 B10
Hachinohe Japan 99 I4
Hadramawt *mountain range* Yemen 89 G9
Haeju North Korea 98 B5
Hafar al Batin Saudi Arabia 89 F5
Hagen Germany 59 B6
Hagi Japan 98 D7
Ha Giang Vietnam 94 D2
Hague, Cap de la *headland* France 54 D2
Haguenau France 55 I3
Haicheng China 97 J4
Haifa Israel 88 D4
Haikou Hainan, China 97 H9
Ha'il Saudi Arabia 89 E5
Hailar China 97 I2
Hainan *island* China 85 F7, 97 H9
Hai Phong Vietnam 85 F7, 94 D2
Haiti *country* C West Indies 23 G11, 37 E5
Hakodate Japan 99 H3
Halaban Saudi Arabia 89 F6
Halaib Egypt 75 E6
Halban Mongolia 97 E2
Halberstadt Germany 59 F6
Halden Norway 49 C10
Halfmoon Bay New Zealand 105 B13
Halifax Nova Scotia, Canada 23 H8, 25 J8
Halla-san *mountain* South Korea 98 B7
Halle Belgium 53 D9
Halle Germany 59 F7
Hallein Austria 61 G4
Halle-Neustadt Germany 59 F7
Hallett, Cape *headland* Antarctica 21 C5
Halls Creek Western Australia, Australia 102 E3
Halmahera *island* Indonesia 95 I7

116 . HALMAHERA SEA–JAROSLAW

Halmahera Sea *sea* Indonesia 95 I7
Halmstad Sweden 49 C11
Hamada Japan 98 E7
Hamadan Iran 89 G3
Hamah Syria 88 D3
Hamamatsu Japan 99 G7
Hamar Norway 49 C8
Hamburg Germany 46 D5, 58 E3
Hämeenlinna Finland 49 G8
Hameln Germany 59 D5
Hamersley Range *mountain range* Western Australia, Australia 102 B4
Hamhung North Korea 98 C4
Hami China 96 E4
Hamilton Victoria, Australia 103 H8
Hamilton Ontario, Canada 25 H9
Hamilton New Zealand 101 F8, 104 G4
Hamm Germany 59 C6
Hammerfest Norway 48 G2
Hampton Virginia, USA 33 H8
Handan China 97 H5
Hangzhou China 97 J6
Hannover Germany 46 D5, 58 D5
Hanoi *country capital* Vietnam 85 F7, 94 D2
Han Shui *river* China 97 H6
Hanzhong China 97 G6
Haora India 93 G6
Haparanda Sweden 48 G5
Happy Valley-Goose Bay Newfoundland & Labrador, Canada 25 J6
Harad Saudi Arabia 89 G6
Haradok Belarus 65 E6
Harare *country capital* Zimbabwe 71 G10, 81 F5
Harbel Liberia 76 D7
Harbin China 85 H5, 97 J2
Hardangervidda *plateau* Norway 49 A9
Harderwijk Netherlands 52 F5
Harelbeke Belgium 53 B9
Harer Ethiopia 75 F9
Hargeysa Somalia 71 H6, 75 G9
Harlingen Netherlands 52 F2
Harney Basin *physical region* Oregon, USA 26 C5
Härnösand Sweden 49 E7
Harper Liberia 76 E8
Harris *island* Scotland, United Kingdom 50 C4
Harrisburg *state capital* Pennsylvania, USA 33 G7
Harstad Norway 48 E3
Hartford Connecticut, USA 33 I6
Harz *mountain range* Germany 59 E6
Hasselt Belgium 53 F9
Hastings New Zealand 105 H6
Hastings England, United Kingdom 51 H12
Hastings Nebraska, USA 29 G6
Hatteras, Cape *headland* North Carolina, USA 23 G9, 31 K3
Hatteras Plain *undersea feature* W Atlantic Ocean 45 C6
Hattiesburg Mississippi, USA 31 G5
Hat Yai Thailand 94 B5
Haugesund Norway 49 A9
Haukeligrend Norway 49 B9
Hauraki Gulf *gulf* New Zealand 104 G3
Havana *country capital* Cuba 23 F11, 36 B3
Havel *river* Germany 58 G5
Havirov Czech Republic 67 E7
Havlickuv Brod Czech Republic 67 C8
Havre Montana, USA 28 C2
Havre-St-Pierre Québec, Canada 25 I7
Hawaii *island* Hawaii, USA 27 C13
Hawaii *state* USA 27 C12
Hawaiian Ridge *undersea feature* N Pacific Ocean 107 E3
Hawea, Lake *lake* New Zealand 105 C10
Hawera New Zealand 105 F6
Hawke Bay *bay* New Zealand 105 H6
Hawra' Yemen 89 G8
Hay New South Wales, Australia 103 H7
Hayma' Oman 89 I7
Hay River Northwest Territories, Canada 24 C5
Hays Kansas, USA 29 G7
Heard & McDonald Islands *island group* S Indian Ocean 83 E8
Heerenveen Netherlands 52 G3
Heerlen Netherlands 53 G9
Hefei China 97 I6
Hegang China 97 J2
Heide Germany 58 D2
Heidelberg Germany 59 C9
Heilbronn Germany 59 D10
Heiligenstadt Germany 59 E7
Heilong Jiang *see* Amur
Heimdal Norway 49 C7
Hejaz *physical region* Saudi Arabia 88 D6
Hekou China 97 G8
Hel Poland 66 F2
Helena *state capital* Montana, USA 28 B3
Helgoland *island* Germany 58 C2
Helgoland Bay *bay* SE North Sea 58 C3
Hell Norway 49 C7
Hellin Spain 57 G6
Helmand *river* Afghanistan 91 D10
Helmond Netherlands 53 G7
Helsingborg Sweden 49 C12
Helsingør Denmark 49 C12
Helsinki *country capital* Finland 47 F3, 49 H9
Helwan Egypt 74 C3
Henderson Nevada, USA 27 E9
Hengelo Netherlands 52 H5
Hengyang China 79 H7
Henry Ice Rise *ice cap* Antarctica 21 B3
Henzada Myanmar 94 B3
Herat Afghanistan 91 D9
Herbertville New Zealand 105 H7
Herford Germany 59 C5
Hermansverk Norway 49 B8
Hermosillo Mexico 23 C9, 34 B2
Herning Denmark 49 B12
Herstal Belgium 53 F9
Hervey Bay Queensland, Australia 103 J5
Herzberg Germany 59 H6
Hettstedt Germany 59 F6
Hialeah Florida, USA 31 J7
Hibbing Minnesota, USA 29 I2
Hicks Bay New Zealand 104 I4
Hidalgo del Parral Mexico 34 C3
Higashi-suido *strait* Japan 98 C7
Hiiumaa *island* Estonia 64 B3
Hildesheim Germany 59 E5
Hilo Hawaii, USA 27 C13
Hilversum Netherlands 52 F5
Himalayas *mountain range* S Asia 84 D6, 96 B5, 92 C3
Himeji Japan 99 F7
Hindu Kush *mountain range* Afghanistan/Pakistan 84 C6, 91 E9
Hinnøya *island* Norway 48 E3
Hirakud Reservoir *reservoir* India 93 F6
Hirosaki Japan 99 H4
Hiroshima Japan 85 H6, 98 E7
Hisar India 92 C4
Hispaniola *island* Dominican Republic/Haiti 37 F5
Hitachi Japan 99 H6
Hitra *island* Norway 49 B6
Hiuch'on North Korea 98 B4
Hjørring Denmark 49 B11
Hkakabo Razi *mountain* China/Myanmar 94 B1
Hobart *state capital* Tasmania, Australia 100 D9, 103 H9
Hobro Denmark 49 B11
Ho Chi Minh Vietnam 85 F8, 94 D5
Hodeida Yemen 89 F9
Hoek van Holland Netherlands 53 D6
Hoeryong North Korea 98 D3
Hof Germany 59 F8
Höfn Iceland 48 C2
Hofu Japan 98 D7
Hohe Tauern *mountain range* Austria 61 G5
Hohhot China 97 H4
Hokitika New Zealand 105 D9
Hokkaido *island* Japan 85 H5, 99 I2
Holguín Cuba 36 D4
Hollabrunn Austria 61 J2
Hollywood Florida, USA 31 J7
Holmestrand Norway 49 C9
Holmsund Sweden 49 F7
Holstebro Denmark 49 B11
Holyhead Wales, United Kingdom 51 E9
Homberg Germany 59 D7
Homburg Germany 59 B9
Homs Syria 88 D3
Homyel Belarus 47 G5, 65 E8
Honduras *country* Central America 23 E12, 35 H7
Honduras, Gulf of *gulf* W Caribbean Sea 35 H6
Hønefoss Norway 49 C9
Hong Gai Vietnam 94 D2
Hong Kong China 85 F7, 97 I8
Honiara *country capital* Solomon Islands 100 D5
Honolulu Hawaii, USA 27 B12
Honshu *island* Japan 85 H5, 99 H5
Hoogeveen Netherlands 52 H4
Hoorn Netherlands 52 E4
Hoover Dam *dam* Nevada/Arizona, USA 27 F9
Hopa Turkey 89 E1
Hopkinsville Kentucky, USA 32 C8
Horlivka Ukraine 65 H10
Hormuz, Strait of *strait* Iran/Oman 89 I5
Horn, Cape *headland* Chile 39 D13, 43 E13, 45 C11
Horsham Victoria, Australia 103 H8
Hotan China 96 B5
Hoting Sweden 49 E6
Hot Springs Arkansas, USA 31 F4
Houlton Maine, USA 33 K3
Houston Texas, USA 23 E10, 31 E6
Hovd Mongolia 96 D2
Hovsgol Nuur *lake* Mongolia 97 F2
Howe, Cape *headland* New South Wales/Victoria, Australia 103 I8
Howland Island *US dependent territory* C Pacific Ocean 101 G4
Höxter Germany 59 D6
Hoy *island* Scotland, United Kingdom 50 F3
Hoyerswerda Germany 59 I7
Hradec Kralove Czech Republic 67 C7
Hranice Czech Republic 67 E8
Hrebinka Ukraine 65 F9
Hrodna Belarus 65 B7
Huai He *river* China 97 H6
Huaihua China 97 H7
Huainan China 97 I6
Huambo Angola 71 E9, 80 B3
Huangshi China 97 I6
Huánucó Peru 40 C5
Huascarán *mountain* Peru 40 C5
Hubbali (Hubli) India 93 C9
Huddersfield England, United Kingdom 51 G9
Hudiksvall Sweden 49 E8
Hudson Bay *bay* Canada 23 F6, 25 F6
Hudson Strait *strait* Hudson Bay/Labrador Sea 23 G5, 25 G5
Hue Vietnam 94 D3
Huelva Spain 56 C7
Huércal-Overa Spain 57 G7
Huesca Spain 57 G3
Huéscar Spain 57 F7
Hughenden Queensland, Australia 103 H4
Huila Plateau *plateau* Angola 80 B4
Hulun Nur *lake* China 97 H2
Humber *river* England, United Kingdom 51 H9
Humboldt *river* Nevada, USA 27 D6
Húnaflói *bay* Iceland 48 B2
Hunedoara Romania 69 F2
Hungary *country* C Europe 47 E6, 67 E11
Hungnam North Korea 98 C4
Hunsrück *mountain range* Germany 59 B9
Huntington West Virginia, USA 32 E8
Huntington Beach California, USA 27 D11
Huntsville Alabama, USA 31 H4
Hurghada Egypt 75 D4
Huron, Lake *lake* Canada/USA 23 G8, 25 G8, 32 E4
Husum Germany 58 D2
Hutchinson Kansas, USA 29 H8
Huy Belgium 53 F10
Hvannadalshnúkur *mountain* Iceland 48 C3
Hvar Croatia 68 C4
Hwange Zimbabwe 80 E5
Hyderabad India 84 D7, 93 D8
Hyderabad Pakistan 84 C6, 91 E12
Hyères, Îles d' *island* France 55 I8
Hyesan North Korea 98 C3
Hyvinkää Finland 49 G9

I

Iasi Romania 46 G6, 69 H1
Ibadan Nigeria 71 C6, 77 H7
Ibagué Colombia 40 C2
Ibb Yemen 89 F9
Ibérico, Sistema *mountain range* Spain 57 F3
Ibiza *island* Balearic Islands, Spain 46 B7, 57 I6
'Ibri Oman 89 I6
Ica Peru 40 C6
Iceland *country* N Atlantic Ocean 46 B1, 48 B2
Iceland *island* N Atlantic Ocean 44 F3
Iceland Basin *undersea feature* N Atlantic Ocean 44 F3
Ichihara Japan 99 H6
Idaho *state* USA 26 F4
Idaho Falls Idaho, USA 26 G5
Idar-Oberstein Germany 59 B9
Idre Sweden 49 D8
Ieper Belgium 53 A9
Iesi Italy 62 E5
Ifôghas, Adrar des *plateau* Mali 77 H4
Iglesias Italy 63 B9
Igoumenitsa Greece 69 E6
Ihosy Madagascar 81 J6
Iisalmi Finland 49 H6
Ijmuiden Netherlands 52 E4
Ijsselmeer *lake* Netherlands 52 F3
Ikaria *island* Greece 69 H8
Ikoli Democratic Republic of Congo 79 F6
Ilagan Philippines 95 G3
Ilam Iran 89 G3
Ilanz Switzerland 60 D5
Ilawa Poland 66 F3
Ile *river* China/Kazakhstan 91 G5
Ilebo Democratic Republic of Congo 78 E7
Ilhéus Brazil 41 J6
Iligan Philippines 95 H5
Illichivsk Ukraine 65 E12
Illinois *river* Illinois, USA 32 B6
Illinois *state* USA 32 B7
Illizi Algeria 73 G6
Iloilo Philippines 95 G5
Ilorin Nigeria 71 C6, 77 H7
Ilulissat Greenland 20 A4
Imatra Finland 49 I8
Imola Italy 62 D4
Imperatriz Brazil 41 H4
Imperia Italy 62 B5
Impfondo Congo 78 D6
Imphal India 93 I5
In Amenas Algeria 73 G5
Inarijärvi *lake* Finland 48 H3
Inch'on South Korea 98 B5
Independence California, USA 27 D9
Independence Missouri, USA 29 I7
India *country* S Asia 84 D7, 93 B6
Indiana *state* USA 32 C6
Indianapolis *state capital* Indiana, USA 23 F9, 32 C7
Indian Ocean *ocean* 75 H12, 82–83, 84 D9
Indian Springs Nevada, USA 27 E9
Indigirka *river* Russian Federation 85 H2, 87 I3
Indonesia *country* SE Asia 85 F9, 94 C8
Indore India 84 D7, 93 C6
Indus *river* S Asia 91 F11, 92 D2
Indus, Mouths of the *delta* Pakistan 91 E12
Ingolstadt Germany 59 F10
Inhambane Mozambique 71 G11, 81 G6
Injune Queensland, Australia 103 I5
Inland Sea *sea* Japan 98 D7
Inn *river* C Europe 60 E5
Inner Hebrides *island group* Scotland, United Kingdom 50 C5
Innsbruck Austria 61 F5
Inowroclaw Poland 66 E4
In Salah Algeria 73 F6
Insein Myanmar 94 B3
Inta Russian Federation 86 D4
Interlaken Switzerland 60 C5
Inuvik Northwest Territories, Canada 24 C3
Invercargill New Zealand 105 B12
Inverness Scotland, United Kingdom 50 E4
Investigator Ridge *undersea feature* NE Indian Ocean 83 G3
Ioannina Greece 69 E6
Ionian Islands *island group* Greece 68 E7
Ionian Sea *sea* C Mediterranean Sea 47 E8, 63 H12, 68 D7
Ios *island* Greece 69 H8
Iowa *state* USA 29 I5
Iowa City Iowa, USA 29 J5
Ipel *river* Hungary/Slovakia 67 F9
Ipoh Malaysia 94 C6
Ipswich Queensland, Australia 103 J6
Ipswich England, United Kingdom 51 I10
Iqaluit Nunavut, Canada 25 H4
Iquique Chile 42 C2
Iquitos Peru 40 C4
Irakleion Greece 47 F9, 69 H9
Iran *country* SW Asia 84 C6, 89 H3
Iranian Plateau *plateau* Iran 89 H4
Iranshahr Iran 89 J5
Irapuato Mexico 34 D5
Iraq *country* SW Asia 84 B6, 89 E4
Irbid Jordan 88 D4
Ireland, Republic of *country* NW Europe 46 B4, 51 B9
Iri South Korea 98 B6
Irian Jaya *political region* Indonesia 85 H9, 95 J7
Iringa Tanzania 79 I8
Iriomote-jima *island* Japan 99 I9
Iriri *river* Brazil 38 F4, 41 G4
Irish Sea *sea* NE Atlantic Ocean 51 D8
Irkutsk Russian Federation 85 F4, 87 G6
Irrawaddy *river* Myanmar 94 B2
Irrawaddy, Mouths of the *delta* Myanmar 94 A4
Irtysh *river* NW Asia 84 D3, 86 D5 *see also* Ertis
Irún Spain 57 G2
Irving Texas, USA 30 E5
Isabela, Isla *island* Galapagos Islands 40 A9
Ísafjördhur Iceland 48 A2
Isar *river* Germany 59 G11
Ischia *island* Italy 63 F8
Ise *bay* Japan 99 G7
Isère *river* France 55 H6
Isernia Italy 63 F7
Ise-wan *strait* Japan 99 G7
Ishigaki-jima *island* Japan 99 I9
Ishim *river* Kazakhstan/Russian Federation 90 E3
Ishim Russian Federation 86 D5
Ishinomaki Japan 99 I5
Isiro Democratic Republic of Congo 79 G6
Iskenderun Turkey 88 D3
Iskur *river* Bulgaria 69 G4
Islamabad *country capital* Pakistan 84 D6, 91 G9
Islay *island* Scotland, United Kingdom 51 D6
Islaz Romania 69 G4
Isle *river* France 54 E6
Isma'iliya Egypt 74 C3
Isoka Zambia 81 G3
Isparta Turkey 88 C2
Israel *country* SW Asia 84 A6, 88 C4
Istanbul Turkey 47 G8, 88 C1
Istra *peninsula* Croatia 68 B3
Italy *country* S Europe 46 E8, 62–63
Itanagar India 92 H5
Itea Greece 69 F7
Itzehoe Germany 58 D3
Ivalo Finland 48 H3
Ivanhoe New South Wales, Australia 103 H7
Ivano-Frankivsk Ukraine 65 B10
Ivanovo Russian Federation 47 H4, 86 B4
Ivory Coast *country* W Africa 71 B6, 77 E7
Iwaki Japan 99 H6
Iwakuni Japan 98 D7
Iwanai Japan 99 H2
Izhevsk Russian Federation 47 I3, 86 C5
Izmayil Ukraine 65 D12
Izmir Turkey 84 A5, 88 B2
Izmit Turkey 88 C1
Izu-shoto *island group* Japan 99 H7
Izyum Ukraine 65 H10

J

Jabalpur India 93 D6
Jaboatão Brazil 38 I5, 41 J5
Jaca Spain 57 G2
Jackson *state capital* Mississippi, USA 23 E10, 31 G5
Jacksonville Florida, USA 23 F10, 31 J5
Jacksonville North Carolina, USA 31 K3
Jacmel Haiti 37 F5
Jacobabad Pakistan 91 E11
Jaén Spain 57 E7
Jaffna Sri Lanka 93 D10
Jagdalpur India 93 E7
Jaipur India 84 D6, 92 C5
Jaisalmer India 92 B5
Jajce Bosnia & Herzegovina 68 D3
Jakarta *country capital* Indonesia 85 F9, 94 D8
Jakobstad Finland 49 G6
Jalalabad Afghanistan 84 D6, 91 F9
Jalandhar India 92 C3
Jalgaon India 93 C7
Jalingo Nigeria 77 J7
Jalu Libya 73 J5
Jamaame Somalia 75 G12
Jamaica *country* W West Indies 23 G12, 36 C5
Jambi Indonesia 94 C7
James *river* North Dakota/South Dakota, USA 29 G3
James Bay *bay* Ontario, Canada 23 G7, 25 G7
James Ross Island *island* Antarctica 21 A2
Jamestown North Dakota, USA 29 G3
Jammu India 92 C3
Jammu and Kashmir *political region* India/Pakistan 92 C2
Jamnagar India 93 A6
Jamshedpur India 93 F6
Janesville Wisconsin, USA 32 B5
Jan Mayen *island* N Atlantic Ocean 44 F2
Jan Mayen *Norwegian dependent territory* N Atlantic Ocean 20 B5
Japan *country* E Asia 85 H5, 99 F6
Japan, Sea of *sea* NW Pacific Ocean 85 H5, 97 K4, 99 E4
Japurá *river* Brazil/Colombia 38 C4, 40 D3 *see also* Caquetá
Jarocin Poland 66 E5
Jaroslaw Poland 67 H7

Jarvis Island *US dependent territory* SW Pacific Ocean 101 H4
Jask Iran 89 I5
Jaslo Poland 67 G8
Jasper Alberta, Canada 24 C7
Jastrowie Poland 66 D3
Jastrzebie-Zdroj Poland 67 E7
Jaunpur India 92 E5
Java *island* Indonesia 83 H4, 85 F9, 94 E9
Java Sea *sea* Indonesia 85 F9, 94 E8
Java Trench *undersea feature* E Indian Ocean 83 G4
Jaya, Puncak *mountain* Indonesia 95 J8
Jayapura Indonesia 95 K7
Jebel Toubkal *mountain* Morocco 72 D4
Jedda Saudi Arabia 84 B7, 88 E7
Jedrzejow Poland 67 G7
Jefferson City *state capital* Missouri, USA 29 J7
Jeju South Korea 98 B7
Jeju-do *island* South Korea 98 B8
Jekabpils Latvia 64 C5
Jelenia Gora Poland 67 C6
Jelgava Latvia 64 B5
Jember Indonesia 95 E9
Jena Germany 59 F7
Jeonju South Korea 98 B6
Jequié Brazil 41 I6
Jerada Morocco 72 E4
Jerba *island* Tunisia 73 H4
Jérémie Haiti 36 E5
Jerez de la Frontera Spain 56 C8
Jericho Queensland, Australia 103 I4
Jerid, Chott El *salt lake* Tunisia 73 G4
Jersey *island* Channel Islands 51 F13
Jersey City New Jersey, USA 33 H6
Jerusalem *country capital* Israel 84 A6, 88 D4
Jesenice Slovenia 61 H6
Jessore Bangladesh 93 G6
Jhansi India 93 D5
Jhelum Pakistan 91 G9
Jhelum *river* Pakistan 91 G9
Jialing Jiang *river* China 97 G6
Jiamusi China 97 J2
Jiangmen China 97 H8
Jiaojiang China 97 J7
Jiaxing China 97 J6
Jicin Czech Republic 67 C7
Jihlava Czech Republic 67 C8
Jilib Somalia 75 G12
Jilin China 85 G5, 97 J3
Jima Ethiopia 75 F7
Jinan China 85 G6, 97 I5
Jinchang China 97 F5
Jindrichuv Hradec Czech Republic 67 C8
Jingdezhen China 97 I7
Jinghong China 97 F9
Jinhae South Korea 98 C7
Jinhua China 97 J6
Jining China 97 H4
Jining China 97 I5
Jinja Uganda 79 H6
Jinju South Korea 98 C6
Jinzhou China 97 I4
Jishou China 97 H7
Jiujiang China 97 I6
Jiuquan China 97 E4
Jixi China 97 K2
Jizan Saudi Arabia 89 F8
Jizzakh Uzbekistan 91 E7
João Pessoa Brazil 39 I5, 41 J5
Jodhpur India 92 B5
Joensuu Finland 49 I7
Joetsu Japan 99 G6
Johannesburg South Africa 71 F11, 81 E7
John o'Groats Scotland, United Kingdom 50 F3
Johnston Atoll *US dependent territory* SW Pacific Ocean 101 G3
Johor Bahru Malaysia 94 C7
Joinville Brazil 41 H8
Joliet Illinois, USA 32 C6
Jolo Island Philippines 95 G6
Jonava Lithuania 65 C6
Jönköping Sweden 49 D11

Jonquière Québec, Canada 25 I7
Joplin Iowa, USA 29 I8
Jordan *country* SW Asia 85 A6, 88 D4
Jos Nigeria 71 D6, 77 I7
Joseph Bonaparte Gulf *gulf* Northern Territory/Western Australia, Australia 102 E2
Jostedalsbreen *glacier* Norway 49 A8
Jotunheimen *mountain range* Norway 49 B8
Juan de Fuca, Strait of *strait* Canada/USA 26 A1
Juan Fernandez Islands *island group* Chile 39 A9
Juàzeiro Brazil 41 I5
Juazeiro do Norte Brazil 41 J5
Juba *river* Ethiopia/Somalia 75 G11
Juba Sudan 71 G7, 75 D10
Júcar *river* Spain 57 G6
Judenburg Austria 61 I5
Juiz de Fora Brazil 41 I7
Juliaca Peru 40 D6
Julian Alps *mountain range* Slovenia 61 H6
Junagadh India 93 A6
Juneau Alaska, USA 23 C5
Junggar Basin *physical region* China 96 D3
Junín Argentina 43 F6
Jura *island* Scotland, United Kingdom 51 D6
Jura *mountain range* France/Switzerland 55 H5, 60 B5
Jurmala Latvia 64 B5
Juruá *river* Brazil/Peru 38 C5, 40 D4
Juruena *river* Brazil 39 E6, 41 F5
Jutland *peninsula* Denmark 49 B11
Juventud, Isla de la *island* Cuba 36 A3
Jyväskylä Finland 49 H7

K

K2 *mountain* China/Pakistan 91 H8, 96 A5
Kaamanen Finland 48 G3
Kaaresuvanto Finland 48 F3
Kabale Uganda 79 G7
Kabalo Democratic Republic of Congo 79 F8
Kabinda Democratic Republic of Congo 79 F8
Kabul *country capital* Afghanistan 84 D6, 91 F9
Kabwe Zambia 81 E4
Kachchh, Gulf of *gulf* India 93 A6
Kachchh, Rann of *physical region* India/Pakistan 91 E12, 93 A5
Kadavu *island* Fiji 101 H5
Kadoma Zimbabwe 81 F5
Kadugli Sudan 75 C8
Kaduna Nigeria 71 D6, 77 I6
Kaédi Mauritania 76 D5
Kaesong North Korea 98 B5
Kafue Zambia 81 E4
Kagoshima Japan 98 D9
Kahraman Maras Turkey 88 D2
Kaifeng China 97 H5
Kai Islands *island group* Indonesia 95 I8
Kaikoura New Zealand 105 F8
Kaili China 97 G7
Kaipara Harbour *harbour* New Zealand 104 F3
Kairouan Tunisia 73 H3
Kaiserslautern Germany 59 B9
Kaiyuan China 97 F8
Kajaani Finland 49 H6
Kakamega Kenya 79 G7
Kakhovka Ukraine 65 F11
Kakhovka Reservoir *reservoir* Ukraine 65 G11
Kakinada India 93 E8
Kalahari Desert *desert* Botswana/Namibia 71 F11, 80 C6
Kalai Mor Turkmenistan 91 D8
Kalamata Greece 69 F8
Kalamazoo Michigan, USA 32 D5
Kalburgi (Gulbarga) India 93 D8
Kalémié Democratic Republic of Congo 79 G8

Kalgoorlie Western Australia, Australia 100 B8, 102 C6
Kalimantan *political region* Indonesia 94 E7
Kaliningrad Russian Federation 47 F5, 65 A6, 86 A3
Kalispell Montana, USA 28 B2
Kalisz Poland 67 E5
Kalisz Pomoroski Poland 66 D4
Kalix Sweden 48 G5
Kalixälven *river* Sweden 48 G4
Kalmar Sweden 49 E11
Kaluga Russian Federation 86 B4
Kalush Ukraine 65 B10
Kalyan India 93 B7
Kalymnos *island* Greece 69 H8
Kama *river* Russian Federation 47 I4
Kamchatka Peninsula *peninsula* Russian Federation 85 I4, 87 K4
Kamina Democratic Republic of Congo 79 F8
Kamloops British Columbia, Canada 24 B7
Kampala *country capital* Uganda 71 G7, 79 H6
Kampong Cham Cambodia 94 D4
Kampong Saom Cambodia 94 C5
Kamyanets-Podilskyy Ukraine 65 C10
Kananga Democratic Republic of Congo 71 F8, 79 E8
Kanazawa Japan 99 G6
Kandahar Afghanistan 91 E10
Kandalaksha Russian Federation 86 C2
Kandi Benin 77 H6
Kandy Sri Lanka 93 E11
Kangan Iran 89 H5
Kangaroo Island *island* South Australia, Australia 103 G7
Kanggye North Korea 98 B3
Kankaanpää Finland 49 G8
Kankan Guinea 76 E6
Kano Nigeria 71 D5, 77 I6
Kanpur India 84 D6, 92 D5
Kansas *state* USA 29 G7
Kansas City Kansas, USA 23 E9, 29 I7
Kansk Russian Federation 87 F6
Kanye Botswana 80 D6
Kaohsiung Taiwan 85 G7, 97 J8
Kaolack Senegal 76 C5
Kaoma Zambia 80 D4
Kapoeta Sudan 75 D10
Kaposvar Hungary 67 E11
Kappeln Germany 58 E2
Kapsan North Korea 98 C3
Kapuas *river* Indonesia 94 E7
Kapuas Mountains *mountain range* Indonesia/Malaysia 95 E7
Kara-Balta Kyrgyzstan 91 G6
Karachi Pakistan 84 C6, 91 E12
Karaj Iran 89 H3
Kara-Kol Kyrgyzstan 91 F7
Karakol Kyrgyzstan 91 H6
Karakoram Range *mountain range* C Asia 91 G8
Karamay China 96 C3
Karamea Bight *bay* New Zealand 105 D7
Karasburg Namibia 80 C7
Kara Sea *sea* Arctic Ocean 20 D3, 84 C2, 86 E3
Karasjok Norway 48 G2
Karawanken *mountain range* Austria/Slovenia 61 H6
Karbala' Iraq 89 F4
Karditsa Greece 69 F7
Kariba Zimbabwe 81 E4
Kariba, Lake Zambia 81 E4
Karibib Namibia 80 B6
Karin Sudan 75 H11
Karleby *see* Kokkola
Karlovac Croatia 68 C2
Karlovy Vary Czech Republic 67 A7
Karlskrona Sweden 48 D12
Karlsruhe Germany 59 C10
Karlstad Sweden 49 D9
Karnal India 92 C4
Karnische Alpen *mountain range* Austria/Italy 61 G5
Karpathos *island* Greece 69 I9
Karratha Western Australia, Australia 102 B4
Karst *physical region* Slovenia 61 H6
Karun *river* Iran 89 G4

Karymskoye Russian Federation 87 H6
Karystos Greece 69 G7
Kasai *river* Angola/Democratic Republic of Congo 71 F9, 78 E7
Kasama Zambia 71 G9, 81 F3
Kasane Botswana 80 D5
Kashan Iran 89 H3
Kashi China 96 B3
Kasongo Democratic Republic of Congo 79 F7
Kasos *island* Greece 69 I9
Kassala Sudan 70 G5, 75 E7
Kassandra, Gulf of *gulf* NW Aegean Sea 69 G7
Kassel Germany 59 D7
Kasserine Tunisia 73 G4
Kastoria Greece 69 E6
Katerini Greece 69 F6
Katherine Northern Territory, Australia 103 F2
Kathmandu *country capital* Nepal 84 M7, 92 F4
Katima Mulilo Namibia 80 D5
Katowice Poland 67 F7
Katrineholm Sweden 49 E10
Katsina Nigeria 77 I6
Kattegat *strait* N Europe 49 C11
Kauai *island* Hawaii, USA 27 A12
Kaunas Lithuania 65 C6
Kavala Greece 69 G5
Kavieng Papua New Guinea 100 D5
Kavir, Dasht-e *physical region* Iran 89 H3
Kawasaki Japan 99 H6
Kaya Burkina 77 G6
Kayan *river* Indonesia 95 F7
Kayes Mali 76 D5
Kaynar Kazakhstan 90 G4
Kayseri Turkey 88 D2
Kazakhstan *country* C Asia 84 C4, 90 D4
Kazakh Uplands *physical region* Kazakhstan 84 D4, 90 F4
Kazan Russian Federation 47 I4, 86 C4
Kazbek *mountain* Georgia 88 F1
Kazerun Iran 89 H4
Kea, Mauna *mountain* Hawaii, USA 27 C13
Kebnekaise *mountain* Sweden 48 E4
Kecskemet Hungary 67 F11
Kedainiai Lithuania 65 B6
Kedzierzyn Kozle Poland 67 E7
Kediri Indonesia 94 E9
Keetmanshoop Namibia 80 C7
Kefallinia *island* Greece 69 E7
Keflavik Iceland 48 B3
Keitele *lake* Finland 49 G7
Keith South Australia, Australia 103 G7
Kelo Chad 78 D4
Kelowna British Columbia, Canada 24 B7
Kemerovo Russian Federation 87 K6
Kemi Finland 48 G5
Kemijärvi Finland 48 H4
Kemijoki *river* Finland 48 G5
Kempele Finland 49 G6
Kemp Land *physical region* Antarctica 21 E2
Kempten Germany 59 E12
Kenai Alaska, USA 26 H2
Kendari Indonesia 95 G8
Kenema Sierra Leone 76 D7
Kénitra Morocco 72 D4
Kennewick Washington, USA 26 D3
Kenosha Wisconsin, USA 32 C5
Kentau Kazakhstan 91 E6
Kentucky *state* USA 32 C8
Kenya *country* E Africa 71 H7, 79 I6
Kenya, Mount *see* Kirinyaga
Kepno Poland 67 E6
Kerch Ukraine 65 H12
Kerguelen *island* S Indian Ocean 82 E7
Kerguelen Plateau *undersea feature* S Indian Ocean 82 E7
Kerinci, Gunung *mountain* Indonesia 94 C7
Kerki Turkmenistan 91 E8
Kerkrade Netherlands 53 G9
Kerkyra Greece 68 E6

Kermadec Islands *NZ dependent territory* SW Pacific Ocean 101 G7
Kermadec Trench *undersea feature* SW Pacific Ocean 107 E6
Kerman Iran 89 I4
Kesennuma Japan 99 I5
Keszthely Hungary 67 D11
Ketrzyn Poland 66 G3
Key Largo Florida, USA 31 J7
Khabarovsk Russian Federation 85 H4, 87 J6
Khambhat, Gulf of *gulf* India 93 A7
Khandwa India 93 C6
Khanewal Pakistan 91 G10
Khanka, Lake *lake* China/Russian Federation 97 K2
Khanty-Mansiysk Russian Federation 86 D5
Kharagpur India 93 G6
Kharkiv Ukraine 47 H5, 65 G9
Khartoum *country capital* Sudan 70 G5, 75 D7
Khartoum North Sudan 75 D7
Khaskovo Bulgaria 69 H5
Kherson Ukraine 65 F11
Khilok Russian Federation 87 H6
Khmelnytskyy Ukraine 65 C10
Khon Kaen Thailand 94 C3
Khorramabad Iran 89 G3
Khorramshahr Iran 89 G4
Khorugh Tajikistan 91 F8
Khouribga Morocco 72 D4
Khrebet Cherskogo *mountain range* Russian Federation 85 H3
Khujand Tajikistan 91 F7
Khujayli Uzbekistan 91 C6
Khulna Bangladesh 93 G6
Khuzdar Pakistan 91 E11
Khvoy Iran 89 F2
Kicevo Macedonia 69 E4
Kidal Mali 77 G4
Kiel Germany 58 E2
Kiel Bay *bay* SE North Sea 58 E2
Kielce Poland 67 G6
Kiev *country capital* Ukraine 47 G6, 65 E9
Kiev Reservoir *reservoir* Ukraine 65 E9
Kiffa Mauritania 76 D4
Kifisos *river* Greece 69 F7
Kigali *country capital* Rwanda 71 G8, 79 G7
Kigoma Tanzania 79 G7
Kihei Hawaii, USA 27 B12
Kii-suido *strait* Japan 99 F7
Kikwit Democratic Republic of Congo 78 D7
Kilchu North Korea 98 D3
Kilimanjaro *mountain* Tanzania 71 H8, 79 I7
Kilkenny Republic of Ireland 51 C10
Kilkis Greece 69 F5
Killarney Republic of Ireland 51 A10
Kilmarnock Scotland, United Kingdom 51 E6
Kimberley South Africa 80 D7
Kimberley Plateau *plateau* Western Australia, Australia 100 A6, 102 D3
Kimch'aek North Korea 98 C3
Kinabalu, Gunung *mountain* Malaysia 95 F6
Kindia Guinea 76 D6
Kindu Democratic Republic of Congo 79 F7
King Island *island* Tasmania, Australia 103 H8
Kingman Reef *US dependent territory* C Pacific Ocean 101 H4
King's Lynn England, United Kingdom 51 H10
Kings Sound *sound* Western Australia, Australia 102 C2
Kingston Ontario, Canada 25 H9
Kingston *country capital* Jamaica 23 G12, 36 D5
Kingston New Zealand 105 B11
Kingston-upon-Hull England, United Kingdom 51 H8
Kingstown *country capital* St Vincent & the Grenadines 37 J7

Kinshasa *country capital* Democratic Republic of Congo 71 E8, 78 D7
Kintyre *peninsula* Scotland, United Kingdom 51 D7
Kirghiz Steppe *physical region* Kazakhstan 84 C4, 90 D4
Kiribati *country* C Pacific Ocean 101 G5
Kirikkale Turkey 88 D2
Kirinyaga *mountain* Kenya 71 H7, 79 I6
Kirkenes Norway 48 H2
Kiritimati *island* Kiribati 101 I4
Kirksville Missouri, USA 29 J6
Kirkuk Iraq 89 F3
Kirkwall Scotland, United Kingdom 50 F3
Kirov Russian Federation 47 I3, 86 C4
Kirovohrad Ukraine 65 F10
Kiruna Sweden 48 F4
Kisangani Democratic Republic of Congo 71 F7, 79 F6
Kismaayo Somalia 71 H7, 75 G12
Kisumu Kenya 71 G7, 79 H6
Kitakyushu Japan 98 D7
Kitami Japan 99 I2
Kitchener Ontario, Canada 25 H9
Kitwe Zambia 71 F9, 81 E3
Kitzbühel Austria 61 G4
Kivu, Lake *lake* Democratic Republic of Congo/Rwanda 79 G7
Kladno Czech Republic 67 B7
Klagenfurt Austria 61 I5
Klaipeda Lithuania 64 A5
Klamath Falls Oregon, USA 26 B5
Klang Malaysia 94 C6
Klarälven *river* Norway/Sweden 49 D9
Klatovy Czech Republic 67 A8
Klerksdorp South Africa 80 E7
Klodzko Poland 67 D7
Kluczbork Poland 67 E6
Knin Croatia 68 C3
Knittelfeld Austria 61 I4
Knoxville Tennessee, USA 31 I3
Kobe Japan 99 F7
Koblenz Germany 59 B8
Kobra India 93 E6
Kobryn Belarus 65 C8
Kocani Macedonia 69 F5
Kocevje Slovenia 61 I7
Kochi Japan 99 E8
Kochkor Kyrgyzstan 91 G6
Kodiak Island *island* Alaska, USA 22 B4, 26 H2
Köflach Austria 61 I5
Kofu Japan 99 G6
Kohima India 92 I5
Kohtla-Jarve Estonia 64 D3
Koidu Sierra Leone 76 D7
Kokkola Finland 49 G6
Kokpekti Kazakhstan 90 H4
Kokshetau Kazakhstan 90 F3
Kola Peninsula *peninsula* Russian Federation 47 G2, 86 C3
Kolari Finland 48 G4
Kolda Sengal 76 C6
Kolding Denmark 49 B12
Kolhapur India 93 C8
Kolkata India 84 E7, 93 G6
Kolobrzeg Poland 66 C2
Kolomyya Ukraine 65 C10
Kolwezi Democratic Republic of Congo 71 F9, 79 F9
Kolyma *river* Russian Federation 85 I2, 87 I3
Kolyma Range *mountain range* Russian Federation 85 I3, 87 J3
Komarno Slovakia 67 E10
Kommunizm, Qullai *mountain* Tajikistan 91 F7
Komatsu Japan 99 F6
Komotini Greece 69 H5
Komsomolets, Ostrov *island* Russian Federation 87 F2
Komsomolsk Ukraine 65 F10
Komsomolsk-na-Amure Russian Federation 87 J6
Kongolo Democratic Republic of Congo 79 F7
Kongsberg Norway 49 B9
Konin Poland 66 E5
Konjic Bosnia & Herzegovina 68 D4
Konotop Ukraine 65 F8

Kontiomäki Finland 49 H6
Konya Turkey 88 D2
Koper Slovenia 61 H7
Korab *mountain* Albania/Macedonia 69 E5
Korce Albania 69 E6
Korcula *island* Croatia 68 C4
Kordofan *physical region* Sudan 75 C8
Korea Bay *bay* China/North Korea 97 J4, 98 A4
Korea Strait *channel* Japan/South Korea 98 C7
Korff Ice Rise *ice cap* Antarctica 21 B3
Korhogo Ivory Coast 77 E7
Koriyama Japan 99 H5
Korla China 96 C4
Kormend Hungary 67 D10
Koros *river* Hungary/Romania 67 G11
Korosten Ukraine 65 D8
Kortrijk Belgium 53 B9
Kos Greece 69 H8
Kos *island* Greece 69 I8
Kosciuszko, Mount *mountain* New South Wales, Australia 103 I8
Kosice Slovakia 67 G9
Kosong North Korea 98 C5
Kosovo *country* 47 F7, 69 E4
Kosovska Mitrovica Kosovo 69 E4
Kosrae *island* Micronesia 100 E4
Kosti Sudan 75 D8
Kostroma Russian Federation 86 B4
Kostrzyn Poland 66 C4
Koszalin Poland 66 D3
Kota India 93 C5
Kota Bharu Malaysia 94 C6
Kota Kinabalu Malaysia 95 F6
Kotka Finland 49 H9
Kotlas Russian Federation 86 C4
Kotuy *river* Russian Federation 85 F2, 87 G3
Koudougou Burkina 77 F6
Kouvola Finland 49 H8
Kovel Ukraine 65 C8
Koyang South Korea 98 B5
Kozani Greece 69 F6
Kozina Slovenia 61 H7
Kozyatyn Ukraine 65 D9
Kragujevac Serbia 69 F4
Krakow Poland 47 F6, 67 F7
Kraljevo Serbia 69 E4
Kramatorsk Ukraine 65 H10
Kramfors Sweden 49 E7
Kranj Slovenia 61 I6
Krasnik Poland 67 H6
Krasnodar Russian Federation 47 H6, 86 A5
Krasnoyarsk Russian Federation 84 E4, 87 F6
Krasnyy Luch Ukraine 65 I10
Krefeld Germany 59 B7
Kremenchuk Ukraine 65 F10
Kremenchuk Reservoir *reservoir* Ukraine 65 F10
Krems an der Donau Austria 61 J3
Kreuztal Germany 59 C7
Krishna *river* India 93 C8
Kristiansand Norway 49 B10
Kristianstad Sweden 49 D12
Kristiansund Norway 49 B7
Kristinestad Finland 49 F8
Krivyy Rih Ukraine 47 H6, 65 F11
Krk *island* Croatia 68 B3
Kroonstad South Africa 80 E7
Krosno Poland 67 H8
Krsko Slovenia 61 J6
Krusevac Serbia 69 F4
Krusne Hory *mountain range* Czech Republic/Germany 67 A7
Krzyz Poland 66 D4
Kuala Lumpur *country capital* Malaysia 85 F8, 94 C6
Kuala Terengganu Malaysia 94 C6
Kuantan Malaysia 94 C6
Kuching Malaysia 94 E7
Kudat Malaysia 95 F6
Kufstein Austria 61 G4

Kuhmo Finland 49 I6
Kuito Angola 80 B3
Kuju-san *mountain* Japan 98 D8
Kukes Albania 69 E5
Kulagino Kazakhstan 90 B4
Kula Kangri *mountain* Bhutan/China 92 G4
Kuldiga Latvia 64 B4
Kulmbach Germany 59 F8
Kumamoto Japan 98 D8
Kumanovo Macedonia 69 E5
Kumasi Ghana 77 F7
Kumba Cameroon 78 B5
Kume-jima *island* Japan 99 J8
Kumo Nigeria 77 J7
Kungsbacka Sweden 49 C11
Kunlun Mountains *mountain range* China 84 D5, 96 B5
Kunming China 85 F6, 97 F8
Kuopio Finland 49 H7
Kupang Indonesia 95 H9
Kupyansk Ukraine 65 H9
Kuqa China 96 C4
Kurashiki Japan 99 E7
Kurchum Kazakhstan 90 I4
Kurdzhali Bulgaria 69 G5
Kure Japan 98 E7
Kuressaare Estonia 64 B4
Kurgan Russian Federation 86 D5
Kurile Islands *island group* Russian Federation 85 I5, 87 K4, 106 C2
Kurile Trench *undersea feature* N Pacific Ocean 106 C2
Kurnool India 93 D8
Kuroiso Japan 99 H6
Kurow New Zealand 105 C11
Kursk Russian Federation 47 H5, 86 A4
Kuruman South Africa 80 D7
Kushiro Japan 99 J2
Kussharo-ko *lake* Japan 99 J2
Kütahya Turkey 88 C2
Kutaisi Georgia 89 F1
Kutno Poland 66 F5
Kuusamo Finland 48 H5
Kuwait *country* SW Asia 84 B6, 89 G4
Kuwait *country capital* Kuwait 84 B6, 89 G5
Kuybyshev Russian Federation 86 E4
Kuytun China 96 C3
Kvaløya *island* Norway 48 E2
Kvinesdal Norway 49 A10
Kwango *river* Democratic Republic of Congo 78 D8
Kwekwe Zimbabwe 81 F5
Kwilu *river* Angola/Democratic Republic of Congo 78 D7
Kyancutta South Australia, Australia 103 F7
Kymi Greece 69 G7
Kyoto Japan 85 H6, 99 F7
Kyparissiakos Kolpos *gulf* SE Ionian Sea 69 E8
Kyrgyz Range *mountain range* Kazakhstan/Kyrgyzstan 91 F6
Kyrgyzstan *country* C Asia 84 D5, 91 G6
Kythira *island* Greece 69 G9
Kyushu *island* Japan 98 D8
Kyzyl Russian Federation 87 F6

L

Laâyoune *disputed region capital* Western Sahara 70 A3, 72 B5
Labé Guinea 76 D6
Labrador *cultural region* Newfoundland & Labrador, Canada 23 H6, 25 I6
Labrador Basin *undersea feature* NW Atlantic Ocean 44 D3
Labrador City Newfoundland & Labrador, Canada 25 I6
Labrador Sea *sea* NW Atlantic Ocean 25 I4, 44 C3
Laccadive Islands *island group* India 82 E2, 84 D8, 84 D8
La Ceiba Honduras 35 H7
La Chaux-de-Fonds Switzerland 60 B4
Lachlan *river* New South Wales, Australia 103 H7

La Crosse Wisconsin, USA 32 A4
La Cruz Costa Rica 35 I8
Ladoga, Lake *lake* Russian Federation 47 G3, 86 B3
Ladysmith South Africa 81 F7
Lae Papua New Guinea 100 C5
Lafayette Louisiana, USA 31 F6
Lågen *river* Norway 49 C8
Lages Brazil 41 G8
Lagos Nigeria 71 C6, 77 H7
Lagos Portugal 56 A8
Lagos de Moreno Mexico 34 D5
Lagouira Western Sahara 72 A7
Laholm Sweden 49 C11
Lahore Pakistan 84 D6, 91 G10
Lahr Germany 59 B11
Lahti Finland 49 H8
Lake Charles Louisiana, USA 31 F6
Lake District *physical region* England, United Kingdom 51 F8
Lake Havasu City Arizona, USA 27 F10
Lake King Western Australia, Australia 102 C7
Lakeland Florida, USA 31 J6
Lakewood Colorado, USA 28 E7
Lakonikos Kolpos *gulf* NE Mediterranean Sea 69 F8
Lakselv Norway 48 G2
Lalitpur Nepal 92 F5
La Línea Spain 56 D9
La Louvière Belgium 53 D10
La Mancha *cultural region* Spain 57 F6
La Marmora, Punta *mountain* Italy 63 B9
Lambaréné Gabon 78 B6
Lamego Portugal 56 B4
Lamezia Italy 63 H10
Lamia Greece 69 F7
Lampang Thailand 94 B3
Lampedusa *island* Italy 63 E13
Lancang Jiang *see* Mekong
Lancaster Sound *strait* Nunavut, Canada 25 F3
Lanciano Italy 63 F6
Landeck Austria 61 E5
Land's End *headland* England, United Kingdom 51 D12
Landshut Germany 59 G11
Langøya *island* Norway 48 D3
Langres France 55 H3
Langsa Indonesia 94 B6
Lansing *state capital* Michigan, USA 32 D5
Lanzhou China 85 F6, 97 F5
Laoag Philippines 95 G3
Laohekou China 97 H6
Laon France 55 G2
Laos *country* SE Asia 85 F7, 94 C3
La Paz *legislative and administrative capital* Bolivia 39 C6, 40 D6
La Paz Mexico 34 B4
La Perouse Strait *strait* Japan/Russian Federation 99 H1
Lapland *cultural region* NW Europe 48 F4
La Plata Argentina 39 E10, 43 G6
Lappeenranta Finland 49 I8
Laptev Sea *sea* Arctic Ocean 20 D2, 87 G3
Lapua Finland 49 G7
L'Aquila Italy 63 F6
Laramie Wyoming, USA 28 D6
Laramie Mountains *mountain range* Wyoming, USA 28 D5
Laredo Texas, USA 30 D7
La Rioja Argentina 39 D5
La Rioja *cultural region* Spain 57 E3
Larisa Greece 69 F6
Larkana Pakistan 91 E11
La Rochelle France 54 D5
La Roche-sur-Yon France 54 D5
La Roda Spain 57 F6
La Romana Dominican Republic 37 G5
Larsen Ice Shelf *ice shelf* Antarctica 21 A2
Las Cruces New Mexico, USA 30 B5
La Serena Chile 42 C5
La Seyne-sur-Mer France 55 H8

Lashio Myanmar 94 B2
La Spezia Italy 62 C4
Las Piedras Uruguay 43 G6
Las Tablas Panama 35 J9
Las Tunas Cuba 36 D4
Las Vegas Nevada, USA 23 C8, 27 E9
Latina Italy 63 E7
Latur India 93 C8
Latvia *country* NE Europe 47 F4, 64 C5
Lauenburg Germany 58 E4
Lau Group *island group* Fiji 101 G6
Launceston Tasmania, Australia 100 D8, 103 H9
Lauria Italy 63 G9
Lausanne Switzerland 60 A5
Laval Québec, Canada 25 I8
Laval France 54 D3
La Vega Dominican Republic 37 G5
Lavrio Greece 69 G8
Lawdar Yemen 89 G9
Lawton Oklahoma, USA 30 D4
Layla Saudi Arabia 89 G7
Lázaro Cárdenas Mexico 34 D6
Leba Poland 66 E2
Lebanon *country* SW Asia 84 A6, 88 D3
Lebap Turkmenistan 91 D7
Lebork Poland 66 E2
Lebu Chile 43 B7
Lecce Italy 63 I8
Lecco Italy 62 C3
Leeds England, United Kingdom 46 C4, 51 G8
Leer Germany 58 C4
Leeuwarden Netherlands 52 G2
Leeuwin, Cape *headland* Western Australia, Australia 102 B7
Leeward Islands *island group* E West Indies 37 H4
Lefkada Greece 69 E7
Lefkada *island* Greece 69 E7
Leganés Spain 57 E5
Legaspi Philippines 95 G4
Legnago Italy 62 B3
Legnano Italy 62 D3
Legnica Poland 67 D6
Le Havre France 46 C5, 54 E2
Leibnitz Austria 61 J5
Leicester England, United Kingdom 51 G10
Leiden Netherlands 53 D5
Leinster *cultural region* Republic of Ireland 51 C9
Leipzig Germany 59 G7
Leiria Portugal 56 A5
Leirvik Norway 49 A9
Leksand Sweden 49 D9
Lelystad Netherlands 52 F4
Le Mans France 54 E3
Lena *river* Russian Federation 85 G3, 86 G6
Lennestadt Germany 59 C7
Lens France 55 F1
Lentvaris Lithuania 65 C6
León Mexico 23 D11, 34 D5
León Nicaragua 35 H8
León Spain 56 D2
Leonberg Germany 59 D10
Leonídi Greece 69 F8
Leonora Western Australia, Australia 102 C6
Lepontine Alps *mountain range* Switzerland 60 D6
Lepsi Kazakhstan 90 H5
Le Puy France 55 G6
Lerwick Scotland, United Kingdom 50 G1
Lesbos *island* Greece 69 H7
Les Ecrins *mountain* France 55 I6
Leshan China 97 F7
Lesina, Lake *lagoon* Italy 63 G7
Lesko Poland 67 H8
Leskovac Serbia 69 F4
Lesotho *country* S Africa 71 F12, 81 E7
Lesser Antilles *island group* E West Indies 23 H12, 37 G7

Lesser Khingan Mountains *mountain range* China 97 I1
Lesser Sunda Islands *island group* Indonesia 95 F9
Leszno Poland 66 D5
Lethbridge Alberta, Canada 24 C8
Leuven Belgium 53 E9
Lévêque, Cape *headland* Western Australia, Australia 102 C2
Leverkusen Germany 59 B7
Levice Slovakia 67 E9
Levin New Zealand 105 G7
Levoca Poland 67 G8
Lewis *island* Scotland, United Kingdom 50 D4
Lewiston Idaho, USA 26 E3
Lexington Kentucky, USA 32 D8
Leyte *island* Philippines 95 H4
Lhasa China 96 D7
Lhokseumawe Indonesia 94 B6
L'Hospitalet de Llobregat Spain 57 I3
Lianyungang China 97 I5
Liao He *river* China 97 I3
Liaoyuan China 97 J3
Liberal Kansas, USA 29 F8
Liberec Czech Republic 67 C6
Liberia Costa Rica 35 H8
Liberia *country* W Africa 71 B6, 76 D7
Libreville *country capital* Gabon 71 D7, 78 B6
Libya *country* N Africa 70 E3, 73 I5
Libyan Desert *desert* NE Africa 70 F3, 73 K7, 74 B4
Licata Italy 63 F12
Lichinga Mozambique 81 G3
Lida Belarus 65 C7
Lido di Ostia Italy 63 E7
Liechtenstein *country* C Europe 46 D6, 60 D5
Liège Belgium 53 F10
Lienz Austria 61 G5
Liepaja Latvia 64 B5
Lier Belgium 53 D8
Liezen *river* Austria 61 H4
Liffey *river* Republic of Ireland 51 C9
Ligurian Sea *sea* N Mediterranean Sea 46 D7, 63 B8
Likasi Democratic Republic of Congo 79 F9
Lille France 55 G1
Lillehammer Norway 49 C8
Lillestrøm Norway 49 C9
Lilongwe *country capital* Malawi 71 G10, 81 G4
Lima *country capital* Peru 39 B6, 40 C5
Limassol Cyprus 88 D3
Limerick Republic of Ireland 51 B10
Limnos *island* Greece 69 G6
Limoges France 55 E5
Limón Costa Rica 35 J8
Limpopo *river* S Africa 71 G11, 81 E6
Linares Spain 57 E7
Linchuan China 97 I7
Lincoln *state capital* Nebraska, USA 29 H6
Lincoln City Oregon, USA 26 B4
Lincoln Sea *sea* Arctic Ocean 20 B3
Lindau Germany 59 D12
Lindi Tanzania 79 J9
Lindos Greece 69 I8
Line Islands *island group* Kiribati 101 H12
Linfen China 97 H5
Lingen Germany 58 B5
Linhares Brazil 41 I7
Linhe China 97 G4
Linköping Sweden 49 D10
Linosa *island* Italy 63 E13
Linz Austria 61 I3
Lion, Gulf of *gulf* France 55 G8
Lipcani Moldova 65 C10
Lipetsk Russian Federation 47 H5, 86 B4
Lippe *river* Germany 59 C6
Lira Uganda 79 H6
Lisbon *country capital* Portugal 46 A7, 56 A6
Lisburn Northern Ireland, United Kingdom 51 D8
Lismore New South Wales, Australia 103 J6

Lithuania *country* NE Europe 47 F4, 64 B5
Litomerice Czech Republic 67 B6
Litomysl Czech Republic 67 D7
Little Alfold *physical region* Slovakia 67 E9
Little Andaman *island* Andaman Islands, India 93 H10
Little Colorado *river* Arizona, USA 27 G10
Little Minch, The *channel* Scotland, United Kingdom 50 C4
Little Missouri *river* North Dakota, USA 29 E3
Little Rock Arkansas, USA 31 F4
Liuzhou China 97 H8
Liverpool England, United Kingdom 46 C4, 51 F9
Livingstone Zambia 71 F10, 80 E5
Livno Bosnia & Herzegovina 68 C4
Livojoki *river* Finland 48 H5
Livonia Michigan, USA 32 E5
Livorno Italy 62 C5
Ljubljana *country capital* Slovenia 46 E6, 61 I6
Ljungby Sweden 49 D11
Ljusdal Sweden 49 E8
Ljusnan *river* Sweden 49 D8
Llanelli Wales, United Kingdom 51 E11
Llano Estacado *physical region* New Mexico/Texas, USA 30 C5
Llanos *physical region* Colombia/Venezuela 38 C2, 40 D2
Lleida Spain 57 H3
Llivia Spain 57 I2
Lloydminster Alberta, Canada 24 D7
Loa, Mauna *mountain* Hawaii, USA 27 C13
Lobito Namibia 80 A3
Locarno Switzerland 60 C6
Lodwar Kenya 79 I5
Lodz Poland 47 F5, 67 F5
Lofoten *island group* Norway 47 E2, 48 D3
Logan, Mount *mountain* Yukon Territory, Canada 22 C4, 24 A4
Logone *river* Cameroon, Chad 78 D4
Logroño Spain 57 F2
Loi-Kaw Myanmar 94 B3
Loire *river* France 46 C6, 55 G4
Lokan Tekojärvi *reservoir* Finland 48 H3
Lokeren Belgium 53 C8
Lokoja Nigeria 77 I7
Lolland *island* Denmark 49 B13
Lomami *river* Democratic Republic of Congo 79 F7
Lomas de Zamora Argentina 39 E10, 43 F6
Lombardy *cultural region* Italy 62 B3
Lomblen *island* Indonesia 95 G9
Lombok *island* Indonesia 95 F9
Lomé *country capital* Togo 71 C6, 77 G7
Lommel Belgium 53 F8
Lomond, Loch *lake* Scotland, United Kingdom 51 E6
Lomonosov Ridge *undersea feature* Arctic Ocean 20 C3
Lomza Poland 66 H4
London *country capital* England, United Kingdom 46 C5, 51 H11
London Ontario, Canada 25 H9
Londonderry Northern Ireland, United Kingdom 51 C8
Londonderry, Cape *headland* Western Australia, Australia 102 D2
Londrina Brazil 41 G7
Long Beach California, USA 27 D11
Long Island *island* Bahamas 36 E3
Long Island *island* New York, USA 23 G9, 33 I6
Longmont Colorado, USA 28 E6
Longreach Queensland, Australia 103 H4
Longview Washington, USA 26 B3
Long Xuyen Vietnam 94 D5

Longyearbyen Svalbard 20 C4
Löningen Germany 58 C4
Lop Nur *seasonal lake* China 96 D4
Lorca Spain 57 G7
Lord Howe Island *island* Australia 100 F3
Lord Howe Rise *undersea feature* SW Pacific Ocean 106 D6
Lorient France 54 C4
Los Alamos New Mexico, USA 30 B3
Los Andes Chile 43 C6
Los Angeles Chile 43 C7
Los Angeles California, USA 23 B8, 27 D11
Los Mochis Mexico 34 B4
Lot *river* France 55 F6
Louangphabang Laos 94 C3
Louga Senegal 76 C5
Louisiana *state* USA 31 F6
Louisville Kentucky, USA 32 C8
Lourdes France 54 E8
Loutra Edipsou Greece 69 F7
Lovech Bulgaria 69 G4
Lowell Massachusetts, USA 33 J5
Lower California *peninsula* Mexico 23 C9, 34 A2
Lower Hutt New Zealand 105 F7
Lower Lough Erne *lake* Republic of Ireland 51 C8
Lower Tunguska *river* Russian Federation 85 E3, 87 F4
Lowicz Poland 66 F3
Loyalty Islands *island group* New Caledonia 101 E6
Loznica Serbia 68 E3
Luacano Angola 80 D3
Lualuba *river* Democratic Republic of Congo 71 F8, 79 F7
Luanda *country capital* Angola 71 E9, 80 A2
Luan He *river* China 97 I4
Luanshya Zambia 81 F4
Lubango Angola 80 A4
Lübben Germany 59 H6
Lübbenau Germany 59 H6
Lubbock Texas, USA 30 C4
Lübeck Germany 58 E3
Lublin Poland 67 H6
Lubliniec Poland 67 F6
Lubny Ukraine 65 F9
Lubumbashi Democratic Republic of Congo 71 F9, 79 G9
Lucca Italy 62 C5
Lucenec Slovakia 67 F9
Lucerne Switzerland 60 C5
Lucknow India 92 E5
Lüderitz Namibia 80 B7
Ludhiana India 92 C3
Ludington Michigan, USA 32 C4
Ludvika Sweden 49 D9
Ludwigsburg Germany 59 D10
Ludwigshafen am Rhein Germany 59 C9
Ludwigslust Germany 58 F4
Luena Angola 80 C3
Lugano Switzerland 60 D6
Lugo Italy 62 D4
Lugo Spain 56 C2
Lugovoy Kazakhstan 91 F6
Luhansk Ukraine 65 I10
Lukenie *river* Democratic Republic of Congo 78 E7
Luleå Sweden 49 F5
Luleälven *river* Sweden 48 E4
Lumsden New Zealand 105 B12
Lun Mongolia 97 F2
Lund Sweden 49 C12
Lundy *island* England, United Kingdom 51 E11
Lüneburg Germany 58 E4
Lüneburg Heath *physical region* Germany 58 D4
Luo He *river* China 97 G5
Luoyang China 97 H5
Lusaka *country capital* Zambia 71 F10, 81 F4
Lut, Dasht-e *desert* Syria 89 I4
Luton England, United Kingdom 51 H10
Lutsk Ukraine 65 C9
Luxembourg *country* W Europe 46 D5, 53 G12
Luxembourg *country capital* Luxembourg 46 D5, 53 G12
Luxor Egypt 70 G3, 74 D4

Luz, Costa de la *coastal region* Spain 56 C8
Luzhou China 97 G7
Luzon *island* Philippines 85 G7, 95 G3
Luzon Strait *strait* Philippines/Taiwan 95 G3, 97 J9
Lviv Ukraine 47 F6, 65 B9
Lycksele Sweden 49 E6
Lyme Bay *bay* England, United Kingdom 51 F12
Lynchburg Virginia, USA 33 F8
Lyon France 46 C6, 55 H5
Lysychansk Ukraine 65 H10

M

Ma'an Jordan 88 D4
Maarianhamina *see* Mariehamn
Maas *river* W Europe 53 G7 *see also* Meuse
Maastricht Netherlands 53 F9
McAllen Texas, USA 30 D7
Macao China 97 I8
Macapá Brazil 41 G3
McClintock Channel *channel* Nunavut, Canada 24 E3
McDermitt Nevada, USA 27 D6
Macdonnell Ranges *mountain range* Northern Territory, Australia 103 F4
Macedonia *country* SE Europe 47 F7, 69 F5
Macedonia *cultural region* Greece 69 F5
Maceió Brazil 39 I5, 41 J5
Machakos Kenya 79 I7
Machala Ecuador 40 B4
Machilipatnam India 93 E8
Macia Mozambique 81 F6
Mackay Queensland, Australia 100 D6, 103 I4
Mackay, Lake *seasonal lake* Northern Territory/Western Australia, Australia 102 E4
Mackenzie *river* Northwest Territories, Canada 22 D5, 24 C4
Mackenzie Mountains *mountain range* Yukon Territory/Northwest Territories, Canada 22 D4, 24 B4
McKinley, Mount *mountain* Alaska, USA 22 C4, 26 H2
Macleod, Lake *lake* Western Australia, Australia 102 B5
Macomer Italy 63 B8
Mâcon France 55 H5
Macon Georgia, USA 31 I4
Madagascar *country* SE Africa 71 H11, 81 J4
Madagascar *island* SE Africa 82 C5
Madagascar Basin *undersea feature* W Indian Ocean 82 C5
Madagascar Plateau *undersea feature* W Indian Ocean 82 C6
Madeira *Portuguese dependent territory* NW Atlantic Ocean 70 A2, 72 A4
Madeira *river* Bolivia/Brazil 38 D4, 41 E4
Mädelegabel *mountain* Germany 59 E13
Madison *state capital* Wisconsin, USA 32 B5
Madras *see* Chennai
Madre de Dios *river* Bolivia/Peru 39 C6, 40 D5
Madre, Laguna *lagoon* Mexico 35 E4
Madrid *country capital* Spain 46 B7, 57 E4
Madura *island* Indonesia 95 E9
Madurai India 93 D10
Maebashi Japan 99 H6
Mafeteng South Africa 80 E8
Mafia *island* Tanzania 79 J8
Magadan Russian Federation 87 J4
Magdalena *river* Colombia 40 C2
Magdeburg Germany 59 F6
Magellan, Strait of *strait* Argentina/Chile 39 D13, 43 D12
Magerøya *island* Norway 48 G1

Maggiore, Lake *lake* Italy/Switzerland 60 C6, 62 B2
Magnitogorsk Russian Federation 86 C5
Mahajanga Madagascar 71 I10, 81 J4
Mahakan *river* Indonesia 95 F7
Mahalapye Botswana 80 E6
Mahanadi *river* India 93 F7
Mahia Peninsula *peninsula* New Zealand 105 I6
Mahilyow Ukraine 65 E7
Mahón Balearic Islands, Spain 57 K5
Maiduguri Nigeria 71 E6, 77 J6
Main *river* Germany 59 E9
Main-Donau-Canal *canal* Germany 59 F10
Maine *state* USA 33 J3
Maine, Gulf of *gulf* NE USA 33 J4
Mainland *island* Orkney Islands, Scotland, United Kingdom 50 F3
Mainland *island* Shetland Islands, Scotland, United Kingdom 50 G1
Mainz Germany 59 C9
Maizuru Japan 99 F7
Majorca *see* Mallorca
Majuro *country capital* Marshall Islands 101 F4
Makassar Indonesia 85 G9, 95 G8
Makassar Strait *strait* Indonesia 95 F8
Makeni Sierra Leone 76 D7
Makhachkala Russian Federation 86 A6
Makiyivka Ukraine 65 H10
Makokou Gabon 78 C6
Makumbako Tanzania 79 H8
Makurdi Nigeria 77 I7
Malabar Coast *coastal region* India 93 C9
Malabo *country capital* Equatorial Guinea 71 D7, 78 B5
Malacca, Strait of *strait* Indonesia/Malaysia 83 G3, 94 B6
Maladzyechna Belarus 65 D6
Málaga Spain 46 A8, 56 E8
Malaita *island* Solomon Islands 100 E5
Malakal Sudan 75 D9
Malang Indonesia 95 E9
Malanje Angola 80 B2
Mälaren *lake* Sweden 49 E9
Malargüe Argentina 43 C7
Malatya Turkey 88 E2
Malawi *country* S Africa 71 G9, 81 G3
Malay Peninsula *peninsula* Malaysia/Thailand 94 B5
Malaysia *country* SE Asia 85 F8, 94 C6
Malbork Poland 66 F3
Maldives *country* N Indian Ocean 84 D8, 93 B12
Maldives *island group* N Indian Ocean 83 E3
Male *country capital* Maldives 84 D8, 93 B12
Malegaon India 93 C7
Malheur Lake *lake* Oregon, USA 26 D4
Mali *country* W Africa 70 C4, 77 F5
Malindi Kenya 79 J7
Mallaig Scotland, United Kingdom 50 D5
Mallawi Egypt 74 C4
Mallorca *island* Balearic Islands, Spain 46 C7, 57 J5
Malmberget Sweden 48 F4
Malmédy Belgium 53 G10
Malmö Sweden 46 E5, 49 C12
Malopolska *cultural region* Poland 67 G4
Malta *country* C Mediterranean Sea 46 E9, 63 F13
Malta *island* C Mediterranean Sea 63 F13
Malta Channel *channel* S Mediterranean Sea 63 F13
Malunda Indonesia 95 F8
Malung Sweden 49 D9
Mamberamo *river* Indonesia 95 K7

Mamoré *river* Bolivia/Brazil 40 E6
Mamou Guinea 76 D6
Mamoudzou Mayotte 81 J3
Man Ivory Coast 76 E7
Manacor Balearic Islands, Spain 57 J5
Manado Indonesia 95 H7
Managua *country capital* Nicaragua 23 F12, 35 I8
Manakara Madagascar 81 J6
Manama *country capital* Bahrain 84 B6, 89 H6
Mananjary Madagascar 81 J6
Manaus Brazil 38 E4, 41 F4
Manchester England, United Kingdom 46 C4, 51 F9
Manchester New Hampshire, USA 33 J5
Manchurian Plain *physical region* China 85 G5, 97 I3
Mandalay Myanmar 85 E7, 94 B2
Mandalgovi Mongolia 97 G3
Mandurah Western Australia, Australia 102 B7
Manfredonia Italy 63 G7
Manfredonia, Gulf of *gulf* SW Adriatic Sea 63 G7
Mangalooru (Mangalore) India 93 C9
Mangaweka New Zealand 105 G6
Manhattan Kansas, USA 29 H7
Manicouagan Reservoir *reservoir* Québec, Canada 25 I7
Maniitsoq Greenland 20 A4
Manila *country capital* Philippines 85 G7, 95 G4
Manisa Turkey 88 B2
Man, Isle of *island* United Kingdom 46 C4, 51 E8
Manitoba *province* Canada 25 E7
Manitoba, Lake *lake* Manitoba, Canada 24 E4
Manizales Colombia 40 C2
Mannar, Gulf of *gulf* India/Sri Lanka 93 D11
Mannheim Germany 59 C9
Manokwari Indonesia 95 J7
Manpo North Korea 98 B3
Manresa Spain 57 I3
Mansa Zambia 81 F3
Mansfield England, United Kingdom 51 G9
Mansfield Ohio, USA 32 E6
Manta Ecuador 40 B3
Mantova Italy 62 D3
Manukau Harbour *harbour* New Zealand 104 F4
Manurewa New Zealand 104 G3
Manzanares Spain 57 E6
Manzanillo Cuba 36 D4
Manzhouli China 97 H2
Manzini Swaziland 81 F7
Maoke, Pegunungan *mountain range* Indonesia 95 K8
Maoming China 97 H8
Maputo *country capital* Mozambique 71 G11, 81 F7
Maputo Bay *bay* W Indian Ocean 81 G7
Maqat Kazakhstan 90 B4
Maracaibo Venezuela 40 D1
Maracaibo, Lake *lake* Venezuela 38 C2, 40 C1
Maracay Venezuela 38 C2, 40 D1
Maradah Libya 73 J5
Maradi Niger 77 I6
Maragheh Iran 89 F2
Marajó, Baía de *bay* Brazil 41 H3
Marajó, Ilha de *island* Brazil 38 G3, 41 H3
Marañón *river* Peru 38 B4, 40 C4
Maratea Italy 63 G9
Marbella Spain 56 D8
Marburg Germany 59 C7
Marche-en-Famenne Belgium 53 F11
Marchena, Isla *island* Galapagos Islands 40 B8
Mar Chiquito, Laguna *lake* Argentina 39 D9
Mar del Plata Argentina 39 E10, 43 G7
Margarita, Isla de *island* Venezuela 41 E1

Margow, Dasht-e *desert* Afghanistan 91 D10
Marhanets Ukraine 65 G11
Mariana Trench *undersea feature* W Pacific Ocean 106 C4
Maribor Slovenia 61 J5
Marie Byrd Land *physical region* Antarctica 21 B4
Mariehamn Finland 49 F9
Mariental Namibia 80 C6
Mariestad Sweden 49 D10
Marijampole Lithuania 65 B6
Marikostinovo Bulgaria 69 F5
Marília Brazil 41 G7
Maringá Brazil 41 G7
Maritime Alps *mountain range* France/Italy 55 I7
Maritsa *river* SW Europe 69 H5
Mariupol Ukraine 65 H11
Marka Somalia 75 G11
Markermeer *lake* Netherlands 52 E4
Marktoberdorf Germany 59 E12
Marktredwitz Germany 59 G9
Marmara, Sea of *sea* Aegean Sea/Black Sea 69 I5
Marmaris Turkey 88 C2
Marmolada *mountain* Italy 62 E2
Marne *river* France 55 H3
Maroantsetra Madagascar 81 K4
Maroochydore-Mooloolaba Queensland, Australia 103 J5
Maroua Cameroon 78 C4
Marquesas Fracture Zone *undersea feature* C Pacific Ocean 107 G5
Marquesas Islands *island group* French Polynesia 107 J5
Marrakech Morocco 70 B2, 72 D4
Marree South Australia, Australia 103 G6
Marsa Al Burayqah Libya 73 J5
Marsabit Kenya 79 I6
Marsala Italy 63 E11
Marseille France 46 C7, 55 H8
Marshall Islands *country* W Pacific Ocean 100 D3
Martaban, Gulf of *gulf* Myanmar 94 B3
Martapura Indonesia 95 F8
Martha's Vineyard *island* Massachusetts, USA 33 J6
Martigny Switzerland 60 B6
Martin Slovakia 67 F8
Martinique *French dependent territory* E West Indies 37 J6
Martinique Passage *channel* Dominica/Martinique 37 J6
Mary Turkmenistan 91 D8
Maryborough Queensland, Australia 103 J5
Maryland *state* USA 33 G7
Maryville Missouri, USA 29 I6
Masai Steppe *physical region* Tanzania 71 H8, 79 I7
Masan South Korea 98 C6
Masasi Tanzania 79 I9
Masbate *island* Philippines 95 G4
Mascarene Basin *undersea feature* W Indian Ocean 82 D4
Maseru *country capital* Lesotho 71 F12, 80 E8
Mashhad Iran 84 C5, 89 I2
Masindi Uganda 79 H6
Masirah *island* Oman 89 J7
Masirah, Gulf of *gulf* NW Arabian Sea 89 J7
Mason City Iowa, USA 29 I5
Massa Italy 62 C5
Massachusetts *state* USA 33 I5
Massawa Eritrea 75 F7
Massena New York, USA 33 H4
Massif Central *plateau* France 46 C6, 55 F6
Masterton New Zealand 105 G7
Masty Belarus 65 C7
Masuda Japan 98 D7
Masvingo Zimbabwe 81 F5
Matadi Democratic Republic of Congo 78 C8
Matagalpa Nicaragua 35 I7
Matam Senegal 76 D5
Matamoros Mexico 35 E4
Matanzas Cuba 36 B3
Mataram Indonesia 95 F9
Mataranka Northern Territory, Australia 103 F2
Mataró Spain 57 J3

Mataura *river* New Zealand 105 B12
Matera Italy 63 H8
Mato Grosso, Planalto de *plateau* Brazil 39 E6, 41 G6
Matosinhos Portugal 56 B4
Matsue Japan 98 E7
Matsumoto Japan 99 G6
Matsuyama Japan 98 E7
Matterhorn *mountain* Italy/Switzerland 60 B6
Matto Japan 99 F6
Maturín Venezuela 41 E1
Maui *island* Hawaii, USA 27 B12
Maun Botswana 80 D5
Mauritania *country* W Africa 70 A4, 76 D4
Mauritius *island* W Indian Ocean 82 D5
Maxixe Mozambique 81 G6
Mayagüez Puerto Rico 37 H5
Maydan Shahr Afghanistan 91 F9
Maykop Russian Federation 86 A5
Mayotte *French dependent territory* S Africa 71 I9, 81 J3
May Pen Jamaica 36 D5
Mazabuka Zambia 81 E4
Mazara del Vallo Italy 63 E11
Mazar-e Sharif Afghanistan 91 E8
Mazatlán Mexico 34 C4
Mazeikiai Lithuania 64 B5
Mazuria *cultural region* Poland 66 F4
Mazyr Belarus 65 D8
Mbabane *country capital* Swaziland 71 G11, 81 F7
Mbaiki Central African Republic 78 D5
Mbaké Senegal 76 C5
Mbale Uganda 79 H6
Mbandaka Democratic Republic of Congo 71 E8, 78 D6
M'banza Congo Angola 80 B2
Mbarara Uganda 79 G6
Mbeya Tanzania 79 H8
Mbuji-Mayi Democratic Republic of Congo 71 F8, 79 F8
Mdantsane South Africa 80 E8
Mead, Lake *lake* Arizona/Nevada, USA 27 F6
Mecca Saudi Arabia 84 B7, 88 E7
Mechelen Belgium 53 D8
Meckenheim Germany 59 B8
Mecklenburg Bay *bay* S Baltic Sea 58 F2
Medan Indonesia 85 E8, 94 B6
Medellín Colombia 38 B2, 40 C2
Medford Oregon, USA 26 B5
Medias Romania 69 G7
Medicine Hat Alberta, Canada 24 C8
Medina Saudi Arabia 88 E6
Medina del Campo Spain 56 D4
Mediterranean Sea *sea* E Atlantic Ocean 63 C11, 68 D9
Meekatharra Western Australia, Australia 102 C5
Meerut India 92 D4
Megisti Greece 69 J8
Meiningen Germany 59 E8
Meizhou China 97 I8
Mekele Ethiopia 75 F8
Meknès Morocco 72 D4
Mekong *river* SE Asia 85 F7, 94 C2, 97 E6
Mekong, Mouths of the *delta* Vietnam 94 D5
Melaka Malaysia 94 C7
Melanesia *island group* W Pacific Ocean 100 C4, 106 C5
Melanesian Basin *undersea feature* W Pacific Ocean 106 D4
Melbourne *state capital* Victoria, Australia 100 D8, 103 H8
Melbourne Florida, USA 31 J6
Melekeok (Koror) *country capital* Palau 100 B4
Melilla *Spanish dependent territory* NW Africa 57 F9, 70 C2, 72 E3
Melitopol Ukraine 65 G11
Mellerud Sweden 49 C10
Melo Uruguay 43 H6
Melun France 55 F3

Melville Island *island* Northern Territory, Australia 103 E1
Melville Island *island* Northwest Territories/Nunavut, Canada 22 F4, 24 D2
Melville Peninsula *peninsula* Nunavut, Canada 25 F4
Memmingen Germany 59 E8
Memphis Tennessee, USA 23 F9, 31 G4
Ménaka Mali 77 H5
Mendana Fracture Zone *undersea feature* E Pacific Ocean 107 I5
Mende France 55 G7
Mendeleyen Ridge *undersea feature* Arctic Ocean 20 C3
Mendocina Fracture Zone *undersea feature* N Pacific Ocean 107 F2
Mendocino, Cape *headland* California, USA 27 A6
Mendoza Argentina 43 C6
Menongue Angola 80 B4
Menorca *island* Balearic Islands, Spain 46 C7, 57 K5
Mentawai Islands *island group* Indonesia 94 B7
Menzies Western Australia, Australia 102 C6
Meppel Netherlands 52 G4
Meppen Germany 58 B5
Mequinenza, Embalse de *reservoir* Spain 57 G4
Merano Italy 62 D2
Merced California, USA 27 C8
Mercedes Argentina 43 D6
Mercedes Uruguay 43 G6
Mergui Archipelago *island group* Myanmar 94 B4
Mérida Mexico 35 H5
Mérida Spain 56 C6
Mérida Venezuela 40 D2
Meridian Mississippi, USA 31 G5
Mérignac France 54 D6
Merke Kyrgyzstan 91 G6
Merredin Western Australia, Australia 102 C6
Mersin Turkey 88 D2
Meru Kenya 79 I6
Mesa Arizona, USA 27 G11
Mesolongi Greece 69 F7
Mesopotamia *physical region* Argentina 39 E9, 43 F5
Messina Italy 63 G11
Messina South Africa 81 F6
Messina, Gulf of *gulf* NE Mediterranean Sea 69 F8
Messina, Strait of *strait* Ionian Sea/Tyrrhenian Sea 63 G11
Mestre Italy 62 E3
Meta *river* Colombia/Venezuela 38 C2, 40 D2
Metairie Louisiana, USA 31 G6
Metán Argentina 42 E3
Metz France 55 H2
Meuse *river* W Europe 53 E10, 55 H2 *see also* Maas
Mexicali Mexico 34 A1
Mexican Hat Utah, USA 27 H9
Mexico *country* S North America 23 D11, 34 D4
Mexico City *country capital* Mexico 23 D11, 34 E6
Mexico, Gulf of *gulf* Mexico/USA 23 E10, 31 G7, 35 G4, 45 B6
Meymaneh Afghanistan 91 D8
Miami Florida, USA 23 G11, 31 J7
Mianwali Pakistan 91 F9
Mianyang China 97 G6
Miass Russian Federation 86 C5
Miastko Poland 66 D3
Michalovce Slovakia 67 H9
Michigan *state* USA 32 D4
Michigan, Lake *lake* N USA 23 F8, 32 C5
Micronesia, Fed. States of *country* W Pacific Ocean 100 C4
Micronesia *island group* W Pacific Ocean 100 C3, 106 D4
Mid-Atlantic Ridge *undersea feature* C Atlantic Ocean 44 E5
Middelburg Netherlands 53 C7
Middle America Trench *undersea feature* E Pacific Ocean 107 I4
Middle Andaman *island* Andaman Islands, India 93 I9
Middlesbrough England, United Kingdom 51 G8

Midi, Canal du *canal* France 55 F8
Mid-Indian Basin *undersea feature* C Indian Ocean 83 F4
Mid-Indian Ridge *undersea feature* C Indian Ocean 82 F4
Midland Texas, USA 30 C5
Mid-Pacific Mountains *undersea feature* N Pacific Ocean 106 C3
Midway Islands *US dependent territory* W Pacific Ocean 101 G1
Miercurea Ciuc Romania 69 G2
Mieres Spain 56 D2
Mikkeli Finland 49 H8
Milan Italy 46 D6, 62 C3
Milazzo Italy 63 G11
Mildura Victoria, Australia 103 H7
Miles Queensland, Australia 103 J5
Miles City Montana, USA 28 E3
Milford Sound New Zealand 105 B11
Milk *river* Montana, USA 28 D2
Milos Greece 69 G8
Milove Ukraine 65 I9
Milton New Zealand 105 C12
Milwaukee Wisconsin, USA 23 F8, 32 C5
Minas Uruguay 43 G6
Minch, The *channel* Scotland, United Kingdom 50 D4
Mindanao *island* Philippines 85 G8, 95 H5
Minden Germany 58 D5
Mindoro *island* Philippines 95 G4
Mingaora Pakistan 91 F9
Minicoy Island *island* India 93 B11
Minna Nigeria 77 I7
Minneapolis Minnesota, USA 23 E8, 29 H4
Minnesota *river* Minnesota/South Dakota, USA 29 H4
Minnesota *state* USA 29 H4
Miño *river* Portugal/Spain 56 B3
Minorca *see* Menorca
Minot North Dakota, USA 29 F2
Minsk *country capital* Belarus 47 G5, 65 E7
Mirandola Italy 62 D4
Miri Malaysia 95 E6
Mirim, Lagoa *lagoon* Brazil/Uruguay 39 F9, 43 H6
Mirnyy Russian Federation 87 G3
Mirpur Khas Pakistan 91 F12
Mirtoan Sea *sea* SW Aegean Sea 69 G8
Miskolc Hungary 67 G9
Misool *island* Indonesia 95 I7
Misratah Libya 70 E2, 73 I4
Mississippi *river* C USA 23 E10, 29 I3, 31 G4, 32 A7
Mississippi *state* USA 31 G5
Mississippi Delta *delta* Louisiana, USA 23 E10, 31 G6
Missoula Montana, USA 28 B2
Missouri *river* C USA 23 D7, 28 D2
Missouri *state* USA 29 J7
Mistelbach Austria 61 K2
Mitchell Queensland, Australia 103 I5
Mitchell *river* Queensland, Australia 103 H2
Mitchell South Dakota, USA 29 G5
Mito Japan 99 H6
Mittellandkanal *canal* Germany 59 F5
Mittersill Austria 61 G4
Mittersill Austria 61 G4
Miyako Japan 99 I4
Miyako-jima *island* Japan 99 I9
Miyakonojo Japan 98 D9
Miyazaki Japan 98 D8
Mjøsa *lake* Norway 49 C9
Mlada Boleslav Czech Republic 67 C7
Mljet *island* Croatia 68 D4
Moanda Gabon 78 C7
Moba Democratic Republic of Congo, USA 31 H5
Mobile Alabama, USA 31 H5
Moçambique Mozambique 81 I4
Mocha Yemen 89 F6
Mochudi Botswana 80 E6
Mocuba Mozambique 81 H4
Modena Italy 62 D4
Modesto California, USA 27 B8

Modica Italy 63 F12
Mödling Austria 61 J3
Mogadishu *country capital* Somalia 71 I7, 75 G11
Mohammedia Morocco 72 D4
Mohéli *island* Comoros 81 J3
Mohoro Tanzania 79 J8
Mo i Rana Norway 48 D5
Mojave Desert *desert* California, USA 27 D10
Mokau New Zealand 104 F5
Mokp'o South Korea 98 B7
Mol Belgium 53 E8
Molde Norway 49 B7
Moldova *country* SE Europe 47 G6, 65 D11
Molepolole Botswana 80 E6
Molfetta Italy 63 H7
Mölln Germany 58 F3
Mölndal Sweden 49 C11
Molokai *island* Hawaii, USA 27 B12
Molokai Fracture Zone *undersea feature* N Pacific Ocean 107 F3
Moluccas *island group* Indonesia 85 G9, 95 H7
Molucca Sea *sea* Indonesia 95 H7
Mombasa Kenya 71 H8, 79 J7
Monaco *country* W Europe 46 D7, 55 J7, 62 A5
Monaco *country capital* Monaco 55 J7
Mona Passage *channel* Dominican Republic/Puerto Rico 37 G5
Monastir Tunisia 73 H3
Monbetsu Japan 99 I2
Moncalieri Italy 62 A3
Monclova Mexico 34 D3
Moncton New Brunswick, Canada 25 J8
Mondovi Italy 62 A4
Monforte Spain 56 C2
Mongo Chad 78 D3
Mongolia *country* E Asia 85 F5, 97 F3
Mongu Zambia 80 D4
Monroe Louisiana, USA 31 F5
Monrovia *country capital* Liberia 71 B6, 76 D7
Mons Belgium 53 C10
Montana Bulgaria 69 F4
Montana *state* USA 28 C3
Montauban France 55 F7
Montbéliard France 55 I4
Montceau-les-Mines France 55 G5
Mont-de-Marsan France 54 D7
Montego Bay Jamaica 36 D5
Montélimar France 55 H7
Montenegro *country* SE Europe 68 D4, 69 E4
Montepuez Mozambique 81 H3
Monterey California, USA 27 B9
Monterey Bay *bay* California, USA 27 B9
Monteria Colombia 40 C2
Monterrey Mexico 23 D10, 34 E4
Montes Claros Brazil 41 I6
Montevideo *country capital* Uruguay 39 E10, 43 G6
Montgomery *state capital* Alabama, USA 31 H5
Monthey Switzerland 60 B6
Montluçon France 55 F5
Montpelier *state capital* Vermont, USA 33 I4
Montpellier France 55 G7
Montreal Québec, Canada 23 G8, 25 I8
Montreux Switzerland 60 B5
Montserrat *UK dependent territory* E West Indies 37 J6
Monywa Myanmar 94 B2
Monza Italy 62 C3
Monze Zambia 81 E4
Monzón Spain 57 H3
Moore, Lake *seasonal lake* Western Australia, Australia 102 C6
Moorhead Minnesota, USA 29 H3
Moose Jaw Saskatchewan, Canada 24 D8
Mopti Mali 77 F5
Mora Sweden 49 D8
Moradabad India 92 D4
Morava *river* C Europe 67 D8

Moravia *cultural region* Czech Republic 67 D8
Moray Firth *inlet* NW North Sea 50 E4
Morbegno Italy 62 C2
Morecambe England, United Kingdom 51 F8
Moree New South Wales, Australia 103 I6
Morelia Mexico 34 D5
Morena, Sierra *mountain range* Spain 56 C7
Morioka Japan 99 H4
Mornington Abyssal Plain *undersea feature* SE Pacific Ocean 107 I8
Morocco *country* N Africa 70 B2, 72 D4
Morogoro Tanzania 79 I8
Moron Mongolia 97 F2
Morondava Madagascar 81 J5
Moroni *country capital* Comoros 71 H9, 81 I3
Morotai *island* Indonesia 95 I6
Moroto Uganda 79 H6
Morristown Tennessee, USA 31 I3
Mortes, Rio das *river* Brazil 41 G4
Mortyq Kazakhstan 90 C4
Morvan *physical region* France 55 G4
Moscow *country capital* Russian Federation 47 H4, 86 B4
Mosel *river* W Europe 59 B8 *see also* Moselle
Moselle *river* W Europe 53 H12, 55 H3 *see also* Mosel
Moshi Tanzania 79 I7
Mosjøen Norway 48 D5
Moskenesøy *island* Norway 48 D4
Mosonmagyarovar Hungary 67 D10
Mosquito Coast *coastal region* Nicaragua 35 I8
Mosquito Gulf *gulf* Panama 35 J8
Moss Norway 49 C9
Mossburn New Zealand 105 B12
Mossendjo Congo 78 C7
Mossoró Brazil 41 J4
Most Czech Republic 67 B6
Mostaganem Algeria 73 F3
Mostar Bosnia & Herzegovina 68 D4
Móstoles Spain 56 E5
Mosul Iraq 89 F3
Motril Spain 57 E8
Motueka New Zealand 105 E7
Mouila Gabon 78 B7
Moulins France 55 G5
Moulmein Myanmar 94 B3
Moundou Chad 78 D4
Mount Gambier South Australia, Australia 103 G8
Mount Isa Queensland, Australia 103 G4
Mount Magnet Western Australia, Australia 102 C6
Moura Portugal 56 B7
Mouscron Belgium 53 B9
Moussoro Chad 78 D3
Moyale Ethiopia 75 F11, 79 I5
Moyynqum *desert* Kazakhstan 91 F6
Mozambique *country* S Africa 71 G10, 81 G5
Mozambique Channel *channel* W Indian Ocean 71 H10, 81 I5, 82 C5
Mozambique Plateau *undersea feature* W Indian Ocean 82 B6
Mpanda Tanzania 79 G8
Mpika Zambia 81 F3
Mtwara Tanzania 79 J9
Muck *island* Scotland, United Kingdom 50 D5
Mucojo Mozambique 81 J3
Mudanjiang China 97 J2
Mufulira Zambia 81 E3
Mughshin Oman 89 I7
Mugodzhar Hills *hill range* Kazakhstan 90 C5
Mühlhausen Germany 59 E7
Mukachevo Ukraine 65 B10
Mulhacén *mountain* Spain 57 F8
Mulhouse France 55 I4
Mull *island* Scotland, United Kingdom 51 D6
Multan Pakistan 84 D6, 91 F10
Mumbai India 84 D7, 93 B7

Muna *island* Indonesia 95 G8
Muncie Indiana, USA 32 D6
Mungbere Democratic Republic of Congo 79 G6
Munich Germany 46 D6, 59 F11
Munku-Sardyk, Gora *mountain* Russian Federation 87 G6
Münster Germany 59 C6
Munster *cultural region* Republic of Ireland 51 B10
Muonio Finland 48 G3
Muonioälven *river* NW Europe 49 F3
Mur *river* C Europe 61 J5
Murcia Spain 46 B8, 57 G7
Mures *river* Hungary/Romania 69 F2
Murfreesboro Tennessee, USA 31 H3
Murghob Tajikistan 91 G8
Müritz *lake* Germany 58 G4
Murmansk Russian Federation 47 G2, 86 C2
Muroran Japan 99 H3
Muroto-zaki *headland* Japan 99 E8
Murray *river* SW Australia 100 D8, 103 H7
Murray Bridge South Australia, Australia 103 G7
Murray Fracture Zone *undersea feature* N Pacific Ocean 107 F3
Murska Sobota Slovenia 61 J5
Murupara New Zealand 104 H5
Murwara India 93 E6
Murwillumbah Austria 61 J4
Musala *mountain* Bulgaria 69 G5
Musan North Korea 98 D3
Muscat *country capital* Oman 84 C7, 89 J6
Musi *river* Indonesia 94 C8
Muskogee Oklahoma, USA 31 E4
Mutare Zimbabwe 71 G10, 81 F5
Mutsu-wan *bay* Japan 99 H3
Muzaffarpur India 92 F5
Mwanza Tanzania 71 G8, 79 H7
Mwene-Ditu Democratic Republic of Congo 79 F8
Mweru, Lake *lake* Democratic Republic of Congo/Zambia 79 G8, 81 F2
Myanmar *country* SE Asia 85 E7, 94 A2
Myingyan Myanmar 94 B2
Myitkyina Myanmar 94 B1
Mykolayiv Ukraine 65 F11
Mykonos *island* Greece 69 H8
Mymensingh Bangladesh 93 G5
Mysliborz Poland 66 C4
Mysuru (Mysore) India 93 C9
My Tho Vietnam 94 D5
Mytilini Greece 69 H7
Mzuzu Malawi 81 G3

N

Naberezhnyye Chelny Russian Federation 47 I4, 86 C5
Nacala Mozambique 81 I4
Nadym Russian Federation 86 E4
Nafplio Greece 69 F8
Naga Philippines 95 G4
Naga Hills *hill range* India 92 I5
Nagano Japan 99 G6
Nagaoka Japan 99 G5
Nagasaki Japan 98 C8
Nagercoil India 93 D11
Nagoya Japan 85 H6, 99 G7
Nagpur India 93 E6
Nagpur, Chota *plateau* India 93 E6
Nagykanizsa Hungary 67 D11
Naha Japan 85 I7
Nairobi *country capital* Kenya 71 H8, 79 I7
Najafabad Iran 89 H4
Najin North Korea 98 D3
Najran Saudi Arabia 89 F8
Nakamura Japan 98 E8
Nakhodka Russian Federation 87 J7
Nakhon Ratchasima Thailand 94 C4
Nakhon Sawan Thailand 94 C4

Nakhon Si Thammarat Thailand 94 B5
Nakuru Kenya 79 I6
Nalchik Russian Federation 86 A6
Namangan Uzbekistan 91 F7
Namaqualand *physical region* Namibia 80 B7
Nambala Zambia 80 E4
Nam Dinh Vietnam 94 D3
Namib Desert *desert* Namibia 71 E11, 80 B6
Namibe Angola 71 D10, 80 A4
Namibia *country* S Africa 71 E11, 80 B5
Nampa Idaho, USA 26 E4
Namp'o North Korea 98 B4
Nampula Mozambique 71 H10, 81 H4
Namsen *river* Norway 49 D6
Namsos Norway 49 C6
Namur Belgium 53 E10
Nan *river* Thailand 94 C3
Nanchang China 85 G6, 97 I7
Nanchong China 97 G6
Nancy France 55 H3
Nanded India 93 D7
Nandyal India 93 D9
Nanga Parbat *mountain* Pakistan 91 G9
Nangnim-sanmaek *mountain range* North Korea 98 B4
Nanjing China 85 G6, 97 I6
Nanning China 97 G8
Nanping China 97 I7
Nansen Basin *undersea feature* Arctic Ocean 20 C4
Nansen Cordillera *undersea feature* Arctic Ocean 20 C4
Nantes France 54 C6, 54 D4
Nantucket Island *island* Massachusetts, USA 33 J6
Nanyang China 97 H6
Nao, Cabo de la *headland* Spain 57 H6
Napa California, USA 27 B8
Napier New Zealand 105 H4
Naples Italy 46 E8, 63 E8
Naples Florida, USA 31 J7
Napo *river* Ecuador/Peru 38 B4, 40 C4
Nara Japan 99 F7
Naracoorte South Australia, Australia 103 G8
Narbonne France 55 G8
Nardo Italy 63 I8
Nares Plain *undersea feature* W Atlantic Ocean 45 C6
Narew *river* Belarus/Poland 66 G4
Narmada *river* India 93 C6
Narodnaya, Gora *mountain* Russian Federation 86 D5
Närpes Finland 49 F7
Narva Estonia 63 G2
Narvik Norway 48 E3
Naryn Kyrgyzstan 91 G7
Nashik India 93 B7
Nashua New Hampshire, USA 33 J5
Nashville *state capital* Tennessee, USA 23 F9, 31 H3
Nassau *country capital* Bahamas 23 G11, 36 D2
Nasser, Lake *lake* Egypt 70 G4, 74 D5
Natal Brazil 38 I5, 41 J7
Natal Basin *undersea feature* W Indian Ocean 82 C5
Natitingou Benin 77 G6
Natuna Besar *island* Indonesia 94 D6
Natuna Islands *island group* Indonesia 94 D6
Natuna Sea *sea* Indonesia 94 D6
Nauru *country* SW Pacific Ocean 101 E4
Navapolatsk Belarus 64 D5
Navarra *cultural region* Spain 57 F2
Navassa Island *US dependent territory* C West Indies 36 E5
Nawabshah Pakistan 91 E11
Nawoiy Uzbekistan 91 E7
Naxcivan Azerbaijan 89 F2
Naxos Greece 69 H8
Naxos *island* Greece 69 H8
Nayoro Japan 99 I1
Naze Japan 99 K8
Nazret Ethiopia 75 F9
N'dalatando Angola 80 B2

Ndjamena *country capital* Chad 71 E5, 78 D3
Ndjolé Gabon 78 B6
Ndola Zambia 71 F9, 81 E3
Neagh, Lough *lake* Northern Ireland, United Kingdom 51 C7
Neapoli Greece 69 G8
Nebitdag Turkmenistan 91 B7
Nebraska *state* USA 29 F6
Neckar *river* Germany 59 D10
Necochea Argentina 43 F8
Negele Ethiopia 75 F10
Negomane Mozambique 81 H3
Negombo Sri Lanka 93 D11
Negro *river* N South America 38 D3, 41 E3
Negro, Río *river* Argentina 39 D10, 43 E8
Negros *island* Philippines 95 G5
Neijiang China 97 G7
Neisse *river* Germany 59 I7
Neiva Colombia 40 C3
Nek'emte Ethiopia 75 E9
Nellore India 93 D9
Nelson *river* Manitoba, Canada 25 F6
Nelson New Zealand 105 E7
Nelspruit South Africa 81 F7
Néma Mauritania 76 E5
Neman *river* N Europe 65 B6
Nemuro Japan 99 J2
Nen Jiang *river* China 97 I2
Nepal *country* S Asia 84 D6, 92 E4
Nesebur Bulgaria 69 I4
Neskaupstadhur Iceland 48 D2
Ness, Loch *lake* Scotland, United Kingdom 50 E5
Netherlands *country* NW Europe 46 C5, 52 E5
Netherlands Antilles *Dutch dependent territory* E West Indies 37 I5
Netherlands Antilles *Dutch dependent territory* S West Indies 23 H12, 37 G7
Nettilling Lake *lake* Nunavut, Canada 25 G4
Neubrandenburg Germany 58 H4
Neuchâtel Switzerland 60 B5
Neuchâtel, Lake *lake* Switzerland 60 B5
Neufchâteau Belgium 53 F12
Neumünster Germany 58 E3
Neunkirchen Austria 61 J4
Neuquén Argentina 43 D8
Neuruppin Germany 58 G4
Neusiedler See *lake* Austria/Hungary 61 K3
Neuss Germany 59 B7
Neustrelitz Germany 58 G4
Neu-Ulm Germany 59 E11
Neuwied Germany 59 B8
Nevada *state* USA 27 D8
Nevada, Sierra *mountain range* Spain 57 E8
Nevers France 55 G4
Nevis *island* St Kitts & Nevis 37 J5
Newark New Jersey, USA 33 H6
New Britain *island* Papua New Guinea 100 D5
New Brunswick *province* Canada 25 I7
Newbury England, United Kingdom 51 G11
New Caledonia *French dependent territory* SW Pacific Ocean 100 E6
Newcastle New South Wales, Australia 100 D8, 103 J7
Newcastle South Africa 81 F7
Newcastle-upon-Tyne England, United Kingdom 51 G7
New Delhi *country capital* India 84 D6, 92 E4
New England *cultural region* NE USA 33 I5
New Forest *physical region* England, United Kingdom 51 G12
Newfoundland *island* Newfoundland & Labrador, Canada 23 I7, 25 J6, 44 D4
Newfoundland & Labrador *province* Canada 25 I6
Newfoundland Basin *undersea feature* NW Atlantic Ocean 44 D4

New Georgia Islands *island group* Solomon Islands 100 D5
New Guinea *island* W Pacific Ocean 106 C5
New Hampshire *state* USA 33 I4
New Ireland *island* Papua New Guinea 100 D5
New Jersey *state* USA 33 H7
Newman Western Australia, Australia 102 C4
New Mexico *state* USA 30 B4
New Orleans Louisiana, USA 23 E10, 31 G6
New Plymouth New Zealand 105 F5
Newport Wales, United Kingdom 51 F11
Newport News Virginia, USA 33 H8
New Providence *island* Bahamas 36 D2
Newquay England, United Kingdom 51 G12
Newry Northern Ireland, United Kingdom 51 D8
New Siberian Islands *island group* Russian Federation 87 H2
New South Wales *state* Australia 103 H6
Newtownabbey Northern Ireland, United Kingdom 51 D7
New Ulm Minnesota, USA 29 I4
New York New York, USA 23 G9, 33 I6
New York *state* USA 33 G5
New Zealand *country* SW Pacific Ocean 101 E8, 104–105
Neyshabur Iran 89 I2
Ngaoundéré Cameroon 78 C4
Ngaurahoe, Mount *mountain* New Zealand 105 G5
N'giva Angola 80 B4
Ngourti Niger 77 J5
Nguigmi Niger 77 J5
Nha Trang Vietnam 94 D4
Niagara Falls *waterfall* Canada/USA 33 F5
Niagara Falls New York, USA 33 F5
Niamey *country capital* Niger 71 C5, 77 H6
Nianzishan China 97 I2
Nias *island* Indonesia 94 B7
Nicaragua *country* Central America 23 F12, 35 I8
Nicaragua, Lake *lake* Nicaragua 23 F12, 35 I8
Nice France 46 D7, 55 I7
Nicobar Islands *island group* India 83 G3, 84 E8, 93 I11
Nicosia *country capital* Cyprus 84 A6, 88 D3
Nidzica Poland 66 G4
Niedere Tauern *mountain range* Austria 61 H4
Nienburg Germany 58 D5
Nieuwegein Netherlands 53 E6
Niger *country* W Africa 70 D5, 77 I5
Niger *river* W Africa 70 C5, 77 I5
Niger Delta *delta* Mali 45 G7, 77 F5
Nigeria *country* W Africa 71 D6, 77 I7
Niger, Mouths of the *wetland* Nigeria 77 I8
Niigata Japan 99 H5
Niihama Japan 98 E7
Nijmegen Netherlands 53 G6
Nikko Japan 99 H6
Nikopol Ukraine 65 G11
Niksic Montenegro 68 D4
Nile *river* NE Africa 70 G4, 75 C6
Nile Delta *delta* Egypt 75 C6
Nîmes France 55 G7
Nine Degree Channel *channel* India/Maldives 93 B11
Ninetyeast Ridge *undersea feature* E Indian Ocean 83 F4
Ninety Mile Beach *coastal region* New Zealand 104 E1
Ningbo China 97 J6
Niobrara *river* Nebraska/Wyoming, USA 29 F5
Nioro Mali 76 E5
Niort France 54 D5

Nipigon, Lake *lake* Ontario, Canada 25 F8, 23 F7
Nis Serbia 69 F4
Nishtun Yemen 89 H8
Nitra Slovakia 67 E9
Niue *NZ dependent territory* C Pacific Ocean 101 G6
Nivelles Belgium 53 D10
Nizamabad India 93 D7
Nizhnevartovsk Russian Federation 86 E5
Nizhniy Novgorod Russian Federation 47 H4, 86 B4
Nizhniy Tagil Russian Federation 86 D5
Nizhyn Ukraine 65 F8
Nizwa Oman 89 I6
Nkongsamba Cameroon 78 B5
Nobeoka Japan 98 D8
Nogales Arizona, USA 27 H12
Nogliki Russian Federation 87 J5
Noirmoutier, Île de *island* France 54 C4
Nojima-zaki *headland* Japan 99 H7
Nokia Finland 49 G8
Nome Alaska, USA 26 G1
Nonthaburi Thailand 94 C4
Noordoewer Namibia 80 C7
Noormarkku Finland 49 F8
Nora Sweden 49 D9
Norden Germany 58 B3
Norderstedt Germany 58 E3
Nordhausen Germany 59 E6
Nordhorn Germany 58 B5
Norfolk Nebraska, USA 29 H5
Norfolk Virginia, USA 33 H8
Norfolk Island *Australian dependent territory* SW Pacific Ocean 101 E7
Norilsk Russian Federation 84 E2, 87 F4
Norman Oklahoma, USA 30 E4
Normandy *cultural region* France 54 D3
Normanton Queensland, Australia 103 H3
Norrköping Sweden 49 E10
Norrtälje Sweden 49 E9
Norseman Western Australia, Australia 102 D7
Norte, Punta *headland* Argentina 43 G7
Northam Western Australia, Australia 102 B6
North America *continent* 22–37
Northampton England, United Kingdom 51 G10
North Andaman *island* Andaman Islands, India 93 H9
North Australian Basin *undersea feature* E Indian Ocean 83 H4
North Bay Ontario, Canada 25 H8
North Cape *headland* New Zealand 104 E1
North Cape *headland* Norway 47 F1, 48 G1
North Carolina *state* USA 31 K3
North Charleston South Carolina, USA 31 J4
North Dakota *state* USA 29 F2
North Downs *hill range* England, United Kingdom 51 H11
North-East Canal *canal* Germany 58 D3
Northern Cook Islands *island group* Cook Islands 101 H5
Northern Dvina *river* Russian Federation 47 H2, 86 C3
Northern Ireland *national region* United Kingdom 51 C7
Northern Mariana Islands *US dependent territory* W Pacific Ocean 100 C2
Northern Sporades *island group* Greece 69 G7
Northern Territory *state* Australia 103 F3
North European Plain *physical region* N Europe 47 E5, 66 E4, 86 B4
North Fiji Basin *undersea feature* SW Pacific Ocean 106 D5
North Frisian Islands *island group* N Europe 58 C1
North Island *island* New Zealand 101 F8, 104 E4

North Korea *country* E Asia 85 G5, 98 B4
North Las Vegas Nevada, USA 27 E9
North Little Rock Arkansas, USA 31 F4
North Platte Nebraska, USA 29 F6
North Platte *river* C USA 29 E6
North Pole *pole* Arctic Ocean 20 C3
North Saskatchewan *river* Alberta/Saskatchewan, Canada 24 C7
North Sea *sea* NE Atlantic Ocean 44 G3, 46 D4, 50 H5, 58 B2
North Shore New Zealand 104 F3
North Taranaki Bight *bay* New Zealand 104 E5
North Uist *island* Scotland, United Kingdom 50 C4
Northwest Atlantic Mid-Ocean Canyon *undersea feature* NW Atlantic Ocean 44 D4
North West Cape *headland* Western Australia, Australia 102 A4
Northwest Highlands *mountain range* Scotland, United Kingdom 50 E4
Northwest Pacific Basin *undersea feature* N Pacific Ocean 106 D2
Northwest Territories *province* Canada 24 C4
North York Moors *moorland* England, United Kingdom 51 G8
Norway *country* NW Europe 46 D4, 49 B8
Norwegian Sea *sea* NE Atlantic Ocean 44 G2, 46 D2
Norwich England, United Kingdom 51 I10
Noshiro Japan 99 H4
Notec *river* Poland 66 D4
Noto-hanto *peninsula* Japan 99 F5
Nottingham England, United Kingdom 51 G9
Nouadhibou Mauritania 76 C3
Nouakchott *country capital* Mauritania 70 A4, 76 C4
Nouméa New Caledonia 101 E6
Nova Gorica Slovenia 61 H6
Nova Iguaçu Brazil 39 G7
Nova Kakhovka Ukraine 65 F11
Novara Italy 62 B3
Nova Scotia *province* Canada 25 J8
Nova Ves Slovakia 67 G8
Novaya Zemlya *island group* Russian Federation 47 H1, 86 D3
Nove Zamky Slovakia 67 E9
Novgorod Russian Federation 86 B3
Novi Sad Serbia 68 E3
Novoalekseevka Kazakhstan 90 C4
Novohrad-Volynskyy Ukraine 65 D9
Novokuznetsk Russian Federation 84 E4, 87 E6
Novo Mesto Slovenia 61 I7
Novosibirsk Russian Federation 84 D4, 87 E6
Novovolyusk Ukraine 65 B9
Novyy Urengoy Russian Federation 86 E4
Nowy Sacz Poland 67 G8
Nowy Targ Poland 67 F8
Nubian Desert *desert* Sudan 70 G4, 74 C3
Nueva Lubecka Argentina 43 C10
Nuevo Laredo Mexico 34 E3
Nu Jiang *river* SE Asia 96 D6 *see also* Salween
Nuku'alofa *country capital* Tonga 101 G6
Nullarbor *physical region* Australia 100 B8
Nullarbor Plain *plateau* South Australia/Western Australia, Australia 102 D6
Nunavut *province* Canada 24 E4
Nunivak Island *island* Alaska, USA 26 G2
Nuoro Italy 63 B8
Nuqus Uzbekistan 91 C6

Nuremberg Germany 59 F9
Nurmes Finland 49 I6
Nushki Pakistan 91 E10
Nuuk Greenland 20 A5, 22 H5
Nyala Sudan 75 B8
Nyasa, Lake *lake* E Africa 71 G9, 79 H9, 81 G3
Nyborg Denmark 49 B12
Nyeri Kenya 79 I6
Nyiregyhaza Hungary 67 H9
Nykobing Denmark 49 C13
Nyköping Sweden 49 E10
Nzérékoré Guinea 76 E7

O

Oahe, Lake *lake* North Dakota/South Dakota, USA 29 F3
Oahu *island* Hawaii, USA 27 B12
Oakland California, USA 27 B8
Oak Ridge Tennessee, USA 31 H3
Oamaru New Zealand 105 D11
Oates Land *physical region* Antarctica 21 C5
Oaxaca Mexico 35 F6
Ob *river* Russian Federation 84 D3, 86 D4
Oban Scotland, United Kingdom 51 D6
Oberhausen Germany 59 B6
Oberwald Switzerland 60 C5
Obi *island* Indonesia 95 I7
Obihiro Japan 99 I2
Obo Central African Republic 79 F5
Oborniki Poland 66 D4
Oceanside California, USA 27 D11
Odemira Portugal 56 A7
Odense Denmark 49 B12
Oder *river* C Europe 47 E5, 58 I5, 67 D6
Oderhaff *bay* S Baltic Sea 58 H3
Odesa Ukraine 47 G6, 65 E12
Odessa Texas, USA 30 C5
Odienné Ivory Coast 76 E7
Oeiras Portugal 56 A6
Offenbach am Main Germany 59 C8
Offenburg Germany 59 C11
Oga Japan 99 H4
Ogaden *plateau* Ethiopia/Somalia 71 H6, 75 G10
Ogaki Japan 99 G7
Ogbomosho Nigeria 77 H7
Ogden Utah, USA 27 G6
Ogdensburg New York, USA 33 H4
Ogulin Croatia 68 C3
Ohai New Zealand 105 B12
Ohio *river* N USA 32 C8
Ohrid Macedonia 69 E5
Ohrid, Lake *lake* Albania/Macedonia 69 E5
Ohura New Zealand 104 G5
Oise *river* France 55 G2
Oita Japan 98 D8
Ojiwarongo Namibia 80 B5
Ojos del Salado *mountain* Argentina 39 C8, 42 C4
Oka *river* Russian Federation 47 H4
Okahandja Namibia 80 B6
Okaihau New Zealand 104 F2
Okara Pakistan 91 G10
Okavango Delta *delta* Botswana 71 F10, 80 D5
Okayama Japan 99 E7
Okazaki Japan 99 G7
Okeechobee, Lake *Lake* Florida, USA 31 J7
Okhotsk, Sea of *sea* NW Pacific Ocean 85 I4, 87 J4, 99 J1
Okhtyrka Ukraine 65 F10
Okinawa Japan 99 J8
Okinawa *island* Japan 99 J8
Oki-shoto *island group* Japan 99 E6
Oklahoma *state* USA 30 D4
Oklahoma City *state capital* Oklahoma, USA 23 E9, 30 E4
Oktyabrsk Kazakhstan 90 C4
Oktyabrskoy Revolyutsii, Ostrov *island* Russian Federation 87 F2
Okucani Croatia 68 D3
Okushiri-to *island* Japan 99 H3

Öland *island* Sweden 47 E4, 49 E12
Olavarría Argentina 43 F7
Olbia Italy 63 B8
Oldenburg Germany 58 C4
Olekma *river* Russian Federation 87 H5
Olekminsk Russian Federation 87 H5
Oleksandriya Ukraine 65 F10
Olenek *river* Russian Federation 85 G2, 87 G3
Oléron, Île d' *island* France 54 D5
Olesnica Poland 67 D6
Olgiy Mongolia 96 D2
Olhão Portugal 56 B8
Olinda Brazil 41 J5
Olivet France 55 F4
Ollagüe Chile 42 C2
Olmaliq Uzbekistan 91 F7
Olomouc Czech Republic 67 D8
Olsztyn Poland 66 G3
Olsztynek Poland 66 G3
Olt *river* Romania 69 F6
Olten Switzerland 60 C4
Olympia *state capital* Washington, USA 26 C4
Olympic Mountains *mountain range* Washington, USA 26 B1
Olympus *mountain* Greece 69 E5
Olympus, Mount *mountain* Washington, USA 26 B1
Omagh Northern Ireland, United Kingdom 51 C7
Omaha Nebraska, USA 29 H6
Oman *country* SW Asia 84 C7, 89 I7
Oman, Gulf of *gulf* N Arabian Sea 82 D1, 89 J6
Omarama New Zealand 105 C10
Omdurman Sudan 70 G5, 75 D7
Omo Wenz *river* Ethiopia 75 E10
Omsk Russian Federation 84 D4, 86 D6
Ondangwa Namibia 80 B5
Ondorhaan Mongolia 97 G3
Onega, Lake *lake* Russian Federation 47 G3, 86 C3
Onesti Romania 69 H2
Ongjin North Korea 98 B5
Ongole India 93 D9
Onitsha Nigeria 77 J8
Ontario *province* Canada 25 F7
Ontario, Lake *lake* Canada/USA 23 G8, 25 H9, 33 G4
Ontong Java Rise *undersea feature* W Pacific Ocean 106 D5
Oodnadatta South Australia, Australia 103 F5
Oosterhout Netherlands 53 E7
Oosterschelde *inlet* Netherlands 53 C7
Opatow Poland 67 G6
Opole Poland 67 E6
Opunake New Zealand 105 F6
Oradea Romania 69 F2
Oral Kazakhstan 90 B3
Oran Algeria 70 C2, 73 E3
Orán Argentina 42 E2
Orange New South Wales, Australia 103 J6
Orange France 55 H7
Orangeburg South Carolina, USA 31 J4
Orange River *river* Namibia/South Africa 71 E12, 80 C7
Oranienburg Germany 58 H5
Oranjestad Aruba 37 G4
Orbetello Italy 63 D6
Ordos Desert *desert* China 97 G4
Ordu Turkey 88 I4
Örebro Sweden 49 D10
Oregon *state* USA 26 C4
Orel Russian Federation 86 B4
Orem Utah, USA 27 G7
Orenburg Russian Federation 47 J4, 86 C5
Orhei Moldova 65 D11
Orihuela Spain 57 G7
Orinoco *river* Colombia/Venezuela 38 D2, 40 E2
Oristano Italy 63 B9
Orivesi *lake* Finland 49 I7
Orizaba Mexico 35 F6
Orizaba, Pico de *volcano* Mexico 23 D11, 35 E6

Orkney Islands *island group* Scotland, United Kingdom 46 C3, 50 E2

Orlando Florida, USA 31 J6

Orléans France 55 F3

Ormoc Philippines 95 H5

Örnsköldsvik Sweden 49 E7

Orsha Belarus 65 E6

Orsk Russian Federation 86 C6

Ortles *mountain* Italy 62 D2

Orumiyeh Iran 89 F2

Oruro Bolivia 40 E6

Orvieto Italy 63 D6

Osaka Japan 85 H6, 99 F7

Osh Kyrgyzstan 91 F7

Oshakati Namibia 80 B5

Oshawa Ontario, Canada 25 H9

Oshkosh Wisconsin, USA 32 B4

Oshogbo Nigeria 77 H7

Osijek Croatia 68 D2

Oskarshamn Sweden 49 E11

Oskemen Kazakhstan 90 H4

Oslo *country capital* Norway 46 E3, 49 C9

Osnabrück Germany 58 C5

Osorno Chile 43 C8

Osorno Spain 56 E2

Oss Netherlands 53 F6

Ossa, Mount *mountain* Tasmania, Australia 103 H6

Ostend Belgium 53 A8

Östersund Sweden 49 D7

Ostrava Czech Republic 67 E7

Ostroda Poland 66 F3

Ostroleka Poland 66 G4

Ostrow Wielkopolski Poland 67 E5

Ostuni Italy 63 I8

Otago Peninsula *peninsula* New Zealand 105 D12

Otaru Japan 99 H2

Oti *river* W Africa 77 G6

Otranto Italy 63 I8

Otranto, Strait of *strait* Adriatic Sea/Ionian Sea 68 D6

Otsu Japan 99 F7

Ottawa *country capital* Ontario, Canada 23 G8, 25 H8

Ottawa Kansas, USA 29 I7

Otway, Cape *headland* Victoria, Australia 103 G6

Ötztaler Alpen *mountain range* Austria/Italy 61 E5

Ouachita Mountains *mountain range* Arkansas/Oklahoma, USA 31 E4

Ouagadougou *country capital* Burkina 71 G5, 77 G6

Ouahigouya Burkina 77 F6

Oualâta Mauritania 77 E5

Ouargla Algeria 73 G4

Ouarzazate Morocco 72 D4

Oudenaarde Belgium 53 C9

Oudtshoorn South Africa 80 D9

Ouessant, Île d' *island* France 54 B3

Ouésso Congo 78 D6

Oujda Morocco 72 E2, 74 F4

Oulu Finland 47 F2, 49 G5

Oulujärvi *lake* Finland 49 H6

Ounasjoki *river* Finland 48 G4

Ourense Spain 56 B3

Ouse *river* England, United Kingdom 51 G8

Outer Hebrides *island group* Scotland, United Kingdom 46 C3, 50 C5

Outjo Namibia 80 B5

Ovalle Chile 42 C5

Ovamboland *physical region* Namibia 80 B5

Ovar Portugal 56 B4

Overland Park Kansas, USA 29 I7

Oviedo Spain 56 D2

Owando Congo 78 D6

Owen River New Zealand 105 E8

Owensboro Kentucky, USA 32 C8

Owerri Nigeria 77 I8

Owyhee *river* W USA 26 D5

Oxford England, United Kingdom 51 G11

Oxnard California, USA 26 C11

Oyama Japan 99 H6

Oyem Gabon 78 C6

Oyo Nigeria 77 H7

Ozark Plateau *physical region* Arkansas/Missouri, USA 29 J8

Ozieri Italy 63 B8

P

Paarl South Africa 80 C9

Pabna Bangladesh 93 G6

Pachino Italy 63 G12

Pachuca Mexico 35 E5

Pacific-Antarctic Ridge *undersea feature* S Pacific Ocean 106 D8

Pacific Ocean *ocean* 106–107

Padang Indonesia 94 B7

Paderborn Germany 59 D6

Padua Italy 62 D3

Paengnyong-do *island* South Korea 98 A5

Pag *island* Croatia 68 C3

Pagan *island* Northern Mariana Islands 100 C2

Pago Pago *island* American Samoa 101 G6

Paide Estonia 64 C3

Päijänne *lake* Finland 49 H8

Painted Desert *desert* Arizona, USA 27 G9

Paisley Scotland, United Kingdom 51 E6

Pais Vasco *cultural region* Spain 57 F2

Pakistan *country* C Asia 84 C6, 91 D11

Pakxan Laos 94 C3

Pakxe Laos 94 D4

Palana Russian Federation 87 J3

Palapye Botswana 80 E6

Palau *country* W Pacific Ocean 100 B4

Palawan *island* Philippines 95 F5

Palembang Indonesia 85 F9, 94 C8

Palencia Spain 56 E3

Palermo Italy 46 D8, 63 E11

Palikir *country capital* Micronesia 100 D3

Palliser, Cape *headland* New Zealand 105 G8

Palma Balearic Islands 46 C7

Palma de Mallorca Balearic Islands, Spain 57 J5

Palmdale California, USA 27 D10

Palmer Land *physical region* Antarctica 21 A2

Palmerston New Zealand 105 D11

Palmerston North New Zealand 105 G7

Palmira Colombia 40 C3

Palm Springs California, USA 27 E11

Palmyra Atoll *US dependent territory* SW Pacific Ocean 101 H4

Palos, Cabo de *headland* Spain 57 G7

Palu Indonesia 95 G7

Pamirs *mountain range* C Asia 91 G8

Pampa Texas, USA 30 C4

Pampas *physical region* Argentina 39 D10, 43 D8

Pamplona Spain 57 G2

Panaji India 93 B8

Panama *country* Central America 23 F13, 35 J9

Panama Canal *canal* Panama 35 K8

Panama City *country capital* Panama 23 G13, 35 K9

Panama City Florida, USA 31 H6

Panama, Gulf of *gulf* Panama 35 K9

Panay *island* Philippines 95 G4

Pancevo Serbia 69 E3

Panevezys Lithuania 65 C5

Pangkalpinang Indonesia 94 D8

Panipat India 92 C4

Panjakent Tajikistan 91 E7

Pantanal *wetland* Brazil 41 F7

Pantelleria *island* Italy 63 D12

Panzhihua China 97 F7

Papakura New Zealand 104 G4

Papeete French Polynesia 101 I6

Papenburg Germany 58 B4

Papua New Guinea *country* SW Pacific Ocean 100 C5

Paraburdoo Western Australia, Australia 102 B4

Paracel Islands *disputed region* SE Asia 94 E3

Paraguay *country* C South America 39 E7, 42 F2

Paraguay *river* C South America 39 E7, 42 G3

Parakou Benin 77 H7

Paramaribo *country capital* Surinam 38 F2, 41 G2

Paraná Argentina 42 F5

Paraná *river* C South America 39 F7, 41 G7, 42 G4

Paranaíba *river* Brazil 41 G7

Parbhani India 93 C7

Pardubice Czech Republic 67 C7

Parepare Indonesia 95 G8

Parikkala Finland 49 I8

Paris *country capital* France 46 C6, 55 F3

Parkano Finland 49 G8

Parkersburg West Virginia, USA 33 E7

Parma Italy 62 C4

Parnaíba Brazil 41 I4

Parnaíba *river* Brazil 41 H5

Parnassus New Zealand 105 E9

Parnu Estonia 64 C3

Paros *island* Greece 69 H8

Parry Islands *island group* Northwest Territories/Nunavut, Canada 22 F4, 24 E2

Partinico Italy 63 E11

Pasadena California, USA 27 D11

Pasadena Texas, USA 31 E6

Pasewalk Germany 58 H4

Pasley, Cape *headland* Western Australia, Australia 102 D7

Passau Germany 59 H11

Passero, Capo *headland* Italy 63 G12

Passo Fundo Brazil 41 G8

Pasto Colombia 40 C3

Patagonia *physical region* Argentina/Chile 39 C12, 43 C11

Patan Nepal 92 F5

Paterna Spain 57 H5

Paterno Italy 63 G12

Paterson New Jersey, USA 33 H6

Patiala India 92 C4

Patna India 84 E6, 92 F5

Patos, Lagoa dos *lagoon* Brazil 39 F9, 41 G9

Patra Greece 47 F8, 69 F7

Patuca *river* Honduras 35 I7

Pau France 54 D8

Pavia Italy 62 B3

Pavlodar Kazakhstan 90 G3

Pavlohrad Ukraine 65 G10

Pavullo nel Frignano Italy 62 C4

Paxoi *island* Greece 68 E7

Payne's Find Western Australia, Australia 102 C6

Paysandú Uruguay 43 G6

Pazardzhik Bulgaria 69 G5

Peace *river* Alberta/British Columbia, Canada 23 D6, 24 C6

Peak District *mountain range* England, United Kingdom 51 G9

Péc Kosovo 68 E4

Pechora Russian Federation 86 D4

Pechora *river* Russian Federation 47 H2, 86 D3

Pecos *river* New Mexico/Texas, USA 30 C5

Pecos Texas, USA 30 C5

Pecs Hungary 67 E12

Pedra Lume Cape Verde 76 A4

Pedro Juan Caballero Paraguay 42 G2

Pegasus Bay *bay* New Zealand 105 E9

Pegnitz Germany 59 F9

Pegu Myanmar 94 B3

Peipus, Lake *lake* Estonia/Russian Federation 64 D3

Pekanbaru Indonesia 94 C7

Pelagic Islands *island group* Italy 63 E13

Peleng *island* Indonesia 95 H7

Peloponnese *peninsula* Greece 69 F8

Pematangsiantar Indonesia 94 B6

Pemba *island* Tanzania 79 J7, 81 I3

Penambo Range *mountain range* Indonesia/Malaysia 94 E6

Penas, Gulf of *gulf* Chile 43 B11

Pendleton Oregon, USA 26 D3

Peniche Portugal 56 A5

Penmarch, Pointe de *headland* France 54 B3

Pennine Alps *mountain range* Italy/Switzerland 60 B6

Pennines *mountain range* England, United Kingdom 51 F7

Penong South Australia, Australia 103 F6

Pensacola Florida, USA 31 H6

Penticton British Columbia, Canada 24 B7

Penza Russian Federation 47 I5, 86 B5

Penzance England, United Kingdom 51 D12

Peoria Illinois, USA 32 B6

Pereira Colombia 40 C2

Pergamino Argentina 43 F6

Périgueux France 55 F6

Perleberg Germany 58 F4

Perm Russian Federation 47 J3, 86 C4

Pernik Bulgaria 69 F4

Perpignan France 55 G8

Perth *state capital* Western Australia, Australia 100 A8, 102 B7

Perth Scotland, United Kingdom 51 F6

Perth Basin *undersea feature* E Indian Ocean 83 H5

Peru *country* W South America 39 B5, 40 C5

Peru-Chile Trench *undersea feature* E Pacific Ocean 107 J5

Perugia Italy 63 E6

Pervomaysk Ukraine 65 E10

Pesaro Italy 62 E5

Pescara Italy 63 F6

Peshawar Pakistan 84 D6, 91 F9

Pessac France 54 D6

Pétange Luxembourg 53 G13

Petén *cultural region* Guatemala 35 G6

Peterborough England, United Kingdom 51 H10

Petropavl Kazakhstan 90 E2

Petropavlovsk-Kamchatskiy Russian Federation 87 K4

Petrozavodsk Russian Federation 86 C3

Pevek Russian Federation 87 I2

Pezinok Slovakia 67 D9

Pforzheim Germany 59 C10

Phan Thiet Vietnam 94 D5

Phetchaburi Thailand 94 B4

Philadelphia Pennsylvania, USA 23 G9, 33 H6

Philippeville Belgium 53 D11

Philippine Basin *undersea feature* S Philippine Sea 106 B4

Philippines *country* SE Asia 85 G8, 95 F5

Philippine Sea *sea* W Pacific Ocean 85 H7, 100 B3, 106 B4

Phnom Penh *country capital* Cambodia 85 F8, 94 C4

Phoenix *state capital* Arizona, USA 23 C9, 27 G11

Phoenix Islands *island group* Kiribati 101 G5

Phuket Thailand 94 B5

Piacenza Italy 62 C3

Piatra-Neamt Romania 69 H2

Pichanal Argentina 42 E2

Pichilemu Chile 43 C6

Pico Duarte *mountain* Dominican Republic 37 F5

Picton New Zealand 105 F7

Piedmont *cultural region* Italy 62 A3

Piedmont *physical region* South Carolina, USA 31 I4

Piedras Negras Mexico 34 E3

Pielinen *lake* Finland 49 I6

Pierre *state capital* South Dakota, USA 29 G4

Piestany Slovakia 67 E9

Pietermaritzburg South Africa 71 G12, 81 F8

Pietersaari *see* Jakobstad

Pietersburg South Africa 81 E6

Pietrasanta Italy 62 C5

Pila Poland 66 D4

Pilcomayo *river* C South America 39 D7, 42 F3

Pinar del Rio Cuba 36 A3

Pindus Mountains *mountain range* Greece 69 F6

Pine Bluff Arkansas, USA 31 F4

Pineios *river* Greece 69 F6

Pine Ridge South Dakota, USA 29 F5

Pinerolo Italy 62 A4

Ping *river* Thailand 94 B3

Pingdingshan China 97 H6

Pingxiang China 97 I7

Pinsk Belarus 65 C8

Pinta, Isla *island* Galapagos Islands 40 A8

Pinto Argentina 42 E4

Piombino Italy 63 C6

Piotrkow Trybunalski Poland 67 F6

Piraeus Greece 69 G7

Pisa Italy 62 C5

Pisek Czech Republic 67 B8

Pistoia Italy 62 D5

Pisz Poland 66 H3

Pit *river* California, USA 27 B6

Pitcairn Island *island* Pitcairn Islands 101 J7

Pitcairn Islands *UK dependent territory* C Pacific Ocean 101 K7

Piteå Sweden 49 F5

Pitesti Romania 69 G3

Pittsburg Kansas, USA 29 I8

Pittsburgh Pennsylvania, USA 33 F6

Piura Peru 40 B4

Plainview Texas, USA 30 C4

Plano Texas, USA 30 E5

Plasencia Spain 56 D5

Plata, Río de la *estuary* Argentina/Uruguay 39 E10, 43 G6

Platte *river* Nebraska, USA 29 G6

Plauen Germany 59 G8

Plauer See *lake* Germany 58 G4

Plenty, Bay of *bay* New Zealand 104 H4

Plesetsk Russian Federation 86 C3

Pleven Bulgaria 69 G4

Plock Poland 66 F4

Ploiesti Romania 69 H3

Plonsk Poland 66 G4

Ploty Poland 66 C3

Plovdiv Bulgaria 47 F7, 69 G5

Plunge Lithuania 64 B5

Plymouth England, United Kingdom 51 E12

Plzen Czech Republic 67 B7

Po *river* Italy 46 D6, 62 B3

Pobeda, Gora *mountain* Russian Federation 87 I3

Pobedy, Pik *mountain* China/Kyrgyzstan 91 H6 *see also* Tomur Feng

Pocatello Idaho, USA 26 G5

Pocohontas Arkansas, USA 31 F3

Podgorica *country capital* Montenegro 68 E5

Pohnpei *island* Micronesia 100 D4

Poinsett, Cape *headland* Antarctica 21 E4

Pointe-Noire Congo 71 D8, 78 C7

Point Fortin Trinidad & Tobago 37 J8

Poitiers France 54 E5

Pokhara Nepal 92 F4

Pola de Siero Spain 56 D2

Poland *country* C Europe 47 E5, 66 E5

Polatsk Belarus 65 D6

Pol-e Khomri Afghanistan 91 E8

Poltava Ukraine 65 G9

Polynesia *island group* C Pacific Ocean 101 H5, 107 F5

Pomerania *cultural region* Poland 66 C3

Pomeranian Bay *bay* S Baltic Sea 58 H2, 66 B2

Ponca City Oklahoma, USA 30 E3

Ponce Puerto Rico 37 H5

Pondicherry India 93 D10

Ponferrada Spain 56 C2

Ponta Grossa Brazil 41 H8

Ponte da Barca Portugal 56 B3

Pontevedra Spain 56 B2

Pontianak Indonesia 94 D7

Pontoise France 55 F2

Ponziane Islands *island group* Italy 63 E8

Poopó, Lake *lake* Bolivia 40 E7

Popayán Colombia 40 C3

Poplar Bluff Missouri, USA 29 K8

Popocatépetl *volcano* Mexico 23 D11, 34 E6

Poprad Slovakia 67 G8

Porbandar India 93 A6

Pordenone Italy 62 E3

Pori Finland 49 F8

Porirua New Zealand 105 F7

Porpoise Bay *bay* Antarctica 21 E4

Porsangen *fjord* Norway 48 G1

Portadown Northern Ireland, United Kingdom 51 D8

Portalegre Portugal 56 B6

Portales New Mexico, USA 30 C4

Port Angeles Washington, USA 26 B1

Port Arthur Texas, USA 31 F6

Port Augusta South Australia, Australia 103 G6

Port-au-Prince *country capital* Haiti 23 H12, 37 F5

Port Blair Andaman Islands, India 93 H10

Port-de-Paix Cuba 37 F4

Port Elizabeth South Africa 71 F13, 80 D9

Port-Gentil Gabon 71 D8, 78 C7

Port Harcourt Nigeria 71 D7, 77 I8

Port Hedland Western Australia, Australia 102 C4

Port Hope Simpson Newfoundland & Labrador, Canada 25 J6

Portimão Portugal 56 A8

Portland Victoria, Australia 103 G6

Portland Maine, USA 33 J4

Portland Oregon, USA 23 C7, 26 B3

Portland Bill *headland* England, United Kingdom 51 F12

Port Laoise Republic of Ireland 51 C9

Port Lincoln South Australia, Australia 103 F7

Port Macquarie New South Wales, Australia 103 J6

Port Moresby *country capital* Papua New Guinea 100 C5

Porto Portugal 46 A7, 56 B4

Porto Alegre Brazil 39 F9, 41 G9

Port-of-Spain *country capital* Trinidad & Tobago 37 J8

Porto-Novo *country capital* Benin 71 C6, 77 H7

Porto Tolle Italy 62 E4

Porto Torres Italy 63 B8

Pórto Velho Brazil 40 E5

Port Pirie South Australia, Australia 103 G7

Port Said Egypt 70 G3, 74 C3

Portsmouth England, United Kingdom 51 G12

Portsmouth Virginia, USA 33 H9

Port Sudan Sudan 70 G4, 75 D3

Portugal *country* SW Europe 46 A7, 56 B5

Portugal Portugal 56 B5

Port-Vila *country capital* Vanuatu 101 E6

Porvoo Finland 49 H9

Posadas Argentina 42 G4

Poso Indonesia 95 G7

Postojna Slovenia 61 H7

Potenza Italy 63 G8

Potosí Bolivia 40 E7

Potsdam Germany 58 G5

Póvoa de Varzim Portugal 56 B3

Powell, Lake *lake* Utah, USA 27 H8

Poyang Hu China 97 I7

Poza Rica Mexico 35 E5

Poznan Poland 47 E5, 66 D5

Prachuap Khiri Khan Thailand 94 B4

Prague *country capital* Czech Republic 46 E6, 67 B7

Praia *country capital* Cape Verde 76 A5

Prato Italy 62 D5

Prerov Czech Republic 67 D8

Prescott Arizona, USA 27 G10

Presidencia Roque Sáenz Peña Argentina 42 F4
Presov Slovakia 67 G8
Prespa, Lake *lake* SE Europe 69 E6
Presque Isle Maine, USA 33 K2
Preston England, United Kingdom 51 F8
Pretoria *administrative capital* South Africa 71 F11, 81 E7
Preveza Greece 69 E7
Priboj Serbia 68 E4
Pribram Czech Republic 67 B7
Prievidza Slovakia 67 E9
Prijedor Bosnia & Herzegovina 68 C3
Prilep Macedonia 69 F5
Prince Albert Saskatchewan, Canada 24 D7
Prince Charles Island *island* Nunavut, Canada 25 G4
Prince Edward Island *province* Canada 25 J7
Prince George British Columbia, Canada 24 B6
Prince Of Wales Island *island* Queensland, Australia 103 H1
Prince of Wales Island *island* Nunavut, Canada 22 F4, 25 E3
Prince Rupert British Columbia, Canada 24 A6
Princess Charlotte Bay *bay* Queensland, Australia 103 H2
Princess Elizabeth Land *physical region* Antarctica 21 E3
Principe *island* São Tomé & Príncipe 78 B6
Prinses Margriet Canal *canal* Netherlands 52 F3
Pripet *river* Belarus/Ukraine 65 D8
Pripet Marshes *marsh* Belarus/Ukraine 65 C8
Pristina *country capital* Kosovo 47 F7, 69 E4
Prizren Kosovo 69 E5
Prokopyevsk Russian Federation 87 E6
Prome Myanmar 94 B3
Proserpine Queensland, Australia 103 I4
Prosna *river* Poland 66 E5
Prostejov Czech Republic 67 D8
Provence *cultural region* France 55 H8
Providence *state capital* Rhode Island, USA 33 J5
Provo Utah, USA 27 G7
Prudhoe Bay Alaska, USA 26 H1
Prut *river* E Europe 65 D12, 69 H1
Pryluky Ukraine 65 F9
Przemysl Poland 67 H7
Psara *island* Greece 69 H7
Pskov Russian Federation 86 B3
Pskov, Lake *lake* Estonia/Russian Federation 64 D4
Ptuj Slovenia 61 J6
Pucallpa Peru 40 C5
Pudasjärvi Finland 49 H5
Puebla Mexico 35 E6
Pueblo Colorado, USA 28 E7
Puerto Aisén Chile 43 C10
Puerto Baquerizo Moreno Galapagos Islands 40 B9
Puerto Barrios Guatemala 35 H7
Puerto Deseado Argentina 43 E11
Puertollano Spain 56 E6
Puerto Montt Chile 43 C9
Puerto Natales Chile 43 C12
Puerto Princesa Philippines 95 F5
Puerto Rico *US dependent territory* C West Indies 23 H12, 37 H5
Puerto Rico Trench Plain *undersea feature* W Atlantic Ocean 45 C6
Puerto San Julián Argentina 43 D11
Puerto Santa Cruz Argentina 43 D11
Puerto Vallarta Mexico 34 C5
Pukekohe New Zealand 104 G4
Pula Croatia 68 B3
Pulawy Poland 67 H6
Pultusk Poland 66 G4
Pune India 93 B7

Punta Arenas Chile 43 D12
Puntarenas Costa Rica 35 I8
Puri India 93 F7
Purmerend Netherlands 52 E4
Purus *river* Brazil/Peru 38 D5, 40 E4
Puspokladany Hungary 67 G10
Putian *lake* China 97 J7
Puttgarden Germany 58 F2
Putumayo *river* NW South America 38 B4, 40 C4
Pyhäjoki Finland 49 G6
Pylos Greece 69 F8
Pyongyang *country capital* North Korea 85 G5, 98 B4
Pyramid Lake *lake* Nevada, USA 27 C7
Pyrenees *mountain range* France/Spain 46 B7, 54 D8, 57 G2
Pyrgos Greece 69 F8

Q

Qaanaaq Greenland 20 B3
Qaidam Basin *physical region* China 96 D5
Qalaikhum Tajikistan 91 F8
Qalat Afghanistan 91 E10
Qaleh-ye Now Afghanistan 91 D9
Qapshaghay Kazakhstan 91 G6
Qaqortoq Greenland 20 A5
Qara Kazakhstan 90 G3
Qaraghandy Kazakhstan 90 F4
Qaraghayly Kazakhstan 90 G4
Qarokul Tajikistan 91 G7
Qarshi Uzbekistan 91 E7
Qatar *country* SW Asia 84 B6, 89 H6
Qattara Depression *physical region* Egypt 74 B3
Qazaly Kazakhstan 91 D5
Qazvin Iran 89 G3
Qena Egypt 74 D4
Qeshm *island* Iran 89 I5
Qilian Shan *mountain range* China 97 E5
Qingdao China 85 G5, 97 I5
Qinghai Hu *lake* China 97 F5
Qinhuangdao China 97 I4
Qinzhou China 97 H8
Qiqihar China 85 G4, 97 I2
Qizilqum *desert* Kazakhstan/Uzbekistan 91 D6
Qom Iran 84 B6, 89 H3
Qomisheh Iran 89 H4
Qonduz Afghanistan 91 F8
Qostanay Kazakhstan 90 D3
Quanzhou China 97 J7
Quartu Sant'Elena Italy 63 B9
Québec Québec, Canada 25 I8
Québec *province* Canada 23 H8
Queen Charlotte Islands *island group* British Columbia, Canada 23 B2, 24 A6
Queen Elizabeth Islands *island group* Nunavut, Canada 22 F3, 25 E2
Queensland *state* Australia 103 H4
Queenstown New Zealand 105 B11
Queenstown South Africa 80 E8
Quelimane Mozambique 71 G10, 81 H5
Querétaro Mexico 34 E5
Quetta Pakistan 91 E10
Quibdó Colombia 40 C2
Quilon India 93 C11
Quilpie Queensland, Australia 103 H5
Quimper France 54 B3
Quito *country capital* Ecuador 38 A3, 40 B3
Qujing China 97 G8
Qulsary Kazakhstan 90 B5
Qunghirot Uzbekistan 91 C6
Quqon Uzbekistan 91 F7
Qurghonteppa Tajikistan 91 F9
Quy Nhon Vietnam 94 D4
Quzhou China 97 I7
Qyzylorda Kazakhstan 91 E6

R

Raab *river* Austria/Hungary 61 J5
Raahe Finland 49 G6

Raba *river* Austria/Hungary 67 D10
Rabat *country capital* Morocco 70 C2, 72 D4
Rabaul Papua New Guinea 100 D5
Rabigh Saudi Arabia 88 E6
Rabka Poland 67 F8
Race, Cape *headland* Newfoundland & Labrador, Canada 25 K7
Radom Poland 67 G6
Radstadt Austria 61 H4
Radzyn Podlaski Poland 67 H5
Rafaela Argentina 42 F5
Rafhah Saudi Arabia 89 F5
Ragusa Italy 63 F12
Rahimyar Khan Pakistan 91 F11
Raichur India 93 D8
Rainier, Mount *mountain* Washington, USA 23 C7, 26 C2
Raipur India 93 E7
Rajahmundry India 93 E8
Rajang *river* Malaysia 95 E7
Rajapalaiyam India 93 D10
Rajkot India 93 B6
Rajshahi Bangladesh 93 G6
Rakvere Estonia 64 D3
Raleigh *state capital* North Carolina, USA 31 J3
Ralik Chain *island group* Marshall Islands 101 E3
Ramnicu Valcea Romania 69 G3
Ranau Malaysia 95 F6
Rancagua Chile 43 C6
Ranchi India 93 F7
Randers Denmark 49 B11
Rangiora New Zealand 105 E9
Rangoon *see* Yangon
Rangpur Bangladesh 92 G5
Rapallo Italy 62 B4
Rapid City South Dakota, USA 29 E4
Rarotonga *island* Cook Islands 101 H4
Rasa, Punta *headland* Argentina 39 E11, 43 F8
Ras Dashen *mountain* Ethiopia 71 H5, 75 E8
Rasht Iran 89 G2
Ratak Chain *island group* Marshall Islands 101 E3
Ratan Sweden 49 D7
Rättvik Sweden 49 D8
Rauma Finland 49 F8
Raurkela India 93 F7
Ravenna Italy 62 E4
Ravi *river* India/Pakistan 91 G10
Rawalpindi Pakistan 91 G9
Rawicz Poland 67 D5
Rawlins Wyoming, USA 28 D5
Rawson Argentina 43 E9
Rayong Thailand 94 C4
Raysut Oman 89 I8
Razgrad Bulgaria 69 H4
Raz, Pointe du *headland* France 54 B3
Reading England, United Kingdom 51 G11
Rebun-to *island* Japan 99 H1
Rechytsa Belarus 65 E8
Recife Brazil 38 I5, 41 J5
Recklinghausen Germany 59 B6
Reconquista Argentina 42 F4
Red Bluff California, USA 27 B7
Red Deer Alberta, Canada 24 C7
Redding California, USA 27 B6
Red Hill *mountain* Hawaii, USA 27 B12
Red River *river* Canada/USA 29 H2
Red River *river* China/Vietnam 94 C2, 97 F8
Red River *river* S USA 30 D4
Red Sea *sea* NW Indian Ocean 70 G4, 75 E6, 82 C2, 84 B7, 89 D6
Reefton New Zealand 105 D8
Ree, Lough *lake* Republic of Ireland 51 C9
Regensburg Germany 59 G10
Reggane Algeria 73 E6
Reggio di Calabria Italy 63 G11
Reggio nell' Emilia Italy 62 C4
Regina Saskatchewan, Canada 24 D8
Rehoboth Namibia 80 B6
Ré, Île de *island* France 54 D5
Reims France 55 G2

Reina Adelaida, Archipiélago *island group* Chile 39 C13, 43 C12
Reindeer Lake *lake* Manitoba/Saskatchewan, Canada 23 E6, 24 E6
Remscheid Germany 59 B7
Rendsburg Germany 58 E2
Rennes France 46 C6, 54 D3
Reno *river* Italy 62 D4
Reno Nevada, USA 27 C7
Republican *river* Kansas/Nebraska, USA 29 G5
Resistencia Argentina 42 F4
Resita Romania 69 F3
Resolution Island *island* New Zealand 105 A12
Rethymnon Greece 69 G9
Retsag Hungary 67 F10
Réunion *island* W Indian Ocean 82 D5
Reus Spain 57 I4
Reutlingen Germany 59 D11
Revillagigedo, Islas *island group* Mexico 34 A5
Reykjanes Ridge *undersea feature* N Atlantic Ocean 44 E3
Reykjavik *country capital* Iceland 46 B1, 48 B3
Reynosa Mexico 35 E4
Rezekne Latvia 64 D5
Rhaetian Alps *mountain range* Italy/Switzerland 60 E6
Rheine Germany 58 B5
Rhine *river* W Europe 46 D6, 53 F6, 55 I3, 59 C10, 60 C4
Rhode Island *state* USA 33 J6
Rhodes Greece 69 I8
Rhodes *island* Greece 47 G9, 69 I8
Rhodope Mountains *mountain range* Bulgaria/Greece 69 G5
Rhön *mountain range* Germany 59 E8
Rhône *river* France/Switzerland 46 C7, 55 H7, 60 B6
Rhum *island* Scotland, United Kingdom 50 D5
Riau Islands *island group* Indonesia 94 C7
Ribeirão Prêto Brazil 39 G7, 41 H7
Ribnica Slovenia 61 I7
Ribnita Moldova 65 D11
Riccione Italy 62 E5
Richard Toll Senegal 76 C5
Richmond Queensland, Australia 103 H4
Richmond *state capital* Virginia, USA 33 G8
Ricobayo, Embalse de *reservoir* Spain 56 C3
Rieti Italy 63 E6
Riga *country capital* Latvia 47 F4, 64 C4
Riga, Gulf of *gulf* E Baltic Sea 64 B4
Riihimäki Finland 49 G8
Riiser-Larsen Ice Shelf *ice shelf* Antarctica 21 B1
Riiser-Larsen Peninsula *peninsula* Antarctica 21 D1
Rijeka Croatia 46 E7, 68 B3
Rimavska Sobota Slovakia 67 F9
Rimini Italy 62 E5
Ringebu *river* Norway 49 C8
Ringsted Denmark 49 C12
Ringvassoy *island* Norway 48 E2
Rinteln Germany 59 D5
Rio Branco Brazil 40 D5
Río Colorado Argentina 43 E8
Río Cuarto Argentina 43 E6
Rio de Janeiro Brazil 39 H8, 41 I7
Río Gallegos Argentina 43 D12
Rio Grande Argentina 43 D13
Rio Grande Brazil 41 G9
Rio Grande Rise *undersea feature* SW Atlantic Ocean 45 E10
Riohacha Colombia 40 D1
Rionero in Vulture Italy 63 G8
Ripoll Spain 57 I3
Rishiri-to *island* Japan 99 H1
Riva Italy 62 D3
Rivera Uruguay 42 G5
Riverside California, USA 27 D11
Rivne Ukraine 47 F6, 65 C9
Rivoli Italy 62 A3
Riyadh *country capital* Saudi Arabia 84 B6, 89 G6

Roanoke Virginia, USA 33 F8
Roan Plateau *plateau* Utah, USA 27 H7
Rochefort France 54 D5
Rochester Minnesota, USA 29 I4
Rochester New York, USA 33 G5
Rockford Illinois, USA 32 B5
Rockhampton Queensland, Australia 102 B7
Rockingham Western Australia, Australia 102 B7
Rock Springs Wyoming, USA 28 C6
Rocky Mountains *mountain range* Canada/USA 22 D5, 24 B5, 26 F2, 28 B2, 30 A1
Rødbyhavn Denmark 49 C13
Rodez France 55 F7
Rodnyy Kazakhstan 90 D3
Roermond Netherlands 53 G8
Roeselare Belgium 53 B9
Rogers, Mount *mountain* Virginia, USA 33 F9
Roggeveen Basin *undersea feature* E Pacific Ocean 107 I6
Rolvsoya *island* Norway 48 G1
Roma Queensland, Australia 103 I5
Roman Romania 69 H2
Romania *country* SE Europe 47 F7, 69 G2
Rome *country capital* Italy 46 D7, 63 E7
Romny Ukraine 65 F9
Ronda Spain 56 D8
Ronne Denmark 49 D13
Ronne Ice Shelf *ice shelf* Antarctica 21 B2
Ronse Belgium 53 C9
Roosendaal Netherlands 53 D7
Roosevelt Island *island* Antarctica 21 C4
Røros Norway 49 C7
Rosario Argentina 39 E9, 43 E6
Rosarno Italy 63 G10
Roscoff France 54 B3
Roseau *country capital* Dominica 37 J6
Roseburg Oregon, USA 26 B4
Rosenheim Germany 59 G12
Roses Spain 57 J3
Rossano Italy 63 H9
Ross Ice Shelf *ice shelf* Antarctica 21 C4
Ross Island *island* Antarctica 21 C4
Ross Sea *sea* Antarctica 21 C4
Rosso Mauritania 76 C5
Rostock Germany 58 G3
Rostov-na-Donu Russian Federation 47 H6, 86 A5
Røsvatnet *lake* Norway 49 D5
Roswell New Mexico, USA 30 B4
Rotenburg Germany 58 D4
Rotherham England, United Kingdom 51 F10
Rotorua New Zealand 104 H5
Rotorua, Lake *lake* New Zealand 104 H4
Rottenmann Austria 61 I4
Rotterdam Netherlands 53 D6
Roubaix France 55 G1
Rouen France 55 F2
Rovaniemi Finland 48 G4
Rovigo Italy 62 D3
Rovuma *river* Mozambique/Tanzania 81 H3
Roxas City Philippines 95 G4
Roxburgh New Zealand 105 C11
Royan France 54 D6
Roznava Slovakia 67 G9
Ruacana Namibia 80 B5
Ruapehu, Mount *mountain* New Zealand 105 G6
Rubtsovsk Russian Federation 86 E6
Rudolstadt Germany 59 F8
Rufiji *river* Kenya 79 I9
Rufino Argentina 43 E6
Rügen *island* Germany 58 H2
Rumford Maine, USA 33 J4
Rumoi Japan 99 I2
Rundu Namibia 80 C5
Ruoqiang China 96 D4
Rupel *river* Belgium 53 D8
Ruse Bulgaria 69 H4
Russian Federation *country* Asia/Europe 47 H3, 84 D3, 86 E4
Rustavi Georgia 89 F1

Rutland Vermont, USA 33 I4
Ruvuma *river* Mozambique/Tanzania 79 I9
Rwanda *country* C Africa 71 G7, 79 G7
Ryazan Russian Federation 47 H4, 86 B4
Rybinsk Russian Federation 86 B4
Rybnik Poland 67 E7
Ryki Poland 67 H5
Ryotsu Japan 99 G5
Rypin Poland 66 F4
Ryukyu Islands *island group* Japan 99 I9
Rzeszow Poland 67 H7

S

Saale *river* Germany 59 F6
Saalfeld Germany 59 F8
Saarbrücken Germany 59 B10
Saaremaa *island* Estonia 64 B3
Sabac Serbia 68 E3
Sabadell Spain 57 I3
Sabah *political region* Malaysia 95 F6
Sabha Libya 73 I6
Sabine *river* Louisiana/Texas, USA 31 E5
Sable, Cape *headland* Nova Scotia, Canada 25 J8
Sable, Cape *headland* Florida, USA 31 J7
Sabzevar Iran 89 I3
Saco Montana, USA 28 D2
Sacramento *river* California, USA 27 B7
Sacramento *state capital* California, USA 27 B8
Sacramento Mountains *mountain range* New Mexico, USA 30 B4
Sado-shima *island* Japan 99 G5
Säffle Sweden 49 C10
Safi Morocco 72 C4
Saga Japan 98 D8
Sagami-nada *inlet* Japan 99 H7
Sagar India 93 D6
Saginaw Michigan, USA 32 D5
Sagres Portugal 56 A8
Sagunto Spain 57 I5
Sahara *desert* N Africa 70 C4, 72 C6, 77 G4, 78 D2
Sahel *physical region* W Africa 70 D5, 77 G5, 78 D3
Sahiwal Pakistan 91 G10
Saïda Algeria 73 F4
Saidpur India 92 G5
Saimaa *lake* Finland 49 H8
St Anton Switzerland 60 E5
St Barthélémy *French dependent territory* E West Indies 37 J5
St-Brieuc France 54 C3
St Catharines Ontario, Canada 25 H9
St-Chamond France 55 H6
Saint Charles Missouri, USA 29 K7
Saint Cloud Minnesota, USA 29 I3
St-Dié France 55 I3
Saintes France 54 D5
St-Étienne France 55 G6
St Gallen Switzerland 60 D4
Saint George Queensland, Australia 103 I6
St George's *country capital* Grenada 37 J8
St George's Channel *channel* Celtic Sea/Irish Sea 51 D10
St Helena *island* SW Africa 45 E8
Saint Helens, Mount *mountain* Washington, USA 26 B3
St Helier Jersey, Channel Islands 51 G13
St John New Brunswick, Canada 25 J8
St John's *country capital* Antigua & Barbuda 37 J5
St John's Newfoundland & Labrador, Canada 25 K6
Saint Joseph Missouri, USA 29 I7
Saint Kilda *island* Scotland, United Kingdom 50 B4

St Kitts *island* St Kitts & Nevis 37 J5

St Kitts & Nevis *country* E West Indies 23 I12, 37 J6

St Lawrence *river* Canada/USA 23 H8, 25 I7

St Lawrence, Gulf of *gulf* Canada 23 H7, 25 J7

St Lawrence Island *island* Alaska, USA 22 B3, 26 G2

St-Lô France 54 D2

Saint-Louis Senegal 76 C5

Saint Louis Missouri, USA 23 F9, 29 K7

St Lucia *country* SE West Indies 37 J7

St Lucia *island* SE West Indies 23 I12

St-Malo France 54 D3

St-Malo, Gulf of *gulf* France 54 C2

St Marc Dominican Republic 37 F5

St Martin *Dutch and French dependent territory* E West Indies 37 J5

St Michael im Langau Austria 61 H5

St Moritz Switzerland 60 D6

St-Nazaire France 54 C4

St-Niklaas Belgium 53 D8

Saint Paul *state capital* Minnesota, USA 23 F8, 29 I4

St Paul Island *island* C Indian Ocean 83 E6

St Peter Port Guernsey, Channel Islands 51 F13

St Petersburg Russian Federation 47 G4, 86 B3

Saint Petersburg Florida, USA 31 I6

St Pierre & Miquelon *island* NE North America 25 K7

St Pierre & Miquelon *French dependent territory* NE North America 23 I7

St Pölten Austria 61 J3

St-Quentin France 55 G2

St-Tropez France 55 I8

St Veit an der Glan Austria 61 I5

St Vincent *island* St Vincent & the Grenadines 37 J7

St Vincent & the Grenadines *country* SE West Indies 23 I12, 37 J7

St Vincent Passage *channel* St Lucia/St Vincent & the Grenadines 37 J7

Saipan *island* Northern Mariana Islands 100 C3

Sajama, Nevado *mountain* Bolivia 39 C7, 40 D6

Sakai Japan 99 F7

Sakakawea, Lake *lake* North Dakota, USA 29 F2

Sakata Japan 99 H5

Sakhalin *island* Russian Federation 85 H4, 87 J5

Sala Slovakia 67 F9

Sala Sweden 49 E9

Salado *river* Argentina 39 D8, 42 E4

Salalah Oman 89 I8

Salamanca Spain 56 D4

Saldanha South Africa 80 C8

Saldus Estonia 64 B5

Sale Victoria, Australia 103 I8

Salé Morocco 72 D4

Salekhard Russian Federation 86 E4

Salem India 93 D10

Salem *state capital* Oregon, USA 26 B3

Salerno Italy 63 F8

Salerno, Gulf of *gulf* E Tyrrhenian Sea 63 F8

Salgotarjan Hungary 67 F9

Salihorsk Belarus 65 D7

Salima Malawi 81 G4

Salina Utah, USA 27 G8

Salinas California, USA 27 B9

Salisbury Plain *physical region* England, United Kingdom 51 G11

Salmon *river* Idaho, USA 26 E3

Salmon River Mountains *mountain range* Idaho, USA 26 E4

Salo Finland 49 G9

Salt *river* Arizona, USA 27 H11

Salta Argentina 42 D3

Saltillo Mexico 34 E4

Salt Lake City *state capital* Utah, USA 27 G6

Salto Uruguay 43 G5

Salton Sea *lake* California, USA 27 E11

Salum Egypt 74 B3

Salvador Brazil 39 I6, 41 J6

Salween *river* Myanmar/Thailand 94 B2 *see also* Nu Jiang

Salzach *river* Austria/Germany 61 G3

Salzburg Austria 61 G4

Salzgitter Germany 59 E6

Salzwedel Germany 58 F5

Samar *island* Philippines 95 H4

Samara Russian Federation 47 I4, 86 B5

Samarinda Indonesia 95 F7

Samarqand Uzbekistan 91 E7

Samarra' Iraq 89 F3

Sambalpur India 93 F7

Sambre *river* Belgium/France 53 E10

Samfya Zambia 81 F3

Samoa *country* C Pacific Ocean 101 G5

Samos Greece 69 H7

Samos *island* Greece 69 H7

Samothrace *island* Greece 69 H6

Samsun Turkey 88 D1

San *river* Poland 67 H7

Sana *country capital* Yemen 84 B7, 89 F9

Sanandaj Iran 89 G3

San Andrés Mexico 35 F6

San Angelo Texas, USA 30 D5

San Antioco *island* Italy 63 A10

San Antonio Texas, USA 23 D10, 30 D6

San Antonio Abad Balearic Islands, Spain 57 I6

San Antonio Oeste Argentina 43 E8

San Benedetto del Tronto Italy 63 F6

San Benedicto, Isla *island* Mexico 34 B5

San Bernado Chile 43 C6

San Bernardino California, USA 27 D11

San Blas, Cape *headland* Florida, USA 31 H6

San Carlos Philippines 95 G5

San Carlos de Bariloche Argentina 43 C9

San Clemente California, USA 27 D11

San Clemente *island* California, USA 27 C11

San Cristobal *island* Solomon Islands 100 E5

San Cristóbal Venezuela 40 D2

San Cristóbal, Isla *island* Galapagos Islands 40 B9

Sancti Spiritus Cuba 36 C3

Sancy, Puy de *mountain* France 55 F6

Sandakan Malaysia 95 F6

San Diego California, USA 23 C9, 27 D12

Sandnes Norway 49 A9

Sandoway Myanmar 94 A3

Sandvika Norway 49 C9

Sandviken Sweden 49 E9

Sandykgacy Turkmenistan 91 D8

San Fernando Philippines 95 G3

San Fernando Spain 56 C8

San Fernando Venezuela 40 D2

San Francisco Argentina 42 E5

San Francisco California, USA 23 B8, 27 B8

San Francisco de Macoris Dominican Republic 37 G5

Sangir Islands *island group* Indonesia 95 H6

Sangli India 93 C8

Sangre de Cristo Mountains *mountain range* Colorado/New Mexico, USA 28 D7, 30 B3

San Jorge, Gulf of *gulf* Argentina 43 D10

San José *country capital* Costa Rica 23 F13, 35 I8

San Jose California, USA 23 B8, 27 B8

San José de Mayo Uruguay 43 G6

San Juan Argentina 43 D5

San Juan *river* Costa Rica/Nicaragua 35 I8

San Juan Puerto Rico 37 H5

San Juan Mountains *mountain range* Colorado/New Mexico, USA 28 C8

Sankt-Vith Belgium 53 G11

Sanliurfa Turkey 88 E2

San Lucas, Cabo *headland* Mexico 34 B4

San Luis Argentina 43 D6

San Luis Potosí Mexico 34 D5

San Marino *country* S Europe 46 D7, 62 E5

San Marino *country capital* San Marino 62 E5

San Matías, Gulf of *gulf* Argentina 39 D11, 43 E8

Sanmenxia China 97 H5

San Miguel El Salvador 35 H7

San Miguel de Tucumán Argentina 39 D8, 42 D4

San Miguelito Panama 35 K8

San Nicolás de Los Arroyos Argentina 43 F6

Sanok Poland 67 H8

San Pedro Argentina 42 E3

San-Pédro Ivory Coast 77 E8

San Pedros de Macorís Dominican Republic 37 G5

San Pedro Sula Honduras 35 H7

San Rafael Argentina 43 D6

San Remo Italy 62 A5

San Salvador *country capital* El Salvador 23 E12, 35 H7

San Salvador de Jujuy Argentina 42 D3

San Salvador, Isla *island* Galapagos Islands 40 A8

San Sebastián Argentina 43 D12

San Severo Italy 63 G7

Santa Ana El Salvador 35 H7

Santa Ana California, USA 27 D11

Santa Clara Cuba 36 C3

Santa Clarita California, USA 27 D10

Santa Cruz *river* Argentina 43 D11

Santa Cruz Bolivia 39 D7

Santa Cruz Brazil 41 E6

Santa Cruz California, USA 27 B9

Santa Cruz, Isla *island* Galapagos Islands 40 B9

Santa Cruz Islands *island group* Solomon Islands 101 E5

Santa Fé Argentina 42 F5

Santa Fe *state capital* New Mexico, USA 30 B4

Santa Isabel *island* Solomon Islands 100 D5

Santa Maria Brazil 41 G9

Santa Maria California, USA 27 C10

Santa Maria di Leuca, Capo *headland* Italy 63 I9

Santa María, Isla *island* Galapagos Islands 40 A9

Santa Marta Colombia 40 C1

Santander Spain 57 E2

Santanyí Balearic Islands, Spain 57 J5

Santarém Brazil 41 G4

Santarém Portugal 56 B5

Santa Rosa California, USA 27 B8

Santa Rosa *island* California, USA 27 C11

Santa Rosalia Mexico 34 B3

Santiago Cape Verde 76 A5

Santiago *country capital* Chile 39 C9, 43 C6

Santiago Dominican Republic 37 F4

Santiago de Compostela Spain 56 B2

Santiago de Cuba Cuba 36 D4

Santiago del Estero Argentina 42 E4

Santo Domingo *country capital* Dominican Republic 23 H12, 37 G5

Santo Domingo Ecuador 40 B3

Santorini *island* Greece 69 H8

Santos Brazil 41 H8

Santo Tomás *volcano* Galapagos Islands 40 A9

San Vicente de Barakaldo Spain 57 E2

San Vito, Capo *headland* Italy 63 E11

Sanya China 97 H9

São Francisco *river* Brazil 38 H5, 41 I6

São Gonçalo Brazil 39 H8, 41 I7

São João da Madeira Portugal 56 B4

São Luís Brazil 38 H4, 41 I4

São Manuel *river* Brazil 38 E5, 41 F5

São Marcos, Baía de *bay* Brazil 41 I3

Saône *river* France 55 H5

São Paulo Brazil 39 G8, 41 H7

São Roque, Cabo de *headland* Brazil 41 J4

São Tomé *country capital* São Tomé & Príncipe 71 D7, 78 A6

São Tomé *island* São Tomé & Príncipe 71 D7, 78 A6

São Tomé & Príncipe *country* E Atlantic Ocean 71 D7, 78 A6

São Vicente, Cabo de *headland* Portugal 56 A8

Sapporo Japan 85 H5, 99 H2

Sarahs Turkmenistan 91 D8

Sarajevo *country capital* Bosnia & Herzegovina 47 E7, 68 D4

Saran Kazakhstan 90 F4

Sarande Albania 68 E6

Saransk Russian Federation 86 B4

Sarasota Florida, USA 31 I7

Saratov Russian Federation 47 I5, 88 B5

Sarawak *political region* Malaysia 95 E6

Saray Iraq 89 F3

Sardinia *island* Italy 46 D8, 63 B9

Sargasso Sea *sea* W Atlantic Ocean 45 D6

Sargodha Pakistan 91 G10

Sarh Chad 78 D4

Sari Iran 89 H3

Sariwon North Korea 98 B5

Sark *island* Channel Islands 51 F13

Sarmiento Argentina 43 D10

Saronic Gulf *gulf* SW Aegean Sea 69 G7

Sarpsborg Norway 49 C9

Sarqan Kazakhstan 91 H6

Sartène Corsica, France 55 K9

Saryozek Kazakhstan 91 H6

Saryshagan Kazakhstan 90 G5

Sary-Tash Kyrgyzstan 91 G7

Sasebo Japan 98 C8

Saskatchewan *province* Canada 24 D6

Saskatchewan *river* Manitoba/Saskatchewan, Canada 23 E6

Saskatoon Saskatchewan, Canada 23 E7, 24 D7

Sasolburg South Africa 80 E7

Sassandra *river* Ivory Coast 77 E8

Sassari Italy 63 B8

Sassnitz Germany 58 H2

Sata-misaki *headland* Japan 98 C9

Satpayev Kazakhstan 90 E5

Satpura Range *mountain range* India 93 C6

Satu Mare Romania 69 F1

Saudi Arabia *country* SW Asia 84 B6, 89 F7

Sault Ste Marie Ontario, Canada 25 G8

Sault Sainte Marie Michigan, USA 32 D3

Saurimo Angola 80 C3

Sava *river* SE Europe 61 I6, 68 D3

Savaii *island* Samoa 101 G6

Savannah Georgia, USA 31 J5

Savannah *river* Georgia, USA 31 J4

Saveh Iran 89 G3

Savona Italy 62 B4

Saxony *cultural region* Germany 58 E5

Sayak Kazakhstan 90 G5

Sayhut Yemen 89 H8

Saynshand Mongolia 97 G3

Scarborough England, United Kingdom 51 H8

Schaerbeek Belgium 53 D9

Schaffhausen Switzerland 60 C4

Scheldt *river* W Europe 53 C8

Schenectady New York, USA 33 H5

Schiedam Netherlands 53 D6

Schiermonnikoog *island* Netherlands 52 G1

Schleswig Germany 58 D2

Schlüchtern Germany 59 D8

Schmallenberg Germany 59 C7

Schwabach Germany 59 E10

Schwäbische Alb *mountain range* Germany 59 C10

Schwandorf Germany 59 G10

Schwaz Austria 61 F4

Schwedt an der Oder Germany 58 I4

Schweinfurt Germany 59 E9

Schwerin Germany 58 F3

Schweriner See *lake* Germany 58 F3

Sciacca Italy 63 E11

Scilly, Isles of *island group* England, United Kingdom 51 C13

Scotia Sea *sea* SW Atlantic Ocean 45 D12

Scotland *national region* United Kingdom 51 C6

Scottsbluff Nebraska, USA 29 E6

Scranton Pennsylvania, USA 33 H6

Scutari, Lake *lake* Albania/Montenegro 68 E5

Seattle Washington, USA 23 C7, 26 B2

Secunderabad India 93 D8

Segamat Malaysia 94 C6

Ségou Mali 77 E6

Segovia Spain 56 E4

Segre *river* Spain 57 I3

Séguédine Nigeria 77 J4

Segura *river* Spain 57 F6

Seiland *island* Norway 48 F2

Seinäjoki Finland 49 G7

Seine *river* France 46 C6, 55 G3

Sekondi-Takoradi Ghana 77 F8

Sekseeil Kazakhstan 90 D5

Selayar *island* Indonesia 95 G8

Selebi-Phikwe Botswana 80 E6

Selenge Moron *river* Mongolia/Russian Federation 97 F2

Sélibabi Mauritania 76 D5

Selma Alabama, USA 31 H5

Semarang Indonesia 94 E9

Semey Kazakhstan 90 H4

Semnan Iran 89 H3

Senanga Zambia 80 D4

Sendai Japan 85 H5, 99 H5

Sendai Japan 98 D8

Sendai-wan *bay* Japan 99 H5

Senec Slovakia 67 D9

Senegal *country* W Africa 70 A5, 76 C5

Senegal *river* W Africa 70 A5, 76 C5

Senftenberg Germany 59 H6

Senja *island* Norway 48 E3

Sens France 55 G3

Seoul *country capital* South Korea 85 G5, 98 B5

Sept-Isles Québec, Canada 25 I7

Seraing Belgium 53 F10

Seram *island* Indonesia 95 I8

Serang Indonesia 94 D8

Serbia *country* SE Europe 47 F7, 69 E3

Serebryansk Kazakhstan 90 H4

Seremban Malaysia 94 C6

Serengeti Plain *physical region* Tanzania 79 H7

Serenje Zambia 81 F3

Serifos *island* Greece 69 G8

Serowe Botswana 80 E6

Serra Geral *mountain range* Brazil 39 F8, 41 G8

Serres Greece 69 G5

Sète France 55 G8

Setesdal *river* Norway 49 B9

Sétif Algeria 73 G3

Setúbal Portugal 56 A6

Sevastopol Ukraine 47 H7, 65 F13

Severn *river* England, United Kingdom 51 H8

Severnaya Zemlya *island group* Russian Federation 85 F1, 87 F2

Severobaykalsk Russian Federation 87 G6

Sevier Lake *lake* Utah, USA 27 G8

Seville Spain 46 A7, 56 C7

Seychelles *island group* W Indian Ocean 82 D4

Seydhisfjördhur Iceland 48 C2

Sfantu Gheorghe Romania 69 H2

Sfax Tunisia 70 D2, 73 H4

Shahjahanpur India 92 D4

Shahrisabz Uzbekistan 91 E7

Shaki Nigeria 77 H7

Shalqar Kazakhstan 90 C5

Shandan China 97 F5

Shanghai China 85 G6, 97 J6

Shangrao China 97 I7

Shannon *river* Republic of Ireland 51 B9

Shan Plateau *plateau* Myanmar 94 B2

Shantou China 97 I8

Shaoguan China 97 I8

Shaoxing China 97 J6

Shaoyang China 97 H7

Shaqra' Iraq 89 F6

Sharjah United Arab Emirates 89 I6

Shark Bay *bay* Western Australia, Australia 102 A5

Shashemene Ethiopia 75 F9

Shashi China 97 H6

Shasta, Mount *mountain* California, USA 27 B6

Shebeli *river* Ethiopia/Somalia 71 H6, 75 G11

Sheffield New Zealand 105 D9

Sheffield England, United Kingdom 51 G9

Shendi Sudan 75 D7

Shenyang China 85 G5, 97 J3

Shenzhen China 97 I8

Sherbrooke Québec, Canada 25 I7

Sheridan Wyoming, USA 28 D4

's-Hertogenbosch Netherlands 53 F7

Shetland Islands *island group* Scotland, United Kingdom 46 C3, 50 G1

Sheyenne *river* North Dakota, USA 29 G2

Shibam Yemen 89 G8

Shibetsu Japan 99 J2

Shieli Kazakhstan 91 F5

Shihezi China 96 C3

Shijiazhuang China 97 H5

Shikarpur Pakistan 91 F11

Shikoku *island* Japan 98 E8

Shiliguri India 92 G5

Shillong India 92 H5

Shimla India 92 D3

Shimokita-hanto *peninsula* Japan 99 H3

Shimonoseki Japan 98 D7

Shinyanga Tanzania 79 H7

Shiono-misaki *headland* Japan 99 F8

Shiraz Iran 84 B6, 89 H4

Shiretoko-misaki *headland* Japan 99 I1

Shivamogga (Shimoga) India 93 C9

Shizuoka Japan 99 G7

Shkoder Albania 68 E5

Shostka Ukraine 65 F8

Shreveport Louisiana, USA 31 G4

Shrewsbury England, United Kingdom 51 F10

Shu Kazakhstan 91 G6

Shuangyashan China 97 K2

Shubarkuduk Kazakhstan 90 C4

Shumen Bulgaria 69 H4

Shymkent Kazakhstan 91 F6

Siauliai Lithuania 64 C5

Sibenik Croatia 68 C4

Siberia *physical region* Russian Federation 85 F3, 87 G4

Siberut *island* Indonesia 94 B7

Sibiu Romania 69 G2

Sibu Malaysia 94 E7

Sichuan Basin *physical region* China 97 G6

Sicily *island* Italy 46 D8, 63 F11

Sicily, Strait of *strait* S Mediterranean Sea 63 D12

Sidi Barrani Egypt 74 B3

Sidi Bel Abbès Algeria 73 E3

Siedlce Poland 66 H5

Siegen Germany 59 C7

Siem Reap Cambodia 94 C4

Siena Italy 63 D5

eradz Poland 67 E5

erra Leone *country* W Africa 71 A6, 76 D7

erra Madre *mountain range* Guatemala/Mexico 23 D10, 35 F7

erra Madre del Sur *mountain* Mexico 23 D11, 34 E6

erra Madre Occidental *mountain range* Mexico 23 C10, 34 C3

erra Madre Oriental *mountain range* Mexico 34 D3

erra Nevada *mountain range* W USA 27 B6

erre Switzerland 60 B6

fnos *island* Greece 69 G8

glufjördhur Iceland 48 B2

gmaringen Germany 59 D11

guiri Guinea 76 E6

linjärvi Finland 49 H7

kasso Mali 77 E6

lesia *cultural region* Poland 67 D6

mbirsk Russian Federation 47 I4, 86 B5

meulue *island* Indonesia 94 A6

mferopol Ukraine 65 G13

mpson Desert *desert* Northern Territory/South Australia, Australia 103 F5

nai *peninsula* Egypt 74 D3

nanju North Korea 98 B4

ncelejo Colombia 40 C1

nes Portugal 56 A7

nga Sudan 75 D8

ingapore *country* SE Asia 85 F8, 94 C7

ingapore *country capital* Singapore 85 F8, 94 C7

ngen Germany 59 C12

ngida Tanzania 79 H7

ngitic Gulf *gulf* N Adriatic Sea 69 G6

ngkawang Indonesia 94 D7

niscola Italy 63 C8

inop Turkey 88 D1

inpo North Korea 98 C4

intra Portugal 56 A6

'nuiju North Korea 98 A4

ion Switzerland 60 B6

ioux City Iowa, USA 29 H5

ioux Falls South Dakota, USA 29 H5

iping China 97 J3

iple Island *island* Antarctica 21 A4

iracusa Italy 63 G12

ir Edward Pellew Group *island group* Northern Territory, Australia 103 G2

iret *river* Romania 69 H2

irjan Iran 89 I4

irte, Gulf of *gulf* S Mediterranean Sea 70 E2, 73 I4

isak Croatia 68 C3

isimiut Greenland 20 A4

itapur India 92 E5

ittwe Myanmar 94 A2

ivas Turkey 88 D2

iwa Egypt 74 B3

iwalik Range *mountain range* India/Nepal 92 D4

kagerrak *channel* NW Europe 49 B10

keleton Coast *coastal region* Namibia 71 D10, 80 A5

kelleftea Sweden 49 F5

kelleftealven *river* Sweden 49 F5

kibotn Norway 48 F3

kien Norway 49 B9

kierniewice Poland 66 F5

kiftet Kihti *strait* Baltic Sea/Gulf of Bothnia 49 F9

kikda Algeria 73 G3

kopje *country capital* Macedonia 47 F7, 69 F5

kye *island* Scotland, United Kingdom 50 D4

kyros *island* Greece 69 G7

latina Romania 69 H3

lave *river* Alberta/Northwest Territories, Canada 24 D6

lavonia *cultural region* Croatia 68 D3

lavonski Brod Croatia 68 D3

ligo Republic of Ireland 51 B8

liven Bulgaria 69 H4

lobozia Romania 69 H3

Slonim Belarus 65 DC7

Slough England, United Kingdom 51 H11

Slovakia *country* C Europe 47 E6, 67 E9

Slovenia *country* SE Europe 46 E6, 61 I6

Slovyansk Ukraine 65 H10

Slubice Poland 66 C5

Slupsk Poland 66 D2

Slutsk Belarus 65 D7

Smallwood Reservoir *reservoir* Newfoundland & Labrador, Canada 23 H7, 25 I6

Smara Western Sahara 72 C5

Smila Ukraine 65 F10

Smoky Hill *river* Kansas, USA 29 F7

Smøla *island* Norway 49 B6

Smolensk Russian Federation 47 G5, 86 B3

Smolikas *mountain* Greece 69 E6

Snake *river* NW USA 26 D3

Snake River Plain *physical region* Idaho, USA 26 F5

Snezka *mountain* Czech Republic 67 C6

Snowdon *mountain* Wales, United Kingdom 51 E9

Snyder Texas, USA 30 C5

Sobradinho, Represa de *reservoir* Brazil 39 G5, 41 H5

Sobral Brazil 41 I4

Sochaczew Poland 67 C6

Society Islands *island group* French Polynesia 101 I6

Socompa Chile 42 C3

Socorro, Isla *island* Mexico 34 B6

Socotra *island* Yemen 82 D2, 84 C7, 89 I9

Sodankylä Finland 48 G4

Söderhamn Sweden 49 E8

Södertälje Sweden 49 E10

Sofala Bay *bay* W Indian Ocean 81 G5

Sofia *country capital* Bulgaria 47 F7, 69 F4

Sognefjorden *fjord* Norway 49 A8

Sohag Egypt 74 C4

Soignies Belgium 53 D10

Sokch'o South Korea 98 C5

Sokhumi Georgia 89 E1

Sokodé Togo 77 G7

Sokoto Nigeria 77 H6

Solapur India 93 C8

Sol, Costa del *coastal region* Spain 56 E8

Solingen Germany 59 B7

Sollentuna Sweden 49 E10

Solomon Islands *country* SW Pacific Ocean 101 E5

Solomon Sea *sea* W Pacific Ocean 100 D5

Solothurn Switzerland 60 B4

Soltau Germany 58 E4

Solway Firth *inlet* England/Scotland, United Kingdom 51 E7

Solwezi Zambia 80 E3

Somalia *country* E Africa 71 I7, 75 G11

Somalia Tanzania 79 H7

Somali Basin *undersea feature* NW Indian Ocean 82 D3

Sombor Serbia 68 E1

Sombrero Channel *channel* Nicobar Islands, India 93 H11

Somerset Island *island* Nunavut, Canada 25 E3

Somerset-West South Africa 80 C9

Somme *river* France 55 F2

Somoto Nicaragua 35 H7

Sonch'on North Korea 98 B4

Sondrio Italy 62 C2

Songea Tanzania 79 I9

Songhua Jiang *river* China 97 J2

Songnam South Korea 98 B5

Songnim North Korea 98 B4

Son La Vietnam 94 C2

Sonneberg Germany 59 F8

Sonoran Desert *desert* Mexico/USA 27 F12

Sopka Klyuchevskaya *volcano* Russian Federation 87 K4

Sopot Poland 66 E2

Sopron Hungary 67 D10

Sora Italy 63 E7

Soria Spain 57 F3

Soroca Moldova 65 D10

Sorong Indonesia 95 I7

Sorøya *island* Norway 49 F2

Sorsele Sweden 49 E5

Sosnowiec Poland 67 F7

Sotavento, Ilhas de *Cape Verde* 76 A5

Sotkamo Finland 49 H6

Sousse Tunisia 73 H3

South Africa *country* S Africa 71 F12, 80 C8

South America *continent* 38–43

Southampton England, United Kingdom 51 G12

Southampton Island *island* Nunavut, Canada 22 F5, 25 F4

South Andaman *island* Andaman Islands, India 93 H10

South Australia *state* Australia 103 E5

South Australian Basin *undersea feature* SE Indian Ocean 83 I6

South Australian Plain *undersea feature* SE Indian Ocean 83 I7

South Bend Indiana, USA 32 C6

South Carolina *state* USA 31 J4

South China Sea *sea* SE Asia 85 G7, 95 E4, 97 I9

South Dakota *state* USA 29 F4

South Downs *hill range* England, United Kingdom 51 G12

Southeast Indian Ridge *undersea feature* SE Indian Ocean 83 F7

Southeast Pacific Basin *undersea feature* SE Pacific Ocean 107 H4

South East Point *headland* Victoria, Australia 103 H8

Southend-on-Sea England, United Kingdom 51 H11

Southern Alps *mountain range* New Zealand 105 B10

Southern Bug *river* Ukraine 65 E11

Southern Cook Islands *island group* Cook Islands 101 H6

Southern Cross Western Australia, Australia 102 C6

Southern Ocean *ocean* 45 E13, 82 D9

Southern Uplands *mountain range* Scotland, United Kingdom 51 E7

South Fiji Basin *undersea feature* SW Pacific Ocean 106 E6

South Georgia *island* SW Atlantic Ocean 45 E11

South Georgia *UK dependent territory* SW Atlantic Ocean 39 G13

South Indian Basin *undersea feature* SE Indian Ocean 83 G8

South Island *island* New Zealand 101 E8, 105 B9

South Korea *country* E Asia 85 G5, 98 C5

South Orkney Islands *island group* SE South America 45 D12

South Platte *river* Colorado/Nebraska, USA 29 E6

South Pole *pole* Antarctica 21 A4

South Sandwich Islands *island group* SE South America 45 E12

South Saskatchewan *river* Alberta/Saskatchewan, Canada 24 C7

South Taranaki Bight *bay* New Zealand 105 F6

South Uist *island* Scotland, United Kingdom 50 C5

South West Cape *headland* New Zealand 105 B13

Southwest Indian Ridge *undersea feature* SW Indian Ocean 82 C7

Southwest Pacific Basin *undersea feature* S Pacific Ocean 107 F7

Sovetskaya Gavan Russian Federation 87 J6

Soweto South Africa 80 E7

Soya-misaki *headland* Japan 99 H1

Spain *country* SW Europe 46 A7, 56 D5

Spanish Town Jamaica 36 D5

Sparks Nevada, USA 27 C7

Sparta Greece 69 F8

Spartivento, Capo *headland* Italy 63 B10

Spartivento, Capo *headland* Italy 63 H11

Spencer Iowa, USA 29 I5

Spencer Gulf *gulf* South Australia, Australia 103 F7

Spey *river* Scotland, United Kingdom 51 E5

Spiez Switzerland 60 B5

Spijkenisse Netherlands 53 D6

Spitsbergen *island* NW Europe 44 G17

Spittal-an der Drau Austria 61 H5

Split Croatia 46 E7, 68 C4

Spokane Washington, USA 26 E2

Spoleto Italy 63 E6

Spratly Islands *disputed region* SE Asia 95 F5

Spree *river* Germany 59 I6

Springfield Colorado, USA 29 F8

Springfield *state capital* Illinois, USA 32 B7

Springfield Massachusetts, USA 33 I5

Springfield Missouri, USA 29 J8

Springfield Oregon, USA 26 B4

Squillace, Gulf of *gulf* NW Ionian Sea 63 H10

Sri Jayewardenepura Kotte *legislative capital* Sri Lanka 84 D8, 93 D11

Sri Lanka *country* S Asia 84 D8, 93 E11

Sri Lanka *island* S Asia 83 F3

Srinagar India 92 C2

Stadtlohn Germany 59 B6

Stakhanov Ukraine 65 I10

Stalowa Wola Poland 67 H7

Stamford Connecticut, USA 33 I6

Stanley Falkland Islands 39 E13, 43 G12

Stanley Tasmania, Australia 103 H9

Stanovoy Khrebet *mountain range* Russian Federation 85 G4, 87 H5

Starachowice Poland 67 G6

Stara Zagora Bulgaria 69 H4

Stargard Szczecinski Poland 66 C4

Starogard Gdanski Poland 66 E3

Stavanger Norway 46 D4, 49 A9

Stavropol Russian Federation 47 I6, 86 A5

Steinkjer Norway 49 C6

Stendal Germany 58 F5

Sterling Colorado, USA 29 E6

Sterling Illinois, USA 32 B5

Sterling Heights Michigan, USA 32 E5

Stewart Island *island* New Zealand 105 B13

Steyr Austria 61 I3

Stillwater Minnesota, USA 29 I4

Stip Macedonia 69 F5

Stirling Scotland, United Kingdom 51 E6

Stockholm *country capital* Sweden 47 E4, 49 E10

Stockton California, USA 27 B8

Stoke-on-Trent England, United Kingdom 51 F9

Stony Tunguska *river* Russian Federation 85 E3, 87 F5

Store Bælt *channel* Baltic Sea/Kattegat 49 B12

Støren Norway 49 C7

Stornoway Scotland, United Kingdom 50 D4

Storsjön *lake* Sweden 49 D7

Storuman Sweden 49 E6

Strakonice Czech Republic 67 B8

Stralsund Germany 58 H2

Stranraer Scotland, United Kingdom 51 E7

Strasbourg France 46 D6, 55 I3

Stratford New Zealand 105 F6

Streaky Bay South Australia, Australia 103 F6

Stromboli *island* Italy 63 G10

Stromness Scotland, United Kingdom 50 F3

Strömstad Sweden 49 C10

Strömsund Sweden 49 E6

Strumica Macedonia 69 F5

Stryy Ukraine 65 B10

Sturt Desert *desert* Queensland/South Australia, Australia 103 G5

Stuttgart Germany 46 D6, 59 D10

Stykkishólmur Iceland 48 B2

Suakin Sudan 75 E6

Subotica Serbia 68 E2

Suceava Romania 69 H1

Sucre *legal capital* Bolivia 39 D7, 40 E7

Sudan *country* N Africa 71 F6, 75 C7

Sudbury Ontario, Canada 25 G8

Sudd *wetland* Sudan 71 G6, 75 C9

Sudeten *mountain range* Czech Republic/Poland 67 C6

Suez Egypt 70 G3, 74 C3

Suez Canal *canal* Egypt 74 C3

Suhar Oman 89 I6

Suhbaatar Mongolia 97 G2

Suhl Germany 59 F8

Suihua China 97 J2

Suizhou China 97 H6

Sukchon North Korea 98 B4

Sukkur Pakistan 91 F11

Sukumo Japan 98 E8

Sulaiman Range *mountain range* Pakistan 91 F10

Sula Islands *island group* Indonesia 95 H7

Sulawesi *island* Indonesia 85 G9, 95 G8

Sullana Peru 40 B4

Sulmona Italy 63 F7

Sulu Archipelago *island group* Philippines 95 G6

Sulu Sea *sea* Philippines 95 G5

Sulzbach-Rozenberg Germany 59 F9

Sumatra *island* Indonesia 83 G3, 85 F9, 94 C7

Sumba *island* Indonesia 95 G9

Sumbawa *island* Indonesia 95 F9

Sumbawanga Tanzania 79 H8

Sumbe Angola 80 A3

Sumeih Sudan 75 B9

Summel Iraq 89 F3

Sumqayit Azerbaijan 89 G1

Sumy Ukraine 65 G9

Sunch'on South Korea 98 B7

Sunderland England, United Kingdom 51 G7

Sundsvall Sweden 49 E7

Sunnyvale California, USA 27 B8

Suomussalmi Finland 49 H5

Superior Wisconsin, USA 32 A2

Superior, Lake *lake* Canada/USA 23 F8, 25 F8, 32 B2

Sur Oman 89 J6

Surabaya Indonesia 85 F9, 95 E9

Surakarta Indonesia 94 E9

Surat India 84 D7, 93 B7

Surat Thani Thailand 94 B5

Surendranagar India 93 B6

Surgut Russian Federation 86 E5

Surigao Philippines 95 H5

Suriname *country* N South America 38 E3, 41 F2

Surt Libya 73 I5

Susa Italy 62 A3

Susch Switzerland 60 E5

Sutlej *river* India/Pakistan 91 G10

Suva *country capital* Fiji 101 F6

Suwalki Poland 66 H3

Suwon South Korea 98 B5

Suzhou China 97 I6

Svalbard *Norwegian dependent territory* Arctic Ocean 20 C4

Svartisen *glacier* Norway 48 D4

Sveg Sweden 49 D8

Svenstavik Sweden 49 D7

Svitavy Czech Republic 67 D7

Svitlovodsk Ukraine 65 F10

Svobodnyy Russian Federation 87 I6

Svyetlahorsk Belarus 65 E7

Swakopmund Namibia 80 B6

Swan Island *island* Honduras 35 I6

Swansea Wales, United Kingdom 51 E11

Swaziland *country* S Africa 71 G12, 81 F7

Sweden *country* NW Europe 47 E3, 49 D8

Swiebodzin Poland 66 C5

Swindon England, United Kingdom 51 G11

Swinoujscie Poland 66 C3

Switzerland *country* C Europe 46 D6, 60 C5

Sydney New South Wales, Australia 100 D8, 103 I7

Sydney Nova Scotia, Canada 25 J7

Syeverodonetsk Ukraine 65 I10

Syktyvkar Russian Federation 86 C4

Sylhet Bangladesh 93 H5

Sylt *island* Germany 58 C2

Syracuse New York, USA 33 H5

Syr Darya *river* C Asia 84 C5, 91 E6

Syria *country* W Asia 84 B6, 88 D3

Syrian Desert *desert* W Asia 88 E4

Szczecin Poland 66 C3

Szczecinek Poland 66 D3

Szeged Hungary 67 F11

Szekesfehervar Hungary 67 E10

Szekszard Hungary 67 E11

Szolnok Hungary 67 G10

Szombathely Hungary 67 D10

T

Tabas Iran 89 I3

Tabor Czech Republic 67 B8

Tabora Tanzania 79 H7

Tabriz Iran 84 B5, 89 F2

Tabuaeran *island* Kiribati 101 H4

Tabuk Saudi Arabia 88 D5

Täby Sweden 49 E9

Tacheng China 96 C2

Tacloban Philippines 95 H4

Tacna Peru 40 D6

Tacoma Washington, USA 26 B2

Taco Pozo Argentina 42 E3

Tacuarembó Uruguay 43 G5

T'aebaek-sanmaek *mountain range* North Korea/South Korea 98 C4

Tafi Viejo Argentina 42 D4

Taganrog, Gulf of *gulf* NE Sea of Azov 65 I11

Taguatinga Brazil 41 H5

Tagus *river* Portugal/Spain 46 A7, 56 A6

Tahat *mountain* Algeria 73 F7

Tahiti *island* French Polynesia 101 I6

Tahoe, Lake *lake* California/Nevada, USA 27 C7

Tahoua Niger 77 H5

Taichung Taiwan 97 J8

Tainan Taiwan 97 J8

Taipei *country capital* Taiwan 85 G6, 97 J7

Taiping Malaysia 94 C6

Taitao Peninsula *peninsula* Chile 43 B10

Taiwan *country* E Asia 85 G7, 97 J8

Taiwan Strait *strait* China/Taiwan 97 J8

Taiyuan China 85 F7, 97 H5

Ta'izz Yemen 89 F9

Tajikistan *country* C Asia 84 D5, 91 F8

Tajumulco, Volcán *volcano* Guatemala 35 G7

Tak Thailand 94 B3

Takamatsu Japan 99 E7

Takaoka Japan 99 G6

Takasaki Japan 99 H6

Takayama Japan 99 G6

Takikawa Japan 99 I2

Takla Makan Desert *desert* China 84 D5, 96 B4

Talak *physical region* Niger 77 H5

Talas Kyrgyzstan 91 F6

Talaud Islands *island group* Indonesia 95 H6

Talavera de la Reina Spain 56 D5

Talca Chile 43 C7

Talcahuano Chile 43 B7

Taldyqorghan Kazakhstan 91 H5

Tallahassee *state capital* Florida, USA 31 I5

Tallinn *country capital* Estonia 47 F4, 64 C3

Taloqan Afghanistan 91 F8
Talsi Latvia 64 B4
Talwood Queensland, Australia 103 I6
Tamale Ghana 77 G7
Tamanrasset Algeria 73 F7
Tambacounda Senegal 76 D5
Tambao Burkina 77 G5
Tambov Russian Federation 86 B4
Tambura Sudan 75 B10
Tamiahua, Laguna de *lagoon* Mexico 35 E5
Tampa Florida, USA 23 F10, 31 I6
Tampere Finland 47 F3, 49 G8
Tampico Mexico 35 E5
Tamworth New South Wales, Australia 103 J6
Tana *river* Finland/Norway 48 G2 *see also* Tenojoki
Tana Norway 48 H2
Tanabe Japan 99 F7
Tana, Lake *lake* Ethiopia 75 E8
Tanami Desert *desert* Northern Territory, Australia 100 B6, 103 E3
Tanega-shima *island* Japan 98 D9
Tanezrouft *desert* Algeria 72 E6
Tanga Tanzania 71 H8, 79 I7
Tanganyika, Lake *lake* E Africa 71 G8, 79 G8
Tangier Morocco 70 C2, 72 D3
Tangshan China 97 I4
Tanimbar Islands *island group* Indonesia 95 I9
Tanjungkarang-Telukbetung Indonesia 94 D8
Tanjungpandan Indonesia 94 D8
Tanjungredeb Indonesia 95 F7
Tanta Egypt 70 G3, 74 C3
Tan-Tan Morocco 72 C5
Tanzania *country* E Africa 71 G9, 79 H8
Taormina Italy 63 G11
Tapa Estonia 64 C3
Tapachula Mexico 35 G7
Tapajós *river* Brazil 38 E4, 41 F4
Tarakan Indonesia 95 F6
Taranaki *see* Egmont, Mount
Taranto Italy 63 H8
Taranto, Gulf of *gulf* NW Ionian Sea 63 H8
Tarascon France 55 H7
Taraz Kazakhstan 91 F6
Tarbes France 54 E8
Tarcoola South Australia, Australia 103 F6
Targoviste Romania 69 G3
Targu Jiu Romania 69 F3
Targu Mures Romania 69 G2
Tarija Bolivia 40 E7
Tarim Basin *physical region* China 96 C4
Tarim He *river* China 84 D5, 96 C4
Tarin Kowt Afghanistan 91 E9
Tarn *river* France 55 F7
Tarnobrzeg Poland 67 G7
Tarnow Poland 67 G7
Tarragona Spain 57 I4
Tartu Estonia 64 D4
Tartus Syria 88 D3
Tarvisio Italy 62 F2
Tashkent *country capital* Uzbekistan 84 D5, 91 F7
Tasman Bay *bay* New Zealand 105 E7
Tasmania *island* Australia 83 J7, 100 C9
Tasmania *state* Australia 103 H9
Tasman Plateau *undersea feature* SE Indian Ocean 83 K7
Tasman Sea *sea* SW Pacific Ocean 100 E8, 103 J8, 105 A5
Tassili-n-Ajjer *plateau* Algeria 70 D3, 73 G6
Tatabanya Hungary 67 E10
Tathlith Saudi Arabia 89 F7
Tatra Mountains *mountain range* Poland/Slovakia 67 F8
Taunggyi Myanmar 94 B2
Taunton England, United Kingdom 51 F11
Taupo New Zealand 104 G5
Taupo, Lake *lake* New Zealand 104 G5
Tauranga New Zealand 104 G4

Taurus Mountains *mountain range* Turkey 88 C2
Tavira Portugal 56 B8
Tavoy Myanmar 94 B4
Tawitawi *island* Philippines 95 G6
Taymyr Peninsula *peninsula* Russian Federation 85 F1, 87 F3
Tbilisi *country capital* Georgia 84 B5, 89 I1
Tchibanga Gabon 78 B7
Tczew Poland 66 E3
Te Anau New Zealand 105 B11
Te Anau, Lake *lake* New Zealand 105 A11
Te Awamutu New Zealand 104 G4
Tébessa Algeria 73 G3
Tebingtinggi Indonesia 94 B6
Tees *river* England, United Kingdom 51 G8
Tegal Indonesia 94 D9
Tegucigalpa *country capital* Honduras 23 E12, 35 H7
Tehran *country capital* Iran 84 B6, 89 H3
Tehuacán Mexico 35 E6
Tehuantepec, Gulf of *gulf* Mexico 35 F7
Tehuantepec, Istmo de *physical region* Mexico 35 F6
Tejen Turkmenistan 91 C8
Tekapo, Lake *lake* New Zealand 105 C10
Te Kuiti New Zealand 104 G5
Tel Aviv-Yafo Israel 88 D4
Telford England, United Kingdom 51 F10
Telfs Austria 61 F4
Tema Ghana 77 G8
Temirtau Kazakhstan 90 F4
Tempe Arizona, USA 27 G11
Templin Germany 58 H4
Temuco Chile 43 C8
Ten Degree Channel *channel* Nicobar Islands, India 93 H10
Ténéré *physical region* Niger 70 D4, 77 J4
Tengiz, Lake *lake* Kazakhstan 90 E4
Tennant Creek Northern Territory, Australia 103 F3
Tennessee *river* S USA 31 H4
Tennessee *state* USA 31 G4
Tenojoki *river* Finland/Norway 48 G2 *see also* Tana
Teófilo Otoni Brazil 41 I6
Tepic Mexico 34 C5
Teplice Czech Republic 67 B6
Teramo Italy 63 F6
Teresina Brazil 38 H4, 41 I4
Términos, Laguna de *lagoon* Mexico 35 G6
Termiz Uzbekistan 91 E8
Termoli Italy 63 G7
Ternate Indonesia 95 H7
Terneuzen Netherlands 53 C7
Terni Italy 63 E6
Ternopil Ukraine 65 C9
Terracina Italy 63 F7
Terralba Italy 63 B9
Terrassa Spain 57 I3
Terre Haute Indiana, USA 32 C7
Terschelling *island* Netherlands 52 F2
Teruel Spain 57 G5
Tessalit Mali 77 G4
Tete Mozambique 81 G4
Teterow Germany 58 G3
Tetouan Morocco 72 D3
Tetovo Macedonia 69 F5
Texas *state* USA 30 D5
Texel *island* Netherlands 52 E3
Thailand *country* SE Asia 85 F7, 94 B3
Thailand, Gulf of *gulf* SE Asia 85 F8, 94 C4
Thai Nguyen Vietnam 94 D2
Thames New Zealand 104 G4
Thames *river* England, United Kingdom 51 F11
Thana India 93 B7
Thanh Hoa Vietnam 94 D3
Thar Desert *desert* India/Pakistan 88 D6, 91 F11, 92 A5
Thasos *island* Greece 69 G6
Thaton Myanmar 94 B3
Thayetmyo Myanmar 94 B3
The Dalles Oregon, USA 26 C3

The Hague *seat of government* Netherlands 46 D5, 53 D5
Theodore Queensland, Australia 103 J5
Thessaloniki Greece 47 F8, 69 F6
Thessaly *physical region* Greece 69 F6
Thiès Senegal 76 C5
Thika Kenya 79 I6
Thimphu *country capital* Bhutan 84 E6, 92 G4
Thionville France 55 H2
Thisted Denmark 49 B11
Thomson *seasonal river* Queensland, Australia 103 H5
Thonon-les-Bains France 55 I5
Thórshöfn Iceland 48 C2
Thrace *cultural region* Greece/Turkey 69 H5
Thun Switzerland 60 B5
Thunder Bay Ontario, Canada 25 F8
Thuringian Forest *forest* Germany 59 E7
Thurso Scotland, United Kingdom 50 F3
Thurston Island *island* Antarctica 21 A3
Tianjin China 85 G5, 97 I4
Tianjun China 97 F5
Tianshui China 97 G6
Tiaret Algeria 73 F3
Tiber *river* Italy 63 E6
Tibesti *plateau* Chad 70 E4, 78 D1
Tibet, Plateau of *plateau* China 84 E6, 96 C6
Tiburón, Isla *island* Mexico 34 B2
Tidjikja Mauritania 76 D4
Tieling China 97 J3
Tienen Belgium 53 E9
Tien Shan *mountain range* C Asia 84 D5, 91 G7, 96 B4
Tierp Sweden 49 E9
Tierra del Fuego *island* Argentina/Chile 39 D13, 43 D13
Tighina Moldova 65 E11
Tigris *river* SW Asia 84 B6, 89 G4
Tijuana Mexico 34 A1
Tikrit Iraq 89 F3
Tiksi Russian Federation 87 H3
Tilburg Netherlands 53 E7
Tillabéri Niger 77 G5
Tilos *island* Greece 69 I8
Timaru New Zealand 105 D10
Timbuktu Mali 77 F5
Timimoun Algeria 73 E5
Timisoara Romania 47 F7, 69 E2
Timor *island* East Timor/Indonesia 95 H9
Timor Sea *sea* E Indian Ocean 95 H9, 102 D1
Timrå Sweden 49 E7
Tindouf Algeria 72 C5
Tinian *island* Northern Mariana Islands 100 C3
Tinogasta Argentina 42 D4
Tinos *island* Greece 69 H8
Tipperary Republic of Ireland 51 B10
Tirana *country capital* Albania 47 F7, 68 E5
Tiraspol Moldova 65 E11
Tiree *island* Scotland, United Kingdom 51 D5
Tirol *mountain range* Austria 61 E4
Tirso *river* Italy 63 B8
Tiruchchirappalli India 93 D10
Tirunelveli India 93 D11
Tirupati India 93 D10
Tiruppur India 93 D10
Tisa *river* SE Europe 68 E2 *see also* Tisza
Tisza *river* SE Europe 47 F6, 67 G10 *see also* Tisa
Titicaca, Lake *lake* Bolivia/Peru 39 C6, 40 D6
Tivoli Italy 63 E7
Tiznit Morocco 72 C5
Tlaxcala Mexico 35 E6
Tlemcen Algeria 72 E4
Toamasina Madagascar 71 I10, 81 K5
Tobago *island* Trinidad & Tobago 37 K8

Toba Kakar Range *mountain range* Afghanistan/Pakistan 91 E10
Toba, Lake *lake* Indonesia 94 B6
Tobol *river* Kazakhstan/Russian Federation 90 D3
Tocantins *river* Brazil 39 G6, 41 H5
Tocopilla Chile 42 C2
Togo *country* W Africa 71 C6, 77 G7
Tokelau *NZ dependent territory* C Pacific Ocean 101 G5
Tokoroa New Zealand 104 G5
Tokuno-shima *island* Japan 99 K8
Tokushima Japan 99 F7
Tokyo *country capital* Japan 85 H6, 99 H6
Tolanaro Madagascar 81 J7
Toledo Spain 56 E5
Toledo Ohio, USA 32 D6
Toliara Madagascar 81 I6
Tolmezzo Italy 62 E2
Tolmin Slovenia 61 H6
Toluca Mexico 34 E6
Tolyatti Russian Federation 47 I4, 86 B5
Tomakomai Japan 99 I2
Tomar Portugal 56 B5
Tomaszow Mazowiecki Poland 67 F6
Tombigbee *river* Alabama/Mississippi, USA 31 H5
Tombua Angola 80 A4
Tomini, Gulf of *gulf* Indonesia 95 G7
Tomsk Russian Federation 84 E4, 87 E6
Tomur Feng *mountain* China/Kyrgyzstan 96 B3 *see also* Pobedy, Pik
Tonga *country* C Pacific Ocean 101 G6
Tongatapu *island* Tonga 101 G6
Tonga Trench *undersea feature* SW Pacific Ocean 107 E6
Tongchuan China 97 G5
Tonghua China 97 J3
Tongking, Gulf of *gulf* China/Vietnam 94 D3, 97 G9
Tongliao China 97 I3
Tonle Sap *lake* Cambodia 94 C4
Tooele Utah, USA 27 G6
Toowoomba Queensland, Australia 103 J5
Topeka *state capital* Kansas, USA 29 H7
Torgau Germany 59 G6
Torhout Belgium 53 B8
Torneträsk *lake* Sweden 48 F3
Tornio Finland 48 G5
Tornionjoki *river* NW Europe 48 G4
Toronto Ontario, Canada 23 G8, 25 H9
Tororo Uganda 79 H6
Torrelavega Spain 56 E2
Torremolinos Spain 56 E8
Torrens Creek Queensland, Australia 103 I4
Torrens, Lake *seasonal lake* South Australia, Australia 100 C8, 103 G6
Torrente Spain 57 G5
Torreón Mexico 34 D4
Torres Strait *strait* Australia/Papua New Guinea 103 H1
Torres Vedras Portugal 56 A6
Torrevieja Spain 57 G7
Tortoli Italy 63 C9
Tortona Italy 62 B4
Tortosa Spain 57 H4
Torun Poland 66 E4
Tosa-wan *bay* Japan 99 E8
Tottori Japan 99 F6
Touggourt Algeria 73 G4
Toulon France 55 I8
Toulouse France 46 C7, 55 F7
Toungoo Myanmar 94 B3
Tourcoing France 55 G1
Tournai Belgium 53 B10
Tours France 55 E4
Townshend, Cape *headland* Queensland, Australia 103 J4
Townsville Queensland, Australia 100 C6, 103 I3
Toyama Japan 99 G6

Toyama-wan *bay* Japan 99 G6
Toyohashi Japan 99 G7
Toyota Japan 99 G7
Trabzon Turkey 89 E1
Tralee Republic of Ireland 51 A10
Transantarctic Mountains *mountain range* Antarctica 21 C3
Transylvania *cultural region* Romania 69 F2
Transylvanian Alps *mountain range* Romania 69 E3
Trapani Italy 63 E11
Trasimeno, Lake *lake* Italy 63 D5
Traunsee *lake* Austria 61 H3
Traunstein Germany 59 G12
Travemünde Germany 58 E3
Traverse City Michigan, USA 32 D4
Trbovlje Slovenia 61 I6
Trebic Czech Republic 67 C8
Trebinje Bosnia & Herzegovina 68 D4
Trelleborg Sweden 49 C12
Trencin Slovakia 67 E8
Trent *river* England, United Kingdom 51 G9
Trento Italy 62 D2
Trenton New Jersey, USA 33 F6
Tres Arroyos Argentina 43 F7
Tres Marias, Islas *island group* Mexico 34 C5
Tres Puntas, Cabo *headland* Argentina 43 E10
Treuchtlingen Germany 59 E10
Treviso Italy 62 D3
Trichur India 93 C10
Trier Germany 59 A9
Trieste Italy 62 F3
Triglav *mountain* Slovenia 61 H6
Trinidad *island* Trinidad & Tobago 37 K8
Trinidad & Tobago *country* SE West Indies 23 I13, 37 K8
Tripoli Greece 69 F8
Tripoli Lebanon 88 D3
Tripoli *country capital* Libya 70 E2, 73 H4
Tripolitania *cultural region* Libya 73 H5
Tristan da Cunha *island* SW Africa 45 F10
Trivandrum India 93 C11
Trnava Slovakia 67 E9
Trois-Rivières Québec, Canada 25 I8
Trollhättan Sweden 49 C10
Tromsø Norway 48 F2
Trondheim Norway 46 E3, 49 C7
Trondheimsfjorden *fjord* Norway 49 B6
Troyes France 55 G3
Trujillo Honduras 35 I7
Trujillo Peru 40 B5
Truro England, United Kingdom 51 D12
Tsarevo Bulgaria 69 I5
Tsetserleg Mongolia 97 F3
Tshabong Botswana 80 D7
Tshikapa Democratic Republic of Congo 78 E8
Tshuapa *river* Democratic Republic of Congo 79 E6
Tsu Japan 99 F7
Tsuchiura Japan 99 H6
Tsugaru-kaikyo *strait* Japan 99 H3
Tsumeb Namibia 80 B5
Tsuruga Japan 99 F6
Tsushima *island group* Japan 98 C7
Tuamotu Islands *island group* French Polynesia 101 I6
Tuatapere New Zealand 105 B12
Tübingen Germany 59 D11
Tubruq Libya 73 K4
Tucson Arizona, USA 27 H12
Tucuruí, Represa *reservoir* Brazil 41 H4
Tuktoyaktuk Northwest Territories, Canada 24 C3
Tukums Latvia 64 B4
Tula Russian Federation 47 H5, 86 B4
Tulcea Romania 69 I3
Tulln Austria 61 J3
Tulsa Oklahoma, USA 30 E3
Tumbes Peru 40 B4
Tun Sweden 49 C10

Tunis *country capital* Tunisia 70 D2, 73 H3
Tunisia *country* N Africa 70 D2, 73 G4
Tunja Colombia 40 C2
Tura Russian Federation 87 E5
Turangi New Zealand 105 G5
Turan Lowland *physical region* C Asia 91 C7
Turayf Saudi Arabia 88 E4
Turbat Pakistan 91 D12
Turda Romania 69 G2
Turin Italy 46 D7, 62 A3
Turkana, Lake *lake* Ethiopia/Kenya 71 G7, 79 I6
Turkey *country* Asia/Europe 84 A5, 88 C2
Turkistan Kazakhstan 91 E6
Turkmenbashy Turkmenistan 91 B7
Turkmenistan *country* C Asia 84 C5, 91 C7
Turks & Caicos Islands *UK dependent territory* N West Indies 23 H11, 37 I3
Turku Finland 47 F3, 49 G9
Turnhout Belgium 53 E8
Turpan China 96 D4
Turpan Basin *physical region* China 96 D4
Turukhansk Russian Federation 87 F4
Tuscaloosa Alabama, USA 31 H5
Tuscany *cultural region* Italy 62 C5
Tuticorin India 93 D11
Tuttlingen Germany 59 C11
Tuvalu *country* C Pacific Ocean 101 F5
Tuxtla Mexico 35 G6
Tuzla Bosnia & Herzegovina 68 D3
Tuz, Lake *lake* Turkey 88 D2
Tver Russian Federation 47 H4, 86 B4
Tweed *river* England/Scotland, United Kingdom 51 F6
Twin Falls Idaho, USA 26 F5
Tychy Poland 67 F7
Tyler Texas, USA 31 E5
Tynda Russian Federation 87 I5
Tyne *river* England, United Kingdom 51 F7
Tyrrhenian Sea *sea* N Mediterranean Sea 46 D8, 63 E9
Tyumen Russian Federation 84 C3, 86 D5

U

Ubangi *river* C Africa 78 E5
Ube Japan 98 D7
Uberaba Brazil 41 H7
Uberlândia Brazil 39 G7, 41 H7
Ubon Ratchathani Thailand 94 C4
Ucayali *river* Peru 38 B4, 40 C4
Uch Adzhi Turkmenistan 91 D8
Uchiura-wan *bay* Japan 99 H3
Uchquduq Uzbekistan 91 D6
Udaipur India 93 C5
Uddevalla Sweden 49 C10
Udine Italy 62 E2
Udon Thani Thailand 94 C3
Ueda Japan 99 G6
Uele *river* Democratic Republic of Congo 71 F7, 79 F5
Uelzen Germany 58 E4
Ufa Russian Federation 47 J4, 86 C5
Uganda *country* E Africa 71 G7, 79 H6
Uige Angola 80 B2
Uijongbu South Korea 98 D5
Uinta Mountains *mountain range* Utah, USA 27 H6
Uitenhage South Africa 80 D7
Ujjain India 93 C6
Ukhta Russian Federation 86 D4
Ukmerge Lithuania 65 C6
Ukraine *country* SE Europe 47 G6, 65 E9
Ulaangom Mongolia 96 E2
Ulan Bator *country capital* Mongolia 85 F4, 97 I2
Ulanhot China 97 I2
Ulan-Ude Russian Federation 87 G6
Uliastay Mongolia 97 E2

Ulung-Do *island* South Korea 98 D5
Ulm Germany 59 E11
Ulsan South Korea 98 C6
Ulster *cultural region* Republic of Ireland/United Kingdom 51 C8
Ulundi South Africa 81 F7
Uluru *rocky outcrop* Northern Territory, Australia 103 E5
Uman Ukraine 65 E10
Umeå Sweden 49 F6
Umeälven *river* Sweden 49 E6
Umtata South Africa 81 E8
Unayzah Saudi Arabia 89 F6
Ungava Bay *bay* Québec, Canada 25 H5
Ungava Peninsula *peninsula* Québec, Canada 23 G6, 25 G5
Ungheni Moldova 65 D11
Uniontown Pennsylvania, USA 33 F7
United Arab Emirates *country* SW Asia 84 C7, 89 H6
United Kingdom *country* NW Europe 46 C4, 51 E7
United States of America *country* N North America 26–33
Upington South Africa 80 C7
Upper Lough Erne *lake* Republic of Ireland/United Kingdom 51 C8
Uppsala Sweden 49 E9
Upua New Zealand 104 F2
Ural *river* Kazakhstan/Russian Federation 47 J4, 84 B4, 86 C5, 90 B4
Ural Mountains *mountain range* Asia/Europe 47 I1, 84 C3, 86 D4
Urawa Japan 99 H6
Urbino Italy 62 E5
Urengoy Russian Federation 87 E4
Urganch Uzbekistan 91 D7
Uritskiy Kazakhstan 90 E3
Urmia, Lake *lake* Iran 89 F2
Urosevac Kosovo 69 E5
Uroteppa Tajikistan 91 J7
Uruguay *country* S South America 39 E9, 43 G6
Uruguay *river* S South America 39 F9, 41 G8, 42 G4
Urumqi China 84 E5, 96 D3
Usak Turkey 88 C2
Usedom *island* Germany 58 H3
Ushuaia Argentina 43 D13
Ussuri *river* China/Russian Federation 97 K2
Ussuriysk Russian Federation 87 J7
Ustica *island* Italy 63 E10
Ust-Ilimsk Russian Federation 87 G5
Usti nad Labem Czech Republic 67 B6
Ustka Poland 66 D2
Ust-Kamchatsk Russian Federation 87 K3
Ustrzyki Dolne Poland 67 H8
Ustyurt Plateau *plateau* Kazakhstan/Uzbekistan 91 B6
Usumacinta *river* Guatemala/Mexico 35 G6
Utah *state* USA 27 G8
Utica New York, USA 33 H5
Utiel Spain 57 G5
Utrecht Netherlands 53 E5
Utsjoki Finland 48 G2
Utsunomiya Japan 99 H6
Uvs Nuur *lake* Mongolia 96 E2
Uyo Nigeria 77 I8
Uzbekistan *country* C Asia 84 C5, 91 D7
Uzhhorod Ukraine 65 A10

V

Vaal *river* South Africa 71 F12, 80 D7
Vaasa Finland 49 F7
Vac Hungary 67 F10
Vacaville California, USA 27 B8
Vadodara India 93 B6
Vadsø Norway 48 H2
Vaduz *country capital* Liechtenstein 46 D6, 60 D5
Vah *river* Slovakia 67 E9

Valdecañas, Embalse de *reservoir* Spain 56 D5
Valdepeñas Spain 57 E6
Valdés, Península *peninsula* Argentina 43 E9
Valdivia Chile 43 C8
Valdosta Georgia, USA 31 I5
Valence France 55 H6
Valencia Spain 46 B7, 57 H5
Valencia Venezuela 38 C2, 40 D1
Valencia, Gulf of *gulf* Spain 57 H6
Valenciennes France 55 G1
Valentine Nebraska, USA 29 F5
Valera Venezuela 40 D1
Valga Estonia 64 C4
Valladolid Spain 46 B7, 56 D3
Valledupar Venezuela 40 C1
Vallejo California, USA 27 B8
Vallenar Chile 42 C4
Valletta *country capital* Malta 46 E9, 63 F13
Valmiera Estonia 64 C4
Valparaíso Chile 43 C6
Valverde del Camino Spain 56 C7
Van Turkey 89 F2
Vanadzor Armenia 89 F1
Vancouver British Columbia, Canada 23 C6, 24 B7
Vancouver Washington, USA 26 B3
Vancouver Island *island* British Columbia, Canada 23 C6, 24 A7
Vancouver, Mount *mountain* Yukon Territory, Canada 24 A4
Van Diemen Gulf *gulf* Northern Territory, Australia 103 E1
Vänern *lake* Sweden 46 E4, 49 C10
Vänersborg Sweden 49 C10
Vangaindrano Madagascar 81 J6
Van, Lake *lake* Turkey 89 F2
Vannes France 54 C4
Vanrhynsdorp South Africa 80 C8
Vantaa Finland 49 H9
Vanua Levu *island* Fiji 101 F6
Vanuatu *country* SW Pacific Ocean 100 E6
Varanasi India 93 E5
Varangerfjorden *fjord* Norway 48 H2
Varano, Lake *lagoon* Italy 63 G7
Varazdin Croatia 68 C2
Varberg Sweden 49 C11
Varde Denmark 49 A12
Varese Italy 62 B3
Varkaus Finland 49 H7
Varna Bulgaria 69 I4
Vasa *see* Vaasa
Vaslui Romania 69 H2
Västerås Sweden 49 E9
Vasto Italy 63 F6
Vatican City *country* S Europe 46 D7, 63 E7
Vatican City *country capital* Vatican City 63 E7
Vatnajökull *glacier* Iceland 48 C2
Vättern *lake* Sweden 46 E4, 49 D10
Växjö Sweden 49 D11
Veenendaal Netherlands 53 F6
Vega *island* Norway 49 C5
Vejle Denmark 49 B12
Veles Macedonia 69 F5
Vélez-Málaga Spain 56 E8
Veliko Turnovo Bulgaria 69 H4
Vellore India 93 D9
Velsen-Noord Netherlands 52 E4
Venado Tuerto Argentina 43 F6
Vendas Novas Portugal 56 B6
Venezuela *country* N South America 38 D2, 40 D2
Venezuela, Gulf of *gulf* Colombia/Venezuela 40 D1
Venice Italy 62 E3
Venice, Gulf of *gulf* NW Adriatic Sea 62 E3
Venlo Netherlands 53 G7
Ventspils Estonia 64 B4
Vera Argentina 42 F5
Veracruz Mexico 35 F6
Veraval India 93 A7
Vercelli Italy 62 B3
Verdalsøra Norway 49 C6
Verde, Costa *coastal region* Spain 56 D1
Verden Germany 58 D4
Vereeniging South Africa 81 E7

Verkhoyanskiy Khrebet *mountain range* Russian Federation 87 H4
Vermont *state* USA 33 I4
Vernon Texas, USA 30 D4
Vernon, Mount Illinois, USA 32 B7
Veroia Greece 69 F6
Verona Italy 62 D3
Versailles France 55 F3
Verviers Belgium 53 G10
Vesoul France 55 H4
Vesterålen *island group* Norway 47 F1, 48 D3
Vestfjorden *fjord* Norway 48 D4
Vestmannaeyjar Iceland 48 B3
Vestmann Islands *island group* Iceland 48 B3
Vestvagøy *island* Norway 48 D3
Vesuvius *volcano* Italy 63 F8
Veszprem Hungary 67 E10
Vetlanda Sweden 49 D11
Veurne Belgium 53 A8
Viana do Castelo Portugal 56 B3
Viareggio Italy 62 C5
Viborg Denmark 49 B11
Vibo Valentia Italy 63 H10
Vicenza Italy 62 D3
Vichy France 55 G5
Victoria *river* Northern Territory, Australia 103 E2
Victoria *state* Australia 103 H7
Victoria British Columbia, Canada 24 B7
Victoria Falls *waterfall* Zambia/Zimbabwe 71 F10, 80 E5
Victoria Island *island* Northwest Territories/Nunavut, Canada 22 E4, 24 D3
Victoria, Lake *lake* E Africa 71 G7, 79 H7
Victoria Land *physical region* Antarctica 21 C4
Victoria River Roadhouse Northern Territory, Australia 103 E2
Vidin Bulgaria 69 F3
Viedma Argentina 43 E8
Vienna *country capital* Austria 46 E6, 61 J3
Vienne *river* France 55 E5
Vientiane *country capital* Laos 85 F7, 94 C3
Vierwaldstätter See *lake* Switzerland 60 C5
Vietnam *country* SE Asia 85 F7, 94 D4
Vignemale *mountain* France 54 E8
Vigo Spain 56 B3
Vijapura (Bijapur) India 93 C8
Vijayawada India 93 E8
Vik Iceland 48 B3
Vikna *island* Norway 49 C6
Vila do Conde Portugal 56 B4
Vila Nova de Gaia Portugal 56 B4
Vila Real Portugal 56 B4
Vila Real de Santo António Portugal 56 B8
Vilhelmina Sweden 49 E6
Viljandi Estonia 64 C4
Villach Austria 61 H5
Villahermosa Mexico 35 G6
Villa María Argentina 43 E6
Villaputzu Italy 63 B9
Villarrica Paraguay 42 G3
Villarrobledo Spain 57 F6
Villavicencio Colombia 40 C2
Villeurbanne France 55 H5
Vilnius *country capital* Lithuania 47 F5, 65 C6
Viluyy *river* Russian Federation 85 G3, 87 H4
Viña del Mar Chile 43 C6
Vinarós Spain 57 H4
Vincent, Gulf St *gulf* South Australia, Australia 103 F7
Vindhya Range *mountain range* India 93 C6
Vinh Vietnam 94 D3
Vinnytsya Ukraine 65 D10
Vinson Massif *mountain* Antarctica 21 B3
Virginia *state* USA 33 F8
Virginia Beach Virginia, USA 33 H9
Virgin Islands *US dependent territory* E West Indies 37 I5
Virovitica Croatia 68 D2
Vis *island* Croatia 68 C4

Visakhapatnam India 93 E8
Visby Sweden 49 E11
Viscount Melville Sound *strait* Northwest Territories/Nunavut, Canada 24 D3
Viseu Portugal 56 B4
Visoko Bosnia & Herzegovina 68 D3
Vistula *river* Poland 47 E5, 66 E4, 67 G7
Viterbo Italy 63 D6
Viti Levu *island* Fiji 101 F6
Vitim *river* Russian Federation 87 H6
Vitória Brazil 41 I7
Vitória da Conquista Brazil 41 I6
Vitoria-Gasteiz Spain 57 F2
Vitsyebsk Belarus 47 G4, 65 E6
Vittangi Sweden 48 F4
Vittoria Italy 63 F12
Vjose *river* Albania/Greece 68 E6
Vlaardingen Netherlands 53 D6
Vladikavkaz Russian Federation 86 A6
Vladimir Russian Federation 86 B4
Vladivostok Russian Federation 85 H5, 87 J7
Vlieland *island* West Frisian Islands 52 E2
Vlissingen Netherlands 53 C7
Vlore Albania 68 E6
Vltava *river* Czech Republic 67 B7
Vocklabruck Austria 61 H3
Voghera Italy 62 B3
Voinjama Liberia 76 D7
Vojvodina *cultural region* Serbia 68 E2
Volga *river* Russian Federation 47 G4, 86 B5
Volgograd Russian Federation 47 I5, 86 B5
Vologda Russian Federation 86 C4
Volos Greece 69 F6
Volta, Lake *lake* Ghana 71 C6, 77 G7
Volyn-Podolian Upland *hill range* Ukraine 65 D9
Vorkuta Russian Federation 86 D4
Voronezh Russian Federation 47 H5, 86 B4
Voru Estonia 64 D4
Vosges *mountain range* France 55 I3
Voss Norway 49 A8
Voznesensk Ukraine 65 E11
Vranje Serbia 69 F4
Vratsa Bulgaria 69 G4
Vrbas Serbia 68 E2
Vryburg South Africa 80 D7
Vukovar Croatia 68 D3

W

Waal *river* Netherlands 53 E6
Waalwijk Netherlands 53 E7
Wabash *river* N USA 32 C7
Waco Texas, USA 30 E5
Waddan Libya 73 I5
Waddenzee *sea* Netherlands 52 E2
Waddington, Mount *mountain* British Columbia, Canada 24 B7
Wadi Halfa Sudan 75 C5
Wad Medani Sudan 75 D8
Wagga Wagga New South Wales, Australia 103 I7
Wagin Western Australia, Australia 102 C7
Wah Pakistan 91 G9
Waiau *river* New Zealand 105 B12
Waigeo *island* Indonesia 95 I7
Waikato *river* New Zealand 104 G4
Waikerie South Australia, Australia 103 G7
Waimangaroa New Zealand 105 D8
Waiouru New Zealand 105 B12
Waipara New Zealand 105 E9

Waipu New Zealand 104 F2
Waipukurau New Zealand 105 H6
Wairoa New Zealand 105 H5
Waitakere New Zealand 104 F3
Wakasa-wan *bay* Japan 99 F6
Wakatipu, Lake *lake* New Zealand 105 B11
Wakayama Japan 99 F7
Wake Island *US dependent territory* SW Pacific Ocean 101 E2
Wakkanai Japan 99 I1
Walachia *cultural region* Romania 69 G3
Walbrzych Poland 67 D6
Wales *national region* United Kingdom 51 E10
Walgett New South Wales, Australia 103 I6
Wallis & Futuna *French dependent territory* C Pacific Ocean 101 F5
Walpole Western Australia, Australia 102 C7
Walvis Bay Namibia 71 E11, 80 B6
Walvis Ridge *undersea feature* SE Atlantic Ocean 45 G9
Wanaka New Zealand 105 C11
Wanaka, Lake *lake* New Zealand 105 B11
Wandel Sea *sea* Arctic Ocean 20 C4
Wanganui *river* New Zealand 105 G6
Wanganui New Zealand 105 G6
Wanxian China 97 G6
Warangal India 93 D8
Warburg Germany 59 D6
Warnemünde Germany 58 G3
Warrego *seasonal river* New South Wales/Queensland, Australia 103 H5
Warren Michigan, USA 32 E5
Warri Nigeria 77 I8
Warsaw *country capital* Poland 47 F5, 66 G5
Warta *river* Poland 66 D4, 67 F6
Warwick Queensland, Australia 103 J6
Washington *state* USA 26 C2
Washington D.C. *country capital* District of Columbia, USA 23 G9, 33 G7
Washington, Mount *mountain* New Hampshire, USA 33 I4
Wash, The *bay* England, United Kingdom 51 H9
Waterbury Connecticut, USA 33 I6
Waterford Republic of Ireland 51 C10
Waterloo Iowa, USA 29 J5
Watertown New York, USA 33 H4
Watertown South Dakota, USA 29 H4
Watford England, United Kingdom 51 H11
Watsa Democratic Republic of Congo 79 G6
Watson Lake Yukon Territory, Canada 24 B5
Watzmann *mountain* Germany 59 G2
Wau Sudan 75 C10
Wawa Ontario, Canada 25 G8
Weald, The *physical region* England, United Kingdom 51 H11
Weddell Plain *undersea feature* C Southern Ocean 45 E12
Weddell Sea *sea* SE Southern Ocean 45 D13
Wedel Germany 58 E3
Weert Netherlands 53 G8
Wei He *river* China 97 G6
Weinan China 97 H6
Welkom South Africa 80 E7
Wellesley Islands *island group* Queensland, Australia 103 G3
Wellington *country capital* New Zealand 101 F8, 105 F7
Wellington, Isla *island* Chile 39 C12, 43 C11
Wellsford New Zealand 104 F3
Wels Austria 61 H3
Wenzhou China 97 J7

Werra *river* Germany 59 E8
Weser *river* Germany 58 C4
Wessel Islands *island group* Northern Territory, Australia 103 G1
West Cape *headland* New Zealand 105 A12
Western Australia *state* Australia 102 C5
Western Desert *desert* Egypt 74 B4
Western Dvina *river* W Europe 47 F4, 65 D5
Western Ghats *mountain range* India 84 D7, 93 B7
Western Sahara *disputed region* Morocco 70 A3, 72 B6
Westerschelde *inlet* S North Sea 53 C7
West Falkland *island* Falkland Islands 39 E13, 43 F12
West Frisian Islands *island group* Netherlands 52 E2
West Indies *island group* Caribbean Sea 23 G11, 36 E2, 45 C6
West Mariana Basin *undersea feature* W Pacific Ocean 106 C4
West Palm Beach Florida, USA 31 J7
Westport New Zealand 105 D8
West Siberian Plain *physical region* Russian Federation 84 D3, 86 D4
West Virginia *state* USA 33 E7
Wetar *island* Indonesia 95 H9
Wetzlar Germany 59 C8
Wewak Papua New Guinea 100 C5
Wexford Republic of Ireland 51 D10
Weymouth England, United Kingdom 51 F12
Whakatane New Zealand 104 H4
Whangarei New Zealand 104 F2
Wharton Basin *undersea feature* E Indian Ocean 83 G5
Wheatland Wyoming, USA 28 E5
Wheeler Peak *mountain* New Mexico, USA 30 B3
Whitehorse Yukon Territory, Canada 24 B4
White Mountains *mountain range* Maine/New Hampshire, USA 33 I4
White Nile *river* Sudan 71 G6, 75 D8
White Sea *sea* Russian Federation 20 D5, 47 G2, 86 C3
White Volta *river* Burkina, Ghana 77 G7
Whitney, Mount *mountain* California, USA 23 C8, 27 D9
Whyalla South Australia, Australia 103 G7
Wichita Kansas, USA 29 H8
Wichita Falls Texas, USA 30 D4
Wick Scotland, United Kingdom 50 F3
Wicklow Mountains *mountain range* Republic of Ireland 51 D9
Wielkopolska *cultural region* Poland 66 E4
Wiener Neustadt Austria 61 J3
Wiesbaden Germany 59 C8
Wight, Isle of *island* England, United Kingdom 51 G12
Wilcannia New South Wales, Australia 103 H6
Wildon Switzerland 61 J5
Wildspitze *mountain* Austria 61 E5
Wilhelmshaven Germany 58 C3
Wilkes Land *physical region* Antarctica 21 D4
Willemstad Netherlands Antilles 37 G8
Wilhelm II Land *physical region* Antarctica 21 E3
Williston North Dakota, USA 29 E2
Willmar Minnesota, USA 29 H4
Wilmington Delaware, USA 33 H7
Wilmington North Carolina, USA 31 K4
Wilson North Carolina, USA 31 J3

Wilson, Mount *mountain* Colorado, USA 28 C7

Wiluna Western Australia, Australia 102 C5

Windhoek *country capital* Namibia 71 E11, 80 B6

Windsor Ontario, Canada 25 G9

Windward Islands *island group* E West Indies 37 J8

Windward Passage *channel* Cuba/Haiti 37 E4

Winnemucca Nevada, USA 27 D6

Winnipeg Manitoba, Canada 23 E7, 25 E8

Winnipeg, Lake *lake* Manitoba, Canada 23 E7, 24 E7

Winnipegosis, Lake *lake* Manitoba, Canada 24 E7

Winona Minnesota, USA 29 J4

Winschoten Netherlands 52 I2

Winsen Germany 58 E4

Winston-Salem North Carolina, USA 31 J3

Winterthur Switzerland 60 C4

Winton Queensland, Australia 103 H4

Wisconsin *state* USA 32 A3

Wisconsin Rapids Wisconsin, USA 32 B4

Wismar Germany 58 F3

Wittenberg Germany 59 G6

Wittenberge Germany 58 F4

Wittstock Germany 58 G4

Wladyslawowo Poland 66 E2

Wloclawek Poland 66 F4

Wlodawa Poland 67 I6

Wodonga Victoria, Australia 103 I7

Wodzislaw Slaski Poland 67 E7

Wolds, The *hill range* England, United Kingdom 51 H9

Wolfsberg Austria 61 I5

Wolfsburg Germany 58 F5

Wolf, Volcán *volcano* Galapagos Islands 40 A8

Wolin Poland 66 C3

Wollaston Lake *lake* Saskatchewan, Canada 24 E6

Wollongong New South Wales, Australia 100 D8, 103 I7

Wolverhampton England, United Kingdom 51 F10

Wonju South Korea 98 C5

Wonsan North Korea 98 C4

Woods, Lake *seasonal lake* Northern Territory, Australia 103 F3

Woods, Lake of the *lake* Canada/USA 25 E8, 29 H2

Worcester South Africa 80 C9

Worcester England, United Kingdom 51 F10

Worcester Massachusetts, USA 33 I5

Wörgl Austria 61 G4

Worms Germany 59 C9

Wrangel Island *island* Russian Federation 85 K2, 87 I1

Wrath, Cape *headland* Scotland, United Kingdom 50 E3

Wrexham Wales, United Kingdom 51 F9

Wroclaw Poland 47 E5, 67 D6

Wrzesnia Poland 66 E5

Wubin Western Australia, Australia 102 B6

Wuhai China 97 G4

Wuhan China 85 F6, 97 H6

Wuhu China 97 I6

Wunstorf Germany 58 D5

Wuppertal Germany 59 B7

Würzburg Germany 59 E9

Wurzen Germany 59 G7

Wusuli Jiang *see* Ussuri

Wuwei China 97 F5

Wuxi China 97 J6

Wuzhou China 97 H8

Wyndham Western Australia, Australia 102 E2

Wyoming *state* USA 28 C5

Wyszkow Poland 66 G4

X

Xai-Xai Mozambique 81 G6

Xalapa Mexico 35 F6

Xanthi Greece 69 G5

Xiamen China 97 I8

Xi'an China 85 F6, 97 G6

Xiangfan China 97 H6

Xiangtan China 97 H7

Xian Jiang *river* China 97 H8

Xianyang China 97 G6

Xichang China 97 F7

Xigaze China 96 C7

Xi Jiang *river* China 97 H8

Xilinhot China 97 H3

Xingtai China 97 H5

Xingu *river* Brazil 38 F4, 41 G4

Xining China 97 F5

Xinxiang China 97 H5

Xinyang China 97 H6

Xixabangma Feng *mountain* China 96 C7

Xuwen China 97 H9

Xuzhou China 97 I5

Y

Yabelo Sudan 75 E10

Yablonovyy Khrebet *mountain range* Russian Federation 85 F4, 87 G7

Yaizu Japan 99 G7

Yakeshi China 97 I2

Yakima Washington, USA 26 C3

Yakmach Pakistan 91 D11

Yaku-shima *island* Japan 98 C9

Yakutsk Russian Federation 85 G3, 87 H4

Yalong Jiang *river* China 97 E6

Yalta Ukraine 65 G13

Yalu *river* China/North Korea 97 J4

Yamagata Japan 99 H5

Yamaguchi Japan 98 D7

Yamal Peninsula *peninsula* Russian Federation 84 D2, 86 E4

Yambio Sudan 75 C10

Yambol Bulgaria 69 H4

Yamoussoukro Ivory Coast 71 B6, 77 E7

Yamuna *river* India 92 D4

Yanan China 97 G5

Yancheng China 97 J6

Yangambi Democratic Republic of Congo 79 F6

Yangon *country capital* Myanmar 85 E7, 94 B3

Yangquan China 97 H5

Yangtze *river* China 85 F6, 97 I6

Yantai China 97 J4

Yaoundé *country capital* Cameroon 71 D7, 78 C5

Yap *island* Micronesia 100 B3

Yapen *island* Indonesia 95 J7

Yaqui *river* Mexico 34 B3

Yarmouth Nova Scotia, Canada 25 J8

Yaroslavl Russian Federation 47 H4, 86 B4

Yatsushiro Japan 98 D8

Yazd Iran 89 H4

Yecheng China 96 B4

Yekaterinburg *river* Russian Federation 84 C4

Yellowknife Northwest Territories, Canada 24 D5

Yellow River *river* China 85 F5, 97 G5

Yellow Sea *sea* E Asia 85 G6, 97 J5, 98 A6

Yellowstone *river* Montana/Wyoming, USA 28 D3

Yemen *country* SW Asia 84 B7, 89 F8

Yenakiyeve Ukraine 65 H10

Yenisey *river* Mongolia/Russian Federation 84 E3, 87 F5

Yerevan *country capital* Armenia 84 B5, 89 F2

Yevpatoriya Ukraine 65 F12

Yibin China 97 G7

Yichang China 97 H6

Yichun China 97 J2

Yinchuan China 97 G5

Yining China 96 C3

Yiyang China 97 H7

Yogyakarta Indonesia 94 E9

Yokkaichi Japan 99 G7

Yokohama Japan 99 H7

Yokote Japan 99 H4

Yonago Japan 99 E7

Yonkers New York, USA 33 I6

Yonne *river* France 55 G3

York England, United Kingdom 51 G8

York, Cape *headland* Queensland, Australia 100 C5, 103 H1

York Peninsula *peninsula* South Australia, Australia 103 G7

Yoshkar-Ola Russian Federation 86 C4

Yos Sudarso *island* Indonesia 95 J8

Yosu South Korea 98 B7

Youngstown Ohio, USA 33 F6

Yrghyz Kazakhstan 90 D4

Ystad Sweden 49 D12

Ysyk-Kol *lake* Kyrgyzstan 91 H6

Yucatan Channel *channel* Cuba/Mexico 35 H5, 36 A3

Yucatan Peninsula *peninsula* Guatemala/Mexico 23 E11, 35 H5

Yucca Valley California, USA 27 E11

Yueyang China 97 H7

Yukon *river* Canada/USA 24 B4, 26 H1

Yukon Territory *province* Canada 24 B4

Yulin China 97 H8

Yuma Arizona, USA 27 F12

Yumen China 96 E4

Yuzhno-Sakhalinsk Russian Federation 87 K6

Yverdon Switzerland 60 A5

Z

Zaanstad Netherlands 52 E4

Zabol Iran 89 J4

Zabrze Poland 67 E7

Zacatecas Mexico 34 D5

Zadar Croatia 68 C3

Zafra Spain 56 C6

Zagreb *country capital* Croatia 46 E7, 68 C2

Zagros Mountains *mountain range* Iran 89 G4

Zahedan Iran 89 J4

Zaire *see* Democratic Republic of Congo

Zajecar Serbia 69 F4

Zakhmet Turkmenistan 91 D8

Zakopane Poland 67 F8

Zakynthos Greece 69 E8

Zakynthos *island* Greece 69 E8

Zalaegerszeg Hungary 67 D11

Zalantun China 97 I2

Zalau Romania 69 F1

Zalim Saudi Arabia 89 F6

Zambezi *river* S Africa 71 F10, 80 D4

Zambezi Zambia 80 D4

Zambia *country* S Africa 71 F10, 80 D4

Zamboanga Philippines 95 G5

Zambrow Poland 66 H4

Zamora Spain 56 D3

Zamora de Hidalgo Mexico 34 D5

Zamosc Poland 67 I6

Zanjan Iran 89 G3

Zanzibar Tanzania 71 H8, 79 J8

Zanzibar *island* Tanzania 79 J8

Zaozhuang China 97 I5

Zapala Argentina 43 C8

Zaporizhzhya Ukraine 65 G11

Zarafshon Uzbekistan 91 D7

Zaragoza Spain 46 B7, 57 G3

Zaranj Afghanistan 91 D10

Zareh Sharan Afghanistan 91 F9

Zaria Nigeria 71 D6, 77 I6

Zary Poland 67 C5

Zawiercie Poland 67 F7

Zaysan Kazakhstan 90 I4

Zaysan, Lake *lake* Kazakhstan 90 I4

Zdunska Wola Poland 67 F5

Zealand *island* Denmark 49 C12

Zeebrugge Belgium 53 B7

Zeid-Willemsvaart Canal *canal* Netherlands 53 F7

Zeist Netherlands 53 F5

Zemun Serbia 69 E3

Zenica Bosnia & Herzegovina 68 D3

Zeven Germany 58 D4

Zgierz Poland 66 F5

Zgorzelec Poland 67 C6

Zhangiztobe Kazakhstan 90 H4

Zhangjiakou China 97 H4

Zhanjiang China 97 H9

Zhaodong China 97 J2

Zhaotong China 97 F7

Zhengzhou China 97 H5

Zhengzhou *river* China 85 F6

Zhezqazghan Kazakhstan 90 E5

Zhlobin Belarus 65 E7

Zhodzina Belarus 65 D6

Zhosaly Kazakhstan 91 D5

Zhuzhou China 97 H7

Zhytomyr Ukraine 65 D9

Zibo China 97 I5

Zielona Gora Poland 66 C5

Zigong China 97 G7

Ziguinchor Senegal 76 C6

Zilina Slovakia 67 E8

Zimbabwe *country* S Africa 71 F10, 81 F5

Zinder Niger 77 I6

Zinjibar Yemen 89 F9

Zi Shui *river* China 97 H7

Zlin Czech Republic 67 E8

Znojmo Czech Republic 67 C8

Zoetermeer Netherlands 53 D5

Zomba Malawi 81 G4

Zonguldak Turkey 88 D1

Zouérat Mauritania 76 D3

Zrenjanin Serbia 69 E3

Zufar *physical region* Oman 89 H8

Zug Switzerland 60 C4

Zugspitze *mountain* Austria/Germany 59 E12, 61 F4

Zula Eritrea 75 F7

Zunyi China 97 G7

Zürich Switzerland 60 C4

Zürichsee *lake* Switzerland 60 C4

Zutphen Netherlands 53 G5

Zvolen Slovakia 67 F9

Zvornik Bosnia & Herzegovina 68 D3

Zwickau Germany 59 G8

Zwolle Netherlands 52 G4

Zyryanovsk Kazakhstan 90 I4

Zywiec Poland 67 F8